Science ⟷ Children

Readings in Elementary Science Education

Science ⟷ Children

Readings in Elementary Science Education

RONALD G. GOOD

Florida State University—Tallahassee

WM. C. BROWN COMPANY PUBLISHERS

Dubuque, Iowa

Copyright ©1972 by Wm. C. Brown Company Publishers

Library of Congress Catalog Card Number: 77—178190

ISBN 0—697—06222—8

Printed in the United States of America

Dedicated to –

Mom and Dad,

Elaine

&

Becky

&

Dave

Contents

PART TWO

Thinking in Children: Implications for Science Education

PART FOUR
Evaluation—Objectives

Preface

This book is intended for those persons interested in science education for elementary school children. A specific point of view is evident throughout and no apology is made for the neglect of "other points of view." Too many books of this type attempt to give equal representation to all current ideas, thus ending up by not saying very much of anything about any of them.

The readings rely heavily on ideas about the intellectual development of children, specifically the ideas of Jean Piaget; and ideas about the nature and purposes of science, as related to elementary school. Definitely, this is not a text on how to teach elementary school science! It is a source of ideas—hopefully thought-provoking ideas—to be considered personally and along with other individuals who likewise are interested in helping children participate in science at the elementary school level. The beliefs about the nature of science and children held by prospective teachers and in-service teachers directly influence resultant classroom behaviors. If these people in conjunction with others, who are involved in influencing the kind of "science" that goes on in classrooms, are vitally interested in providing the best possible science experiences for children, new points of view should be constantly considered. Different types of learning will likely be facilitated in different ways, however, and one's conception of science for elementary school children will be a governing factor in making curriculum and instructional decisions. A final solution for elementary science at some point in the future is extremely unlikely. What is most important is that we continue to probe alternatives that seem to offer assistance in the attainment of our goals. In short, an open, thinking approach must be maintained in the teaching-learning process.

PART ONE

"Science Is...?"

The learning environment established in a classroom obviously depends on many factors. One of the most important of these factors affecting elementary science education is the conception of just what it is that constitutes "science." Science for many persons consists of a large body of facts and concepts that are understood only by a few rather strange individuals who work in white coats at universities and other research laboratories. These white coat scientists are most certainly brainy, non-social, little men who run around with a slide rule in one hand and very complicated books in the other. The likelihood that they are like other individuals in terms of human emotions and personal needs is practically nonexistent, primarily because emotions and "science" just do not mix.

Prior to this century the contingency of becoming fairly well-informed of the facts and concepts accumulated by scientists in a particular field of study like physics or chemistry was comparatively great. However, during the twentieth century, the abundance of this accumulating information has ruled out that possibility.

If science still consists of learning facts and concepts which have already been identified by our white-coat scientists, the problem now becomes one of deciding which information is most important for children to learn in our schools. Only the tiniest fraction of the available facts and concepts can be used in the time available for elementary school science. Which "things" do we choose?

Perhaps we could define science in a different way—for instance—what does science mean to you? Try defining science at this point before you read about some of the ideas other people have suggested about science. In the articles that follow, a point of view regarding the nature of science should become fairly evident to you and this author hopes questions will be raised in your mind that might stimulate discussion with others and continue further thinking on your part.

1 | RICHARD P. FEYNMAN

What Is Science?

"Science is the belief in the ignorance of experts." The author of the following article makes this statement as a part of his ideas about the nature of science. Try to decide what you believe could be meant by such a statement after reading Feynman's ideas. It is also suggested by this Nobel Prize winner in physics that "mathematics is looking for patterns." Is this what you would have said if asked to define mathematics? How about energy? Can you define energy?

When you discover what Feynman calls his "best definition" of science, do not hurry over the words without some reflection. This and many other ideas contained in this article deserve much individual and group consideration. Questions are listed following the article that are intended to stimulate thought and discussion.

I thank Mr. DeRose for the opportunity to join you science teachers. I also am a science teacher. I have much experience only in teaching graduate students in physics, and as a result of the experience I know that I don't know how to teach.

I am sure that you who are real teachers working at the bottom level of this hierarchy of teachers, instructors of teachers, experts on curricula, also are sure that you, too, don't know how to do it; otherwise you wouldn't bother to come to the Convention.

The subject "What Is Science" is not my choice. It was Mr. DeRose's subject. But I would like to say that I think that "what is science" is not at all equivalent to "how to teach science," and I must call that to your attention for two reasons. In the first place, from the way that I am preparing to give this lecture, it may seem that I am trying to tell you how to teach science—I am not at all in any way, because I don't know anything about small children. I have one, so I know that I don't

Reprinted from *The Physics Teacher,* Vol. 7, issue 6, 1968, pp. 313-320, by permission of the editor and the author. Dr. Feynman received the Nobel Prize in physics in 1965 and presently serves as Richard Chase Talman Professor of theoretical physics.

know. The other is I think that most of you (because there is so much talk and so many papers and so many experts in the field) have some kind of a feeling of lack of self-confidence. In some way you are always being lectured on how things are not going too well and how you should learn to teach better. I am not going to berate you for the bad work you are doing and indicate how it can definitely be improved; that is not my intention.

As a matter of fact, we have very good students coming into Caltech, and during the years we found them getting better and better. Now how it is done, I don't know. I wonder if you know. I don't want to interfere with the system; it is very good.

Only two days ago we had a conference in which we decided that we don't have to teach a course in elementary quantum mechanics in the graduate school any more. When I was a student, they didn't even have a course in quantum mechanics in the graduate school; it was considered too difficult a subject. When I first started to teach, we had one. Now we teach it to undergraduates. We discover now that we don't have to have elementary quantum mechanics for graduates from other schools. Why is it getting pushed down? Because we are able to teach better in the university, and that is because the students coming up are better trained.

What is science? Of course you all must know, if you teach it. That's common sense. What can I say? If you don't know, every teacher's edition of every textbook gives a complete discussion of the subject. There is some kind of distorted distillation and watered-down and mixed-up words of Francis Bacon from some centuries ago, words which then were supposed to be the deep philosophy of science. But one of the greatest experimental scientists of the time who was really doing something, William Harvey, said that what Bacon said science was, was the science that a lord-chancellor would do. He spoke of making observations, but omitted the vital factor of judgment about what to observe and what to pay attention to.

And so what science is, is not what the philosophers have said it is, and certainly not what the teacher editions say it is. What it is, is a problem which I set for myself after I said I would give this talk.

After some time, I was reminded of a little poem:

A centipede was happy quite, until a toad in fun Said, "Pray, which leg comes after which?" This raised his doubts to such a pitch He fell distracted in the ditch Not knowing how to run.

All my life, I have been doing science and known what it was, but what I have come to tell you—which foot comes after which—I am unable to do, and furthermore, I am worried by the analogy with the poem, that when I go home I will no longer be able to do any research.

There have been a lot of attempts by the various press reporters to get some kind of a capsule of this talk; I prepared it only a little time ago, so it was impossible; but I can see them all rushing out now to write some sort of headline which says: "The Professor called the President of NSTA a toad."

Under these circumstances of the difficulty of the subject, and my dislike of philosophical exposition, I will present it in a very unusual way. I am just going to tell you how I learned what science is. That's a little bit childish. I learned it as a child. I have had it in my blood from the beginning. And I would like to tell you how it got in. This sounds as though I am trying to tell you how to teach, but that is not my intention. I'm going to tell you what science is like by how I learned what science is like.

My father did it to me. When my mother was carrying me, it is reported—I am not directly aware of the conversation—my father said that "if it's a boy, he'll be a scientist." How did he do it? He never told me I should be a scientist. He was not a scientist; he was a businessman, a sales manager of a uniform company, but he read about science and loved it.

When I was very young—the earliest story I know—when I still ate in a high chair, my father would play a game with me after dinner.

He had brought a whole lot of old rectangular bathroom floor tiles from some place in Long Island City. We sat them up on end, one next to the other, and I was allowed to push the end one and watch the whole thing go down. So far, so good.

Next, the game improved. The tiles were different colors. I must put one white, two blues, one white, two blues, and another white and then two blues—I may want to put another blue, but it must be a white. You recognize already the usual insidious cleverness; first delight him in play, and then slowly inject material of educational value!

Well, my mother, who is a much more feeling woman, began to realize the insidiousness of his efforts and said, "Mel, please let the poor child put a blue tile if he wants to." My father said, "No, I want him to pay attention to patterns. It is the only thing I can do that is mathematics at this earliest level." If I were giving a talk on "what is mathematics," I would already have answered you. Mathematics is looking for patterns. (The fact is that this education had some effect. We had a direct experimental test, at the time I got to kindergarten. We had weaving in those days. They've taken it out; it's too difficult for children.

We used to weave colored paper through vertical strips and make patterns. The kindergarten teacher was so amazed that she sent a special letter home to report that this child was very unusual, because he seemed to be able to figure out ahead of time what pattern he was going to get, and made amazingly intricate patterns. So the tile game did do something to me.)

Mathematics is looking for patterns.

I would like to report other evidence that mathematics is only patterns. When I was at Cornell, I was rather fascinated by the student body, which seems to me was a dilute mixture of some sensible people in a big mass of dumb people studying home economics, etc. including lots of girls. I used to sit in the cafeteria with the students and eat and try to overhear their conversations and see if there was one intelligent word coming out. You can imagine my surprise when I discovered a tremendous thing, it seemed to me.

I listened to a conversation between two girls, and one was explaining that if you want to make a straight line, you see, you go over a certain number to the right for each row you go up, that is, if you go over each time the same amount when you go up a row, you make a straight line. A deep principle of analytic geometry! It went on. I was rather amazed. I didn't realize the female mind was capable of understanding analytic geometry.

She went on and said, "Suppose you have another line coming in from the other side, and you want to figure out where they are going to intersect. Suppose on one line you go over two to the right for every one you go up, and the other line goes over three to the right for every one that it goes up, and they start twenty steps apart," etc.—I was flabbergasted. She figured out where the intersection was! It turned out that one girl was explaining to the other how to knit argyle socks.

I, therefore, did learn a lesson: The female mind is capable of understanding analytic geometry. Those people who have for years been insisting (in the face of all obvious evidence to the contrary) that the male and female are equally capable of rational thought may have something. The difficulty may just be that we have never yet discovered a way to communicate with the female mind. If it is done in the right way, you may be able to get something out of it.

Now I will go on with my own experience as a youngster in mathematics. Another thing that my father told me—and I can't quite explain it, because it was more an emotion than a telling—was that the ratio of the circumference to the diameter of all circles was always the same, no matter what the size. That didn't seem to me too unobvious, but the ratio had some marvelous property. That was a wonderful number, a deep number, pi. There was a mystery about this number that I didn't quite understand as a youth, but this was a great thing, and the result was that I looked for pi everywhere.

When I was learning later in school how to make the decimals for fractions, and how to make 3 1/8, I wrote 3.125, and thinking I recognized a friend wrote that it equals pi, the ratio of circumference to diameter of a circle. The teacher corrected it to 3.1416.

I illustrate these things to show an influence. The idea that there is a mystery, that there is a wonder about the number was important to me, not what the number was. Very much later when I was doing experiments in the laboratory—I mean my own home laboratory—fiddling around—no, excuse me, I didn't do experiments, I never did; I just fiddled around. Gradually through books and manuals I began to discover there were formulas applicable to electricity in relating the current and resistance, and so on. One day looking at the formulas in some book or other, I discovered a formula for the frequency of a resonant circuit

> There was a mystery about this number that I didn't understand as a youth, but this was a great thing, and the result was that I looked for pi everywhere.

which was $f = 1/2 \pi \sqrt{LC}$, where L is the inductance and C the capacitance of the circle? You laugh, but I was very serious then. Pi was a thing with circles, and here is pi coming out of an electric circuit. Where was the circle? Do those of you who laughed know how that comes about?

I have to love the thing. I have to look for it. I have to think about it. And then I realized, of course, that the coils are made in circles. About a half year later, I found another book which gave the inductance of round coils and square coils, and there were other pi's in those formulas. I began to think about it again, and I realized that the pi did not come from the circular coils. I understand it better now; but in my heart I still don't quite know where that circle is, where that pi comes from.

When I was still pretty young—I don't know how old exactly—I had a ball in a wagon I was pulling, and I noticed something, so I ran up to my father to say that "When I pull the wagon, the ball runs to the back, and when I am running with the wagon and stop, the ball runs to the front. Why?"

How would you answer?

He said, "That nobody knows!" He said "It's very general, though, it happens all the time to anything; anything that is moving tends to keep moving; anything standing still tries to maintain that condition. If you look close you will see the ball does not run to the back of the wagon where you start from standing still. It moves forward a bit too, but not as fast as the wagon. The back of the wagon catches up with the ball which has trouble getting started moving. It's called inertia, that principle." I did run back to check, and sure enough the ball didn't go backwards. He put the difference between what we know and what we call it very distinctly.

Regarding this business about names and words, I would tell you another story. We used to go up to the Catskill Mountains for vacations. In New York, you go the Catskill Mountains for vacations. The poor husbands had to go to work during the week, but they would come rushing out for weekends and stay with the families. On the weekends, my father would take me for walks in the woods. He often took me for walks, and we learned all about nature, and so on, in the process. But the other children, friends of mine also wanted to go, and tried to get my father to take them. He didn't want to, because he said I was more advanced. I'm not trying to tell you how to teach, because what my father was doing was with a class of just one student; if he had a class of more than one, he was incapable of doing it.

So we went alone for our walk in the woods. But mothers were very powerful in those days as they are now, and they convinced the other fathers that they had to take their own sons out for walks in the woods. So all fathers took all sons out for walks in the woods one Sunday afternoon. The next day, Monday, we were playing in the fields and this boy said to me, "See that bird standing on the wheat there? What's the name of it?" I said, "I haven't got the slightest idea." He said, "It's a brown-throated thrush. Your father doesn't teach you much about science."

I smiled to myself, because my father had already taught me that that doesn't tell me anything about the bird. He taught me "See that bird? It's a brown-throated thrush, but in Germany it's called a halzen-flugel, and in Chinese they call it a chung ling and even if you know all those names for it, you still know nothing about the bird. You only know something about people; what they call that bird."

"Now that thrush sings, and teaches its young to fly, and flies so many miles away during the summer across the country, and nobody knows how it finds its way," and so forth. There is a difference between the name of the thing and what goes on.

The result of this is that I cannot remember anybody's name, and when people discuss physics with me they often are exasperated when they say "the Fitz-Cronin effect"—and I ask "What is the effect?" and I can't remember the name.

I would like to say a word or two—may I interrupt my little tale—about words and definitions, because it is necessary to learn the words.

It is not science. That doesn't mean just because it is not science that we don't have to teach the words. We are not talking about what to teach; we are talking about what science is. It is not science to know how to change Centigrade to Fahrenheit. It's necessary, but it is not exactly science. In the same sense, if you were discussing what art is, you wouldn't say art is the knowledge of the fact that a 3-B pencil is softer than a 2-H pencil. It's a distinct difference. That doesn't mean an art teacher shouldn't teach that, or that an artist gets along very well if he doesn't know that. (Actually you can find out in a minute by trying it; but that's a scientific way that art teachers may not think of explaining.)

In order to talk to each other, we have to have words, and that's all right. It's a good idea to try to see the difference, and it's a good idea to know when we are teaching the tools of science, such as words, and when we are teaching science itself.

To make my point still clearer, I shall pick out a certain science book to criticize unfavorably, which is unfair, because I am sure that with little ingenuity, I can find equally unfavorable things to say about others.

There is a first-grade science book which, in the first lesson of the first grade, begins in an unfortunate manner to teach science, because it starts off on the wrong idea of what science is. There is a picture of a dog, a windable toy dog, and a hand comes to the winder, and then the dog is able to move. Under the last picture, it says "What makes it move?" Later on, there is a picture of a real dog and the question "What makes it move?" Then there is a picture of a motor bike and the question "What makes it move?" and so on.

I thought at first they were getting ready to tell what science was going to be about: physics, biology, chemistry. But that wasn't it. The answer was in the teachers edition of the book; the answer I was trying to learn is that "energy makes it move."

Now energy is a very subtle concept. It is very, very difficult to get right. What I meant is that it is not easy to understand energy well enough to use it right, so that you can deduce something correctly, using the energy idea. It is beyond the first grade. It would be equally well to say that "God makes it move," or "spirit makes it move," or "movability makes it move." (In fact one could equally well say "energy makes it stop.")

Look at it this way: That's only the definition of energy. It should be reversed. We might say when something can move that it has energy in it, but not "what makes it move is energy." This is a very subtle difference. It's the same with this inertia proposition. Perhaps I can make the difference a little clearer this way:

If you ask a child what makes the toy dog move, you should think about what an ordinary human being would answer. The answer is that you wound up the spring; it tries to unwind and pushes the gear around.

What a good way to begin a science course. Take apart the toy; see how it works. See the cleverness of the gears; see the ratchets. Learn something about the toy, the way the toy is put together, the ingenuity of people devising the ratchets and other things. That's good. The question is fine. The answer is a little unfortunate, because what they were trying to do is teach a definition of what is energy. But nothing whatever is learned.

Suppose a student would say, "I don't think energy makes it move." Where does the discussion go from there?

I finally figured out a way to test whether you have taught an idea or you have only taught a definition. Test it this way: You say, "Without using the new word which you have just learned, try to rephrase what you have just learned in your own language." Without using the word "energy," tell me what you know now about the dog's motion." You cannot. So you learned nothing about science. That may be all right. You may not want to learn something about science right away. You have to learn definitions. But for the very first lesson is that not possibly destructive?

I think, for lesson number one, to learn a mystic formula for answering questions is very bad. The book has some others—"gravity makes it fall;" "the soles of your shoes wear out because of friction." Shoe leather wears out because it rubs against the sidewalk and the little notches and bumps on the sidewalk grab pieces and pull them off. To simply say it is because of friction, is sad, because it's not science.

My father dealt a little bit with energy and used the term after I got a little bit of the idea about it. What he would have done I know, because he did in fact essentially the same thing—though not the same example of the toy dog. He would say, "It moves because the sun is shining," if he wanted to give the same lesson. I would say "No. What has that to do with the sun shining? It moved because I wound up the springs."

"And why, my friend, are you able to move to wind up the spring?"
"I eat."
"What, my friend, do you eat?"
"I eat plants."
"And how do they grow?"
"They grow because the sun is shining."

And it is the same with the dog. What about gasoline? Accumulated energy of the sun which is captured by plants and preserved in the ground. Other examples all end with the sun. And so the same idea about the world that our textbook is driving at is phrased in a very exciting way.

All the things that we see that are moving, are moving because the sun is shining. It does explain the relationship of one source of energy to another, and it can be denied by the child. He could say, "I don't think it is on account of the sun shining," and you can start a discussion. So there is a difference. (Later I could challenge him with the tides, and what makes the earth turn, and have my hand on mystery again.)

That is just an example of the difference between definitions (which are necessary) and science. The only objection in this particular case was that it was the first lesson. It must certainly come in later, telling you what energy is, but not to such a simple question as "What makes a dog move?" A child should be given a child's answer. "Open it up; let's look at it."

During those walks in the woods, I learned a great deal. In the case of birds, for example, I already mentioned migration, but I will give you another example of birds in the woods. Instead of naming them, my father would say, "Look, notice that the bird is always pecking in its feathers. It pecks a lot in its feathers. Why do you think it pecks the feathers?"

I guessed it's because the feathers are ruffled, and he's trying to straighten them out. He said, "Okay, when would the feathers get ruffled, or how would they get ruffled?"

"When he flies. When he walks around, it's okay; but when he flies it ruffles the feathers."

Then he would say, "You would guess then when the bird just landed he would have to peck more at his feathers than after he has straightened them out and has just been walking around the ground for a while. Okay, let's look."

So we would look, and we would watch, and it turned out, as far as I could make out, that the bird pecked about as much and as often no matter how long he was walking on the ground and not just directly after flight.

So my guess was wrong, and I couldn't guess the right reason. My father revealed the reason.

It is that the birds have lice. There is a little flake that comes off the feather, my father taught me, stuff that can be eaten, and the louse eats it. And then on the louse, there is a little bit of wax in the joints be- tween the sections of the leg that oozes out, and there is a mite that lives in there that can eat that wax. Now the mite has such a good source of food that it doesn't digest it too well, so from the rear end there comes a liquid that has too much sugar, and in that sugar lives a tiny creature, etc.

The facts are not correct. The spirit is correct. First I learned about parasitism, one on the other, on the other, on the other.

Second, he went on to say that in the world whenever there is any source of something that could be eaten to make life go, some form of life finds a way to make use of that source; and that each little bit of left over stuff is eaten by something.

Now the point of this is that the result of observation, even if I were unable to come to the ultimate conclusion, was a wonderful piece of gold, with marvelous results. It was something marvelous.

Suppose I were told to observe, to make a list, to write down, to do this, to look, and when I wrote my list down, it was filed with 130 other lists in the back of a notebook. I would learn that the result of observation is relatively dull, that nothing much comes of it.

I think it is very important—at least it was to me—that if you are going to teach people to make observations, you should show that something wonderful can come from them. I learned then what science was about. It was patience. If you looked, and you watched, and you paid attention, you got a great reward from it (although possibly not every time). As a result, when I became a more mature man, I would painstakingly, hour after hour, for years, work on problems—sometimes many years, sometimes shorter times—many of them failing, lots of stuff going into the wastebasket; but every once in a while there was the gold of a new understanding that I had learned to expect when I was a kid, the result of observation. For I did not learn that observation was not worthwhile.

Incidentally, in the forest we learned other things. We would go for walks and see all the regular things, and talk about many things; about the growing plants, the struggle of the trees for light, how they try to get as high as they can, and to solve the problem of getting water higher than 35 or 40 ft., the little plants on the ground that look for the little bits of light that come through, all that growth, and so forth.

One day after we had seen all this, my father took me to the forest again and said, "In all this time we have been looking at the forest we have only seen half of what is going on, exactly half."

I said, "What do you mean?"

He said, "We have been looking at how all these things grow; but for each bit of growth, there must be the same amount of decay, otherwise the materials would be consumed forever. Dead trees would lie there having used up all the stuff from the air, and the ground, and it wouldn't get back into the ground or the air, and nothing else could grow, because there is no material available. There must be for each bit of growth exactly the same amount of decay."

There then followed many walks in the woods during which we broke up old stumps, saw funny bags and fungusses growing—he couldn't show me bacteria, but we saw the softening effects, and so on. I saw the forest as a process of the constant turning of materials.

There were many such things, descriptions of things, in odd ways. He often started to talk about a thing like this: "Suppose a man from Mars were to come down and look at the world. For example when I was playing with my electric trains, he told me that there is a great wheel being turned by water which is connected by filaments of copper, which spread out and spread out and spread out in all directions; and then there are little wheels, and all those little wheels turn when the big wheel turns. The relation between them is only that there is copper and iron, nothing else, no moving parts. You turn one wheel here, and all the little wheels all over the place turn, and your train is one of them. It was a wonderful world my father told me about.

You might wonder what he got out of it all. I went to MIT. I went to Princeton. I came home, and he said, "Now you've got a science education. I have always wanted to know something that I have never understood; and so, my son, I want you to explain it to me." I said yes.

He said, "I understand that they say that light is emitted from an atom when it goes from one state to another, from an excited state to a state of lower energy."

I said, "That's right."

"And light is a kind of particle, a photon, I think they call it."

"Yes."

"So if the photon comes out of the atom when it goes from the excited to the lower state, the photon must have been in the atom in the excited state."

I said, "Well, no."

He said, "Well, how do you look at it so you can think of a particle photon coming out without it having been in there in the excited state?"

I thought a few minutes, and I said, "I'm sorry; I don't know. I can't explain it to you."

He was very disappointed after all these years and years of trying to teach me something, that it came out with such poor results.

What science is, I think, may be something like this: There was on this planet an evolution of life to a stage that there were evolved animals, which are intelligent. I don't mean just human beings, but animals which play and which can learn something from experience (like cats). But at this stage each animal would have to learn from its own experience. They gradually develop, until some animal could learn from experience more rapidly and could even learn from another's experience by watching, or one could show the other, or he saw what the other one did. So there came a possibility that all might learn it, but the transmission was inefficient and they would die, and maybe the one who learned it died too, before he could pass it on to others.

Science is the belief in the ignorance of experts.

The question is: is it possible to learn more rapidly what somebody learned from some accident than the rate at which the thing is being forgotten, either because of bad memory or because of the death of the learner or inventors?

So there came a time, perhaps, when for some species the rate at which learning was increased, reached such a pitch that suddenly a completely new thing happened; things could be learned by one individual animal, passed on to another, and another fast enough that it was not lost to the race. Thus became possible an accumulation of knowledge of the race.

This has been called time-binding. I don't know who first called it this. At any rate, we have here some samples of those animals, sitting here trying to bind one experience to another, each one trying to learn from the other.

This phenomenon of having a memory for the race, of having an accumulated knowledge passable from one generation to another, was new in the world. But it had a disease in it. It was possible to pass on ideas which were not profitable for the race. The race has ideas, but they are not necessarily profitable.

So there came a time in which the ideas, although accumulated very slowly, were all accumulations not only of practical and useful things, but great accumulations of all types of prejudices, and strange and odd beliefs.

Then a way of avoiding the disease was discovered. This is to doubt that what is being passed from the past is in fact true, and to try to find out *ab initio,* again from experience, what the situation is, rather than trusting the experience of the past in the form in which it is passed down. And that is what science is; the result of the discovery that it is worthwhile rechecking by new direct experience, and not necessarily trusting the race experience from the past. I see it that way. That is my best definition.

I would like to remind you all of things that you know very well in order to give you a little enthusiasm. In religion, the moral lessons are taught, but they are not just taught once, you are inspired again and again, and I think it is necessary to inspire again and again, and to remember the value of science for children, for grown-ups, and everybody else, in several ways; not only that we will become better citizens, more able to control nature and so on. There are other things.

There is the value of the world view created by science. There is the beauty and the wonder of the world that is discovered through the results of these new experiences. That is to say, the wonders of the content which I just reminded you of; that things move because the sun is shining. (Yet, not everything moves because the sun is shining. The earth rotates independent of the sun shining, and the nuclear reaction recently produced energy on the earth, a new source. Probably volcanoes are generally moved from a source different from the shining sun.)

The world looks so different after learning science. For example, trees are made of air, primarily. When they are burned, they go back to air, and in the flaming heat is released the flaming heat of the sun which was bound in to convert the air into tree, and in the ash is the small remnant of the part which did not come from air that came from the solid earth, instead.

These are beautiful things, and the content of science is wonderfully full of them. They are very inspiring, and they can be used to inspire others.

Another of the qualities of science is that it teaches the value of rational thought as well as the importance of freedom of thought; the positive results that come from doubting that the lessons are all true. You must here distinguish—especially in teaching—the science from the forms or procedures that are sometimes used in developing science. It is easy to say, "We write, experiment, and observe, and do this or that." You can copy that form exactly. But great religions are dissipated by following form without remembering the direct content of the teaching of the great leaders. In the same way, it is possible to follow form and call it science, but that is pseudoscience. In this way, we all suffer from the kind of tyranny we have today in the many institutions that have come under the influence of pseudoscientific advisers.

We have many studies in teaching, for example, in which people make observations, make lists, do statistics, and so on, but these do not thereby become established science, established knowledge. They are merely an imitative form of science—analogous to the South Sea islands airfields, radio towers, etc., made out of wood. The islanders expect a great airplane to arrive. They even build wooden airplanes of the same shape as they see in the foreigner's airfields around them, but strangely enough, their wood planes do not fly. The result of this pseudoscientific imitation is to produce experts, which many of you are. You teachers who are really teaching children at the bottom of the heap can maybe doubt the experts once in a while. Learn from science that you must doubt the experts. As a matter of fact, I can also define science another way: Science is the belief in the ignorance of experts.

When someone says, "Science teaches such and such," he is using the word incorrectly. Science doesn't teach anything; experience teaches it. If they say to you, "Science has shown such and such," you might ask, "How does science show it? How did the scientists find out? How? What? Where?" It should not be "science has shown," but "this experiment, this effect, has shown." And you have as much right as anyone else, upon hearing about the experiments (but be patient and listen to all the evidence) to judge whether a sensible conclusion has been arrived at.

In a field which is so complicated that true science is not yet able to get anywhere, we have to rely on a kind of old-fashioned wisdom, a kind of definite straightforwardness. I am trying to inspire the teacher at the bottom to have some hope, and some self-confidence in common sense and natural intelligence. The experts who are leading you may be wrong.

I have probably ruined the system, and the students that are coming into Caltech no longer will be any good. I think we live in an unscientific age in which almost all the buffeting of communications and television words, books, and so on are unscientific. As a result, there is a considerable amount of intellectual tyranny in the name of science.

Finally, with regard to this time-binding, a man cannot live beyond the grave. Each generation that discovers something from its experience must pass that on, but it must pass that on with a delicate balance of respect and disrespect, so that the race (now that it is aware of the disease to which it is liable) does not inflict its errors too rigidly on its youth, but it does pass on the accumulated wisdom, plus the wisdom that it may not be wisdom.

It is necessary to teach both to accept and to reject the past with a kind of balance that takes considerable skill. Science alone of all the subjects contains within itself the lesson of the danger of belief in the infallibility of the greatest teachers of the preceding generation.

So carry on. Thank you.

NOTE

A film entitled "Strangeness Minus Three" gives an account of the search for a nuclear particle "called omega minus" in which Richard Feynman had some part. He discusses the nature of science in general and other scientists involved reflect upon their roles in the project. Check your media center for this film.

Also, another excellent source of ideas closely related to the nature of science involves the brief paperback by Watson entitled *The Double Helix*. It is a personal account of the events leading up to the discovery of the molecular structure of

DNA by one of the two Nobel Prize winning discoverers. Perhaps most important are the insights given into the personal lives of scientists who were involved in the exciting search to decode the life-controlling molecule, DNA.

Another account of a scientist's ideas about science is entitled *To Know a Fly*. Vincent Dethier has recorded in a very interesting and humorous way his experiences as a scientist who wants to know more about a fly. Holden-Day is the publisher.

---

1. Can you think of examples that substantiate the idea of mathematics as looking for patterns?
2. Would it be appropriate to begin teaching the concept of energy in grade two? How would one approach such a task? Can you define energy and give a few examples?
3. Why do you think Feynman says, "Science alone of all the subjects contains within itself the lesson of the danger of belief in the infallibility of the greatest teachers of the preceding generation?"
4. "Science doesn't teach anything; experience teaches it." Does this mean that to learn something about science, we must experience it? Can you detect any implications for elementary school science?

2 ALBERT SZENT-GYORGYI

Teaching and the Expanding Knowledge

Another Nobel Prize winner offers some insight about the nature of science. He talks of generalizations, the role of books, learning in schools, and humanism in relation to science. Like Richard Feynman, Gyorgi suggests an active kind of role for the scientist who is trying to make more sense out of nature. If you were able to read The Double Helix *before encountering this article you will probably have a better feeling for some of the ideas. In any case, the perceptions of this man should raise some questions or suggest alternatives that will help to stimulate further considerations about science.*

The simplification that comes with expanding knowledge enables teaching to encompass this knowledge.

Our attempt to harmonize teaching with expanding—or rather exploding—knowledge would be hopeless should growth not entail simplification. I will dwell on this sunny side. Knowledge is a sacred cow, and my problem will be how we can milk her while keeping clear of her horns.

One of my reasons for being optimistic is that the foundations of nature are simple. This was brought home to me many years ago when I joined the Institute for Advanced Studies in Princeton. I did this in the hope that by rubbing elbows with those great atomic physicists and mathematicians I would learn something about living matters. But as soon as I revealed that in any living system there are more than two electrons, the physicists would not speak to me. With all their computers they could not say what the third electron might do. The remarkable thing is that it knows exactly what to do. So that little electron knows something that all the wise men of Princeton don't, and this can

Reprinted from *Science*, Vol. 146, December 4, 1964, pp. 1278-1279, by permission of the editor and the author. Dr. Gyorgyi received the Nobel Prize for Physiology and Medicine in 1937 and is one of the best known biochemists in the world.

only be something very simple. Nature, basically, must be much simpler than she looks to us. She looks to us like a coded letter for which we have no code. To the degree to which our methods become less clumsy and more adequate and we find out nature's code, things must become not only clearer, but very much simpler, too.

Science tends to generalize, and generalization means simplification. My own science, biology, is today not only very much richer than it was in my student days, but is simpler, too. Then it was horribly complex, being fragmented into a great number of isolated principles. Today these are all fused into one single complex with the atomic model in its center. Cosmology, quantum mechanics, DNA and genetics, are all, more or less, parts of one and the same story—a most wonderful simplification. And generalizations are also more satisfying to the mind than details. We, in our teaching, should place more emphasis on generalizations than on details. Of course, details and generalizations must be in a proper balance: generalization can be reached only from details, while it is the generalization which gives value and interest to the detail.

After this preamble I would like to make a few general remarks, first, about the main instrument of teaching; books. There is a widely spread misconception about the nature of books which contain knowledge. It is thought that such books are something the contents of which have to be crammed into our heads. I think the opposite is closer to the truth. Books are there to keep the knowledge in while we use our heads for something better. Books may also be a better place for such knowledge. In my own head any book-knowledge has a half-life of a few weeks. So I leave knowledge, for safe-keeping, to books and libraries and go fishing, sometimes for fish, sometimes for new knowledge.

I know that I am shockingly ignorant. I could take exams in college but could not pass any of them. Worse than that: I treasure my ignorance; I feel snug in it. It does not cloud my naiveté, my simplicity of mind, my ability to marvel childishly at nature and recognize a miracle even if I see it every day. If, with my 71 years, I am still digging on the fringes of knowledge, I owe it to this childish attitude, "Blessed are the pure in heart, for they shall see God," says the Bible. "For they can understand Nature," say I.

I do not want to be misunderstood—I do not depreciate knowledge, and I have worked long and hard to know something of all fields of science related to biology. Without this I could do no research. But I have retained only what I need for an understanding, an intuitive grasp, and in order to know in which book to find what. This was fun, and we must have fun, or else our work is no good.

My next remark is about time relations. The time spent in school is relatively short compared to the time thereafter. I am stressing this because it is widely thought that everything we have to know to do our job well we have to learn in school. This is wrong because, during the long time which follows school, we are apt to forget, anyway, what we have learned there, while we have ample time for study. In fact, most of us have to learn all our lives, and it was with gray hair that I took up the study of quantum mechanics, myself. So what the school has to do, in the first place, is to make us learn how to learn, to whet our appetites for knowledge, to teach us the delight of doing a job well and the excitement of creativity, to teach us to love what we do, and to help us to find what we love to do.

My friend Gerard quoted Fouchet as advising us to take from the altar of knowledge the fire, not the ashes. Being of more earthly disposition, I would advise you to take the meat, not the bones. Teachers, on the whole, have a remarkable preference for bones, especially dry ones. Of course, bones are important, and now and then we all like to suck a bit on them, but only after having eaten the meat. What I mean to say is that we must not *learn* things, we must *live* things. This is true for almost everything. Shakespeare and all of literature must be *lived*, music, paintings, and sculptures have to be *made*, drama has to be *acted*. This is even true for history: we should live through it, through the spirit of the various periods, instead of storing their data. I am glad to say that this trend—to live things—is becoming evident even in the teaching of science. The most recent trend is not to *teach* the simpler laws of nature, but to make our students *discover* them for themselves in simple experiments. Of course, I know data are important. They may be even interesting, but only after we have consumed the meat, the substance. After this we may even become curious about them and retain them. But taught before this they are just dull, and they dull, if not kill, the spirit.

It is a widely spread opinion that memorizing will not hurt, that knowledge does no harm. I am afraid it may. Dead knowledge dulls the spirit, fills the stomach without nourishing the body. The mind is not a bottomless pit, and if we put in one thing we might have to leave out another. By a more live teaching we can fill the soul and reserve the mind for the really important things. We may even spare time we need for expanding subjects.

Such live teaching, which fills both the soul and the mind, may help man to meet one of his most formidable problems—what to do with himself. The most advanced societies, like ours, can already produce more than they can consume, and with advancing automation the discrepancy is increasing rapidly. We try to meet the challenge by producing useless things, like armaments. But this is no final answer. In the end we will have to work less. But then, what will we do with ourselves? Lives cannot be left empty. Man needs excitement and challenge, and in an affluent society everything is within easy reach. And boredom is dangerous, for it can easily make a society seek excitment in political adventure and in brinkmanship, following irresponsible and ignorant leaders. Our own society has recently shown alarming signs of this trend. In a world where atomic bombs can fly from one end to the other in seconds, this is tantamount to suicide. By teaching live arts and science, the schools could open up the endless horizons and challenges of intellectual and artistic life and make whole life an exciting adventure. I believe that in our teaching not only must details and generalizations be in balance, but our whole teaching must be balanced with general human values.

I want to conclude with a few remarks on single subjects, first, science. Science has two aspects: it has to be part of any education, of humanistic culture. But we also have to teach science as preparation for jobs. If we distinguish sharply between these two aspects then the talk about the "two cultures" will lose its meaning.

A last remark I want to make is about the teaching of history, not only because it is the most important subject, but also because I still have in my nostrils the acid smell of my own sweat which I produced when learning its data. History has two chapters: National History and World History. National history is a kind of family affair and I will not speak about it. But what is world history? In its essence it is the story of man, how he rose from his animal status to his present elevation. This is a fascinating story and is linked to a limited number of creative men, its heroes, who created new knowledge, new moral or ethical values, or new beauty. Opposing this positive side of history there is a negative, destructive side linked to the names of kings, barons, generals, and dictators who, with their greed and lust for power, made wars, fought battles, and mostly created misery, destroying what other men had built. These are the heroes of the history we teach at present as world history. Not only is this history negative and lopsided, it is false, too, for it omits the lice, rats, malnutrition, and epidemics which had more to do with the course of things than generals and kings, as Zinsser ably pointed out. The world history we teach should also be more truthful and include the stench, dirt, callousness, and misery of past ages, to teach us to appreciate progress and what we have. We need not falsify history; history has a tendency to falsify itself, because only the living return from the battlefield to tell stories. If the dead could return by once and tell about their ignominious end, history and politics would be different today. A truer history would also be simpler.

As the barriers between the various sciences have disappeared, so the barriers between science and humanities may gradually melt away. Dating through physical methods has become a method of research in history, while x-ray spectra and microanalysis have become tools in the study of painting. I hope that the achievements of human psychology may help us, also, to re-write human history in a more unified and translucent form.

The story of man's progress is not linked to any period, nation, creed, or color, and could teach to our youngsters a wider human solidarity. This they will badly need when rebuilding political and human relations, making them compatible with survival.

In spite of its many chapters, our teaching has, essentially, but one object, the production of men who can fill their shoes and stand erect with their eyes on the wider horizons. This makes the school, on any level, into the most important public institution and the teacher into the most important public figure. As we teach today, so the morrow will be.

---

1. Gyorgyi stated that "books are there to keep the knowledge in while we use our heads for something better." Does this have any implications for science textbooks in elementary school science? Secondary school? College?
2. Do you note any similarities or differences in the thinking of Feynman and Gyorgyi as to the nature of science?
3. "This was fun, and we must have fun, or else our work is no good." Could a scientist's work be fun?
4. Can we learn things without living them?

3   PAUL WESTMEYER

Man-Made Science

It might be argued that mathematics is nonexistent until man "makes it up." The product is an abstraction, not necessarily related to the real world as we know it. How about science? Is science invented or discovered? Are there really electrons, or are they merely an invention to satisfy an explanation made up by man? Do ideas in science change as the ideas of scientists change? What is science?

Consider the following ideas carefully for they provide a somewhat different answer to the question we are pursuing.

At 3:20 P.M. on December 2, 1942, reaction in the world's first atomic pile became self-sustaining. It was a dramatic moment but Fermi (leading the group which conducted the test) and the other scientists watching intently knew that it would work.[1] Why did they know? They knew because the science which supported the physical structure, the pile, was theirs—they had made it up.

Man began to construct this science long ago. It was given a very special building block in 1912 when Rutherford invented the heavy unitary nucleus and another in 1932 when Chadwick proposed a particle called the neutron. In 1939 Hahn and Strassman observed that barium was present in the residue of experiments in which uranium was bombarded with neutrons.

Lise Meitner attempted mathematical analysis of these experiments and found that the total of the atomic masses of the residual elements was less than the atomic mass of uranium. She and her nephew, O. R. Frisch, put this information and Einstein's 1905 theory equating mass

This paper was presented at a symposium on elementary science at the forty-third annual meeting of the National Association for Research in Science Teaching, 1970 and is published with the author's permission. Dr. Westmeyer is widely known in the field of science education and is presently the Head of the Department of Science Education at Florida State University.

1. See account in *The First Reactor*, U. S. Atomic Energy Commission/Division of Technical Information, November, 1968.

and energy together and made up the explanation that under neutron bombardment uranium nuclei split, forming two nuclei each approximately half the mass of the uranium nucleus, and in the process some of the nuclear mass is converted into energy.

Finally, Fermi and Bohr conceived the idea that neutrons are emitted during nuclear fission and hence a chain reaction is possible. All that remained was precise calculations and trial of the experiment, but they knew it would work—they had made it all up.

Yes, the nuclear atom is an invention of man and furthermore, in a recent publication Dewey Larson has said, ". . . when the arguments in favor of the nuclear atom concept, developed fifty years ago on the basis of a very limited amount of experimental information, are re-examined in the light of the immense store of factual knowledge now available, they collapse completely and leave the theory entirely without support."[2] Larson has published at least four books in which he insists that many of our present scientific explanations are in need of total change—not revision, *total* change.

Everybody knows that mathematics is a man-made device but they aren't so sure about science. Richard Feynman who said in an NSTA[3] talk, "Mathematics is looking for patterns," also said, "Science is the belief in the ignorance of experts." He said further, ". . . science is . . . the result of the discovery that it is worthwhile rechecking by new direct experience, and not necessarily trusting the race experience from the past." And finally, ". . . you have as much right as anyone else, upon hearing about . . . experiments (but be patient and listen to *all* the evidence) to judge whether a sensible conclusion has been arrived at."

"But," you say, "can't theories be proven?" Let me tell you a story.

The American Indians of a century and a half ago observed that meat boiled in water high up on a mountain was not tender and edible as it was when cooked at the base of the mountain. Furthermore, the Indians observed that the tenderness decreased steadily as the meat was boiled at locations farther and farther up the mountain. So they invented an explanation, which was that evil spirits prevent meat from cooking and the density of evil spirits increases as altitude increases. This was a plausible and probably useful explanation. As a matter of fact, it could be "proven." All they had to do was clamp a lid on the cooking pot atop the mountain and *seal* it. This would keep out evil spirits and

2. Dewey B. Larson. *The Case Against the Nuclear Atom* (North Pacific Publishers, Portland, Oregon, 1963).
3. National Science Teacher's Association.

the meat should be well done. (It would be.) So you can't prove a thing you can only *not disprove* it.

So—if science is man-made then anyone can make up science. Oh that doesn't mean that just any explanation for a set of observations is all right, but it does mean that any explanation that fits the observation, is useful for predictions, and stands the test of trial should not be discouraged.

Can students actually make up science? Let me tell you another story—this one of a chemistry student in a CBA[4] class several years ago. This girl was given a cylindrical "black box," 18 inches long and 2 inches in diameter, and told me to make a mental model to explain its behavior. She rotated the box and found that something inside seemed to *roll* in this direction. She tipped the box and the thing inside *slid* and struck the end of the box. She tipped it the other way and the thing slid again but seemed to hit that end of the box much more quickly than it hit the end on the first tip. She repeated these observations several times and then the teacher took the box away, saying, "That's all the data you have to work with."

She pondered the observation for a time and finally proposed her explanation—"The box contains a cylinder which is shorter on one end than the other."

Did it explain? It seemed to.

Testable? No. The box was no longer available to her.

Real? Hardly.

Invention? You bet!

---

1. Do you think that Einstein's 1905 theory might someday be found wrong? Why?
2. Are there theories in science that are correct for all time? Can you identify some that would probably fall into that category?
3. Try to make up a different explanation for the "black box" experiment. Is yours better? Why?

4. Chemical Bond Approach.

4 RAYMOND J. SEEGER

Scientists Are People

What are scientists like? Is there a typical childhood that is characteristic of scientists? While hundreds of biographies and autobiographies have been written about the lives of scientists, somehow, most people are uninformed about the personal lives of scientists. The human side is typically neglected because the emphasis has been allocated to discoveries (inventions?) and the professional side of things.

Although Dr. Seeger's words were originally directed toward educators who prepare science teachers, the ideas are pertinent for our inquiry into the nature of science.

The 15 scientists considered could easily be categorized as "giants" in the field of science. Their contributions have greatly influenced the course of events in man's attempt to understand his physical environment. Some names such as Galileo and Newton will probably be quite familiar to you while others such as Herschel and Young may not be as well-known. All fifteen present a unique *look at* unique *individuals.*

Many paperbacks have been written about famous scientists that are quite readable and readily available in most bookstores. If such biographies or autobiographies become of interest to you as a result of reading Dr. Seeger's paper, it would probably be well worth your time to choose one or two of these paperbacks and read them in order to gain more detailed insight into the humanistic side of scientists.

A major problem of modern education is the general *drop-out* from school: of the students in fifth grade a few years ago about 72% will graduate from high school and 40% will enter college, but only 20% will graduate from it. A minor problem is the special *stay-out* from certain disciplines, particularly physics. During the past five years the

Reprinted from The Physics Teacher, Vol. 6, issue 9, 1968, pp. 454-465 by permission of the editor and the author. Dr. Seeger has had a distinguished career as a theoretical physicist and is presently a senior staff associate for research at the National Science Foundation.

Editor's Note: This article was presented as an invited address at the annual meeting of Association for the Education of Teachers in Science—National Science Supervisors Association 1 April, 1968, Washington, D. C.

number of college students receiving a bachelor's degree in physics has decreased 10%. Over the past 15 years even the high school enrollment in physics has decreased 1%, whereas in science, generally, it has increased 9% and in mathematics 11%. It is sometimes argued that the mathematical requirements for modern physics are a deterrent for students contemplating this subject. If so, then the very increase in students taking mathematics in secondary schools should alleviate the problem instead of aggravating it. Evidently the primary need now is better coordination between mathematics courses and physics courses in high school, with more emphasis upon applications of mathematical reasoning to understanding natural phenomena.

Although we are not particularly concerned in this article with the factors that contribute to the physics stay-out, in passing, I should like to call attention to a few. In the first place, there is the stereotype image of the scientist. In an opinion poll[1] about one-third of the high school students blamed the difficulties encountered in science on their own poor academic background coupled with the apparent inadequacy of their intellectual capacity (the supposed need to be a "genius"). They complained, furthermore, of scientists being a group of "odd" people, who jealously guard their own interests and fail to sacrifice for other people, who have no time to enjoy life and can't even have a normal family. Ten percent of the students claimed that scientists are inherently dishonest and evil. These conclusions, unfortunately, are abetted by the narrow opinions of many professional counsellors, whose guidance too often reflects merely their own lack of adequate scientific experience. Of equal importance are the careless actions of many physicists who frequently fail to communicate the spiritual depth of their own research interests. What is of most concern to me, however, is the lack of any evident improvement in such attitudes from the first year of high school through the senior year.[2] In view of the relatively few students taking physics during this educational phase, physics teachers cannot be entirely to blame. Perhaps teachers of biology and of chemistry have an even greater responsibility—not to mention the influence of teachers in other disciplines inasmuch as they have these students for most of their high school career.

A second stay-out factor is the practical one of scheduling. Most high school biology today is obviously more or less a compromise between traditional natural history and modern molecular biology. It is

1. "Physical Science Aptitude and Attitudes Toward Occupations," Lafayette, Ind., Purdue Opinion Panel Research Report, 45 (July 1956).
2. Dorothy G. Rogers, "An Analysis of Attitudes Toward Science," Lafayette, Ind., Purdue Opinion Panel Research Report 58-41 (May 1958).

usually based upon modern chemistry, which some of the students get in their junior year. (The chemistry, in turn, is based upon modern physics, which the student gets only in his senior year—if at all.) This sequence is obviously the reverse of any educationally sound approach to modern biology, which is founded largely upon biochemistry and biophysics.

The perennial need for motivation is highly significant; its correction, therefore, will afford some degree of a practicable solution to the stay-out problem. Let us briefly analyze this factor from the point of view of science as experience combined with reason and imagination. Of primary importance is developing curiosity about phenomena themselves. Unfortunately, modern urbanization with its increasing loss of blue skies and green fields restricts opportunities for people even to notice particularly interesting things. At the same time, the complex gadgetry in "black" boxes does not always invite an inquiring mind in school. Sometimes, however, motivation is association more with the eternal quest for comprehensive understanding, for an over-all view. In this instance there is unquestionably a potential for stimulating student interest, inasmuch as theoretical concepts are nowadays emphasized more frequently than empirical approaches. An over-emphasis, however, upon the status quo is also a danger signal, warning that it is not only important to know where we are, but also where we expect to be. To get a sense of direction, indeed, we need at least two points; the one where are we and the other, where we were: the line joining them indicates a probable future outlook. Students must be taught not merely to understand the science of today, but even more to be prepared for its inevitable change 25 years hence. The science of tomorrow, we can be certain, will be as different from today's science as the latter is from the science of yesterday. A third factor in motivation is the fellowship of imaginative persons (living and dead). Some years ago I came across a book with the interesting title, *Children Are People*.[3] So, too, I mused, students are people, teachers are people, scientists are people! What I propose, therefore, is an emphasis upon people-to-people communication, one to another. Let us not try to classify all students, all teachers, all scientists, but rather regard each one as an individual person. I am convinced that the most important contribution a high school teacher can make to education is the personal motivation of students. You may recall the prophet Jeremiah brooding about the ruins of Jerusalem. What would happen now, he wondered, to the promised land that had just been destroyed by the conqueror, to the promise made

3. Emily Post, *Children Are People* (New York: Funk and Wagnalls, 1940).

to the people recently taken captive to Babylon? It occurred to Jeremiah that, although the covenant between God and the people of Israel could not now be in effect owing to the very dissolution of the nation, nevertheless, through individuals, the existent remnant, a new covenant could be made—this time between God and each person. In this spirit, therefore, I propose a teenager-to-teenager communication, a bridge between young people of today with those young people of yesterday who became scientists, who themselves had seemingly formidable problems as growing persons. We shall find that their predicaments were not too different from those encountered by teenagers today. Accordingly, I have selected, somewhat at random, 15 well-known scientists, and have grouped them roughly into the advantaged, the undecided, and the frustrated. Let us look at each of these scientists when he was a teenager.

The first of the advantaged I shall call genius "X." He was born in 1623 in Clermont near the volcanic Auvergne. His father was a magistrate who went to live in Paris in 1631, but had to go into hiding (1638) because of certain demonstrations against the government. Upon being pardoned later that year he became a tax collector at Rouen. The mother, who had some interest in mathematics, died when the child was three. The family were Jansenists. As a baby the boy was sickly; his abdomen was puffed and hardened. (After 18 years of age he is said to have spent no day without pain.) His early instruction was given entirely at home, where his father taught him grammar, ecclesiastical history, and some science. (Latin and mathematics were deferred until a later time.) The boy benefited much by self study. Despite his father's restriction on geometry, at 12 he was found ferreting out theorems with his own charcoal diagrams. At 16 he wrote a one-page treatise on conic sections, in which he utilized the then new mathematics (projective geometry) of Gerard Desargues (not fully appreciated until 200 years later). At 19 he had to help his father with calculations for tax assessments. Anxious to escape this drudgery, he designed the first calculating machine (10 of the 50 constructed are extant). His scientific achievements were outstanding. At 24 he made major contributions to the physics of fluids and at 31 laid down the foundations of probability. Meanwhile, however, he had dedicated his life wholly to religion. His writing of the "Lettres provinciales" at 33 has earned him recognition as the father of modern French prose. Having to wait on occasions with others for individual carriages, at 35 he conceived the omnibus (for all), a suggestion which was taken up and put into practice—at five sous a ride. He died at 39. This scientist "X" was truly a genius, this religious man of science—Blaise Pascal.[4]

4. Morris Bishop, *Pascal* (Baltimore: Williams and Wilkins, 1936).

We shall consider precocious "Y" as our second advantaged person. He was born in 1773 at Milverton (near Taunton, Somerset). The boy was the first of ten children. His father was a mercer (cloth merchant), a banker, and a Quaker. He learned to read at the age of two (he actually attended a village school then). By four he had read the whole Bible twice, together with some of Isaac Watts' hymns. At five he could recite Oliver Goldsmith's "The Deserted Village." At six he began his study of Latin. He was then sent to a boarding grammar school at 6 plus, but became homesick. Returning home he read about science in the library there. At 8 plus he again went away to boarding school, where he heard his first lectures on natural philosophy and where he enjoyed making telescopes and binding books. By 13 he would read Latin and Greek, French and Italian, as well as Hebrew. At 14 he was hired as a tutor—companion for a Barclay grandson. In this capacity he read English, French, and Italian classics. (He translated some English classics into Greek.) He also read Isaac Newton's "Principia" and "Opticks." At 16, stirred by the Negro trade, as a Quaker, he abstained from sugar. At this stage modern guidance counsellors would undoubtedly have recommended that he embark upon a literary career. During that very year, however, he became ill and was treated by an uncle (Dr. Brocklesby), who persuaded him to study medicine. The boy attended lectures on chemistry and performed some simple experiments on his own, although he was never particularly interested in experiments per se. At 19 he began his higher education in the Hunterian School of Anatomy in London. At 20 he entered St. Bartholomew's Hospital and gave a paper on "Observations on Vision," which was published by the Royal Society the following year. (He was elected a fellow of the Royal Society.) He then continued his medical education at the University of Edinburgh. Because of his developing interest in music, dancing, and the theater, he separated himself from the Quakers. At 22 he went to the University of Göttingen (founded in 1733 by George II). Here his curiosity was aroused about sound, particularly its production and propagation—the beginning of his interest in physics. At 24, a converted Anglican, he entered Emmanual College at Cambridge to receive its prestigious degree (at 25) preparatory to becoming a practising physician. As for his scientific accomplishments, at 27 he became Professor of Physics at the Royal Institution (1800-1802). His lectures there on Natural Philosophy were published in 1807; in them he argued convincingly for the wave theory of light, based upon a thought experiment involving the phenomenon of interference. Meanwhile, the Egyptian Rosetta stone, discovered by France in 1799 and obtained by England in 1811, presented an unusual problem of linguistic interpretation inasmuch as it was written in some undeciphered languages: hieroglyphic, Egyptian, and Encorial inscriptions. This scholar made some translations of them; six turned out to be correct, four partially correct, and four wrong. He died at 56. A medallion commemorates him in the Westminster Abbey. This scientific man of medicine "Y" was truly precocious —Thomas Young.[5]

Our last instance of an advantaged person is a gentleman and scholar "Z." He was born in 1831 at Edinburgh. As Laird of an estate inherited from a brother, the father was a sportsman with practical interests, but at the same time quite unworldly (he was an elder in the Scottish Church). His mother, whose father had been prominent, was a gentlewoman, a pious Anglican, who composed for the organ, but who unfortunately died when the boy was only nine. Being an only child he enjoyed a close relationship with his father. In the pregrammar school period the boy was wont to ask, "What's the go o' that?" At eight he had some knowledge of the Scriptures and Milton; he could repeat the lengthy 119th Psalm. He was accurate in drawing. While at home he was accustomed to wandering. At ten he went to a Scottish day school in Edinburgh, where he lived with an aunt. He had to attend both St. Andrew's Presbyterian Church and St. John's Anglican Church. Shy and dull at school, he consequently had few friends, particularly in view of his lack of interest in sports. At 13 he made some models of the five regular solids and become interested in geometry. Although he was only 11th in the list of scholars the next year, he obtained first prize in English, as well as a prize for English verse and a mathematics medal. At 15 he wrote a paper on "Oval Curves," which was read at the Royal Society of Edinburgh. He did not receive a medal that year, but did become interested in magnetism and electricity. At 16 he received first prizes in English and in Mathematics (and almost in Latin). His higher education began with his entrance to the University of Edinburgh at 17. Here he studied logic, mathematics, and natural philosophy. At 18 he wrote a paper on rolling curves, and at 19, one on elastic solids. During that year he entered Peterhouse College at Cambridge (he should have probably gone there a year earlier). He later transferred to Trinity College, where the Master was William Whewell. He did not, however, receive a scholarship until 21. He was noted for his verse, usually humorous, sometimes ironical; nevertheless, he wrote a "Student's Evening Hymn." At 23 he was awarded the distinction of second Wrangler and tied with the first Wrangler, Edward John Routh, for the coveted Smith prize. By this time he had developed his life-long interest in electricity

5. Alexander Wood and Frank Oldham, Thomas Young (New York: Cambridge University Press, 1954).

and magnetism, as well as an ingenious color top. At 24 he was elected a
fellow of Trinity College. Although aways receptive as a student, he
managed to put his own stamp on all his work. Later he always acknowl-
edged appreciatively his education. He became Professor of Physics at
Marischal College (Aberdeen), then at King's College (London, 1860-
65), where he had contacts with Michael Faraday. Later he was called
to the University of Cambridge, where he was responsible for building
the world-famous Cavendish Laboratory. He received the Adams prize
for his essay on Saturn's Rings, was one of the founders of the kinetic
theory of gases, and wrote the classical "Treatise on Electricity and
Magnetism" (1873), in which he summarized previous experimental
findings in mathematical terms and formulated the electromagnetic
theory of light—confirmed experimentally in 1888. This professor of experimental physics "Z" was truly a gentleman and a scholar—James Clerk
Maxwell.[6]

Let us consider a few cases in the undecided class. We shall begin
with ministerial student "A." He was born in 1571 at Weil der Stadt. A
Lutheran grandfather had been a bookbinder and mayor, but was apparently never particularly interested in this child. His father at first
assisted the grandfather, but then devoted most of his life to soldiering;
he was rude and rough to his wife and actually abandoned his family
in 1583. His mother in later life was jailed for 14 months and then tried
as a witch; she died obscurely. A brother (epileptic) was a good-for-
nothing and ran away; another, however, was a respectable craftsman
(a pewterer); a sister married a clergyman. The child himself almost
died with smallpox while his parents were away engaged in war in the
Netherlands. His early education was in a German school in Württem-
berg. At seven he attended a Latin school, where continual moving and
hard agricultural labor necessitated his spending five years to complete
the normal three-year course. He did, however, show evidence of a keen
intellect, primarily in the state examinations. At 13, accordingly, he was
enrolled in a convent school at Adelberg. At 15, he was admitted to a
higher seminary located in an old Cistercian Monastery. He was a con-
scientious student, but quite introspective. He exhibited keen spiritual
anxiety and became increasingly disturbed about religious controversies.
He was always busy, but unable to stick long at any one thing. At 17
he passed the entrance examination for the University of Tübingen on
the Neckar, but returned for another year to the seminary at Maulbronn.
At 18 he entered the University, specifically the Stift Seminary, where

6. Lewis Campbell and Wm. Garnett, *The Life of James Clerk Maxwell* with se-
lections from his correspondence and occasional writings. New ed. rev. (London:
Macmillan and Company, Ltd., 1884); Richard Tetley Glazebrook, *James Clerk
Maxwell and Modern Physics* (New York: The Macmillan Company, 1896).

his life was wholly regulated. In philosophy there he preferred Plato to Aristotle, and became interested in the mystic Nicholas of Cusa. A teacher, Michael Maestlin, stimulated his interest in mathematics and astronomy, particularly in Euclid and Apollonius, Archimedes, Ptolemy and Copernicus. He became increasingly discouraged in theology, owing to constant squabbling; indeed, he developed a bitter distaste for all such controversy. At 23, the faculty unexpectedly recommended him as a mathematics teacher to the Graz Seminary (protestant). His parents would have preferred the prestige of a priest, but deferred to the advice of the faculty. At this time, he abandoned his native land forever. Later he became assistant to the celebrated astronomer Tycho Brahe at Prague, and eventually himself became Imperial Mathematician. He completed the Rudolphine astronomical tables and formulated the three laws of planetary motion. In 1604 he detected a new star (nova); he later studied optics with particular interest in the design of telescopes. On the side, however, he maintained a practical interest in astrology. This undecided ministerial student "A" became the diligent mathematical astronomer, Johannes Kepler.[7]

Let us next consider a premedical drop-out "B." He was born at Pisa in 1564 (a memorable year for births and deaths of celebrities). His father was of an impoverished lower nobility and had to resort to trade (cloth) for his living. The father, however, was interested in language, mathematics, and music, particularly the lute. The boy went initially to school at Pisa and with his father's help studied some classics. He made toy machines, which did not always work. He then attended the monastery school at Vallombrosa, where he learned to enjoy the classics and Italian Poetry, particularly Dante, Petrarch, and Ariosto. He learned to play the lute and organ. He liked to draw and paint; he admitted later he would have chosen art for his life's work had he been free to do so. At 17 plus, as a premedical student, he entered the University of Pisa. Overhearing a mathematics tutor, at 18 he found himself suddenly fascinated by mathematics. With the consent of his father, he decided not to study medicine. Being attentive to the lectures was not enough to win the professors' good will and a much needed scholarship, inasmuch as he was also quite argumentative. At 20, therefore, owing to financial straits, he had to return to his family at Florence; he never graduated. At 21 he wrote a paper on the center of gravity, and at 22, one on "The Little Balance." At 25 he was appointed Professor at the University of Pisa, the very institution from which he had dropped out. He later became Professor at the University of Padua and finally Chief Mathema-

7. Max Caspar, *Kepler,* translated and edited by C. D. Hellman (London: Abelard Schuman, 1959).

tician for the Grand Duke of Tuscany. He is largely responsible for the so-called scientific method as we know it today, for the application of mathematics to observations, for the interaction of experiment with theory. He was unqualifiedly the founder of dynamics and acoustics, as well as the first to design a thermoscope, a telescope, and a compound microscope. He was always a sharp, aggressive opponent of all authoritarianism, both in philosophy and theology; he was an enthusiastic proponent of the Copernican system. This undecided premedical drop-out "B" became the founder of modern physics, Galileo Galilei.[8]

We now come to a farm boy "C," who was born on Christmas at Woolsthorpe, seven miles south of Grantham, the very year that Galileo died. His father, who had a small manor (a poor estate), died three months before the boy was born. Within two years the mother married a clergyman, by whom she had three children. Meanwhile the boy had to live with his grandmother and an uncle. As a premature child, he was quite frail; in his early years he had to wear a bolster about his neck to support his head. He attended day schools at Skillington and Stoke. At 12 he entered King's School at Grantham, where he was placed in the lowest form, indeed, next to the last in his class. It is said that the boy who ranked above him one day kicked him in the stomach. He fought the boy and determined to beat him also in studies. Ultimately he became first in school. Nevertheless, he showed no unusual ability. At 16 he had to return home to help farm and manage the estate (his stepfather had died in 1656), but he was quite negligent of the animals —a total failure at farming (he studied mathematics while supposedly at work). At 18, accordingly, he returned to King's School to prepare for Cambridge, where he entered Trinity College the next year; a shy diffident country lad; he found it populous and busy. His first years were spent without distinction, undoubtedly owing to the keen competition of the better prepared public school boys. As a sizar, moreover, he had to work for his room and board by performing menial services. He was not popular; on the one hand, he was shunned by fellow students because of his lack of interest in physical exercise and sports; and, on the other, he was not attractive to older men, inasmuch as he was not sociable, talkative, or witty. At 21 one of the teachers, Isaac Barrow, gave some lectures on natural philosophy, including optics, which greatly interested the young man. Together with 44 other students he received a scholarship, and at 22 obtained the bachelor's degree—without any distinction being noted. He returned to

---

8. J. J. Fahie, *Galileo* (London: John Murray, 1903); Laura Fermi and Gilberto Bernadini, *Galileo and the Scientific Revolution* (New York: Basic Books, Inc., 1961); Raymond J. Seeger, *Galileo Galilei, His Life and His Works* (Oxford, England: Pergamon Press, Inc., 1966).

Woolsthorpe, where he sat out the great (black) bubonic plague until the University re-opened. It was during this time that he meditated on calculus (fluxions), the nature of white light, and universal gravitation. His outstanding scientific accomplishment was the publication of the "Philosophiae Naturalis Principia Mathematica" in 1687, which included the fundamental laws of motion, and which has been acclaimed as "the greatest intellectual feat in the history of science." In 1703 he wrote a book on "Opticks." Meanwhile, at 26 he had been appointed Lucasian Professor of Mathematics at Trinity. Later, he became warden of the mint, then its master, a member of Parliament in 1701, President of the Royal Society in 1703; he was knighted two years later. He died at the age of 84 and was buried in Westminster Abbey. This undecided farm boy "C" became the foremost theoretical physicist (and mathematician), Isaac Newton.[9]

Let us now consider the musician deserter "D," born at Hanover in 1738. His father was an oboeist in the Guards. His mother had ten children, of which he was the fourth. She was opposed to learning and made it impossible for her daughters to learn French or dancing. She herself could not write. The boy attended a garrison school until 14, where he learned some French and later, on the outside, Latin and arithmetic. His father taught him to play the oboe, the violin, and the organ. At 17 he, too, became an oboeist in the Guards and toured England for a year. He participated in the campaign of 1759, but the next year, at 19, he decided on "removal" (desertion), ostensibly because of poor health; penniless, he returned to England. (On his first official visit to the King of England in 1789, he was presented with a formal pardon.) At 22, he took charge of the music for the militia of Durham. Essentially a free lance, he found himself involved with pupils, concerts, and compositions. At 28 he became organist at the octagon chapel in fashionable Bath, where he was engaged in both composition and teaching. By himself he studied Italian, Greek, and mathematics. He became interested in the applicability of mathematics to optics in general, and then to astronomy in particular. At 36 he made a Gregorian telescope. A year later he used a Newtonian telescope to survey the whole sky and to locate planets and stars above the 4th magnitude. At 41 he joined the new Philosophical Society at Bath, and at 44 decided to devote full time to astronomy. Scientifically, his most notable discovery was the planet Uranus in 1781, the first since "shepherds watched their flocks by night." Subsequently, he was made a fellow of the Royal Society and received the Copley medal. At the same time he continued to identify nebulae

9. E. N. DaC. Andrade, *Isaac Newton* (New York: Chanticlear, 1950); Louis Trenchard Moore, *Isaac Newton* (New York: Dover Publications, Inc., 1934, 1962).

and star clusters; he proposed a structure of the universe. He was knighted in 1816 and died in 1822. A memorial stone has been set in Westminister Abbey's floor near his son's tomb. This undecided musician deserter "D" became the astronomical explorer, Frederick William Herschel.[10]

Next we shall consider an adventurer "E," born in 1753 at North Woburn, Massachusetts. His father was a fifth-generation American farmer. Unfortunately he died when the child was only two; the mother remarried. The boy went to school until 13. Nothing of genius was evident; indeed, he was said to be "indolent, flighty, unpromising." With the aid of an older boy, however, he did manage some self-education. At 14 he became an apprentice to a dry goods merchant in Salem, where he exhibited good draftsmanship. At 16 he transferred to a dry goods merchant in Boston, where he once walked to Harvard to hear Professor John Winthrop lecture on natural philosophy. He tried to make a perpetual motion machine. He is said to have participated in the Boston "massacre" (1770). The fireworks he prepared for a Stamp Act celebration blew up and badly burned him. His employer, concerned about such a risk in his store, fired the boy. He became an itinerant teacher. At 19 he went to Rumford (later Concord), New Hampshire, where he taught for a clergyman. An aggressive daughter, a 32-year-old widow with the largest fortune in town, arranged a marriage with the adventurer. They had only one child. He himself used his position to become commissioned by the Governor at Portsmouth as a major in the Second Provincial Regiment. His aristocratic airs, however, earned him the epithet "dandy and upstart;" he was unpopular and at 22 was regarded as unfriendly to the popular cause of liberty. (He was actually a spy, and from time to time sent information to General Thomas Gage in Boston.) He was "tried" but found "not guilty." Nevertheless, there was considerable agitation to have him tarred and feathered. He escaped—never to return. At 23 when the British evacuated Boston he went with a group to England. Owing to some successful experiments with gunpowder, at 27 he became a fellow of the Royal Society. The next year he was made a lieutenant colonel in the British Army and returned with its New York regiment to America. A year later, as a colonel he returned to England. At 31 he went to serve the Bavarian Elector at Munich. Meanwhile, he had been knighted by George III. At 32 he returned again to Munich and was made there a Count of the Holy Roman Empire of the German nation. At 52 he married Antoine Laurent Lavoisier's widow. He died in France at 61. His scientific achievements were not of a major character, although he did

10. Angus Armitage, *William Herschel* (London: Thomas Nelson and Sons, 1962).

make a significant contribution to the understanding of heat. He was primarily important for his organizing activities; for example, he was one of the founders of the Royal Institution in London (corresponding to the later Smithsonian Institution in Washington, established by an Englishman) in 1799. This undecided adventurer "E" became the well-known physicist, Sir Benjamin Thompson, Count Rumford.[11]

We come now to a country gentleman "F," born at Shrewsbury in 1809. His father, a successful country physician, married a daughter of the potter Josiah Wedgewood. They had six children, of whom he was the fourth. The mother died when he was eight, so that he was brought up mainly by his older sister. In the same year he was sent to day school (Unitarian), where he was slower at learning even than his younger sister. He did, however, show interest in collecting plants and eggs, pebbles and shells. His father's judgment at that time was the following: "You care for nothing but shooting dogs, and will be a disgrace to yourself and your family." At 9 he went to school under Samuel Butler, grandfather of the author of "Erewhon." Later he himself reflected that "the school as a means of education to me was simply a blank." At 16 he went to the University of Edinburgh to study medicine. He found the lectures there incredibly dull, with the exception of those on chemistry. He was actually rebuked by another student for investigating biological phenomena in what the student regarded as his own pre-empted field. Aware of his father's property, the young man made no great effort to prepare himself for a career in medicine. His father, therefore, proposed holy orders. And so at 18 he entered Christ College, Cambridge. He regarded his years there "wasted" as far as academic studies were concerned, "as completely as at Edinburgh and as at school." He continued shooting and hunting—and collected beetles. The Reverend John Steven Henslow, however, stimulated his interest in botany. At 22 he graduated 10th among those not seeking honors. He did, however, make a geological excursion into Wales with Professor Adam Sedgwick. He then sought a job as naturalist aboard the ship Beagle. His father, however, questioned such an experience for a potential clergyman, owing to the disrepute and discomfort associated with it. An uncle, however, argued that natural history may not be unsuitable for a clergyman. The young man, meanwhile, had been rejected by the ship's captain owing to his physiognomy (a poor nose shape did not seem suitable for the hardships that would be encountered), but was later accepted. He determined to make collections on the journey. At 27 he returned to England eager to pursue an entirely different career,

11. Sanborn C. Brown, *Benjamin Thompson—Count Rumford* (Oxford England: Pergamon Press, Inc., 1967).

namely, that of a man of science. He was elected a fellow of the Royal Society at 29 plus. Having poor health he elected to live in a country house (Downs) near Seven Oaks in Kent with a Wedgewood daughter, whom he married in 1839. His publications, "Journal of Researches" (1839), "On the Origin of The Species" (1859), and "The Descent of Man" (1871), all have had wide-reaching significance. He received the Copley Medal in 1864. Although buried in Westminster Abbey in 1862, he was never honored otherwise by the Government. This undecided country gentleman "F" became the revolutionary biologist, Charles Darwin.[12]

We shall conclude this group of the undecided with runaway "G," born at Boston in 1706. His father, an emigrant from Banbury, England, was a chandler. His mother, a second wife, had ten children. The boy learned to read early and attended what is now known as the Boston Latin School; he was head of his class. Noting the ultimate cost of college education, even in those days, the father withdrew the boy at nine and sent him to a day school where he learned to write, but failed in arithmetic. At ten he was withdrawn from this school, too, to assist his father and to learn to handle tools. At 12 he was apprenticed to a printer (his brother) to learn this trade. He was fond of reading; he borrowed books and even bought some of them with money saved on food. At 16 under a pseudonym he wrote for a newspaper. At 17 he sold some of his books and set out to seek his fortune elsewhere. He walked to New York and from there to Philadelphia, where he arrived with one Dutch dollar and one copper shilling. Whereas at Boston his studies had been his major concern, in Philadelphia his interest turned to friends (he married there at 24.) At 18 he made a trip to London, where he became stranded and had to practice the trade of printing to obtain funds. Returning at 20, he made some quantitative observations of oceanic properties on this trip. It was not, however, until the age of 40 that he had sufficient leisure to pursue freely his curiosity about natural phenomena. A lecture on electricity stimulated his interest. As he returned from England on his last voyage, at 79, he was still measuring the temperature of the air and of the water. Scientifically, he can be said to have been only an amateur; nature was only a secondary interest. As a physicist, however, he did postulate the increasingly significant principle of conservation of electric charge on the basis of an acceptable electrostatic theory he himself had devised. In 1753 he became the first foreigner to receive the Copley medal; in 1756 he was made a fellow of

12. Gavin De Beer, *Charles Darwin* (Garden City: Doubleday and Company, Inc., 1964); Julian Huxley and H. B. D. Kettlewell, *Charles Darwin and His World* (New York: The Viking Press, 1965).

the Royal Society. In general, he was a philanthropist, involved in the founding of the University of Pennsylvania and the American Philosophical Society (1768), as well as a patriot and a writer. This undecided runaway "G" became the outstanding United States scientist of the 18th century, Benjamin Franklin.[13]

Our last group of teenagers who became scientists concerns the frustrated. We begin with No. 1, a laborer, born in 1766 at Eaglesfield in West Cumberland. His father was a poor hand-loom weaver, who made the popular gray wool coats. He lived in a thatched cottage, where the sleeping room was 15 ft $\times$ 6 ft $\times$ 6 ft. The mother was quite active; she had three children who lived, this one not being the oldest. The family (Quakers) sent the boy to a Quaker school master, who was more than the ordinary run of North Country teachers. He was found to be "not a brilliant nor quick boy," but steadfast in purpose and in power of abstract thought. At 11 he attracted the interest of a local meteorologist and instrument maker, who taught him some mathematics. At 12 he himself opened a school for children from infancy to 17. It was not a success. Accordingly, at 14 he had to work as a laborer with a plow. At 15 he decided to seek his fortune elsewhere. So with a new umbrella in hand and with his underclothes under an arm, he walked 44 miles through the Lake District to Kendal, where he worked for his brother in a school. On the side, he made barometers and thermometers. At 19 the brothers themselves took over the school. The income, however, was so small that they had to borrow money continually, even from their poor parents. They were not popular, owing largely to their uncouth manners. At 21 the young man was solving various mathematical problems for a journal and making barometric measurements of his own. He gave 12 public lectures, which had an unfavorable response. At 24 he had to collect flora and flies to make money. At 27 he decided to become a tutor in a then essentially secondary school, Manchester College, which later (1889) moved to Oxford. At 30 he found himself interested in chemistry, and three years later, accordingly, gave up his regular position. He became a private teacher, instructing very young children, in order that he might carry on private research in his small room in the back of the boarding house. Scientifically, he is noted for the first (1794) paper on color blindness (his own). In 1808 he published his famous "New System of Chemical Philosophy," for which he was made a member of the French Academy of Sciences in 1816, six years before he was selected as a fellow of the Royal Society. In 1832 he received a

13. *The Autobiography of Benjamin Franklin* (New York: Pocket Books, Inc., 1952); Carl Van Doren, *Benjamin Franklin* (New York: The Viking Press, 1938, 1965).

DCL from Oxford University. He died in 1844. This frustrated laborer No. 1 became the founder of modern atomic science, John Dalton.[14]

The bookbinder, No. 2, was born in London in 1791. His father was a blacksmith, who had to emigrate in 1791 from the country to London. When the boy was five, he lived above a coach house. The father being in poor health, the family had to go on relief when the boy was ten. The mother was a country girl; she and her husband were Sandemanians. He had an uncle who was a shoemaker and one who was a shopkeeper, another uncle who was a packer, still another a slater; his brother was a gas fitter—all good occupations, but hardly to be associated with intellectual accomplishments. The boy went to a common day school, where he learned the three R's. At 13, however, he had to take a full-time job; he became an errand boy delivering newspapers. At 14 he was apprenticed to a bookbinder, and qualified as a journeyman seven years later. Most of his education now was done by himself, mainly by reading, but including some simple experiments on chemistry and electricity, which he repeated. At 20 he was fortunate to be given some tickets for scientific lectures by the fashionable Sir Humphrey Davy. At 21 he enthusiastically wrote a letter to Sir Joseph Banks, President of the Royal Society, to ascertain if he could find employment in science—no reply. He did, however, manage to become an assistant to Davy at the Royal Institution in 1813—and its Director 20 years later. His scientific discoveries include the motor, the dynamo, and the transformer (no patents), as well as electric and magnetic properties of matter, in particular, the relationship of magnetism to light. He refused the Presidency of the Royal Society, of which he became a member at 36. At the founding of the United States National Academy of Sciences (1863), when he was 72, he was made a foreign member. He enjoyed lecturing both to adults and to juveniles. Thus this frustrated bookbinder No. 2 became the foremost experimental physicist (and chemist), Michael Faraday.[15]

Our next case was a revolutionist (No. 3) born in 1811 at Bourg-La-Reine (France). His father was head of a boys' school after deposition as mayor. Discouraged by the loss of his social position, the father later committed suicide, when the boy was 18. His mother tutored him from time to time. At 12 he passed an examination for entrance to a secondary school, Lycée Louis-le-Grand, in Paris. At 13 in the midst of a school rebellion, he was saved from expulsion only by his absence on a critical day of action. At 16 he was put back in a rhetoric class, where he was bored; accordingly, he took mathematics for relief. Finding that

14. Sir Henry E. Rascal, *John Dalton and the Rise of Modern Chemistry* (London: Cassel, 1901).
15. John Tyndall, *Faraday as Discoverer* (New York: Apollo, 1961).

the class had already reached the half-way mark of André Marie Legendre's geometry (normally a two-year course), he proceeded to read the book on his own—and finished it in two nights. He became interested in the solution of algebraic equations and later received the second prize in mathematics (his explanation was said to have been insufficient for the first). At 17 he continued to study mathematics—to the neglect of the rest of his subjects. Nevertheless, he failed the entrance examination in mathematics for the Ecole Polytechnique. When asked by the examiner why he had not taken the customary preparatory course, he replied frankly, "I studied by myself." This sensitive young man, moreover, failed to give a complete answer to a certain question because it had been formulated so poorly. In the same year he published his first paper, which was unimportant—and unnoticed. At 18, however, he sent to Augustin-Louis Cauchy a significant article which, unfortunately, was "lost." During that year he again failed the Polytechnique examination: this time the examiner kept insisting upon a fuller explanation for a particular statement which the young man regarded as "obvious." Finally, in despair, he hit the examiner with a sponge. At 19 he published three short papers and entered the Ecole Normale Supérieure. There he stirred up trouble with respect to the succession of Louis Philippe to the throne in place of the exiled Charles X. He was expelled and then joined the National Guard. At 20 he offered a public course in mathematics, which had to be dropped owing to the lack of attendance. Another paper was sent to the French Academy of Sciences; it was rejected by Siméon Denis Poisson, who noted the correctness of the result but complained of the briefness of the proof. He attended a banquet and gave a toast for Louis Philippe with a glass in one hand and a dagger in the other. He was arrested. The verdict was "not guilty." A preventive arrest was made later on the pretext of his wearing the uniform of the dissolved National Guard. After waiting four months for trial he was convicted and given a six-months imprisonment. At the end of the fourth month he became ill and was sent to a nursing home. There he became interested in a girl visiting his roommate. He fell in love with her only to find out later that she was the mistress of an absent boy friend. Upon this disclosure he gave way to an outburst and was subsequently challenged by the lover. The duel occurred on May 30, 1832. Wounded, he was left to die. The whole affair is believed to have been a frame-up. On the night before his duel, however, he wrote a scientific testament with the following pathetic notation in the margin: "I have no time." His work was neglected until 1846 and received full recognition only in 1870. Thus this frustrated revolutionist No. 3 revolutionized all mathematics with his group theory; he himself became recognized as one of the top four mathematicians in the 19th century, Evariste Galois.[16]

A girl, No. 4, was born at Warsaw in 1867. Her father was a professor of physics and an under-inspector of schools. Later retiring from the latter position involving boarding students he had to take a smaller apartment. The mother, well-born, pious and active, herself director of a private school, died from tuberculosis when the girl was 11. At 14 she was brilliant at the government gymnasium but neglected at home. At 16 she graduated with a gold medal. In this respect, however, she was not unlike other gifted students in her group, e.g., her brother and sister, who also received gold medals. At 17 she did some tutoring, but gave it up owing to the tardiness of the students and the even greater delay of their payments. Having a disdain for frivolity she adopted a severe mode of dress and had her hair cut almost to the roots. Her formal education stopped at this time owing to the policy of the Russian-controlled University of Warsaw not to admit women. At 18, therefore, she became a governess for the family of a lawyer who, though rich, was quite stingy, as well as vulgar and petty. At 19 she became governess for an estate administrator 60 miles north. Here she freely taught the peasants the Polish language. She fell in love with the son of the owner, but was forbidden marriage because of her inferior social position as a governess. After two years she returned to her family. And so, at 22 this young woman was unhappy in love, disappointed intellectually, and hard-up materially. She had to help financially both at home and in Paris with her sister's education. At 24, however, her sister, having married, freed her of the latter obligation. At last the young woman herself was able to go to Paris—third class—to continue her own studies. At 25 she entered the University and lived near the Sorbonne—on three francs a day. Her room had no water, no heat, no light. One day, having fainted, she was found alone in her room with only one packet of tea for food. Later she received a scholarship from a group at Warsaw; she passed first in the physics examination. At 28 she married a physicist, who was killed by a carriage 11 years later. About 30 plus she discovered new chemical elements, which she named radium and polonium. After four years, with the help of her husband, she managed to separate radium from uranium (no patent was ever sought for the novel method employed). At 36 she received the Ph.D. with the notation "très honorable." In that same year she received the Nobel prize. This frustrated

16. Leopold Infeld, *Whom the Gods Love* (New York: McGraw-Hill Book Company, 1948).

girl No. 4 became the only person ever to win the Nobel prize twice for scientific achievements—Marie Sklodovsky Curie.[17]

Finally, we shall consider a high school drop-out No. 5. He was born in 1879 at Ulm on the Danube. His father owned a small electrochemical factory, which was transferred to Munich when the child was two. When the boy was 15, the father had to move his works again to Milan, owing to failure. The father was undoubtedly a free thinker; the mother, however, was of the Jewish faith. She had a sense of humor and played the piano. An uncle engineer early stimulated the boy's interest in mathematics. Although he was slow in learning to speak, he was apt with violin lessons, which he began at the age of six. He attended a primary Catholic school, but was not at all a prodigy; indeed, he continued to lack fluency in speech. At ten he entered the gymnasium for general education. Later he noted that, whereas the elementary school teachers had performed like sergeants, those in the gymnasium behaved like lieutenants; both, however, were of the military type. At 12 he began to study geometry and was so fascinated that he could not put the textbook down. At 14 he performed chamber music. At 15 he received Jewish instructions; he liked the Old Testament proverbs and ethics, but not the ritual. At this time he was far ahead of his class in mathematics, but far behind in the classics, which he complained were taught primarily for the purpose of examination. He determined to leave school supposedly on account of a nervous breakdown, but actually to be with his family in Milan. He learned, however, that the faculty had already acted and were requesting him to withdraw from school inasmuch as his fellow students were losing respect for their teachers owning to his own pronounced aversion to drill. At this time he legally renounced both his German citizenship and his Jewish religion. He failed the entrance examinations (modern languages and natural science) for the Swiss Federal Polytechnic School in Zurich. (The University there was closed to him inasmuch as he had no gymnasium diploma.) He was advised to complete his secondary education at a Cantonal school about 30 miles northwest. There, because of the independence and interest of the teachers, he experienced less aversion to school. At 17, upon graduation, he entered the Polytechnic automatically without examination. He elected the course for "training teachers in physical and mathematical subjects." Unfortunately, here he lost his interest in mathematics owing to its poor teaching by Hermann Minkowski; the physics, moreover, was out of date (he studied this subject independently). At 21 he graduated,

17. Eve Curie, *Madame Curie*, translated by V. Sheehan (Garden City: Doubleday and Company, 1943).

but was unemployed for six months. Was it because of his Jewish background or his colleagues' jealousy that he received no assistantship? Neither could he obtain a teaching position in a secondary school. He did, however, manage to become a tutor for two students in a grammar school, but was fired when he tried to become the boys' sole teacher. Eventually he had to resort to a job in the Berne Patent Office. As to his scientific accomplishments, at the age of 26 while at the Patent Office, he wrote three papers, any one of which would have won him world renown. The one on the photoelectric effect was based upon the recent quantum theory and was the primary basis later for his receiving the Nobel prize in physics. The second, on Brownian movements was subsequently used for direct experimental confirmation of the century-old atomic theory. The third, quite original, was on relativity. He became professor at the Universities of Zurich and of Prague, at the Prussian Academy of Sciences and at the Institute for Advanced Study in Princton. He was a pacifist and a Zionist; he is frequently remembered in the United States for a letter he wrote recommending the construction of an atomic bomb to President Franklin D. Roosevelt. Thus the frustrated high school drop-out No. 5 revolutionized all physics in the 20th century —Albert Einstein.[18]

Each teenager is concerned today with the question: How far will I get? He is told that his progress will depend upon his heredity and his environment. Probably it is fortunate that our personal heredity is so largely unknown and that very few of us ever reach its limits. It is profitable, therefore, to consider the experiences of other individuals[19] such as the advantaged, the undecided, and the frustrated, who, although they may have lived in a different social scene, as human beings, nevertheless, performed on a similar stage. Each one was confronted with personal difficulties and indecisions, which he overcame by energetic perseverance and enthusiastic interest. Such lives can be object lessons to us all. They suggest clues for solving our own problems. A student of mine once looked questioningly when I handed out some homework and said indignantly, "Who do you think I am, Einstein?" I replied, "No, Einstein would probably not be taking this physics course the fourth time." It is not always the obviously bright who go the farthest. You recall the story of the race between the tortoise and the hare. On that beautiful spring day if you had been betting on the basis of heredity and environment you would undoubtedly have selected the hare—and

18. Philipp Frank, *Einstein*, translated by G. Rosen, edited and revised by S. Kusaka (New York: Alfred A. Knopf, Inc., 1947).
19. F. Sherwood Taylor, *An Illustrated History of Science* (London: William Heinemann, 1955).

lost. I, myself, had a similar experience some years ago. Getting into my car at night to drive some 200 miles from Washington to Durham, N. C., I suddenly realized that my headlights shone only 200 feet. How could I go the necessary 200 miles? Going those 200 feet, however, I noticed that the lights still shone another 200 feet. Thus by always going the distance that I could see, I ended my journey at a point that had been far beyond my vision. It is said of an alpine climber that he was last seen going forward.

As a graduate student I had occasion to hear a professor of eugenics speak on the subject, "Who Shall Inherit the Earth?" He argued that obviously the sons and daughters of the learned, the well-to-do, the leaders of society, *et al.*, would inherit the earth. When he had finished, an editor of one of the New Haven newspapers said, "Professor, you are correct. Those are the ones that will inherit the earth. But allow me to tell you who will take it away from them: the sons and daughters of the Irish charwomen on State Street." (That man was the father of Thornton Wilder.)

Some years ago I heard a story about an Indian, which seems to summarize succinctly what I have been trying to say about motivation. A secondary school teacher of music happened to visit a small town some hundreds of miles from Mexico City to give a concert. Seeing a 10-year-old barefoot Indian boy, he asked if the boy would help pump the organ at the evening concert. The teacher became interested in the boy and inquired the next day if the boy could go along with him as a personal valet. The mother and father were thrilled: it would be a rise in the social scale, for the boy could now wear shoes (furthermore, the family was again "expecting"—number 17). The boy was discovered to have some musical talent, and later, at 19, performed in the presence of President Parferia Diaz. The President, who had been told the story, offered the young man a scholarship to study music at the Paris Conservatory of Music; the Conservatory, however, turned him down owing to his "advanced" age. Nevertheless, the boy became. a concert violinist, Director of the Symphony of Mexico City, the Dean of the University's School of Music. Records of his analysis of the songs of birds are to be found in the Library of Congress. His son graduated from Harvard with a Ph.D. in soil mechanics, and became President of the University of Mexico—he told me the whole story himself.

May I remind you of a perennial challenge, as stated some years ago by James B. Conant: "To find and educate the gifted youth is essential for the welfare of the country, we cannot afford to leave undeveloped the greatest resource of the country."

1. Can you identify any common childhood experiences that characterize the fifteen scientists?
2. Do you think you could pick a scientist out of a crowd in a supermarket?
3. Are scientists born or "made"?

5 JAMES T. ROBINSON

Science Teaching and
the Nature of Science

*The "structure" of science as well as representative "processes"
involved are analyzed by Dr. Robinson. The product-process controversy has been debated by advocates of each side. Should subject matter content (product) be the determining factor in curriculum development or should the processes of science provide the focus for new
science curricula?*

*Interrelationships between structure and process in science should
become more visible as you read this paper. Remember, the ideas were
"made up" by an individual and in no way should they be considered
"the last word." Ponder the ideas openly and objectively during your
pursuit of the question—"what is science?"*

Today's teachers of science are confronted with an almost overwhelming volume of materials—texts, programs, pamphlets, etc.—purporting
to provide information which will enable the student "to understand
science." Science kits with packaged laboratory exercises in many forms
are available. It is suggested that by using these materials the student
will learn how to "inquire," will learn the "process" of science. The
possibilities of keeping students actively engaged in laboratory activities and well-supplied with reading material in most of the fields of
science is no longer a problem. Rather, the problems reside in much
more profound questions: Have the students, as a result of doing the
activities, reading and discussing what they have read, indeed increased
their "understanding of science?" What is the nature of science which
they are to understand? Can aspects of the nature of science be identified and so specified as to provide for guidance in the selection and
organization of elements which are to be included in science curricula?

Reprinted from *The Journal of Research in Science Teaching*, Vol. 3, issue 1, 1965, pp. 37-50, by
permission of the editor. Dr. Robinson has worked in science education with the Los Angeles County
Superintendent of Schools Office and this paper was developed from an unpublished doctoral
dissertation.

Many articles in the professional literature suggest that it is the "processes" of science which are most important in teaching science rather than the teaching of the "products" of science. Other articles suggest that the "structure of science" as a discipline and the "processes of inquiry" are of the greatest importance. Many science guides developed within school districts emphasize the teaching of "science concepts" as well as "science processes."

These many suggestions, and others could be cited, raised numerous questions for the writer. Not all of these questions have been fully explored, and for many it has been possible only to refine them for further investigation. Implicit in the suggestions for science teaching cited above was the separability, identifiability, and teachability of the processes and products of science. But can process be separated from product in science? How do product and process relate to the structure of science, and what is meant by the structure of science? Does this structure become most significantly stated as an array of products, concepts, facts, theories, and laws of nature? The list of questions may be expanded almost indefinitely; the study reported here makes its central contribution in relation to the nature of what may be termed in current parlance "the structure of science."

In order to make some entry into this field of interrelated problems, and with the purpose of searching for eventual clarification of the nature or structure of scientific knowledge which might become a framework to provide guidance in curriculum development in the secondary schools, an investigation into the nature of scientific knowledge seemed in order. With such a framework one might be able to develop answers to such questions as the following: Is the language used in instructional materials consistent with the structure of science? Are the scientific relationships developed in materials consistent with relationships which characterize the structure of science? While these questions were initial goals of the inquiry, more specific questions were to be found that could be formulated and more fruitful answers were to be proposed as a consequence of the study.

The dissertation was based upon an analysis of six writings concerned with the nature and organization of scientific knowledge: three written by physical scientists(1-3) and three written by biological scientists.(4-6) These writings were selected from a working bibliography of more than one hundred works. A preliminary list of writings was selected from the bibliography on the basis of publication date, authorship by men who had taken a Ph.D. or received recognition in biology, chemistry, or physics, and who had a special interest in the nature and organization of scientific knowledge. The list of writings of physical scientists was sent to a selected group of physical scientists and the list by biologists was sent to a selected group of biological scientists. The final selection of the six works used in the investigation was made on the basis of the responses of the scientists, the recency of publication, a balance of works by biologists and physical scientists, and the writer's judgment.

The framework or structure of science which will be presented below must be considered as preliminary, since it has been based on a limited number of writings and represents the writer's selection of those aspects of the writings which he evaluated as central to the formulation of a structure of science which would be relevant to education in the sciences.

The reporting of the findings from this dissertation will be carried forward in two phases. First, four aspects of the structure of science will be discussed. At the present time, it is these four aspects which the writer feels have particular significance for curriculum implementation: (1) the distinctions as between the correlational and the exact sciences, (2) the constructional nature of scientific reality (including the circuit of verification and the inextricable interrelationships of the processes of induction and deduction), (3) the processes of observation and the emergence of rules of correspondence, and (4) the considerations which lead to the verification and acceptance of scientific theories. Second, the writer will present a statement of selected understandings which characterize an individual who is growing in scientific literacy. While only four aspects of these understandings will be discussed in phase one in any detail, the reader is referred to the dissertation and the six original works upon which it was based for substantiation of the additional emphases in these understandings.

Correlational and Exact Sciences

Although the sciences may be seen to consist of observations, experiments, theories, and hypotheses, the findings of this investigation support a necessity to go beyond this simple formulation in developing an understanding of the structure of science. First, a distinction must be made between correlational and exact procedures in the sciences; for the discussion in this article will be concerned primarily with the methodologies of the exact sciences. The history of science provides evidence that the various sciences began with observation and speculation, moved to the correlational level, and are developing, albeit at varying rates of speed, toward a theoretical or exact level.

Correlational procedures are characterized by data collection and by comparisons. Such comparisons may result in groupings or classifications, for example, the groupings of organisms into the categories plants, animals, or protists. Correlations of quantitative data may result in a mathematical relation, the correlation coefficient, developed by agreed upon rules of procedure. The biological sciences are characterized by correlational procedures. The inductive generalizations resulting from these procedures may summarize or describe, but they do not predict, and thus do not seem to satisfy investigators as they search for basic explanations. As Margenau indicates, ". . . they feel the urge to probe more deeply, to *derive* . . . (these uniformities) of experience from principles not immediately given."(7) In support of this observation Margenau gives the example of the use of the three-four-five rule by Egyptians as a correlational procedure but states that we honor Pythagoras for his mathematical demonstration for ". . . through his act a *theory* was born; the surface of mere correlation was broken, subsurface explanation had begun. To put it another way; the contingency of correlation had given way to logical necessity."(7)

This search for subsurface explanation was evinced by Paul Weiss in the transcript of the Lee Conference at which "Concepts of Biology" were discussed. Weiss asked if there might be relationships in the morphology of a flock of starlings and a slime mold colony. He explains these phenomena by stating:

> The outline of the starling cloud is very sharp, nearly spherical. Now, when this is broken in two, each half almost simultaneously rounds up into a separate unit. It isn't exact; it has almost an ameboid motion, with distortions and elongations. The remarkable thing is that despite these deformations, they cohere and retain a very sharp outline. We don't know what the communication system could be that would tell a bird the differential equation of a smooth, spherical surface. This is the analogy I wanted to investigate because that is what really happens.(8)

Frank Brink, Jr. continued the discussion and extended the analysis by stating:

> . . . the similarity here is a little bit like certain mathematical formulations; you have an operator, differential equations with the function in which it is going to operate not specified physically. . . (9)

Paul Weiss related this comment to concerns in biological studies:

> . . . isn't a lot of our present biological work impoverished by the fact that people don't look for these operators? Take endocrinology—how much we know about the agents, which we can purify and extract and even synthesize, and how comparatively few people worry about their mode of action. Not until we know both do we have a complete and consistent understanding. (9)

This illustration points up the qualities of thought which characterize the movement from correlational to exact or theoretical procedures.

The biological sciences have been predominantly correlational, but the thrust of these sciences, as with the physical sciences, has been toward exact or theoretical procedures. A discussion of a limited number of these procedures is the central purpose of this paper; for such procedures serve to form the paradigm of science and this may be considered of greatest importance in the search for the nature or structure of science.

The distinctions between inductive generalizations and the generalizations of the exact sciences are more clearly delineated by Frank Brink, Jr. when he commented regarding the framework of biological principles developed at the Lee Conference:

> I am trying to get my own ideas straight as to what kind of generalizations these are. With other generalizations that occur in science, and perhaps a subsidiary set of rules of procedure, one can go back to the instances that suggested the generalization. . . . It's not clear that I can do this and, therefore, I am not sure that this is a basic set of generalizations. But if it is a basic set of generalizations, what must be added to it in the way of rules of procedure? Without these formal symbolisms, and rules for manipulating the symbols, it doesn't seem to me that you can work backwards to the instances that suggested general principles. (10)

In this statement several of the essential characteristics of the exact sciences are presented: a basic set of generalizations is presented with formal symbolisms and rules of procedure by which one may go back to the specific instances that are suggested by the general principles.

The findings reported in the dissertation were formulated into statements of understandings which would characterize those individuals who are increasing their understanding of the structure of science as developed from this study. Each major aspect of the nature or structure of science was followed by a summary in the form of understandings. Understandings which relate to the distinctions as between the exact and correlational sciences are as follows:

Accordingly, an individual who is developing scientific literacy will increasingly

> *understand* that the thrust in all sciences is for them to become increasingly theoretical and exact, the biological sciences being currently more correlational and the physical sciences more exact,
>
> > understand the current theoretical framework of the exact sciences, and where such frameworks are developed in predominantly correlational sciences, and
> >
> > understand the limitations of current patterns of explanation in the biological sciences and understand the attempts to devise

explanatory systems in the biological sciences which will be predictive.[1]

The writings of Morton Beckner reflected a point of view which was more expressive of the correlational than the exact thrust in science. He was concerned with documenting and clarifying the processes for rationalizing data now current in the field of organismic biology. In the transcript of the Lee Conference(11) some of the same strands of thought were in evidence. The general statements of the biological sciences are most characteristically inductive generalizations rather than theoretical systems of explanation, and thus the biological sciences are more generally correlative or descriptive rather than exact sciences. But the thrust of the biological sciences is clearly toward the methodologies of the exact sciences.

In attempting to understand the nature of organisms, the biological sciences began with description and classification. This taxonomic stage of investigation was supplemented by morphological investigations and then progressed into investigations of the dynamics of living systems. The complexities of living systems has led some biologists to investigate organisms through levels of organization: molecular, organelle, cell, organ, individual organism, small group, population, and community. The investigations at the molecular level have utilized the methodologies of the exact sciences more fully than those investigations at the "higher" levels of organization. Investigations at each of these levels has produced large bodies of discrete facts and concepts, but the ordering of these facts and concepts into theoretical frameworks has lagged. The thrust of biological investigation toward the logico-mathematical systems characterizing the physical sciences is coupled with a belief by some biologists in the uniqueness of life and the questioning of the usability of such methodologies, especially at the higher levels of organization.

Some biologists evince concern with the fragmentation of their discipline into many non-communicating sub-disciplines with special concepts and special language. The breakdown of existing disciplinary boundaries with a reorganization into a "levels" organization has been given impetus by advances in information theory, systems analysis, symbolic logic, and the application of the methodologies of the exact sciences to living things. Such a movement to a more unified discipline with greater attention to deductive systems of explanation was commented upon by Margenau who, in discussing "causation in biology," stated:

---

1. The "understands" presented in this paper represent a selection from, and in some instances a revision and reordering of, a longer and more comprehensive development in the dissertation.

In biology, multiplicity of causal schemes is probably important enough to be studied in its own right. It may give rise to levels of explanation, perhaps to an entire hierarchy of explanations, each a causal one, and each at a different stage of organizational integration. Thus there may be encountered a theory framable in terms of molecules and molecular forces, another one in terms of thermodynamic systems, another in which cells and cytological interaction are basic concepts, and perhaps one that speaks of stimuli and responses. If a prognosis can be based on physics, one may judge it to be a very long time before the vertical connections between these schemes are completely understood. (12)

Thus, an understanding of science in this period of history must include understanding the divergent ways of thought which characterize contemporary biology.

Accordingly, an individual who is developing scientific literacy will increasingly

understand the development of inquiry in biology with movement from simple observation to taxonomy, to descriptive morphology, to comparative morphology, and to the addition of analysis to description,

understand the diversity of methodological approaches by which practicing biologists are attempting to explain living systems,

understand that some biologists accept inductive generalizations as being currently satisfactory for living systems, and

understand that inductive generalizations formed into law-like statements preclude prediction in the sense usually required by the exact sciences;

understand the logical, mathematical, and syntactical structure of the physical sciences since the physical sciences are being used as a paradigm of the exact, or deductive, sciences,

Understand that there are divergencies in biological thought as to the applicability of deductive patterns to all levels of biological organization,

understand that some areas of biological investigation are currently more deductively fruitful (genetics, open systems analysis) than are some other areas of inquiry, and

understand that a system of classification is not a deductive system although it may provide suggestions as to relevant relationships.

The processes of scientific thought have been considered in rather broad perspective and some aspects of the constructionist nature of scientific knowledge have been considered. A more detailed analysis of these topics will now be developed in the hope of clarifying these general considerations.

The Constructional Nature of Scientific Knowledge

As has been indicated, the organization of thought in the physical sciences may be used as a paradigm of the model of the exact sciences. One way of illustrating this organization is proposed in Figure 1.

This circle of thought "begins," "ends," and "continues" in the area of observation and thus emphasizes the empirical roots of the physical sciences. But observations are not given in nature. They are selected by the scientist—selected against the background of contemporary theory, general and metaphysical principles, and pragmatic considerations. The level of sense observation has been designated as the P field in Figure 1 and the area of verbal description, the conceptual or constructional area, as the C field.[2]

The exact sciences are characterized by inductions which include inventive, imaginative qualities going beyond the observations which generated their development. Such inductions have been variously referred to as "hypotheses," "concepts," or "constructs."[3] The statements constructed by inductions from sense observations are not produced at random but emerge under the constraints of the theory within which they are being formed. The logical, mathematical, and metaphysical constraints which function throughout the invention and development of constructs continue to function in the processes of verification to which constructs are subjected. They continue to function as the construct is tested further throughout the total area of discourse in which it is relevant. Metaphor and analogy often accompany the early phases of construction, but as testing proceeds, increasing the precision of terminology and reducing its ambiguity, removing metaphor and analogy become important parts of the formalization process.

Bridgman illustrates this use of analogy with the concept of light as a "thing traveling."

> There have been a number of different physical pictures of the nature of light, all of which have had the feature in common that light is to be regarded as in some way a "thing traveling." This statement obviously is applicable to the old corpuscular theory of light; it is true

2. The usage of "P field" and "C field" follows that developed by Margenau.
3. The writer will follow Margenau's use of "construct."

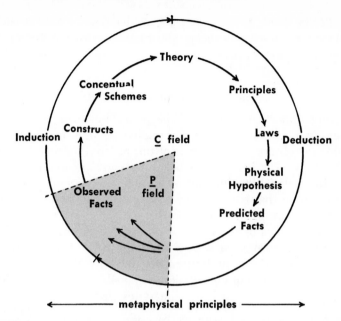

FIGURE 1. A schemata of the organization of thought in the physical sciences.

for the electromagnetic theory where the "thing" is a phase in the electromagnetic field, which may be followed in thought as it moves, as in Einstein's special relativity; or finally we have the "thing travelling" picture of the photons of quantum mechanics. . . . But we cannot see a photon in flight nor does it create a wind. (13)

These analogies (instrumental operations produce "things lighted," not "light travelling") are not currently capable of instrumental verification, but they do serve to stimulate experimentation.

Verification proceeds from the P field through operational definitions to the C field wtih its network of accepted constructs where it moves into what are generally referred to as deductive processes—the prediction of new and non-trivial observations in the P field. The predicted observations must fall within the probability prescribed by the theory of which they are a part. When this circuit is successfully completed, the entire set of constructs involved is said to be verified.

It is now possible to indicate that *an individual who is developing scientific literacy will increasingly*

understand that the relevance and validity of the constructs of a science are determined by the theoretical structure of the science, and understand that no construct is considered valid until it can be fitted into an existing theory and function successfully in facilitating scientific prediction.

The Processes of Observation

Newtonian mechanics accepted the premise of man as a unique discontinuity in a continuous and orderly universe. Man the spectator could independently observe the spectacle of this ordered universe; his removal from the scene was believed to be of no consequence. But events of the past fifty years have brought about a reexamination of this premise and a realization that Newton's laws were valid not absolutely but relative to the system of fixed stars.

The relationships of observer and observed is dramatically illustrated by the problems associated with establishing the "existence" of "empty space." The introduction of instruments to verify that the purportedly empty space is really empty precludes the possibility of its being "empty." In discussing this dilemma Bridgman states that:

> . . . within the last few years we have the quantum mechanical concept of a fluctuating zero point electrostatic field in otherwise empty space. If the theory is correct, it means that it will be found as a matter of experiment that it never occurs that there are places where all physical instruments give no readings, so that "empty" space corresponds as little to the physical actuality as do the simultaneous position and momentum prohibited by the Heisenberg principle of interdetermination. In this denial of the legitimateness of the concept of empty space it seems to me that we have as dramatic a demonstration as can be imagined of the impossibility of divorcing our concepts from the operations by which they are generated and of the impossibility of speaking of things existing of themselves in their own right. (14)

With the physicists' invasion of the microscopic realm the effect of the investigator on what is observed could not be ignored. Man, the ordered observer, enters into the construction of scientific knowledge as he observes phenomena and *selects* those aspects of experience which may be constructed into the ordered formalisms which scientists consider to be explanatory. Such selection does not occur *in vacuo* but is guided by theory, for without theory the scientist does not know what to observe. Observations may generate hypotheses which may be extensions of existing theory or they may become generative of new experiments and hypotheses which may eventuate in the modification or replacement of the theory within which they had their origins.

Within the structure of science, the processes of induction and deduction are seen to enter in the form of a web-like rather than linear order. The scientist collects observations and then proceeds by induction to constructs (hypotheses). This creation, or construction, from observational material of a structure of "linguistic material" includes more than the observational material, for theories, conjectures, and thoughts play an essential role in induction, furnishing raw materials which may be shaped by imagination into new constructs.

The inductions which lead eventually to deductions within established theory have been distinguished from those inductive generalizations which summarize or describe but do not predict. This distinction is a crucial one which partly explains the difficulty of "discovery" in modern science, for discovery develops within accepted theory—discoveries come to the well-prepared mind.

Correspondences between constructs and observations provide connections between the logical, rational areas of thought, and the empirical, observational areas which give substance to constructs. The establishment and formalization of these rules of correspondence, including operational definitions, is another important aspect of the inductive-deductive cycle. As scientists have probed into the microcosm, the relations between the operations used to produce observables and the nature of the observables produced have had to be more rigorously examined.

P. W. Bridgman has contributed greatly to the understanding of these relations by his analyses of the operations which are involved in the content, definitions, and extensions of some of our physical concepts. He states:

> The fundamental idea back of an operational analysis is simple enough; namely, that we do not know the meaning of a concept unless we specify the operations which were used by us or our neighbour in applying the concept in any concrete situation. (15)

Various kinds of operations—instrumental, verbal, and mathematical —are employed together in a way to mutually reinforce and supplement one another to produce the observable properties from which physical objects are constructed. A great deal of latitude is allowed to the verbal and mathematical operations but such freedom is restricted by the requirement that these operations must be capable of eventually making connections with instrumental operations. This requirement is based on the premise that:

> . . . the broadest basis on which we can hope for an eventual understanding is *invariable correlation between the results of instrumental operations*. Given invariable correlation, we can find how to predict, and prediction is perhaps the most searching criterion of understanding. (16)

As verification proceeds, correlation between constructs may result in relations expressible in the form of differential equations—the criterion for a law of nature as it is used in its most precise formulation.

The passage from data to constructs to the prediction of new facts within a formal system comprises the inductive-deductive cycle. However, for the verification of predictions, purely logical deductions are correlated with physical objects by means of rules of correspondence. Thus the goal of scientific explanation is seen to be the development of a coherent logico-mathematical system of relations between symbols, and rules of correspondence for those symbols, developed in such a way that the logical conclusions drawn from these statements become statements about observable facts that are confirmed by actual sense observations. The development of such a deductive system serves not only to predict new facts but it also serves to guide the knower in carrying out observations.

The acceptance of those deductive theories which correspond closely to data, *i.e.*, are more "concrete" than "abstract," is based primarily upon the logical, semantical, and empirical relations of the theory. As more abstract theories are formulated, acceptance is based upon more than scientific criteria; the psychological and sociological climate in which they are formulated become a part of the criteria for acceptance.

Accordingly, an individual who is developing scientific literacy will increasingly

> *understand* the distinctions in structure and development as between the inductive and deductive aspects of theory,
>
> > understand that if it were not for both of these phases, all statements regarding a theory would be analytically equivalent,
> >
> > understand that all conceptual schemes are built up from inductions which in turn have been in part achieved through prior deductions from existing theories,
> >
> > understand that the working scientists invents his signs in order to make representations of phenomena—the relationship between these signs and symbols is the semantical component of science,
> >
> > understand that scientists have selected as their criteria for truth sense data which can be comprehended and checked by everybody with the appropriate training, and
> >
> > understand that the principles of physics can only be valid when they refer to a system, or systems, of reference;

understand the role of the ordered observer as a constructor of reality;

understand the relationship of theory to observation—without theory man does not know what to observe;

understand the role of operational analysis as it has come to be a part of the methodology of the physical sciences;

understand the function of operational definitions in prediction, for prediction is only possible when the terms within the principles of science have been given their operational definitions,

understand the way in which different operations reinforce and supplement each other in many ways, and

understand the critical role of instrumental operations in developing physical content in physical concepts;

understand the impossibility of divorcing physical concepts from the operations by which they are generated and of the impossibility of speaking of things existing by themselves in their own rights, and

understand that no observation record is understandable without knowledge of the theory which underlies the instruments used in observation.

The Verification and Acceptance of Theories

The search for sciences of increasingly precise predictability, rather than correlational or descriptive sciences, was evidenced in each of the works investigated. That prediction does not seek to merely call forth the original observation but must also have the power, the deductive fertility, to be extended to as yet unknown phenomena was stressed by those writers who delved deepest into its meanings. The difficulties of prediction in biology, where the unique event is of interest, brings additional difficulties to this field which are as yet unresolved through available mathematical and logical techniques. That the symbolization denoting the entities of complex systems and rules for manipulating these symbols provided by the Boole-Frege movement offer an as yet unexploited methodological system was illustrated by Woodger's axiomatization of Mendelian genetics.(17)

The validation of theories which predict involves a threefold process. First, the constructs within theories must undergo the imposition of certain metaphysical principles. Second, they must successfully complete the circuit of verification. The circuit of verification begins in the *P field* (see Fig. 1), the field of perception, proceeds by rules of correspondence in the *C* field, the constructional field, and then returns to the *P* field by a different pathway. Third, verification also includes the establishment of rules of correspondence which link data to constructs. Working always within theory, the linking of constructs to the *P* field and establishing relations among constructs assures the validation of constructs and theory. As Margenau indicates, the processes of verification have enabled the exact sciences ". . . to develop *theories* furnishing criteria for the rejection of illusory data."(18) As illustrated in Figure 1 and as discussed throughout this paper, prediction involves both empirical and rational knowledge; neither is sufficient alone. Through the development of operational definitions, correspondence between the rational and the empirical is maintained; throughout this circuit, the observer is an integral part of both what is observed and constructed. One has only to recall the changes in man's conception of the universe which followed the Copernican Revolution to appreciate the importance of the constructional nature of science.

Theories of high generality such as relativity, quantum theory, Newton's theory of gravitation, etc., are not uniquely determined by their logical consistency, as developed through the circuit of verification and their agreement with observed fact. Sociological and psychological factors, C. S. Pierce's pragmatic component of science,(19) enter into acceptance when several theories may be valid. As Frank points out, Francis Bacon preferred the Ptolemaic theory over the Copernican theory ". . . because it is more in agreement with common sense."(20) This illustration helps further to clarify the influence of the pragmatic component for "common sense" is shaped by the climate of opinion which prevails at a particular time in history. Bridgman provides a further clarification of theory acceptance in discussing Ostwald's proposal of fifty years ago that the concept of atoms was superfluous when he observed that "it may well be, however, that one of two alternative points of view is so much more congenial to the commonsense way of looking at things, *the commonsense point of view itself being recognized as at bottom a construction* (italics mine), that we shall adopt it in preference to the other.(26) In this instance further experimental discoveries became so overwhelming that Ostwald's proposal has been discarded.

The currents of scientific thought which questioned the organismic universe of the Greek's and resulted in the Copernican revolution and the world machine of Newton took place over centuries within the fabric of the evolving society of western civilization. We may thus consider theories as being constructed, and their validity may be considered adequate so long as their predictions are confirmed in experiment. An understanding of the constructed nature of theories and of the inter-relationships of scientific thought with the social milieu in which they are imbedded is a necessary part of education in the sciences. It also becomes essential that education in the sciences provide ways for individuals to learn that the very "seeing" and "recording" that man does have been influenced by his past.

Accordingly, an individual who is developing scientific literacy will increasingly

understand the inextricable relationship of the knower and the known, and

understand the way in which other areas of human thought or beliefs in religion, logic, mathematics, technology, etc., may influence his views in science;

understand that those aspects of experience of interest to science are those which satisfy the available procedures for rationalizing data;

understand that prediction is only possible when the terms within the principles of science have been given their operational definitions,

understand that a prediction to be of value and interest in science must be able to predict a large number of apparently unrelated observations,

understand that prediction is more difficult in biology and that appropriate logical, mathematical, and syntactical procedures will be needed to cope with deductive theories and processes concerning the living state; and understand the differences in criteria used for verifying and for accepting a theory.

A Summary of Additional Understandings with Regard to the Nature of Science

Imbedded in the discussion of the four areas of concern to which the writer has devoted the largest measure of his attention in this article, and which were selected for emphasis because of his judgment as to their central importance to science curriculum, there has been stated central understandings which emerged from this study. These understandings were stated so as to characterize an individual who will be in process of growth toward a more mature conception of the nature and structure of science.

In this concluding section additional understandings will be presented without elaboration except in the last instance.[4] Four of the areas will deal further with the constraints within scientific reasoning which both serve to facilitate this reasoning and to characterize it as "scientific" when contrasted with other modes of thought. A brief discussion of intuition and discovery is included since much current writing in science education relates to these processes, and it is the judgment of the writer that the works studied in this dissertation cast thoughtful light on some essential distinctions with regard to these processes.

Constraints: metaphysical principles
Accordingly, an individual who is developing scientific literacy will increasingly

> *understand* the continuing role that certain metaphysical principles have had in directing inquiry;

> *understand* the relative longevity of metaphysical principles, theories, laws of nature, and constructs within the evolution of scientific knowledge;

> *understand* that certain assumptions serve as constraints and guides in the evolution of scientific knowledge and thus become a part of the structure of science.

Constraints: language
Accordingly, an individual who is developing scientific literacy will increasingly

> *understand* the indispensability of language as well as instruments in the development of scientific knowledge—that the recording of observations and the construction hypotheses is impossible without each;

> *understand* the decreasing utility of the natural language as science develops and understand the requirements for developing a more precise language, and

>> understand the pitfalls into which one may fall in the use of natural language in science—dualistic thinking, unwarranted use of metaphor, elliptical expression;

---

4. The reader is referred to the dissertation, or the individual works analyzed in it, for substantiation of the statements.

understand the role of man as an interpreter of nature and that as a consequence, the study of language is as essential to the scientist as the study of observation, and

understand the advantages of the extensional point of view in developing scientific statements;

understand the metaphysical and organismic interpretations which were a part of man's attempt to construct explanatory schemes and that the contemporary sciences still exhibit such reasoning, and

understand that philosophical interpretations of theories grow out of analogies to daily life and are not uniquely determined by theory;

understand the use of metaphor and analogy when speaking of "directiveness" in organisms as being like "conscious purposing" in man, a yet to be clarified area of methodological concern in biology, and

understand the use of analogy as a method of discovery, but also understand its lack of complete and unique correspondence.

Constraints: logical and mathematical

Accordingly, an individual who is developing scientific literacy will increasingly

understand that the essential relationships within all exact, or deductive, sciences are logical and mathematical, and

understand that without the utilization of set theory the biologist is left with properties which he often treats as though they were entities;

understand the "haziness" of measurement and the logical hiatus between measurements and their mathematical expression in numbers;

understand the development of a natural law as a statement which has evolved from a definition to a differential equation in which each term has independent instrumental significance.

Constraints: models and visualizations

Accordingly, an individual who is developing scientific literacy will increasingly understand that models may be used in science to represent various sets of relationships and may be mechanical, linguistic, mathematical, etc.;

understand that as the sciences have developed, models have become increasingly theoretical and abstract—physical models give way to mathematical models;

understand the use of models and visualizations by the scientist as a means of assisting him in organizing his relationships into a unified whole and to assist him in formulating hypotheses, and

understand that models are idealizations that are widely used as pedagogical devices but that models are not the physical reality itself;

understand the term "model" which may be used in the biological sciences in the phrase "a family of models" as defining a biological theory which serves to interrelate concepts at different levels of organization.

Intuition and discovery

The impossibility of separating intuition and discovery from the matrix of thought patterns and processes which characterize scientific reasoning has been apparent from the six writings investigated, for each works within the total fabric of thought. One becomes convinced from these writings that intuition and discovery in science are the fruit of imagination working with the well-prepared mind. Both involve the ability to see relationships previously unseen, but both must work within the semantical, logical, and pragmatic constraints of scientific reasoning.

Intuition particularly functions in the inductive phases of inquiry when, as Woodger notes,(22) the particularity of observation records is transformed by the formulation of a newer, verifiable hypothesis which speaks of "all" in reference to a given set of phenomena.

Discovery, too, functions within the inductive phases of inquiry and can, also, be an outgrowth of the deductive phases as whole new cosmologies may be constructed. Discovery is frequently aided in the inductive phase by analogy and metaphor as the scientist seeks to transcend his observations and achieve a more general statement.

Every individual scientific discovery refers, beyond the factual circumstances in which it arises, to some universal for its *significance*. The difference between noting a fact and making a discovery centers precisely in this crucial condition: that a discovery suggests a fairly general postulational proposition which presses for tentative acceptance, while the fact allows mere inductive generalization. The postulate, when analyzed, is replete with deductive consequences, each of which says more than the original discovery; the inductive generalization as such can say nothing save what might happen when similar facts are inspected. (23)

In the last analysis, the insights gained from both intuition and discovery must be integrated and formalized into the accepted patterns of reasoning if they are in time to become a part of the deductive structure of a particular scientific discipline.

Accordingly, an individual who is developing scientific literacy will increasingly

understand the use of imagination, intuition, and construction which are essential characteristics of the processes of discovery in science,

understand the use of analogy as a method of discovery, but understand its lack of complete and unique correspondence,

and understand the relationship between discovery and the well-prepared mind of the inquiring scientist.

Summary

The necessary interrelationships as between structure and process as they emerge from the findings of this investigator are presented in Figure 2. This schemata attempts to represent the pervasive influences of the metaphysical principles and the circuit of verification as they have developed historically and are expressed in contemporary experimental inquiry.

This paper has reported selected findings from a doctoral dissertation concerned with the nature or structure of science. Four aspects of the emergent structure of science were briefly discussed and a statement of selected understandings which characterize an individual who is growing in scientific literacy have been presented. The dichotomy of products and processes of the scientific enterprise has been replaced by a unity in which the knower and the known are inextricably intertwined.

The writer proposes that the series of understandings may provide, after further investigation, a basis for the development of science curricula which makes the structure of science more explicit and provides for uniting the methods of inquiry with the knowledge produced—science curricula which would reflect the nature and organization of scientific knowledge as developed in this study.

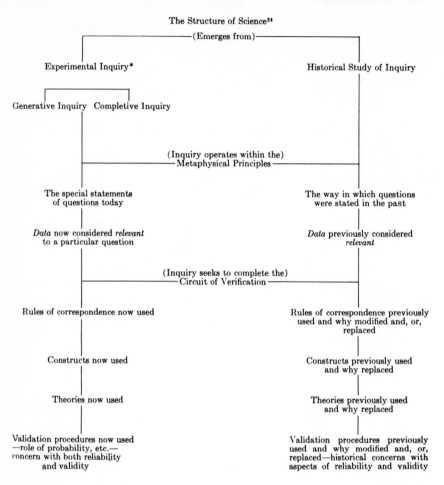

FIGURE 2.   A schemata of the nature of science.

*J. J. Schwab made similar distinctions as to type of inquiry in a recent pub-
lication, "Education and the Structure of the Disciplines," a paper prepared
for the Project on the Instructional Program of the Public Schools, National
Education Association, Washington, D. C., 1961.

The writer uses the term "generative" in preference to Schwab's "fluid"
and "completive" in preference to "stable" in the belief that these terms convey more of the findings of this study than do Schwab's terms. Schwab also
uses "inquiry into inquiries" in a way somewhat parallel to "Historical Study
of Inquiry."

REFERENCES

1. Margenau, Henry. *The Nature of Physical Reality: A Philosophy of Modern
   Physics.* New York: McGraw Hill, 1950.
2. Frank, Philipp. *Philosophy of Science: The Link Between Science and Philosophy.* Englewood Cliffs, New Jersey: Prentice Hall, 1957.

3. Bridgman, Percy W. *The Nature of Some of Our Physical Concepts.* New York: Philosophical Library, 1952.
4. Woodger, J. H. *Biology and Language.* Cambridge, England: Cambridge University Press, 1959.
5. Beckner, Morton. *The Biological Way of Thought.* New York: Columbia University Press, 1952.
6. Gerard, Ralph W. ed. "Concepts of Biology." *Behavioral Science* 3 (1958): 93-215.
7. Margenau, *op. cit.* p. 28.
8. Gerard, *op. cit.*, pp. 168-169
9. *Ibid.* p. 173.
10. *Ibid.* p. 157.
11. *Ibid.* pp. 93-215.
12. Margenau, *op. cit.*, p. 417.
13. Bridgman, *op. cit.*, p. 20.
14. *Ibid.* p. 19.
15. *Ibid.* p. 7.
16. *Ibid.* pp. 17-18.
17. Woodger, *op. cit.*, pp. 95-218.
18. Margenau, *op. cit.*, p. 463.
19. Frank, *op. cit.*, p. 349.
20. *Ibid.* p. 353.
21. Bridgman, *op. cit.*, p. 22.
22. Woodger, *op. cit.*, p. 32.
23. Margenau, *op. cit.*, p. 249.
24. Robinson, James T., "An Investigation of Selected Frameworks of Science," unpublished Ed. D. dissertation, School of Education, Stanford University, 1964. p. 381.

---

1. What are the differences between correlational and exact sciences?
2. What is a theory?
3. Compare inductive and deductive aspects of a theory.
4. Where do intuition and discovery enter into the development of a theory?

6 HARRY S. BROUDY

Science, Art
and Human Values

For two decades following World War II science was vaulted to the forefront in the minds of most people in this country. Scientists "never had it so good" during those golden years. Then, for numerous and complex reasons, science relinquished its favorable position during the last half of the 1960s. Dr. Broudy looks at some possible reasons for this decline and suggests future alternatives. Science and the humanities are viewed as a joint enterprise where values must be taken into account.

C. P. Snow's analysis of the scientific community in our culture parallels and expands upon many of the ideas presented by Broudy.[1]

Anyone in 1960 predicting that high school and college students would in a few years lose some of their enthusiasm for science would have been ridden out of the academic community on a rail. But it has happened, and with the prescience of hindsight one can point to portents that should not have been ignored.

There is little question but that in the late '50s and in the early '60s scientists, especially natural scientists, were well on the way to achieving the status of a priesthood. They were to be our intercessionaries with the secret powers of nature, not only for the good life, but for life itself. Their knowledge was esoteric; their *sacra* were displayed in bewildering instrumentation; and their "augury" was fascinatingly unintelligible to the man on the street. Under these circumstances it was not—and indeed even now it is not—inappropriate to speak of science as if it were a religion, with its hierarchies of priests, acolytes, colleges of cardinals, and assorted bishops. As far as the average man is concerned, the scientific establishment is as occult as the most arcane church.

Reprinted from *The Science Teacher,* Vol. 36, No. 3, 1969, pp. 23-28, by permission of the editor. Dr. Broudy is a Professor of Philosophy of Education at the University of Illinois, Urbana.

1. C. P. Snow, *The Two Cultures: And A Second Look* (New York: The New American Library, 1963).

Academically, any criticism of science still smacks of obstructionism, obscurantism, or just plain heresy. The scientific church, so far as I know, never bothers to persecute or harass heretics—it can afford to ignore them.

As usual, the members of the congregation exact a price for their homage, namely, help in their pursuit of happiness. Accordingly, when it became apparent that the evils of the world—especially those of war —were not being exorcised by science, disenchantment and some disaffection ensued. But disaffection has gone beyond science; all rational discourse as a means of coping with the evils of the world is now suspect. The demand for immediate control of events by action has taken its place.

I should like to suggest that the current loss of confidence in reason may be blamed on the failure of the intellectual in the exploration of values; more specifically, on the failure of academicians to search for new behavioral forms that would be really consistent with what I believe to be the invariant principles of human excellence: the virtues of courage, temperance, wisdom, and justice. I would hold that when one speaks of "revolutions" in values or morality, it is the special behavioral forms of courage, temperance, wisdom, and justice, which fluctuate with the times that are the target, not the virtues themselves. For the latter are not things, but forms of action and life that define *human* nature, so that if we were to encounter creatures who did not exhibit these forms we would call them depraved and wicked, and if they did not know what we were talking about—however intelligent they otherwise might be—we would call them nonhuman. Those who regard the current protests against sundry establishments as a rejection of the virtues or of the human nature they define are just as wrong, I believe, as those who believe that the virtues must be identified with the peculiar behaviors in which they are expressed in a given generation.

Young people are about convinced, and with some reason, that their professors are *not* exploring these new behavioral forms. Professors in both humanities and science exemplify the same value syndrome: respect for truth according to the cannons of one's discipline; the joy of discovery; the importance of dealing with ideas; faith in the rational powers of man—all important values, and as ultimate as any other. Good students are not insensitive to them. However, devotion to test tubes or literary footnotes may be regarded by the sensitive young student as a shrieking, outrageous irrelevance: irrelevant to cruelty, the threat of war, the whip of discrimination, the alienation of man *from* man. The intellectual values are not, for him, the existential ones.

Nevertheless, that science is nonmoral and, therefore, can only be relevant to means is less than half of the truth. Granted that science cannot tell us directly what ought to be the case, there are at least two senses in which science, in finding out what *is* the case, becomes relevant to what ought to be the case.

In the more obvious sense, science, by establishing the facts, can be decisive as to which policy is preferable. If science shows that the introduction of fluorides in drinking water is the most efficient preventive of tooth decay—assuming, as I am, that there is no disagreement about the desirability of preventing tooth decay—this fact can be decisive with respect to choosing among alternative policies about preventing tooth decay. For among the moral imperatives there is none higher than to act on the best knowledge available to us. Not to take account of science where it is relevant is, therefore, immoral.

But there is another important sense in which science is morally relevant. If the field of our moral obligation is defined by those value possibilities that can and ought to be realized, then every time new power is put into our hands by scientifically based technology, a shift in the moral economy occurs. For, although we are not morally obligated to do all that one can do, all we are obligated to do must be possible.

In this sense, scientists, with complicated assists from technologists, have removed "impossibility" as a valid ground of exculpation in such matters as race discrimination, peace, and social justice. Delaying actions, counsels of moderation, and linguistic evasions therefore, are seen ever more clearly for what they are. The brighter the students, the more clearly they see and the quicker their indignation.

Because one is never obligated to do the impossible, and since all that is possible is not necessarily obligatory, the value quest is more than a search for means to given ends. Both ends and means are transformed by expansions and contractions in the spheres of possibility. For example, the fight against cancer was not a duty for Socrates, but it may well be for us. The abolition of poverty, overpopulation, pollution of air and water, and the abatement of ignorance are all matters of our obligation not only because their desirability is obvious, but especially because the power for their accomplishment is clearly available. Once technology makes social justice possible, we cannot get by with good intentions.

If the role of science in shaping the ends of action has been underestimated, its role as a dynamic for reaching our goals has been overvalued. The commitment to achievement is not of itself a scientific task. Commitment is shaped and triggered by human desire, and human desire—as distinguished from merely animal desire—is shaped by the beauty of envisioned life as well as by its possibility. Commitment is primarily a function of feeling.

The influence of feeling covers a tremendously wide range. At one end is raw emotional discharge; at the other is the subtle shaping by art, made possible by the human impulse to form and order. We touch here upon the great mystique of art. The first clue to rightness and wrongness with existence is still a sense of aesthetic propriety.

The inveterate susceptibility of man to the aesthetic mode of experience gives art great power and responsibility. Art for art's sake rejects this responsibility, but its effects remain real and important nevertheless. The persuasive power of the modern mass media needs no further comment, save to note that this power operates through images that present value commitments directly to feeling and will. As such they are invitations to emulation and commitment. (Art works its way with varying degrees of subtlety. A patch of blue may evoke an evanescent image of feeling; a picture like *Guernica* can evince a powerful passion.) The effect of great personalities on the values of an age also depends on their aesthetic impact, for it is by art that a personality is celebrated as a culture hero.

The really influential personalities—Socrates, Jesus, Ghandi—are outsize figures, and until their behavior transcends the limits of ordinary men they do not serve as effective models. It is precisely this extremism that makes them suitable for the artistic imagination. The myth-making power of the artist selects those features of the hero's life that enhance the deviations from the ordinary, and so the hero becomes a legend, a remote but powerful object of imitation.

Folk art or popular art, not to speak of Madison Avenue, is forever engaged in model building; one wonders how many American men's lives were affected by the 150 or so variants of the Horatio Alger hero. It is not a question whether art will or will not shape the values of the people, but rather which art—the serious art or the popular art. Just as scientific illiteracy throws the people back on vulgarization, so does aesthetic illiteracy surrender the field of feeling formation to the mass taste-makers.

If I have stressed the role of art as a means to commitment, it was not to denigrate its power to reveal new possibilities of human experience that could shape its aspirations. My purpose is to show that allotting means solely to science and ends solely to art and the humanities is a mistake.

The exploration of value, then, is a joint enterprise for science and the humanities, but in what sense can they collaborate? Certainly not in the sense that science becomes art or *vice versa*, or that science ceases to be scientific and art artistic. Both are rightly insistent on their autonomy. and there is little hope or advantage in appealing to either scientists or artists to abandon specialization.

The enterprise can be joint in two ways: first in that both scientists and humanists are human and men. This gives both a concern for the exploration. The second way involves what must be called, despite all circumlocutions, metaphysics. It has to do with the argument for a common assumption about the inherent rationality and coherence of a world that makes the specialized search of both scientists and humanists worth undertaking in the first place. (I shall touch on this second point in the discussion of Polanyi's notion of tacit knowledge.)

However, the problem of specialization is the more immediate one, and it is wider than that of academic specialization. Every citizen, sooner or later, either has to undertake his own exploration of value or utilize the findings of others who have undertaken it. Both require a kind of schooling other than that which produces specialists at various stages of arrested development. So the tired old question arises again: What sort of schooling will function in the exploration of value? Clearly the customary mix we call liberal education or the set of hard subjects required for admission to college is no longer adequate, if, indeed, it ever was.

Suffice it to note that in no epoch was liberal education sufficient to prevent revolting atrocities against the human spirit, and the humanities were no more potent in this regard than the sciences. Every despot, malignant or benign, has been able to recruit intellectuals to his cause. Schooling has not been a decisive factor in producing social good and evil for at least three reasons: (1) There is a long interval between the end of formal schooling and mature adult life; (2) other institutional influences are more direct and constant; and (3) commitment uses knowledge in ways that are quite different from the ways schools teach it.

Life is packaged in predicaments that are intellectually messy; the clean, highly abstract, logical systems we call the intellectual disciplines are very late and very artificial ways of organizing thought about life rather than life itself. This discrepancy has always been a problem for formal instruction, but as the disciplines become more fragmented, more specialized, and more abstract, the problem is exacerbated.

The most distinctive (not necessarily the most successful) response in our time, has been the activity approach to instruction. For the lower schools it was formulated by W. H. Kilpatrick on the theoretical structure provided by Dewey's description of the complete act of thought. It has been called the project method, the activity program, and many unkind things besides. But its essence is to organize instruction in terms of life problems rather than in terms of intellectual disciplines.

In higher education this approach was and still is rigorously opposed by the disciplinarians, but professional schools and countless new institutes and centers are witness to the fact that the modern university cannot organize all its research and teaching on a straight disciplinary basis. The current clamor of the student for relevance in his studies is further witness of the same trend.

Unfortunately, the life problem approach does not solve the educational dilemma, which may be summed up in a paraphrase of Kant's dictum: Disciplinary study without life problems is nonfunctional; problem study without disciplinary knowledge is superficial. Without the generalizations from formal study of the disciplines, discussion of life problems remains at a mediocre common sense level, and there is no way of inducing these generalizations reliably or economically from common sense discussions of ordinary life problems.

The way out of the impasse is to abandon the attempt—at least for the foreseeable future—to make problem-solving or discipline mastery accrue as a by-product of each other. Instead, we may as well plan to make provision for both types of instruction. Of every discipline we must then ask the following question: How is your discipline to be taught so that it will function in the intelligent structuring and discussion of the societal problems that confront the citizen in a modern society? And of every problem-solving activity we can then ask to what extent it embodies or reflects disciplinary knowledge.

A possible approach to the questions is suggested by the following two-part hypothesis.

1. That general education presupposes an interpretive use of knowledge
2. That the interpretive use of knowledge is a species of what Polanyi has called "tacit knowing"

When I say that science, for example, in general education is used interpretively, I intend to deny that it represents primarily three other possible uses: the applicative, the replicative, and the associative. The replicative use we often call rote memory. By the associative use I mean the rearousal of learnings by a wide range of clues that are related to the learning by the laws of association. And by the applicative use of schooling I mean the solving of a problem by bringing it under a more general theoretical framework, for example, applying the principles of organic chemistry to the problem of air and water pollution or the principles of mechanics to designing new systems of transportation.

I have argued elsewhere in some detail that although application has been the customary justification for the teaching of the disciplines, as a matter of fact, about the only time we use schooling applicatively is in our field of specialization. To apply knowledge entails far more

than being familiar with the appropriate theory. It entails familiarity
with a domain of particular problems of practice and the theoretical
as well as the technological resources for translating theory into operational procedures.[2]

The more typical use of science by the educated citizen is to read
scientific literature or to converse about problems to which science is
relevant. In such activities the categorical structure of science rather
than its technological applications or experimental details is the operative factor. One hopes that the discourse of an educated citizen in this
respect can be clearly differentiated not only from that of a witch
doctor, but also from that of any contemporaries who have not studied
science at all.

The spate of recent talk about the "structure of knowledge" refers
to the set of constructs and their relationships that characterize a given
discipline. Atoms, molecules, energy, neutrons, electrons, mesons, and
other particles, together with the laws that relate them, make up the
structure of the discipline we call physics. Each discipline, regardless
of its resemblance to others in the same family (e.g., the physical sciences
or the social sciences), is distinctive by virtue of the special constructs
and relations that are its building blocks, so to speak. This is important
in education because it renders virtually futile the attempt to reduce
all science instruction to the understanding of scientific method in general. Such a generalized description is a convenient shorthand for talking about science, but it is of no use in talking about or understanding
the phenomena with which sciences are concerned.[3] I am convinced,
therefore, that general education, if it is to be useful in helping the
citizen to understand the problems that plague him, must teach the key
concepts of the basic disciplines and not be content to teach the logical
properties common to their several modes of inquiry.

The role of the cognitive and evaluative structures provided by the
sciences and the humanities for the citizen is the same: namely, to sort
experience for perception, reflection, discourse, and judgment. This sorting is indispensable, for we are told that there is no perception, not to
speak of more discursive operations, without some kind of preliminary
organization of the field. The question for society and for education is

2. Harry S. Broudy; B. Othanel Smith; and Joe R. Burnett. *Democracy and Excellence in American Secondary Education* (Chicago: Rand McNally, 1964). *See also
Philosophy and Education,* Proceedings International Seminar. Monograph Series
No. 3 Ontario Institute for Studies in Education, 1967, pp. 59-71.
3. This is not to deny the fact that two or more disciplines can translate some of
their constructs and laws into each other's language or into a language common to
them all. But biophysics, biochemistry, and physical chemistry, which exemplify
such coalescence, are neither additive combinations of their partners nor applications
of one to the other.

which sorter the citizen will employ. An advanced culture offers at least two alternatives in this regard: the stereotypes of popular science and art, or the more refined, more sophisticated, more reflected categories that are embodied in the intellectual disciplines. Inasmuch as absorbing the popular culture requires less endowment and effort than is required to absorb the more organized kind, formal schooling in the disciplines always encounters the principle of least cognitive strain. The history of education is largely the record of ingenious attempts to counteract this principle.

The problem would not be so urgent if we could good-naturedly bumble along, with the masses using mass stereotypes and the experts using the categories of the intellectual disciplines. We could manage, perhaps, if we gave up the goal of a democratic society in which large decisions are to be made by the masses as well as the experts. But in our stage of technological development, all major policy decisions demand that the masses think with the categories of the intellectual disciplines, both cognitive and affective. General education, on these terms, has little choice: It has to include the formal systematic study of the basic disciplines for all children. Individual differences in interest and ability will have to be met by varying the tactics of instruction rather than the subjects of instruction. If my hypothesis is correct, then the crucial question for science teaching is how to teach the structure of the discipline for interpretive rather than applicative use. Motivating the student to stay awake and attentive is an important tactical consideration, but not the main strategic issue. The problem is whether we can teach the categorical scheme of a science so that it (if there must be a choice), rather than the technical details, will function in adult life. This suggests concentration on a minimal set of key concepts, but also the use of problems somewhat different from those customarily found at the end of each chapter of science textbooks. Reading and discussing an article in the *Scientific American* or even in *The New York Times* Sunday science section is a more appropriate test problem than is calculating the points at which two ballistic missiles will meet or the probable yield of a chemical equation, indispensable as such competency is for the prospective major in physics or chemistry.

The reference to tasks appropriate to estimating the efficacy of general education brings us to an important but touchy point. For a whole clutch of reasons the efficiency criterion has become a virtually unchallengeable dogma in education as well as in industry and in many governmental agencies. To test efficiency, both causes and effects must be identified and explicit. The school, following the import of this doctrine, has adopted the slogan: Down with nonbehavioral objectives. This would not be so bad if it were not interpreted to mean that all non-explicit, nonformalizable objectives or effects are nonbehavioral and, therefore, somehow illegitimate.

This view is reinforced by the scientific tradition in which occult entities and mysteries are eschewed and by the ambitions of computer-aided programmed instruction, which can deal only with that which is formulable into explicit bits and rules. In the replicative and applicative uses of knowledge, precise, detailed, explicit knowledge is a *sine qua non*. But is this also the case with the associative and interpretive uses of knowledge?

Experience would indicate that it is not the case. The categories of chemistry and physics function in the thought of the general medical practitioner long after he has forgotten the specific constants and equations that he learned in high school and college. Michael Polanyi has called this kind of functioning tacit knowing. It occurs when we apprehend a whole or a pattern or a relationship by means of details to which we do *not* attend. Thus, in order to ride a bicycle properly it is important *not* to concentrate on the component movements of bicycle riding; in order to get the effects of a stereopticon we must *not* attend to the two slightly different images of the object. These details. Polanyi would say, function "subsidiarily."

I believe that much of our longstanding difficulty with defining and evaluating general education stems from the fact that so much of it functions tacitly (subsidiarily) rather than explicitly (focally).[4]

Thus a citizen to use the concept of oxidation to interpret rusting and burning need not be *focally* aware of all the details that went into the study of oxidation in his high school or college chemistry courses. If he had not learned these details focally at one time, however, he might not now be aware of them subsidiarily or tacitly. Using recall of the details to test the functionality of the concept by the citizen as a non-specialist is, therefore, just as much a mistake as dispensing with study of these details might be.

Our researchers have not been overly interested in determining the optimum mix of principles-details study for the interpretive use of science, but it seems to me to be the crux of the problem of defining general education. My own suspicion as to the cause of the current, and one hopes transient, disenchantment with science is not so much that science is not well-taught, as Skinner and others would have us

---

4. Michael Polanyi. *Personal Knowledge.* (Chicago: University of Chicago Press, 1958) and "Logic and Psychology." *American Psychologist* 23:1, 27-43; January 1968, p. 31.

believe,[5] as that the wrong things are taught too efficiently. If, for example, a large number of technical details, procedures, and rules are overlearned for replication or application, the student or citizen who wants to interpret his world scientifically may be frustrated by inability to cease focusing on the details rather than using them in a subsidiary way. It may then be a case of not seeing the forest for the trees.

Tacit knowing is especially important in making judgments of relevance and such judgments are crucial in problem solving. Yet, the processes whereby the mind makes these judgments are precisely what remain tacit, and for this reason, according to at least one commentator, cannot in principle be simulated on the computer.[6]

Tacit knowing operates in general education in two ways. First, it uses details that are learned as means to perceive wholes that go beyond the details, a fact made amply familiar by Gestalt psychology. Second, the whole, also in a tacit way, prestructures the kind of details that will be perceived as being relevant, in accordance with the doctrines of selective perception.

Polanyi insists that the great discoveries of science, e.g., those of Kepler and Einstein, depended heavily on the tacit components, among the most important of which is a conviction that reality will not only confirm one's own theory, but that it will be the source and validator of further and as yet unmade discoveries in the same domain. This insight is not built up logically out of painstaking observations and tests, Polanyi argues, but rather guides and gives sense to observation, experiment, and theorizing. For this reason Polanyi regards all knowledge as "personal knowledge" involving moral and aesthetic, as well as cognitive, factors.

The consequences of these remarks for the teaching of science are of several kinds. If the observations about the interpretive use of knowledge are sound, and if the comments about the tacit element in science are relevant, then explicitness in either outcomes or tests is not the center of gravity of science teaching. Doing well on the kind of objective tests now in vogue for science courses may not be the most relevant measure of adequacy. On the contrary, as has been mentioned, the facile and apt use of scientific concepts in reading and discussion of moral problems becomes the more relevant test.

Another type of consequence is hinted at in Polanyi's theory as to the role of metaphysics in the scientific vision and discovery. If, as he

5. B. F. Skinner. "Teaching Science in High School—What is Wrong?" *Science* 159: (February 16, 1968) 704-10.
6. Hubert L. Dreyfus. "Why Computers Must Have Bodies to Be Intelligent." *The Review of Metaphysics* 21:1, 13-33; September 1967.

holds, deep conviction in a coherent reality of infinite cognitive potential is a necessary condition for the deepest scientific exploration, then what is one to make of the positivistic spirit of science that pervades science curricula? (I refer, of course, to the notion that scientific discovery consists of a standard series of hypothetico-deductive steps that are carried on dispassionately by the scientist wholly independent of his metaphysical commitments.)

It is this notion of science, fruitful though it is, that has isolated science from value and value from science. Positivism makes the knowledge of fact objective and impersonal at the cost of rendering judgments of value incorrigibly subjective and idiosyncratic. But if reality is a coherent whole, then its value components are no less objective than are its fact components, and science has its passion as well as art.

In other words, if Polanyi is right, a better understanding of the value components of scientific effort would leave the pupil with a sense of the unity of science with life as a whole, a sense that is now damped and muted. The faith that scientific reflection and loyalty to the truth will be confirmed more and more by a reality we did not invent is the link between science, art, and value.

The goal of science in general education is not the production of scientific workers at the applicational or routine investigational level, important, no doubt, as that is. That is a job for special education. Nor is its aim the production of Nobel Laureates, although this might be a gratifying albeit remote, by-product of good general education. The target is, rather, the exploration of value, including its scientific components. Surely no task is more urgent than this, and by now we should have learned that no magic device or scheme will engender interdisciplinary thinking as an automatic, effort-free dividend of either specialized disciplinary training or common sense discussion of current events. Somewhere in the school this interdisciplinary exploration of value has to be undertaken deliberately and systematically. Until this is done, we shall have no way of studying just how well the various disciplines are functioning, tacitly or explicitly, in the exploration of value. The use of exploration of value as a test task in school is especially important because it so closely resembles the sort of thinking, deliberating, and choosing that will be required of one as a citizen in what one hopes will have some resemblance to a humane and democratic world.

It is by now a cliché that our future depends on the bulk—not an elite handful—of our citizens being able to carry on interdisciplinary thinking or the exploration of value. Whether science will have its proper share in that enterprise depends not only on the specialized training we give our future scientists, but on the way the interpretive schema of the citizen incorporates the scientific disciplines. Above all, these schema must not irremediably bifurcate fact and value. A world that will continue inexhaustibly to confirm, to produce, to yield to our inquiry the truths and imperatives that do cohere is the mainspring not only of science but of art and, in its purest sense, religion as well.

---

1. What do you think are some reasons for the loss of confidence and interest in science?
2. Who should be held responsible for: (1) bombing Hiroshima, (2) chemical warfare, (3) air pollution, and (4) other events made possible by science?
3. How can the sciences and humanities combine to produce greater relevancy?
4. Broudy suggests that religion, in its purest sense, along with art and science are involved in truths and imperatives in our world. How is religion related to science?

7 MORRIS H. SHAMOS

Science and
the Humanities

Dr. Shamos offers additional ideas related to science and humanities. He suggests that science is "the search for order in nature" and then tries to coordinate such a definition with the humanities. Dr. Shamos also identifies differences between the sciences and the humanities. Testing the truth or validity of statements in science takes a form that is somewhat meaningless for the humanities.

The launching of the first Soviet Sputnik was a forceful reminder that man has not yet succeeded in defining the common ground between his two great areas of knowledge, science and the humanities, for the resultant clamor for improved science education in the United States and greater support for science, generally, touched off an immediate and typical reaction from those whose interests lie chiefly, perhaps even solely, in the humanities. They agreed, not that humanistic studies are more important to mankind, but that they should not be ignored in the rush for international supremacy in science. They were right, of course, but it almost appeared as though battle lines were being drawn once again, with the humanities on one side and science forced to the other.

This is an old controversy that dates back roughly to the beginning of the modern period in science. It seems that, from the time science first exerted a noticeable influence on the affairs of men, it clashed with the traditional forms of liberal culture. There can be little doubt that the conflict stems more from a misunderstanding of the nature of science than from some basic incompatibility between scientific and humanistic pursuits.

Reprinted from the *Fifty-Ninth Yearbook of the National Society for the Study of Education,* 1960, by permission of the editor. Dr. Shamos is a physicist who has been actively involved in science education at all levels.

Modern science is only some three centuries old; yet, in this relatively short time it has made a deep and lasting impression on modern civilization. Virtually no segment of human activity has been left untouched by the results of scientific thought. Whether science has always worked for the over-all good is to some humanists (and scientists) a matter for debate. But it is idle to speculate on this point, for we are unable to turn back the clock. For centuries philosophy was conceived of as embracing all knowledge worthy of interest for its own sake, but the rapid development of science forced its separation from philosophy, a process not completed until the nineteenth century. The conflict between science and the humanities can be traced largely to the importance accorded by science to its experimental aspects as distinguished from its purely speculative nature and to technology, which inevitably grows with a science and which provides it with stimulus for further development.

When Plato discussed how best to educate the future leaders of society, he took the position that, to arrive at an idea of "the good," one must study, among other things, the hypotheses and basic concepts of the natural sciences.[1] Unfortunately, this conception of science was quite different from the modern view. He scorned experiment, thinking that the only true knowledge was that derived from pure philosophical speculation. It was inconceivable to him that, to understand nature, one had to enlist its aid. This would have been totally inconsistent with the teleological scheme of things. After all, was not nature "designed" for the good of mankind? To understand it, therefore, one simply had to seek the ends or purposes which it served, giving free rein to the imagination. This mode of explanation not only appealed to the early Greeks, at least to the followers of Socrates, Plato, and Aristotle, but also set the pattern for centuries of hopeless confusion in science, a pattern finally broken by the intellectual strength of the Renaissance. As science leaned more and more on experiment to add to man's understanding of nature and sought explanations in terms of initial causes of things rather than the ends or "goods" they served, it prospered. Yet it appears that the very factors which led to the explanation of the phenomena of science became the chief source of contention in this strange controversy.

Science came under sporadic attack from those humanists who questioned the intellectual value of a study which they regarded as mechanistic and routine. And as the methods and techniques of scientific investigation grew more precise, these humanists were strengthened in

1. Plato, *The Republic*. Translated by R. Jowett. (New York: Modern Library, 1941.)

their conviction that creative imagination and appreciation of beauty played little, if any, role in the scientific study of nature. With the industrial revolution a new factor was added, namely, the utility of science. Perhaps more than any other aspect of this enterprise, its ulility has conveyed a false impression of the nature of science, particularly in modern times.

The famous French mathematician and philosopher, Henri Poincaré described the true motives of science: "The scientist does not study nature because it is useful; he studies it because he delights in it, and he delights in it because it is beautiful."[2]

The layman, unfortunately, finds it difficult to reconcile this view with the outward impressions he gets of science. He finds himself surrounded by the material products of science. His habits, his mode of living, his health, perhaps even his freedom to enjoy the arts—all are conditioned by advances in technology. He is aware, furthermore, that such advances generally result from specific needs of society rather than the creative spirit of man. Can he be convinced that there is far more to science than the end products that meet his eye or that men do not engage in this pursuit solely to fashion such things as automobiles, radios, and electric lights? Not readily!

The average man, as well as the humanist, has held such a partial view of science. He confuses pure science with applied science or technology. The two strengthen one another but differ greatly in basic values. Not that technology has less value, but it is a kind of value remote from the ken of the humanist and is not what is meant by science. That some humanists hold a totally irrational view of science is clear from the nature of their arguments. They lament the changing scene; they deplore the inroads of technology on nature; they fear that the literary and artistic classics of the past may be lost from view because they will no longer evoke meaningful memories. They regard the whole of science somewhat in the same light as its military potential: a barbaric enterprise destined to halt the cultural development of civilization. No doubt most individuals, scientists included, who have witnessed some of the changes brought on by modern technology, look back with a certain nostalgia to the "simpler life" of earlier times. But the changes mark the direction that civilization has taken, and the poet, rather than cling solely to the cultural riches of the past, must record that which is significant on the contemporary scene.

Perhaps the greatest injustice that can be done to science is to regard it merely as a collection of facts, and the practice of science as little more than the routine accumulation of minutiae. It is true that science

2. H. Poincaré. *The Value of Science.* Translated by George Bruce Halsted. (New York: Science Press, 1907.) p. 8.

deals with hard, inflexible facts, but it has also to do with very general
ideas and abstract principles; and it is the co-ordination of these ideas
and observed facts that is the essence of modern science. Facts alone
do not constitute a science. *Nature study* is not the same as the *study
of nature.*

What, then, is science? It is the search for *order in nature.* The
scientist seeks to account for nature in the simplest possible terms; that
is, with the greatest economy of thought and expression. This is, after
all, what is meant by *explanation* in science. The humanist seeks a similar economy of expression but in a somewhat different sense. The poet,
Coleridge, defined beauty as *unity in variety,* and described the arts,
poetry, painting, music as the search for this unity. The creative artist
seeks to encompass in a single poem, in a painting, in a musical composition, a certain segment of human experience. In much the same way
the scientist seeks for unity amid the great variety of nature. Both study
nature because it is beautiful, but they regard beauty in different ways.
After describing what motivates the scientist to study nature, Poincaré
went on to distinguish these kinds of beauty.

> Of course I do not here speak of that beauty which strikes the senses,
> the beauty of qualities and appearances; not that I undervalue such
> beauty, far from it, but it has nothing to do with science; I mean that
> profounder beauty which comes from the harmonious order of parts
> and which a pure intelligence can grasp.[3]

Were it not that nature works in essentially simple fashion, there
could be no science. Suppose, instead of having roughly one hundred
different chemical elements in nature, we had one hundred billion, all
uniformly distributed. Then as Poincaré pointed out,[4] the chance of
finding two objects in nature bearing some resemblance would be extremely remote. Whatever we might know of parts of nature would avail
us little in our efforts to understand the whole. All things would be
different. Science could be no more than an interminable accumulation
of isolated facts.

Nor could there be any art. Nature, would defy description by the
humanist as well as the scientist. Neither one could evoke memories of
the past nor provide useful ideas for the future. Imagine man's range
of hearing or the spectral limits of his vision to be multiplied a thousand-
fold, and think what effect this would have on music and the visual arts.
That order and simplicity are prerequisite to all forms of knowledge
must be evident.

On the other hand, it should be clear that there are significant differences between the sciences and the humanities. The latter are con-

3. Poincaré, *op. cit.,* p. 8.
4. *Ibid.,* p. 5.

cerned with man himself, with his whole being and his interactions with the world about him; the sciences are more objective, less concerned with the ways of man than with his understanding of the ways of nature. There are no simple definitions of these disciplines. A work of art is a finished thing; it need not build upon the past nor form a foundation for the future. It is complete and unique in itself. Science, however, is tentative and accumulative. Its structure has been built up over the ages, but always of removable bricks, so that the weaker ones, when discovered, may be replaced by stronger. It is the cumulative nature of science, according to Conant,[5] that distinguishes it most from other forms of intellectual activity. He points out that while progress is expected in the sciences, it is not a characteristic of the humanities. The criterion actually goes much deeper. One may question, for instance, whether it is meaningful to speak of progress in connection with the humanities. A more useful, though perhaps related distinction would seem to be the matter of self-consistency. Science has evolved means of testing the truth of its statements about nature. These methods, while not infallible, have on the whole proved successful in guiding science along the correct path to knowledge. The humanities, however, despite frequent claims to *self-evident truths*, have no logical rules for testing its accomplishments. Indeed, the concepts of truth and falsity cannot even be applied to humanistic knowledge, for it is meaningless to ask whether a work of art or a poem can be justified on this ground.

Regardless of these differences, there appear to be no valid reasons for mutual antagonism. Both scientist and humanist, as we have seen, are motivated by a common goal, the search for order. They seek this goal in different ways; but each, to claim achievement, must display creative imagination. The basic difficulty is a lack of mutual understanding. One kind of knowledge cannot replace the other. The major problems of modern civilization will not be solved by science alone but by a combination of science and human wisdom. Each one, scientist and humanist, has the responsibility of seeking the common ground.

---

1. "Nature study is not the same as the study of nature." What do you think was meant by that statement?
2. How is science different from the humanities, according to the author?
3. How do the humanities search for order?
4. How do science and technology differ?

5. James Bryant Conant, *Science and Common Sense.* (New Haven, Connecticut: Yale University Press, 1951.)

8 GEORGE EASTMAN

Scientism in Science Education

In conjunction with the previous two authors, George Eastman examines the connections between the humanities and the sciences. He uses scientism to represent a third party—the people who believe that science is the ultimate way to solve man's problems. Eastman suggests that nonscientific culture seeks complete, eternal truths. Modern science, however, differs from such closure ideas by defining reality as a continuing, dynamic process.

The author suggests that the confusion between science and scientism may be a central cause for the many problems of teaching science.

Snow's "Two Culture" image is now clear: "Literary intellectuals at one pole—at the other scientists . . . [and] between the two a guild of mutual incomprehension . . . hostility and dislike, but most of all lack of understanding."(1) The image has misled on two counts. The important thing is not the contest between literati and scientists, but the conflict between *cultures*. And the conflict is not between two parties, but three: a conflict among the cultures of scientists, non- or anti-scientific humanists, and believers in and practitioners of scientism.[1] The purpose of this paper is to investigate this triangle, first by examining the humanistic and the scientific cultures, then contrasting these with scientism, and concluding with evidence in support of the claim that scientism is often confused with genuine science in our schools and that this fact is deeply damaging to the future of our society.

The dominant culture in the West, right into the second decade of the twentieth century, was humanistic. It accepted a conception of reality rooted in the Greco-Judeo-Christian tradition. "Reality" was

Reprinted from *The Science Teacher*, Vol. 36, No. 4, 1969, pp. 19-22 by permission of the editor. Dr. Eastman is Associate Professor of Social Foundations at State University of New York at Buffalo.

1. As will be more completely defined later, scientism as used in this article refers to the credo that science is the true and ultimate way to solve the problems of nature and man.

largely, if not entirely, completed or worked out. The "nature of things" when uncovered would be found to be perfect, permanent, and universal. Man's task was to uncover these invariable "laws" and to bring his behavior into line with them. The prequantum conception of "complete description," which held that with time all of the laws relevant to the complete description of a phenomenon could be uncovered and thus provide a total explanation, is an expression of the view of reality as fixed, determinate, *and* determinable.

This conception, which we shall call determinate reality (in contrast with indeterminate reality, which characterizes modern science), is a basic postulate, generally tacit, behind humanistic "literary" views, religious views, and economic and political postures which can be called conservative. So long as prequantum, prerelativity science held to a determinate (and determinable) reality concept, it could be romanticized into the role of a handmaiden for those who believed there was one predetermined reality, knowledge of which they had and which, somehow, nicely vindicated their class and intellectual biases.

A humanistic culture(2) holds then to a determinate reality concept, a conception with profound implications for class structure, conceptual ordering, and education. Once one assumes a fixed and knowable reality, there is a tendency to seek those social, political, economic, intellectual, and educational arrangements which are most consistent with this reality. Arbitrary social and intellectual arrangements, maintained because they best serve the self-interest of entrenched elites, are justified on grounds of "naturalness," i.e., correspondence with "natural law" and determinable reality. In a nonscientific culture, truth is reached when enough evidence has been mustered to constitute vindication, and this may be very little and of a suspect kind by the standards of science. Nonscientific culture seeks inclusiveness and totality of explanation but not of control. It seeks to give expression to "eternal verities," to turn the phrase that will encapsulate these universal truths "for all time." The quest is for a complete and definitive explanation of reality; yet, at the same time, it is held that, however complete the explanation, there is a zone that eludes description, a mysterious realm that forever invites the explorer yet resists full disclosure.

Finally, nonscientific culture is marked by a drive for closure, for certain and absolute truth. Maturity—personal, social, intellectual—is defined in terms of completeness, of having *arrived*, of having finished. Our culture abounds in metaphorical uses of finished: A person's career may be finished; a school may be a finishing school; a painting or a novel is, at last, finished; a student finishes a course or a degree. These uses are dominantly nonscientific and assume a conception of "goodness" as final and complete.

But what of modern science? While traditional humanistic culture is involved in vindicative truth-seeking, scientific culture pursues detached truth-seeking. Where the humanist seeks to vindicate his preconceptions, the scientist seeks to confirm or disconfirm a hypothesis. Reality for the modern scientist is indeterminate—it is not fixed and certain or predetermined. The scientist believes that reality is a dynamic process but not necessarily teleological. He is aware of the bias that he, as the observer and, especially, as the conceptualizer, introduces, into his descriptions and explanations. Rather than seek inclusiveness and totality of explanation, science seeks wholeness of explanation with maximum control.(3) In fact, control is more important to science than is explanation. Modern science is closer to the ancient Babylonian's skill in "saving the phenomena" (i.e., calculating the times and dates of astronomical events), than to the Ionian's skill in speculation, theory, and interpretation.(4) B. F. Skinner's views of the nonfunctionality of "explanation" and "interpretation" is a paradigm of a significant direction which modern science is taking: seeking prediction and control, but without explanation or answers to the question, "why?"(5)

Finally, modern science does not seek total, inclusive explanation. Its view of reality as continuous process, and of observation and measurement as indeterminate, leads to an open-ended search for possibilities. The drive is for nonclosure, for keeping the observational situation open and the types of controls numerous. Modern science, in contrast to the traditional, humanistic world view, can be described in terms of negative as opposed to positive entropy. It is an improbable condition, requiring organizing and structuring, and leading to concentration of diffused materials. It operates typically by creating more order at some points at the cost of creating less order elsewhere.

If we characterize modern science as a continuous process of detached truth-seeking after an indeterminate reality over which man seeks to gain maximum control but which he does not necessarily expect or seek to explain, how are we to describe "scientism"? Scientism is the conception of science generally held by the public, by many literati, and by some scientists themselves. It assumes "science" designates *the* true and ultimate way to solve the problems of nature and man. It is, in fact, a scientized scholasticism, a de-Godized religion. "Scientism" is not a methodology, but an ideology.[2] It demands true believers of the true way. It resembles traditional humanist culture in its conviction that there

2. An "ideology" tends to be systematic, tenaciously held, and to require proselytism. A "theory" tends to be systematic, tentatively held, and nonproselytizing. Ideologies result in creeds and doctrines; theories in descriptions and hypotheses. (*See* Eastman, G. "The Ideologizing of Theories: John Dewey's Educational Theory, a Case in Point." *Educational Theory*. 17: 103-119; April 1967.)

is a basic, underlying order that in the end will work itself out to man's benefit. It is the mid-twentieth-century version of eighteenth-century deism. Like the deists, practitioners of scientism have denatured God, but deified nature, assigning to scientism an omnipotent role of solving all problems, clarifying all things.(6) Scientism tends to be based on a naive realist ontology that assumes there are real, isolated entities standing apart from human perceiving and conceiving and which are there waiting to be uncovered, like artifacts of some lost culture. The scientist is seen as one uniquely equipped—like a rainmaker with his twig—to detect these real nuggets and expose them. Bronowski thus describes scientism's conception of the scientist:

> . . . the colorless professionals of science, going off to work in the morning into the universe in a neutral, unexposed state. They then expose themselves like a photographic plate. And then in the darkroom or laboratory they develop the image, so that suddenly and startlingly it appears, printed in capital letters, as a new formula for atomic energy. (7)

In scientism the ultimate, preexisting reality that is to be *un*covered is material, consisting of individual entities to be unearthed, polished, and placed on display as tokens of the triumph of man over ignorance. Scientism holds that "scientific advancement" consists of the accumulation, over time, of these unearthed material truths (i.e., laws, principles, objects, events); that the number of these "truths" is finite; and that man eventually may win all the marbles in nature's bag and place them in his own.

Public education in the United States, from kindergarten through to graduate school, is actively (though in most cases not intentionally) fostering scientism and its correlate of ideological arrogance. When the basic humility and restraint of judgment and action consistent with a view of science as indeterminate, probabilistic, and heuristic are lacking, it is easy to turn to scientism, to find appealing the prospect of becoming part of the priesthood of scientism equipped to perform the sacred rites of *un*covery. What is the evidence that scientism is being taught and is leading to ideological arrogance?

There is, first of all, the testimony of others actively involved in education. Henle charges that both nonscience and science majors tend to be ignorant of the "nature of science itself." We must, he argues

> find a way to present the totality of science as well as its internal variety, to teach the nature of science, to convey the total cultural impact of science—its place in history, the change in the general view of the world and of man from sub-cell to supersociety, from subatomic structure to stellar masses. (8)

Winthrop condemns the type of learning that consists of the accumulation of information and argues for functional thinking, which, he stresses, is characteristic of genuine science. For persons to think functionally, he argues, they must acquire

> the fixed habit of looking at multiple and varied phenomena as components of complex systems in which these same components are in causal relationship with each other, or more sophisticatedly, *in functional relationship with each other.* (9)

What conception of science is being advanced through school textbooks? An examination of science textbook series, and texts in the separate sciences, reveals that they stress either a conception of science as miraculous giver of things, or as a process of thinking, a method, and a set of attitudes. An analysis suggests about a 60-40 percent distribution of these views, with most textbooks stressing science as miraculous giver of things and uncoverer of preexisting reality. One of the more enlightened textbook series states that

> It may be impossible for a civilization to survive without the education of children in science. Since the survival of any society is largely dependent upon the conduct and activities of its members, the urgent need is to develop a population that is able to operate intelligently and resourcefully with the materials and energy of the Universe. (10)

This same source defines "science" as tentative, creative, realistic, and cooperative, and proposes that for each of these characteristics a corresponding behavior be developed in the student. Thus the tentativeness of scientific conclusions will require an open- and critical-mindedness on the part of the student; creativeness in science will require original, imaginative, creative thinking; science deals with forces and problems that will require resourcefulness in the learner; and science as cooperative activity will require responsibleness in its practitioners and learners.

Another textbook series explains— to the teacher who is to use the book, not to the student, it is to be noted—that

> Knowledge grows: Unlike the laws of the Medes and the Persians, the laws of science change as the partial nature of earlier statements becomes evident. The discovery of nature's processes must be gradual with addition of fact to fact. Our statements describing these processes, the laws of science, must also change. (11)

Still a different series asserts that

> What a child learns may be of less value to him than the way he learns it. [He should] be encouraged to develop a critical attitude and an open mind. (12)

These statements, and others like them, are impressive, and certainly suggest genuine science rather than scientism. Such statements, however, are not directed to the students who presumably are to use the textbooks, but are found in the teacher's manual. While these manuals often advance an enlightened conception of science, it is not shared explicitly with the student, nor is it, in most instances, significantly demonstrated in the content and in the organization of the textbooks themselves.(13) In one current textbook series(14), one which illustrates the scientist-as-rainmaker-view, the student is asked: 'How important is the study of science?" The authors reply: "Look about you. Can you find one object which has not been improved by scientists or people with scientific training?" In this same statement to the student we read: "Today, a typical young scientist might be working in the electronics division or synthetic fibers division of a large corporation, or he may be part of a team of scientists at a university or government laboratory studying nuclear fusion or designing instruments for future spaceships." And in still another series, also technology-oriented, we read that "Scientists are very practical people. They take the facts and ideas of science and use them to produce necessities of life."(15)

Still, regardless of the view of science or scientism in the teacher's manual, or in the statement to the student, or as reflected in the organization and content of the textbooks, what view is in fact being taught in the classroom? Here the content and organization of the textbooks is a partial indicator, and these, plus observations of and discussions with science teachers, suggest to the author that scientism is probably being taught in well over half of the classrooms.

Looking at science teachers in our schools and colleges for a moment, we may ask how much thought have they given to their activity as an expression of a new and significant and, perhaps, crucial world view? How many of the undergraduate *or* graduate programs in science require majors to take work in—at least—a philosophy of science course, or a sociology of knowledge course, or a linguistics course that shows the relationship of linguistic symbols to thought processes and thus to reality structuring?

And what of our own experience in school? Were we in any way led to think functionally; or, in fact, to think at all; and least of all to learn to examine our own thinking processes?

We have, as Kenneth Boudling argues, entered a new phase of human life.(16) Call it postcivilization, postmodern, ultramodern—whatever the name—our new age has and is acquiring characteristics that are discontinuous with the past. One way to describe the change is to say that we have moved from hibernation to cybernation—from a condition of suspended animation and only partial awareness of the self and of the world, to a condition of acute self-awareness and unprecedented world control. But this is the rub: The altered nature of knowledge, science, and "reality" demands that we, too, change; yet most of us have not. Each generation grows up resteeped in cultural folk images, largely blind to its own inner life, and burdened down by anachronistic knowledge and ineffectual methodologies. We are trained in scientism, learn to adulate its technological extension, and live for the acquistion of technology's perpetual products. If humanists, we quixotically attack scientism in the mistaken notion that our windmill is the dragon science. The humility that follows from genuine science is never experienced by "technological enthusiasts" whose commitment to scientism leads them to believe that technology will make man's long-standing problems obsolete.

Where formerly the price of not knowing oneself might have been a painful but bearable conformity to a socially imposed role, it is now absorption into an industrial-cultural complex that has as its goal transforming man into the perfect consumer: uncritical, voracious, insatiable, and unhappy. Continuing to teach scientism significantly contributes to one of the most pressing dangers of our time. Those who accept scientism for science are especially likely to fall victim to the grossest dehumanizing and depersonalizing aspects of our postcivilization. They are likely to have a blind faith in the Great God Science (i.e., scientism) and so to uncritically and irrationally absorb its claims and its products and eventually to become its docile pawns.

REFERENCES

1. Snow, C. P. *The Two Cultures and the Scientific Revolution.* New York: Cambridge University Press, 1959, pp. 4-5. In his sequel, *The Two Cultures: And A Second Look.* New York: Cambridge University Press, 1963, Snow corrects his earlier tendency to dichotomize and advances a concept of a "third culture" —a combined humanistic-scientific culture of the kind Bronowski defends. (*See* footnote 2.)
2. Bronowski, Jacob. *Science and Human Values.* Revised Edition. New York: Harper & Row, Publishers, 1965. Bronowski is the most eloquent and articulate exponent of the view that science and genuine humanism are one and the same. The concept of humanism used in this paper is the "old" one that implies opposition with science.
3. The distinction Erik Erikson makes between "wholeness" and "totality" is intended here. By "wholeness" is meant "a sound, organic, progressive mutuality between diversified functions and parts within an entirety, the boundaries of which are open and fluid"; while "totality" involves "an absolute boundary [where] nothing that must be outside can be tolerated inside." (Erikson, E. "Wholeness and Totality—A Psychiatric Contribution." In *Totalitarianism.* C. J. Friedrich, Editor. Cambridge, Massachusetts: Harvard University Press, 1954, pp. 161-162.)

4. Toulmin, S. *Foresight and Understanding.* New York: Harper & Row, 1961, pp. 30-34. Toulmin uses the Babylonian and Ionian astronomers between 600 and 400 B.C. as an example of how one can have foresight in the sense of accumulation of measurements and accurate prediction yet have no understanding in the sense of explanation.
5. Skinner, B. F. "Are Theories of Learning Necessary?" In *Cumulative Record.* New York: Appleton-Century-Crofts, 1961, pp. 39-69; *Science and Human Behavior.* Chapter III. New York: The Macmillan Company, 1953.
6. Becker, Carl L. *The Heavenly City of the Eighteenth-Century Philosophers.* New Haven, Connecticut: Yale University Press, 1932. *See* especially Chapter II, "The Laws of Nature and of Nature's God."
7. Bronowski, *op. cit.,* p. 10.
8. Henle, R. J. "Collegiate Education for Modern Culture." *Educational Record.* Washington, D. C.: American Council on Education, 47 (Summer 1966): 342.
9. Winthrop, Henry. "Needed Reconstruction in Education for a Cybernating Society." *Educational Record.* Fall 1965. Washington, D. C.: American Council on Education, 46: 400-411.
10. Craig, Gerald S., and Bryan, B. C. *Science for You.* Boston, Massachusetts: Ginn and Company, 1965, pp. v-vi.
11. Carroll, Franklin B.; Adams, S.; and Harrison, L. M. *Science in Our World.* New York: J. C. Winston, Company, 1957, p. iv.
12. Thurber, Walter A. *Exploring Science,* Boston, Massachusetts: Allyn and Bacon, Inc., 1962, p. 13.
13. *The Science for You* series (*op. cit.*) comes closest to practicing what it preaches. Book Six, for instance, opens with a section on "Ways of Thinking and Behaving." In a subsection entitled, "Our Behavior Shows," it is pointed out that a visitor to a school "could by observing the behavior of students learn what your school is teaching about health, safety, and good citizenship," p. 22. This section attempts to make explicit, in operational terms appropriate to sixth-graders, what critical mindedness, resourcefulness, responsibleness, and creativeness are.
14. Jacobson, W. J.; Kind, R. N.; and Killie, L. F. *Broadening Worlds of Science.* New York: American Book Company, 1959, p. x.
15. Syrocki, John and Munch, T. W. *Science for a Changing World.* Chicago, Illinois: Benefic Press, 1967, p. 8.
16. Boulding, Kenneth E. *The Meaning of The Twentieth-Century: The Great Transition.* Chapter I. New York: Harper & Row, 1964.

---

1. Compare science with scientism. Can you identify some specific examples in our present society?
2. Are there any differences between Eastman's ideas and the views of Broudy and Shamos?

9 JOHN H. WOODBURN

Science Defined Versus Indefinable: A Personal Attempt to Define Science

The final article in this section represents a systematic attempt by one individual to define science. Sixteen scientists and science educators offered ideas about the nature of science. The "final" definition is, of course, as tentative as any other, but the process of arriving at this definition should not be easily dismissed. Many different points of view were represented and the definition is a compromise from many suggestions. The definition is an active, dynamic one that categorizes science less as a body of content and more as a personal attempt by man to "find out."

Acting as a subtle yet extremely powerful determinant of what a teacher teaches and how it is taught is the definition of science operating in the mind of the teacher. Similarly, the spirit and structure of science courses and curricular programs and how these are to be administered reflect vividly what their creators believe to be the spirit, structure, and function of science. What they hope that young people will gain from their instruction in science reveals what educators believe to be the goals, outcomes, and function of science in our society and culture.

In line with this argument, I have done two things. First, I have tried to understand how scientists, philosophers, logicians, and other scholars define science. Second, through correspondence, I invited 29 scientists and science educators to have a go at shaping up an operational definition of science "for science teachers working at all grade levels." Eight of fifteen scientists and eight of fourteen science educators responded.

Looking forward to a "round robin" pooling of suggestions and criticisms, a definition was cited "to serve as a point of departure." This definition is:

Reprinted from *The Science Teacher*, Vol. 34, No. 8, 1967, pp. 27-30 by permission of the editor. Dr. Woodburn has been active in science education and has done work in this area at Charles W. Woodward School in Rockville, Maryland.

Science is that human endeavor that seeks to describe, with ever-increasing accuracy, the events and circumstances within our natural environment.[1]

A few comments on the conception of this definition. Its origin traces to my interpretations of ideas expressed by scientists and other kinds of scholars who have thought about the fundamental nature of science. Examples of those cited in the above reference follow.

Science is the interpretation of nature and man is the interpretor. G. Gore, 1878.

Science is the attempt to make the chaotic diversity of our sense experience correspond to a logically uniform system of thought. A. Einstein, 1940.

Nature, with all her regularities and irregularities, might have been just as real even if there were no men to observe and study her. But there could have been no science without human beings, or beings like them. It is the spirit of man brooding over the stream of natural events that has given birth to science. A. Wolf, 1925.

Science in itself furnishes none of the ends of action; in so far as the knowledge of the scientist is concerned, it is immaterial whether what we know of high explosives is used to build a great reservoir to make the desert bloom as the rose, or to construct giant shells to snuff out the lives of an entire city. As a man the scientist may, nay, must, make some preference; but the grounds for that preference are not to be found in physics. Columbia Associates in Philosophy, 1923.

These citations are representative of many from which I tried to extract the essence and then synthesize into an operational definition of science.

In general, there seems to be a long way yet to go, as responses to my invitation show. Extreme pessimism asks whether "any definition, however carefully worded, can reflect the nature of science. We need much more than a verbal statement." Slightly less pessimistic is the idea that "perhaps it is impossible to produce a short, simple definition of natural science in operational terms." A similar state of mind is sensed in the comment, "One thing that always troubles me is whether it is either possible or desirable to reduce a description of science to a one sentence definition."

Were it not for one brute fact, I, too, would divorce myself from the nagging urge to synthesize a valid operational definition of science. The fact is that science *is* defined. The word appears in every dictionary. One or another definition of science appears on thousands of chalkboards every autumn. The word shows up in textbook glossaries and more or

1. John H. Woodburn, and Ellsworth S. Obourn. *Teaching the Pursuit of Science.* (New York: Macmillan Company, 1965.) p. 12.

less garbled statements appear in countless university student lecture notes which begin, "Science is . . ."

Furthermore, I feel uneasy to pursue an accurate description of any phenomenon without establishing, at best, temporary boundaries of the domain in which the pursuit will be carried out. I feel urged to advise my students that they cannot pursue their laboratory exercises or small-scale excursions into science without risking loss of efficiency if they allow their activities to stray too far afield from the probable domain of science. And the wisdom of defining one's terms is proverbial.

In his thought-provoking essay "Who Speaks for Science?" Wallace R. Brode[2] discusses several non-pedagogical problems which arise from the increasing confusion regarding a concept of science and the identification of who is a scientist. Most disturbing of these problems stems from the sharp influence science has on our cultural, economic, political, and social life, both nationally and internationally. The "voice of science" stands to affect significantly the judgment of the nation and its guiding leaders. Perhaps less vital is the confusion arising from decisions regarding what kinds of projects belong in the domain of the National *Science* Foundation, attempts to trace trends in the supply of and demand for *scientists*, and proper assignments of individuals in national registers of *scientists*.

There are also elements of optimism among the responses to my initial invitation. For example, "Your attempt to think through the definition of science is commendable but the task is difficult." And, "We must indeed continue trying to refine our definitions." Qualified optimism shows through in suggestions that a definition of science can be framed which will be meaningful at least to people who have participated in science—people who have lived with science.

Some people accept the point-of-departure definition pretty much as it is worded. Others find little of value in the definition. Rejection points sharply to the term "description." One respondee says, "What leaves me most uneasy, however, is your use of the word 'describe' as the key operator in the definition. To limit science to *description* is to miss, I fear, much of its essence. Many sciences start with a description and classification of natural events and circumstances, and some in their infancy even end there, but the more highly developed sciences only *begin* with the description of nature in the form of data." Another says, "Science is a long way from being merely a description. It also 'explains,' provides theoretical structures for organizing, etc." Another respondee criticizes the definition because "It makes no reference to the cause and

2. Wallace R. Brode. "Who Speaks for Science?" *Topic: A Journal of the Liberal Arts* 6 (Spring 1966.): 14-34.

effect, or 'interrelatedness,' concept so dear to scientists in general and chemists in particular." A final example takes the form, "It seems to me that science is, in one extremely important and crucial sense, much more than an attempt to describe events in the natural environment. I would think that your definition would be more consistent with what is often referred to as natural history rather than science."

No one seems to disagree with the inference that the phenomena of nature constitute the raw materials of science.

My original correspondence also invited response to an effort to distinguish among the various branches of science. This distinction is to be achieved by adding separate phrases to a common root definition. This common root derived from the point-of-departure definition is: Science is that endeavor which seeks to describe, with ever-increasing accuracy, the events and circumstances that occur or exist. . . . For biology, the final distinguishing phrase becomes: "in and among living systems." For chemistry, the final phrase would be: "when bonds between atoms are being broken or regenerated." For physics, the phrase, "when energy is transformed," completes the definition. And the complete definition for geology would end with: "the events and circumstances which accompany changes in the earth's rocks, its oceans, and atmosphere."

When commenting on these attempts to distinguish among the various branches of science, one particularly thought-provoking response says, "What needs to be thought about is the question of whether each science is differentiated from the others because of the nature of the systems that are observed or because of the nature of the ideas that are used to interrelate one's observations. One general pattern is that the different disciplines are concerned with somewhat different sets of systems, but they all tend toward the use of the same set of ideas. Probably the principal distinction in ideas is concerned with the level of complexity."

As for the individual distinguishing phrases, one respondee says, "Your final phrase for biology and for geology suit me, too, but I cannot say this with an air of authority. I do feel qualified, however, to criticize your more specific definitions of physics and chemistry. Here you seriously departed, I feel, from your philosophy of 'operational clarity' since you here appeal to quite complicated abstractions, 'bonds,' 'atoms,' and 'energy.' Furthermore, you make a distinction between chemistry and physics that has nothing to do with reality. Many chemists are vigorously engaged in the study of energy transformations; many physicists are concerned with the structure of solids. In fact, there is hardly a way to draw a line between the disciplines. I would urge you to seek some less abstract way of describing the specific interests of chemists and physicists, such as 'the properties of the substances that we find in our environment and the changes that occur in these substances.' . . . Concerning the line of distinction, I have a most radical proposal. I would no longer try to distinguish the two (if you care about representing the facts of our time in your definition). I would suggest lumping them. 'Chemistry and physics are those human endeavors . . .' and then at the end, say something about physics tending to be more concerned with those aspects of nature susceptible to mathematical description."

Colleagues of one respondee express similar ideas when they say, "The definition of physics is not definitive, and it is too restrictive. Energy transformations are important, but that is by no means the only area investigated by physicists—nor is the study of events and circumstances related to energy transformation limited to physics." And for the chemistry definition, these men say, "Chemistry is that human endeavor that seeks to describe the properties of substances and the changes in properties that take place when substances interact. It also seeks to explain these properties and changes in properties with mental models. A useful mental model has both explanatory and predictive value."

Discontent with the distinguishing phrase for geology suggests that "what is needed is a statement related to the earth sciences and here the scope needs to be wider than the earth's rocks, its oceans, and atmosphere."

And now, how to bring these criticisms and suggestions to bear on redoing the point-of-departure definition? To abandon pursuit of a definition is one suggestion I am not yet ready to accept. A few of the respondees attempted the suggested realignment. At the minimum level of reconstruction, I find, "Science is *one* of the human endeavors that seeks . . ." Another realignment suggests, "Science is the exploration of the material universe to seek ever-increasingly accurate explanations of the objects, events, and circumstances that occur or exist within the natural environment." Another response that departs further from the beginning definition reads, "Science involves those methods of study by which man describes and explains his environment and by which man extends and corrects the related fund of knowledge."

Keeping the total array of suggestions and criticisms in mind and, admittedly, husbanding allegiance to the background of experience which produced the original point-of-departure definition, my revision becomes:

> *Science is one of the efforts of man to describe and relate with ever-increasing accuracy and simplicity, and thus explain, the objects and events within our natural environment.*

As there must be, there are elements of compromise in this revision. To insert the word *objects* generates uneasiness because it reduces the emphasis on the dynamic aspect of the pursuit of science. I sense improvement in adding the word *explain,* together with the connotation shown. Syntax, already questionable in the earlier wording, needs to be improved.

The word *effort* may or may not be an improvement over *endeavor.* This choice of word problem is reflected where one respondee says, "My own taste runs to considering science as a process that has two important parts. One part is the exploration of phenomena through observation and experiment, and presumably this includes description. The other part is the interpretation of phenomena by the development of imaginative ideas whose logical consequences are consistent wtih the observations of phenomena. The general result of this process is that diverse phenomena are shown to be interrelated. The interrelationship, however, is not apparent in the phenomena themselves, but only as ideas permit us to develop a logical argument which provides an interrelationship upon interpretation."

The two words *effort* and *endeavor* can carry both verb and noun meanings. So many people, however, are given to thinking of science with only the noun connotation that a word is needed which brings out more emphatically the verb connotation. The word *pursuit* emphasizes the process aspect of science and still retains the product connotation and thus holds promise of being useful in further revisions.

To respond to the suggestions regarding the distinguishing phrases for the separate branches of science, the biology phrase seems to stand as is. For chemistry and physics, the suggested realignment becomes: Chemistry and physics are the efforts of man to describe and relate with ever-increasing accuracy, and thus explain, the objects and events accompanying energy transformations and their interactions with the properties of matter. For geology, the final phrase becomes: "accompanying the origin of the earth and changes in its rocks, oceans, and atmosphere and its relationships with the other bodies in the universe."

Obviously, my quest continues for an operational definition of science "for science teachers at all grade levels" that truly expresses "the spirit and nature of science as practicing scientists understand this spirit and nature to be." The need is urgent. Our students see science defined operationally almost every day in news media, both in their editorial material and in advertisements. They see "science" being credited with all manner of discoveries, inventions, and creations, sometimes to make science the scapegoat, sometimes to give credit where credit is due, and sometimes to add apparent respectability to something that, in reality, contradicts or prostitutes the true spirit, structure, and function of science. Surely science teachers deserve guidance from the scientific fraternity to avoid adding to our students' confusion about what our discipline really is.

AUTHOR'S NOTE

Some comments on the methods used in this study. Personal correspondence proved to be especially effective, but there are problems. To give due credit to respondees is one. Another is the brashness of addressing people with whom the investigator has had little or no prior interaction, a factor which calls for compassion toward the men and women who failed to respond. Finally, I hesitate to quote from personal correspondence because responses may well be the "property" of their authors. A compromise exists in not identifying individual quotations but in listing the sixteen respondees and expressing my sincere thanks for their help. Their names follow:

N. E. Bingham, University of Florida
J. A. Campbell, Harvey Mudd College
Bentley Glass, State University of New York at Stony Brook
Donald F. Hornig, Executive Office of the President
Paul DeHart Hurd, Stanford University
Philip G. Johnson, Cornell University
Chester A. Lawson, University of California, Berkeley
Addison E. Lee, The University of Texas
John R. Mayor, American Association for the Advancement of Science
Linus Pauling, Center for the Study of Democratic Institutions
George C. Pimentel, University of California, Berkeley
Joseph J. Schwab, University of Chicago
Robert C. Smoot, The McDonogh School
Lawrence E. Strong, Earlham College
Jerome B. Wiesner, Massachusetts Institute of Technology
Jerrold R. Zacharias, Massachusetts Institute of Technology

---

1. How does the final definition of science by Woodburn coincide with your past experiences in science courses?
2. If science really is represented by Woodburn's definition, how would you change the science courses you have taken in college?

PART TWO

Thinking in Children:
Implications for Science Education

The nature and structure of science was considered in Part One, but no thought was given to the "recipient" of such ideas. Children of elementary school age represent a very diverse group in terms of their abilities to understand the natural environment.

Until fairly recently, the science curriculum for children consisted wholly of textbooks centered around science content. With various elementary science curriculum projects being developed during the 1960s, alternatives to the textbook approach were made available to schools. Some projects gave more attention to the characteristics of children than did others. The work of Jean Piaget probably had the greatest impact in terms of the cognitive development of children.

Fit the school to the child, not vice-versa. This cliché has been tossed around until it holds no real meaning. It can take on more meaning if specific characteristics of children are taken into account. Trying to teach a child a concept like velocity is surely nonsense if that child cannot deal adequately with either distance or time. Even then, if the child is unable to combine two variables simultaneously, such as distance/time, the learning will most likely be superficial and nontransferable.

An understanding of the child's thinking abilities and the various limitations involved with such are critical in learning about science teaching. Such an understanding has direct implications for both curriculum and instruction. This section is devoted to a look at some ideas related to cognitive development, with major emphasis on various aspects of Piaget's theory.

10 ELEANOR R. DUCKWORTH

Piaget Rediscovered

In 1968, the American Educational Research Association recognized Jean Piaget as the most outstanding contributor to the field of cognitive development in children. He has produced over thirty books and more than 100 articles in this field. His work with conservation *problems is probably best known and pursued in greatest detail by other research- ers. Piaget's early training as a zoologist (Ph.D. at the age of 21) has caused him to view the child as a complex organism functioning as a totality. Shortly after receiving his Ph.D. in zoology in Switzerland, he explored psychology and noticed some puzzling aspects of the think- ing of young children. These early experiences led Piaget to explore the thinking of his own children in great detail and he began to publish books and articles during the 1920s on his observations.*

He presently directs the activities at the Jean-Jacques Rousseau Institute at Geneva University and continues to publish the results of his studies. Miss Duckworth did two years of graduate research at the "Institut des Sciences de l'education in Geneva with Piaget and the following paper is her account of Piaget's contributions to a 1964 con- ference at Cornell University.

Everybody in education realizes that Piaget is saying something that is relevant to the teaching of children. For the most part he is understood to be underestimating the value of teaching. He is understood to be saying something like this: Children go through certain stages of intel- lectual development from birth through adolescence. These stages ma- terialize, fully constructed, when their time has come, and there is little we can do to advance them. What we must do in education is to realize the limits of children's understanding at certain ages, and plan our teach- ing so it falls within these limits.

Reprinted from *The Journal of Research in Science Teaching*, Vol. 2, Issue 3, 1964, pp. 172-175 by permission of the editor. Dr. Duckworth did two years of graduate research with Piaget in Geneva and continues to work in the area of cognitive development.

In two recent conferences, one at Cornell, one at Berkeley, Piaget made clear that the implications of his psychology for education are a good deal more fecund than this. In fact, the only one of these statements that he would support is that children go through certain stages of intellectual development. Contrary to the view most often attributed to him, he maintains that good pedagogy *can* have an effect on this development.

I will start with the essentials of Piaget's theory of intellectual development, as presented at these conferences, and then go on to some implications for education.

Development of intellectual capacity goes through a number of stages whose order is constant, but whose time of appearance may vary both with the individual and with the society. Each new level of development is a new coherence, a new structuring of elements which until that time have not been systematically related to each other.

Piaget discussed four factors contributing to this development: (1) nervous maturation, (2) encounters with experience, (3) social transmission, and (4) equilibration or auto-regulation. While the first three do indeed play a role, Piaget finds each of them insufficient in itself. His findings lead him to conclude that an individual's intellectual development is a process of equilibration, where the individual himself is the active motor and coordinator of his own development.

What the first three factors have in common is that the individual is passive. Something is done to him—his physiological system matures, or he is presented with physical or linguistic material to absorb. But intellectual development is not this passive. Piaget finds it necessary to call upon the factor of the individual's own activity. An individual comes to see the world as coherent, as structured, to the extent that he acts upon the world, transform it, and succeeds in coordinating these actions and transformations.

Development proceeds as partial understandings are revised, broadened, and related to one another. Piaget's model for this is one of auto-regulation to attain ever broader and more stable equilibrium in the individual's dealing with his world.

As far as education is concerned, the chief outcome of this theory of intellectual development is a plea that children be allowed to do their own learning. Piaget is not saying that intellectual development proceeds at its own pace no matter what you try to do. He is saying that what schools usually try to do is ineffectual. You cannot further understandings in a child simply by talking to him. Good pedagogy must involve presenting the child with situations in which he himself experiments, in the broadest sense of that term—trying things to see what happens, manipulating things, manipulating symbols, posing questions and seeking his own answers, reconciling what he finds one time with what he finds at another, comparing his findings with those of other children.

Beyond this general implication, Piaget does not claim to be an educator. During the course of the two conferences he made no single discourse on pedagogy. But he made a number of points which I have gathered together here. Most of them are not new ideas; but it seems to me that it is of importance, somehow, to realize that this is what he is saying.

I shall start with comments on one or two teaching practices often associated with Piaget's name, because of some relationships to his research. One is the head-on attack on a specific notion in a precise and limited way. This is the type of attack engaged in by psychological experimenters, in trying to teach 4 and 5 year olds, for example that the amount of liquid stays the same when poured into a glass of a different shape. (In Piaget's own research, when a child asserts that the same amount of liquid is conserved, this is taken as an indication of a certain structure of mental operations. For this reason, performance on this task is an important indicator of intellectual level.)

Piaget sees little sense in intensive specific training on tasks like this one. His feeling is that no learning of any significance will take place. Even if the child does manage to learn something about this situation, the learning is not likely to have a general effect on his level of understanding.

But notice that he is *not* thereby saying that a young child's mental structure cannot be touched. He is only saying that this type of specific attack is rather trivial. Modifying a child's effective set of mental operations depends on a much wider, longer-lasting and fundamental approach, which involves all of the child's activity.

Piaget amplified this point about the importance of investigative activity in general in reply to a question on cross-cultural comparisons. Montreal psychologists using Piaget's material as tests, found children in Martinique to be delayed several years over children in Montreal. Similarly, there is a significant delay of children in Iranian villages over children in Iranian cities. Piaget was asked what factors in the adult societies might account for these differences.

In reply, he first pointed out that the schools in Martinique follow the same curriculum as the schools in France, so that scholastic preparation was not likely to account for the difference. Then he quoted the psychologist who had done the research in Martinique, who pointed out that the climate is fine, agriculture flourishes and living poses few problems. There seems to be little call for questioning and struggling for solutions—in general, little call for either physical or intellectual activity. Piaget speculated that this could be the significant factor.

Another pedagogical approach often associated with Piaget's name has to do with teaching the "structure" of a subject matter area. This has been associated with him because of the importance that mental structures play in his psychological theory. The word "structure" is seized upon as the link.

The pedagogical idea is that children should be taught the unifying themes of a subject matter area, after which they will be able to relate individual items to this general structure. (This seems to be what Bruner often means by "teaching the structure" in The Process of Education.) Commenting on this procedure, Piaget made the following statement:

> The question comes up whether to teach the structure, or to present the child with situations where he is active and creates the structures himself. . . . The goal in education is not to increase the amount of knowledge, but to create the possibilities for a child to invent and discover. When we teach too fast, we keep the child from inventing and discovering himself. . . . Teaching means creating situations where structures can be discovered; it does not mean transmitting structures which may be assimilated at nothing other than a verbal level.

Piaget addressed two remarks to problems of teacher training. The first is that adults, as well as children, can learn better by doing things than by being told about them. He was talking about teachers in training, when he said, "If they read about it, it will be deformed, as is all learning that is not the result of the subject's own activity."

The second is that prospective teachers ought to spend some time questioning children in a one-to-one situation, in order to realize how hard it is to understand what children mean, and even more, how hard it is to make oneself understood by children. Each prospective teacher should work on an original investigation to find out what children think about some problem—and thus be forced to phrase the problem and establish communication with a number of different children. Facing the difficulties of this type of research will have a sobering effect on a teacher who thinks he is talking successfully to a whole class of children at once.

Permit me one other point of psychological theory, as context for another of Piaget's remarks. Piaget sees the process of equilibration as a process of balance between assimilation and accommodation in a biological sense. An individual assimilates the world—which comes down to saying he sees it in his own way. But sometimes something presents itself in such a way that he cannot assimilate it into his view of things, so he must change his view—he must accommodate if he wants to incorporate this new item.

The question arose in this conference as to whether school situations could lead a child to accommodate wrongly—that is, to change his ideas on the wrong basis. Piaget replied: "This is a very interesting question. This is a big danger of school—false accommodation which satisfies a child because it agrees with a verbal formula he has been given. This is a false equilibrium which satisfies a child by accommodating to words —to authority and not to objects as they present themselves to him. . . . A teacher would do better not to correct a child's schemes, but to provide situations so he will correct them himself."

Here are a few other remarks at random:

> Experience is always necessary for intellectual development. . . . But I fear that we may fall into the illusion that being submitted to an experience (a demonstration) is sufficient for a subject to disengage the structure involved. But more than this is required. The subject must be active, must transform things and find the structure of his own actions on the objects.

> When I say "active," I mean it in two senses. One is acting on material things. But the other means doing things in social collaboration, in a group effort. This leads to a critical frame of mind, where children must communicate with each other. This is an essential factor in intellectual development. Cooperation is indeed cooperation.

(The role of social interaction is important in Piaget's theory of development. A characteristic phenomenon in intellectual difficulties of pre-school children is that they have difficulty conceiving of any point of view other than their own. Coming to an awareness that another child sees something differently from the way he sees it plays an important role in bringing a child to accommodate, to rebuild his point of view, and come closer to a coherent operational structure.)

> The best idea I have heard from a pedagog at the International Bureau of Education in Geneva was made by a Canadian. He said that in his province they had just decided every class should have two classrooms —one where the teacher is, and one where the teacher isn't.

> The teacher must provide the instruments which the children can use to decide things by themselves. Children themselves must verify, experimentally in physics, deductively in mathematics. A ready-made truth is only a half-truth.

One participant asked what Piaget thought of having children of different ages in a class together. He replied that it might be helpful especially for the older ones. They could be given some responsibility of teaching younger ones. "Nobody knows better than a professor that the best way to learn something is to teach it."

Yes, the element of surprise is an essential motive in education and in scientific research in general. What distinguishes a good scientist is that he is amazed by things which seem natural to others. Surprise plays an important role; we might try to develop an aptitude for surprise.

Words are probably not a short-cut to a better understanding. . . . The level of understanding seems to modify the language that is used, rather than vice versa. . . . Mainly, language serves to translate what is already understood; or else language may even present a danger if it is used to introduce an idea which is not yet accessible.

The principal goal of education is to create men who are capable of doing new things, not simply of repeating what other generations have done—men who are creative, inventive, and discoverers. The second goal of education is to form minds which can be critical, can verify, and not accept everything they are offered. The great danger today is of slogans, collective opinions, ready-made trends of thought. We have to be able to resist individually, to criticize, to distinguish between what is proven and what is not. So we need pupils who are active, who learn early to find out by themselves, partly by their own spontaneous activity and partly through material we set up for them; who learn early to tell what is verifiable and what is simply the first idea to come to them.

---

1. "You cannot further understandings in a child simply by talking to him." Do you agree or disagree with this statement? Can you give evidence to support this statement? Can you give evidence to support your position?
2. "What distinguishes a good scientist is that he is amazed by things which seem natural to others." What might be the reasoning behind this statement?
3. Jot down the things in this paper by Miss Duckworth which are not clear to you and try to find some answers in the next few articles. A good introduction to the ideas of Piaget is: *Piaget's Theory of Intellectual Development* by Ginsburg and Opper, 1969.

11 EDWARD A. CHITTENDEN

Piaget and Elementary Science

Although some repetition of content between this paper and the previous one by Duckworth is evident, more detail is used in describing the various stages of development here. Both papers tend to form a sound basis for a better understanding of the paper by Piaget. Chittenden uses examples of interviews that have been used to collect information on the nature of thinking children use to explain various phenomena. Many are quite simple and could be used by anybody interested in studying the thinking of children.

There has been a substantial revival of interest in this country in the research and theory of Jean Piaget, the Swiss child psychologist. This interest probably stems to some extent from the general current concern with questions regarding cognition and the development of intellectual abilities. But it also must stem from a growing awareness that his work represents a major contribution to our understanding of the development of human thought. During 50 years of studies he and his co-workers in Geneva have observed and examined thousands of subjects, ranging in age from the newborn to the adolescent. Some 30 volumes and countless articles on the subject of infant and child thought have been published. As it stands today, Piaget's theory of intelligence is unique in its complexity and comprehensiveness.

Piaget's Methods

In his studies of children's thinking, Piaget has never been especially interested in depicting, in a normative way, the various responses that may occur at particular ages, and one finds few statistical descriptions of children's responses in his books. Instead he has attempted to discover

Reprinted from *Science and Children*, Vol. 8, no. 4, 1970, pp. 9-15 by permission of the editor. Dr. Chittenden is a research psychologist at Educational Testing Service.

the underlying structures which give rise to children's response. When he poses, to a five-year-old child, the task of putting into serial order a set of ten graded sticks, he wants to find out how the child will go about handling the task. He is interested in the kinds of errors the child may make and in the kinds of groupings he may attempt, rather than only the final result or the final arrangement made by the child. It is not surprising, then, that he dismisses the traditional intelligence tests as mere catalogues of behavior, useful for certain purposes, but not very enlightening if we want to know something about the nature of child thought. These points should be stressed because Piaget's early books (4, 5) as well as his later books have sometimes been misinterpreted by people who were looking for normative description. In essence, his books offer theoretical analysis of thought processes, and the data, in the form of children's answers, serve primarily to illustrate and verify his theory.

Piaget's concern with theory can also be seen in his interviewing methods. He has described his method as a "clinical method"(5)—very similar to the procedures of psychiatric examination. The interview with the child must be flexible. The investigator, drawing upon theory, must be ready to vary the form of his questions and tasks depending upon the response of the subject. The good interviewer, says Piaget, must combine two seemingly incompatible qualities. On the one hand, "he must know how to observe, that is to say, to let the child talk freely, without ever checking or side-tracking his utterance." And, on the other hand, the interviewer "must constantly be alert for something definitive, at every moment he must have some working hypothesis, some theory, true or false, which he is seeking to check."(5) He notes the child's verbal reaction to the problem and the child's justification of his solution.

A final point to make about Piaget's methods concerns the distinction between typical and maximal performance. Cronbach(2) suggests that in the usual procedures for testing intelligence we are interested in obtaining evidence of maximal performance—we want to find out whether the child can or cannot handle a particular problem. In personality assessment, on the other hand, we are concerned with typical performance—whether the child does or does not behave in certain ways. The intent of Piaget's interviews seems much closer to personality assessment. The interest is in typical or natural behavior. To illustrate, I once observed a five-year-old boy who was methodically breaking up his cracker into small pieces. I asked him why he was doing this and he answered, without hesitation, "there's more to eat." I quizzed him further, as adults do, trying to get him to admit that breaking the cracker really did not affect quantity. He put up a pretty good argument; "If it's broken up, it takes longer to eat." Finally, after further prodding, he did seem to admit that quantity really would remain unchanged. But in the course of this conversation it became obvious to me that my idea of quantity was not typical of him (at least in the setting of eating). Moreover, he seemed to find this adult concept of quantity to be somewhat puzzling and not terribly useful.

Piaget admits that it is sometimes possible to push children to the point where they express an advanced idea, but such maximal responses tell us a lot less about the nature of thought than do the typical responses. It therefore seems misleading to interpret Piaget as saying that children can or cannot think in certain ways; a more accurate interpretation would be that Piaget tells us how children *typically do or do not think.*

Piaget's theory has been more concerned with understanding, rather than controlling behavior. Intelligence is viewed as a process of organization and adaptation. When a child encounters an object, he will attempt to organize the object into his present schema or structure. When schema are present, assimilation will occur. If the assimilation does not take place, the child is at disequilibrium until present schemas are altered or new ones developed. A group of schema that occur more or less at the same time make up a "stage" in Piaget's model of child development. The clinical methods used by Piaget could be utilized much more frequently in this country. In our research on children's thinking, some of us rely too much on data from rather rigid standardized interviews—others rely too much on the casual observation and anecdote. Piaget's method falls somewhere between and it could serve to correct the distortions inherent in these other approaches.

There are three major periods in Piaget's account of the development of thought. The sensori-motor period, extending from birth to one-and-a-half or two years; secondly, the period in which concrete logical operations emerge, encompassing the years from two to eleven or twelve; and finally, the period of formal logical operations, from eleven or twelve into adolescence. The second period is divided into two major stages: the stage of preoperational thought, from two to around seven years, and the stage of concrete logical operations, from seven to eleven or twelve. (See the chart on page 113.)

Sensori-Motor

The sensori-motor period marks the development from reflexive behavior of the newborn to development of symbolic behavior at one-and-a-half years. At the beginning of this period, the world is undifferentiated from self; at the conclusion of the period, events and objects in the world have some identity of their own. For the young infant, objects seem to have no independent existence. The infant acts as though he "believed that an object is alternately made and unmade."(7) Thus, the six-months-old baby reaches for a bottle held in front of him, but if the bottle is then moved behind an arm of the adult, out of the visual field, the reaching activity ceases. Later in the first year, active search for vanished objects does begin, but with noticeable restrictions. If an object is hidden under a pillow, the ten-months-old baby may reach for and attain it. However, if next, before his eyes, the object is placed under a second pillow, the baby makes his initial search under the first pillow. Such behavior indicates that successive displacements of objects are still not easily handled. Later, around one year, such a problem is solved as long as the displacements of the object are perceptible. Finally, at one-and-a-half, the child can cope with unseen as well as seen displacements. By this time Piaget believes there is evidence of a mature object concept. The object now has its own existence, apart from the child, and its own movement through space.

Toward the end of the sensori-motor period, symbolic behavior appears. Nevertheless, even at its highest level, sensori-motor intelligence is not reflective. Sensori-motor intelligence, Piaget says, "acts like a slow-motion film, in which all the pictures are seen in succession but without fusion, and so without the continuous vision necessary for understanding the whole." Sensori-motor thought is "an intelligence in action and in no way reflective."(6)

Preoperational Thinking

The preoperational stage can be divided into two substages: that of preconceptual thought, from two to four years, and intuitive thought from four to around seven. In general, the characteristics of this stage are more exaggerated or pronounced in the earlier years. Of all the age groups, the intuitive stage has received the most extensive study by Piaget. John Flavell's excellent book on Piaget(3) summarizes some of this vast research.

One general characteristic of preoperational thought is egocentrism. In its more exaggerated form, egocentrism is seen in children's ideas about various natural phenomena. In examples given by Piaget(5) the child claims that the sun moves when he moves. ". . . when one walks, it follows. When one turns round it turns round too. Doesn't it ever follow you too?" the child asks the interviewer. The question of whether the sun really moves or only appears to move is not understood by the child and, according to Piaget, it does not occur to him to think of this question.

Intellectual Development Stages
—Interpreted from Writings of Jean Piaget*

Developmental Stage	General Age Range	Characteristics of Stage Pertaining to Problem-Solving Activities; Comments and Examples
Sensori-motor	Birth to approximately 18 months	—Stage is preverbal —An object "exists" only when in the perceptual field of the child —Hidden objects are located through random physical searching —Practical basic knowledge is developed which forms the substructure of later representational knowledge
Preoperational or "representational"	18 months to 7-8 years	—Stage marks the beginning of organized language and symbolic function, and, as a result, thought and representation develop —The child is perceptually oriented, does not use logical thinking, and therefore cannot reason by implication —The child is simple-goal directed; activity includes crude trial-and-error corrections —The child lacks the ability to coordinate variables, has difficulty in realizing that an object has several properties, and is commonly satisfied with multiple and contradictory formulations —Since the concept of conservation is not yet developed, the child lacks operational reversibility in thought and action
Concrete operations	7-8 years to 11-12 years	—Thinking is concrete rather than abstract, but the child can now perform elementary logical operations and make elementary groupings of classes and relations (e.g., serial ordering) —The concepts of conservation develop (first of number, then of substance, of length, of area, of weight and finally of volume) —The concept of reversibility develops —The child is unable to isolate variables, and proceeds from step to step in thinking without relating each link to all others
Propositional or "formal operations"	11-12 years to 14-15 years	—Stage of formal (abstract) thought marked by the appearance of hypothetical-deductive reasoning based upon the logic of all possible combinations; the development of a combinatorial system and unification of operations into a structured whole —The development of the ability to perform controlled experimentation, setting all factors "equal" but one variable (at 11-12 years to 14-15 years, the child's formal logic is superior to his experimental capacity). Individuals discover that a particular factor can be eliminated to analyze its role, or the roles of associated factors —Reversal of direction between reality and possibility (variables are hypothesized before experimentation). Individuals discover that factors can be separated by neutralization as well as by exclusion
	14-15 years and onwards	—The individual can use interpropositional operations, combining propositions by conjunction, disjunction, negation, and implication (all arise in the course of experimental implications).

*Dyrli, Odvard Egil. *Intellectual Development Stages*, from *Developing Children's Thinking Through Science* by Anderson, DeVito, Dyrli, Kellogg, Kochendorfer, and Weigand. Prentice-Hall, Inc., Englewood Cliffs, New Jersey, 1970, p. 121. Reprinted with permission.

Another example of egocentrism comes from the experiments reported in the *Child's Conception of Space*(8). The subject is shown a display of model mountains. He is then shown photographs that represent these mountains from different viewpoints. The child is seated in one position and a doll in another and the child asked to indicate what the doll will see in various positions. The preoperational subject has great difficulty, on this task, in imagining the succession of perspectives viewed from positions other than his own.

Egocentric orientation is also revealed in children's conversations of this stage. Piaget describes(4) the results of a simple experiment in which one child explains something to another. The explaining child, says Piaget, gives one "the impression of talking to himself, without bothering about the other child. Very rarely did he succeed in placing himself at the latter's point of view." Piaget believes that children fail to communicate for egocentric reasons, "because they think that they do understand one another. The explainer believes from the start that the listener will grasp everything, will almost know beforehand all that should be known, and will interpret every subtlety." When the listener seems puzzled, the explainer may try to clarify simply by repeating what he has said; sometimes he repeats in louder tones as if addressing someone who is hard of hearing. This egocentric conviction that others know what you know is encouraged by the fact that adults in the child's world often do understand what the child is going to say.

Toward the end of the stage egocentrism in communication may not be as pronounced, but it is evident in another form in children's explanations. Recently, as part of a research project(1), we asked children some questions about flotation. Various objects were placed on a table (a small stone, toothpick, block of wood, etc.). A large container of water was set nearby and children were asked to select those objects they thought would float, and those that would sink. They were also asked to explain their predictions. The predictions of the younger, kindergarten subjects and the older, second-grade subjects did not differ in accuracy. Instead, the differences between the kindergarten and older children came in their explanations of their predictions. The younger child would say, "the little stone will sink because it's little," and then, when asked about a big stone, would say, "It will sink because it's big." In other words, two contrasting attributes, big and little, are offered in explanation for the identical action of the objects. Similarly, a toothpick would float because "it's light" and the block of wood would float because "it's heavy." The younger subjects did not seem to be bothered by apparent contradictions. Older children often tried to avoid inconsistent explanations. The toothpick would float "because it's light," and the block of wood "because it's not very heavy." Sometimes the kindergarten children would offer a single explanation for contrasting actions of the objects, asserting that the toothpick would float, because it's light and the nail would sink because it's light. Older children tried to use weight and size terms in a more consistent way even though they could not formulate a weight-per-volume statement about density. This attempt of older children to be more systematic very likely led them to errors in prediction that the younger subjects did not make. Thus, there was a steady decline in accuracy of prediction for the block of wood. Younger children simply asserted that it would float because "it's wood" or because it was big, or heavy, or whatever. Older ones, following a more logical pattern, seemed to conclude wrongly that since it was big or heavy, it should sink.

The young child's reasoning is often more a logic of convenience than a logic of conviction. When asked why an object will float, any convenient attribute is used; any handy characteristic, big, small, fat, light, etc., is referred to. It does not occur to the child of the preoperational stage to look for contradictions in his explanations. This is in line with Piaget's belief that the preoperational child does not examine his own thought processes nor does he feel it necessary to justify his thinking to others. He thinks, but he does not think about his thinking.

Another general characteristic of preoperational thought is the tendency for the child to "center" upon one prominent feature of an object or array of objects, excluding simultaneous consideration of other features. Piaget's conservation experiments can be used here for illustration. In one version the child is shown two identical balls of clay, and he agrees that they are equivalent in amount. In full view of the child, the experimenter then stretches one of the balls of clay into a sausage shape, and asks the child whether the sausage contains as much clay as the remaining ball. "Do they still have the same amount of clay?" Prior to the age of seven, Piaget reports that children are apt to answer "No, the sausage has more clay because it is longer," or, "It has less clay because it is thinner." Either way, the preoperational child is "centering" attention on some particular feature to the neglect of others. He may focus on length and assert that there is more clay because the sausage is longer, or he may center on width and conclude there is less because the sausage is thinner. Unlike the older child, he does not "decenter," or "reverse," and consider the two attributes simultaneously.

Piaget reports that one often finds children moving toward decentration toward the end of the stage. Thus, in the clay experiment, they may at first center on length, but if the clay is stretched even further, they recenter on width, noting the obvious thinness, and conclude that the sausage contains less. Such successive recenterings sometimes lead the child into flagrant contradictions, but they herald the beginnings of logical operations in which coordination of attributes will replace alternating centrations.

The clay experiment shows that the preoperational child does not view quantity as a constant—a constant unaffected by changes in shape and appearance. In Piaget's terms, he does not "conserve" such quantities as mass, weight, or number. If a child counts 14 cubes in a row, and then the experimenter bunches the cubes together, the child may not be sure there are still 14. He may want to count them again. Changes in appearance influence his thinking about number; 14 cubes in a row look quite different from 14 cubes clustered together. Because of this general tendency to center on prominent features, the stage is sometimes described as a stage of perceptual thought.

Centering also takes the form of attending to the beginning or end states of an object rather than to the process of transformation. In the clay experiment, preoperational attention centers on resulting configurations of the clay rather than on the transformation from one state to another. In a different experiment, two model cars are placed in parallel starting positions. They are both moved forward, starting and stopping at the same time. However, one car has been moved faster than the other and its stopping point is further from the start position. The preoperational child, focusing on the unequal stoppping positions, is quite certain that one car has taken longer than the other. Similarly, he finds it very difficult to reconstruct a possible series of positions through which a bar passes when it falls from a vertical to a horizontal state. In all these examples, the focus is on states and not upon transformation from one state to another.

Piaget has also emphasized that thinking of the preoperational stage is ". . . a kind of action carried out in thought."(7) Thought takes the form of imagined representations of concrete events. Reasoning takes the form of a "mental experiment," that is, "an internal imitation of actions and their results." Such thinking is laborious and prone to error and confusion. For example, in a problem involving transitive relations, if A is found shorter than B, and B shorter than C, the preoperational child does not necessarily conclude that A is shorter than C. One reason for the difficulty may be that in reconstructing these events, he must explicitly represent them in thought; A is imagined with B, B with C, etc. Unlike the case of the older child, the observations "shorter than" are not represented as general symbolic statements; rather, they may take the form of imagined replication.

Such thinking moves in one direction only and is irreversible, because the premises with which the child starts cannot remain unaltered through a reasoning sequence.

The child's unstable system of thought leads him into contradiction and conflict. Denied reversible systems, he is buffeted about my appearances of reality. Piaget states that preoperational thought "provides a map of reality, . . . but it is still imaginal, with many blank spaces and without sufficient coordinations to pass from one point to another." (7) Nevertheless, in Piaget's theory, it is this very state of disequilibrium which eventually leads to the resolution of the stage and to the reversible systems of concrete logical operations.

Concrete and Formal Logical Operations

With the emergence of concrete operations, at age seven or so, Piaget reports that a profound reorientation in thinking becomes evident. This is best illustrated in conservation. The seven- or eight-year-old is sure that the amount of clay remains constant. He is surprised that you should even ask such a question. "Of course, they're the same," he says, "you've only changed the shape." Appearances are explicitly denied. On a seriation task, the approach is different from that of a younger child. In putting ten sticks into serial order, the method of the eight-year-old reflects a logical system and a recognition of order. The older child approaches many other problems in a new way; ". . . thought is no longer tied to particular states of the object, but (can) follow successive changes with all their possible detours and reversals; and (thought) no longer issues from a particular viewpoint of the subject, but co-ordinates all the different viewpoints in a system of objective reciprocities."(7) In short, concrete operations represent a much more flexible and comprehensive system.

It should be emphasized that although the transition from preoperational thinking to concrete operations is relatively rapid, this does not mean that the child goes to bed one night, an unsettled preoperational being, and wakes up the next morning with the world put into logical order. Instead, from seven on, operational thought appears in certain areas of experience and only gradually extends to other areas. The logic of the concrete stage is closely tied to the content of the problem. Unlike formal operations of adolescence, it does not constitute a hypothetical system in which the form of the logic can be independent of the particular content of the problem at hand. To illustrate, consider the riddle, "Which is heavier—a pound of feathers or a pound of lead?" In the concrete stage, reason may dictate that a pound is a pound, but it is still a stage in which feathers and lead can very easily interfere with reasoning. For that matter, neither the child nor the adult ever entirely abandons earlier ways of thinking. Rather, the earlier ways appear less frequently for problems where they would be inappropriate.

In the concrete operational stage, the child is able to observe, judge, and evaluate in less egocentric terms and formulate more objective explanations than in the preoperational stage, but even now he cannot verbally express hypotheses following a long series of related ideas, or if concrete referents are not available.

In the formal operational stage the child is emancipated from dependence on direct perception of objects as a mediator of thought. Mental experiences can be carried out as well as actual ones, and probability is well understood.

Implications for Education

There are interesting implications for educators in Piaget's work on preoperational thought, particularly for science educators. For example, consider an experiment conducted by Jan Smedslund(10). The subjects, five- to seven-year-old children, were given a pretest of conservation of weight. Two balls of clay were placed on a platform balance and their equivalence in weight demonstrated. The child was then asked if they would still weigh the same when one of the balls was changed (shaped into a sausage). This pretest identified two groups of subjects; one which conserved and one which did not. Next, training sessions were given to the non-conserving group. Constancy of weight was demonstrated in various ways. After training, these children readily asserted that weight would indeed remain constant. After an interval, a post-test was given to all subjects, those originally conserving and those trained to conserve. The post-test was exactly the same as the pre-test; two equivalent balls of clay were placed on the balance and subjects asked to predict what would happen when one of the balls was changed in some way. All subjects now believed that the pieces would continue to weigh the same. However, and this is the crux of the experiment, the interviewer cheated the subjects; he surreptitiously removed some clay from the changed piece so that when placed on the scale, the pieces actually did not balance. When asked to explain this unexpected event, all the trained subjects quickly reverted back to their original preoperational answers ("it's skinnier, so doesn't weigh as much," etc.), while the majority of the children who had acquired conservation on their own resisted this type of explanation. They generally remarked that something was "fishy," that some clay must have been removed, that something was wrong with the balance, etc.

The findings in this experiment illustrate Piaget's belief that formal instruction cannot accelerate acquisition of operational systems. One cannot speed up this process very much through a formal program of demonstrations.

More generally, if we consider the characteristics of preoperational thought, we might conclude that any instruction which attempts to prove some principle through appeals to logic or scientific experiment would be wasted on children of this stage. Piaget has remarked, for example, that children do not learn conservation of quantity through being shown that quantity is constant. In fact, in the Piagetian model this is a theoretical impossibility because if the child possessed the capacity to understand the implications of such a proof—of such a demonstration— then most likely he would already understand the principle. The conviction in conservation of older children is really a symptom of the development of logical structures and one cannot bring about these structures through teaching the symptom. On the other hand, it does appear that educational experiences for young children aimed at giving them the opportunity to observe and describe on the level of perception would be fruitful. The preoperational child's capacities for observation, for discriminating between fine and gross details, are comparable to abilities of older children. It is when we ask him to put these observations into some logical system that the purpose may escape him. When we ask him to attend, not to the perceived data, but to a system which relates the data, he is puzzled. The characteristics of egocentrism, centration, and unconcern with thought do not readily permit such a shift in cognitive orientation.

What then does account for cognitive growth? for the beginnings of logical operations at age seven? for later extensions of operations? In answering this question, Piaget has pointed to three realms of experience.

First, and possibly the least important, there is social experience. This is the experience of confronting the views and ideas of other children and adults. It serves as an important force in overcoming egocentrism by stimulating the child to consider and adapt to other viewpoints.

Secondly, there is physical experience. This consists of activities aimed at exploring the properties of objects. It is an "acting upon objects in order to find something from the objects themselves."(1) It includes explorations of their color, weight, form, movement in space.

Third, there is what Piaget calls "logico-mathematical experience." "In this case, while the actions are once again carried out on objects, knowledge is derived from the actions which transform the objects, and not from the objects themselves."(1) Thus, if a child counts three groups of two objects and two groups of three, obtaining the same sum, he is learning that sum and the order of counting are independent. He is learning something from the actions themselves, rather than from the particular objects involved in the actions. Activities of bringing together, taking apart, grouping, ordering, counting, are of this type.

No matter what type of experience, it is evident from Piaget's work that cognitive change, in any stage, depends on a long history of transaction with the object world. The infant who demonstrates a persisting fascination with peek-a-boo games, who wants to repeat the game over and over, also demonstrates that the idea of the permanent object does not arise out of a few experiences with disappearing and reappearing objects. The Piagetian child is an active, exploring creature, not a passive receiver of external stimuli. But he is also thorough, and from the adult point of view, somewhat repetitious. Actions performed on objects and activities performed with objects are carried out on all fronts— piling up pots and pans in the kitchen, building with blocks, making colors, squeezing mud, comparing lengths. No one of these explorations, in itself, brings about marked changes in thought. Instead, eventually the actions performed in one setting combine with actions in others, leading to more general systems of ordering, comparing, etc.

Piaget has stated that in school, children should be "allowed a *maximum* of activity of their own, directed by means of materials which permit their activities to be cognitively useful. In the area of logicomathematical structures, children have real understanding only of that which they invent themselves, and each time that we try to teach them something too quickly, we keep them from reinventing it themselves."(1) He points out that the time which seems to be wasted in children's personal explorations is really gained in the construction of methods. The important aspect of the discovery or invention process lies in the actions involved, in the methods, and not in the end product of a concept or fact.

By way of conclusion, a cautionary observation should be made: The most valuable aspect of Piaget's work is not his delineation of the various stages and substages (provocative as it may be) but rather his portrayal of how children go about learning. There is a real danger in focusing only upon the stages for it too readily leads to attempts to categorize children (*late preoperational* or *early concrete*) rather than to observe them for what they are really up to. This focus on stages also leads to unwarranted attempts to speed up the progression to the next stage and to view earlier stages as "bad" ways of thinking, processes that must be gotten over like the measles. Each stage should be viewed as legitimate in its own right, for the ways of learning of each stage make necessary contributions to capabilities at later ages.

REFERENCES

1. Almy, M.; Chittenden, E. A.; and Miller, P. *Young Children's Thinking: Studies of Some Aspects of Piaget's Theory.* New York City: Teachers College Press, 1966.

2. Cronbach, L. J. *Essentials of Psychological Testing.* Second Edition. New York: Harper & Row, 1960.
3. Flavell, J. H. *The Developmental Psychology of Jean Piaget.* Princeton, New Jersey: D. Van Nostrand, 1963.
4. Piaget, J. *The Language and Thought of the Child.* New York City: Harcourt, Brace & Company, 1926.
5. Piaget, J. *The Child's Conception of the World.* New York City: Harcourt, Brace & Company, 1929.
6. Piaget, J. *The Psychology of Intelligence.* London, England: Routledge & Kegan Paul, Ltd., 1950.
7. Piaget, J. *The Construction of Reality in the Child.* New York City: Basic Books, 1954.
8. Piaget, J. and Inhelder, B. *The Child's Conception of Space.* London, England: Routledge & Kegan Paul, Ltd., 1956.
9. Smedslund, J. "The Acquisition of Conservation of Substance and Weight in Children, III: Extinction of Conservation of Weight Acquired 'Normally' and by Means of Empirical Controls on a Balance Scale." *Scandinavian Journal of Psychology* 2 (1961): 85-87.

1. Can you think of any "interviews" that could be done with children to probe the nature of their thinking?
2. Could classroom teachers determine the developmental stages of the children in their classrooms using interviews similar to the few described in this paper?

12 JEAN PIAGET

Development and Learning

During the 1964 Cornell Conference on cognitive development, Piaget delivered a number of talks. This paper represents one of them, in which he dealt with development and learning. Such terms as operation, equilibration, reversibility, assimilation and accommodation require careful thought and perhaps the rereading of certain segments.

Each of the papers in this part of the book will serve to answer some questions that may arise as a result of reading other papers on cognitive development. It should help to discuss some of the ideas with others and share perceptions. One of the keys to comprehending the essence of Piaget's writings is to understand certain terms that he uses repeatedly, a few of which were identified in the previous paragraph.

My dear colleagues, I am very concerned about what to say to you, because I do not know if I shall accomplish the end that has been assigned to me. But I have been told that the important thing is not what you say, but the discussion which follows and the answers to questions you are asked. So this morning I shall simply give a general introduction of a few ideas which seem to me to be important for the subject of this conference.

First I would like to make clear the difference between two problems: the problem of *development* in general and the problem of *learning*. I think these problems are very different, although some people do not make this distinction.

The development of knowledge is a spontaneous process, tied to the whole process of embryogenesis. Embryogenesis concerns the development of the body, but it concerns as well the development of the nervous system and the development of mental functions. In the case of the development of knowledge in children, embryogenesis ends only in

Reprinted from *The Journal of Research in Science Teaching*, Vol. 2, Issue 3, 1964, pp. 176-186, by permission of the editor. Dr. Piaget is undoubtedly the foremost authority on cognitive development and continues to do research at the University of Geneva, Switzerland.

adulthood. It is a total developmental process which we must re-situate in its general biological and psychological context. In other words, development is a process which concerns the totality of the structures of knowledge.

Learning presents the opposite case. In general, learning is provoked by situations—provoked by a psychological experimenter; or by a teacher, with respect to some didactic point; or by an external situation. It is provoked, in general, as opposed to spontaneous. In addition, it is a limited process—limited to a single problem, or to a single structure.

So I think that development explains learning, and this opinion is contrary to the widely held opinion that development is a sum of discrete learning experiences. For some psychologists development is reduced to a series of specific learned items, and development is thus the sum, the cumulation of this series of specific items. I think this is an atomistic view which deforms the real state of things. In reality, development is the essential process and each element of learning occurs as a function of total development, rather than being an element which explains development. I shall begin, then, with a first part dealing with development, and I shall talk about learning in the second part.

To understand the development of knowledge, we must start with an idea which seems central to me—the idea of an *operation*. Knowledge is not a copy of reality. To know an object, to know an event, is not simply to look at it and make a mental copy or image of it. To know an object is to act on it. To know is to modify, to transform the object, and to understand the process of this transformation, and as a consequence to understand the way the object is constructed. An operation is thus the essence of knowledge; it is an interiorized action which modifies the object of knowledge. For instance an operation would consist of joining objects in a class to construct a classification. Or an operation would consist of ordering, or putting things in a series. Or an operation would consist of counting, or of measuring. In other words, it is a set of actions modifying the object, and enabling the knower to get at the structures of the transformation.

An operation is an interiorized action. But, in addition, it is a reversible action; that is, it can take place in both directions, for instance, adding or subtracting, joining or separating. So it is a particular type of action which makes up logical structures.

Above all, an operation is never isolated. It is always linked to other operations, and as a result it is always a part of a total structure. For instance, a logical class does not exist in isolation; what exists is the total structure of classification. An asymmetrical relation does not exist in isolation. Seriation is the natural, basic operational structure. A number does not exist in isolation. What exists is the series of numbers which constitute a structure, an exceedingly rich structure whose various properties have been revealed by mathematicians.

These operational structures are what seem to me to constitute the basis of knowledge, the natural psychological reality, in terms of which we must understand the development of knowledge. And the central problem of development is to understand the formation, elaboration, organization, and functioning of these structures.

I should like to review the stages of development of these structures, not in any detail, but simply as a reminder. I shall distinguish four main stages. The first is a sensory-motor, pre-verbal stage, lasting approximately the first 18 months of life. During this stage is developed the practical knowledge which constitutes the substructure of later representational knowledge. An example is the construction of the schema of the permanent object. For an infant, during the first months, an object has no permanence. When it disappears from the perceptual field it no longer exists. No attempt is made to find it again. Later, the infant will try to find it, and he will find it by localizing it spatially. Consequently, along with the construction of the permanent object there comes the construction of practical or sensory-motor space. There is similarly the construction of temporal succession, and of elementary sensory-motor causality. In other words, there is a series of structures which are indispensable for the structures of later representational thought.

In a second stage, we have pre-operational representation—the beginnings of language, of the symbolic function, and therefore of thought, or representation. But at the level of representational thought, there must now be a reconstruction of all that was developed on the sensory-motor level. That is, the sensory-motor actions are not immediately translated into operations. In fact, during all this second period of pre-operational representations, there are as yet no operations as I defined this term a moment ago. Specifically, there is as yet no conservation which is the psychological criterion of the presence of reversible operations. For example, if we pour liquid from one glass to another of a different shape, the pre-operational child will think there is more in one than in the other. In the absence of operational reversibility, there is no conservation of quantity.

In a third stage the first operations appear, but I call these concrete operations because they operate on objects, and not yet on verbally expressed hypotheses. For example, there are the operations of classification, ordering, the construction of the idea of number, spatial and temporal operations, and all the fundamental operations of elementary logic of classes and relations, of elementary mathematics, of elementary geometry, and even of elementary physics.

Finally, in the fourth stage, these operations are surpassed as the child reaches the level of what I call formal or hypothetic-deductive operations; that is, he can now reason on hypotheses, and not only on objects. He constructs new operations, operations of propositional logic, and not simply the operations of classes, relations, and numbers. He attains new structures which are on the one hand combinatorial, corresponding to what mathematicians call lattices; on the other hand, more complicated group structures. At the level of concrete operations, the operations apply within an immediate neighborhood: for instance, classification by successive inclusions. At the level of the combinatorial, however, the groups are much more mobile.

These, then, are the four stages which we identify, whose formation we shall now attempt to explain.

What factors can be called upon to explain the development from one set of structures to another? It seems to me that there are four main factors: first, of all, *maturation,* in the sense of Gesell, since this development is a continuation of the embryogenesis; second, the role of *experience* of the effects of the physical environment on the structures of intelligence; third, *social transmission* in the broad sense (linguistic transmission, education, etc.); and fourth, a factor which is too often neglected but one which seems to me fundamental and even the principal factor. I shall call this the factor of *equilibration* or if you prefer it, of self-regulation.

Let us start with the first factor, maturation. One might think that these stages are simply a reflection of an interior maturation of the nervous system, following the hypotheses of Gesell, for example. Well, maturation certainly does play an indispensable role and must not be ignored. It certainly takes part in every transformation that takes place during a child's development. However, this first factor is insufficent in itself. First of all, we know practically nothing about the maturation of the nervous system beyond the first months of the child's existence. We know a little bit about it during the first two years but we know very little following this time. But above all, maturation doesn't explain everything, because the average ages at which these stages appear (the average chronological ages) vary a great deal from one society to another. The ordering of these stages is constant and has been found in all the societies studied. It has been found in various countries where psychologists in universities have redone the experiments but it has also been found in African peoples for example, in the children of the Bushmen, and in Iran, both in the villages and in the cities. However, although the order of succession is constant, the chronological ages of these stages varies a great deal. For instance, the ages which we have found in Geneva are not necessarily the ages which you would find in the United

States. In Iran, furthermore, in the city of Teheran, they found approximately the same ages as we found in Geneva, but there is a systematic delay of two years in the children in the country. Canadian psychologists who redid our experiments, Monique Laurendeau and Father Adrien Pinard, found once again about the same ages in Montreal. But when they redid the experiments in Martinique, they found a delay of four years, that is, there are the same stages, but systematically delayed. So you see that these age variations show that maturation does not explain everything.

I shall go on now to the role played by experience. Experience of objects, of physical reality, is obviously a basic factor in the development of cognitive structures. But once again this factor does not explain everything. I can give two reasons for this. The first reason is that some of the concepts which appear at the beginning of the stage of concrete operations are such that I cannot see how they could be drawn from experience. As an example, let us take the conservation of the substance in the case of changing the shape of a ball of plasticene. We give this ball of plasticene to a child who changes its shape into a sausage form and we ask if there is the same amount of matter, that is, the same amount of substance as there was before. We also ask him if it now has the same weight and thirdly if it now has the same volume. The volume is measured by the displacement of water when we put the ball or the sausage into a glass of water. The findings, which have been the same every time this experiment has been done, show us that first of all there is conservation of the amount of substance. At about eight years old a child will say, "There is the same amount of plasticene. Only later does the child assert that the weight is conserved and still later that the volume is conserved. So I would ask you where the idea of the conservation of substance can come from. What is a constant and invariant substance when it doesn't yet have a constant weight or a constant volume? Through perception you can get at the weight of the ball or the volume of the ball but perception cannot give you an idea of the amount of substance. No experiment, no experience can show the child that there is the same amount of substance. He can weigh the ball and that would lead to the conservation of weight. He can immerse it in water and that would lead to the conservation of volume. But the notion of substance is attained before either weight or volume. This conservation of substance is simply a logical necessity. The child now understands that when there is a transformation something must be conserved because by reversing the transformation you can come back to the point of departure and once again have the ball. He knows that something is conserved but he doesn't know what. It is not yet the weight, it is not yet the volume; it is simply a logical form—a logical necessity. There, it seems to me, is an example of a progress in knowledge, a logical necessity for something to be conserved even though no experience can have lead to this notion.

My second objection to the sufficiency of experience as an explanatory factor is that this notion of experience is a very equivocal one. There are, in fact, two kinds of experience which are psychologically very different and this difference is very important from the pedagogical point of view. It is because of the pedagogical importance that I emphasize this distinction. First of all, there is what I shall call physical experience, and, secondly, what I shall call logical-mathematical experience.

Physical experience consists of acting upon objects and drawing some knowledge about the objects by abstraction from the objects. For example, to discover that this pipe is heavier than this watch, the child will weigh them both and find the difference in the objects themselves. This is experience in the usual sense of the term—in the sense used by empiricists. But there is a second type of experience which I shall call logical mathematical experience where the knowledge is not drawn from the objects, but it is drawn by the actions effected upon the objects. This is not the same thing. When one acts upon objects, the objects are indeed there, but there is also the set of actions which modify the objects.

I shall give you an example of this type of experience. It is a nice example because we have verified it many times in small children under seven years of age, but it is also an example which one of my mathematician friends has related to me about his own childhood, and he dates his mathematical career from this experience. When he was four or five years old—I don't know exactly how old, but a small child—he was seated on the ground in his garden and he was counting pebbles. Now to count these pebbles he put them in a row and he counted them one, two, three, up to ten. Then he finished counting them and started to count them in the other direction. He began by the end and once again he found ten. He found this marvelous that there were ten in one direction and ten in the other direction. So he put them in a circle and counted them that way and found ten once again. Then he counted them in the other direction and found ten once more. So he put them in some other arrangement and kept counting them and kept finding ten. There was the discovery that he made.

Now what indeed did he discover? He did not discover a property of pebbles; he discovered a property of the action of ordering. The pebbles had no order. It was his action which introduced a linear order or a cyclical order, or any kind of an order. He discovered that the sum was independent of the order. The order was the action which he introduced among the pebbles. For the sum the same principle applied. The pebbles had no sum; they were simply in a pile. To make a sum, action was necessary—the operation of putting together and counting. He found that the sum was independent of the order, in other words, that the action of putting together is independent of the action of ordering. He discovered a property of actions and not a property of pebbles. You may say that it is in the nature of pebbles to let this be done to them and this is true. But it could have been drops of water, and drops of water would not have let this be done to them because two drops of water and two drops of water do not make four drops of water as you know very well. Drops of water then would not let this be done to them, we agree to that.

So it is not the physical property of pebbles which the experience uncovered. It is the properties of the actions carried out on the pebbles, and this is quite another form of experience. It is the point of departure of mathematical deduction. The subsequent deduction will consist of interiorizing these actions and then of combining them without needing any pebbles. The mathematician no longer needs his pebbles. He can combine his operations simply with symbols, and the point of departure of this mathematical deduction is logical-mathematical experience, and this is not at all experience in the sense of the empiricists. It is the beginning of the coordination of actions, but this coordination of actions before the stage of operations needs to be supported by concrete material. Later, this coordination of actions leads to the logical-mathematical structures. I believe that logic is not a derivative of language. The source of logic is much more profound. It is the total coordination of actions, actions of joining things together, or ordering things, etc. This is what logical-mathematical experience is. It is an experience of the actions of the subject, and not an experience of objects themselves. It is an experience which is necessary before there can be operations. Once the operations have been attained this experience is no longer needed and the coordinations of actions can take place by themselves in the form of deduction and construction for abstract structures.

The third factor is social transmission-linguistic transmission or educational transmission. This factor, once again, is fundamental. I do not deny the role of any one of these factors; they all play a part. But this factor is insufficient because the child can receive valuable information via language or via education directed by an adult only if he is in a state where he can understand this information. That is, to receive the information he must have a structure which enables him to assimilate this information. This is why you cannot teach higher mathematics to a five-year-old. He does not yet have structures which enable him to understand.

I shall take a much simpler example, an example of linguistic transmission. As my very first work in the realm of child psychology, I spent
a long time studying the relation between a part and a whole in concrete experience and in language. For example, I used Burt's test employing the sentence, "Some of my flowers are buttercups." The child
knows that all buttercups are yellow, so there are three possible conclusions: the whole bouquet is yellow, or part of the bouquet is yellow, or
none of the flowers in the bouquet are yellow. I found that up until nine
years of age (and this was in Paris, so the children certainly did understand the French language) they replied, "The whole bouquet is yellow
or some of my flowers are yellow." Both of these mean the same thing.
They did not understand the expression, "some of my flowers." They
did not understand this "of" as a partitive genitive, as the inclusion of
some flowers in my flowers. They understood some of my flowers to be
my several flowers as if the several flowers and the flowers were confused as one and the same class. So there you have children who until
nine years of age heard every day a linguistic structure which implied
the inclusion of a subclass in a class and yet did not understand this
structure. It is only when they themselves are in firm possession of this
logical structure, when they have constructed it for themselves according to the developmental laws which we shall discuss, that they suceed
in understanding correctly the linguistic expression.

I come now to the fourth factor which is added to the three preceding
ones but which seems to me to be the fundamental one. This is what I
call the factor of equilibration. Since there are already three factors,
they must somehow be equilibrated among themselves. That is one reason for bringing in the factor of equilibration. There is a second reason,
however, which seems to me to be fundamental. It is that in the act of
knowing, the subject is active, and consequently, faced with an external
disturbance, he will react in order to compensate and consequently he
will tend towards equilibrium. Equilibrium, defined by active compensation, leads to reversibility. Operational reversibility is a model of an
equilibrated system where a transformation in one direction is compen-
sated by a transformation in the other direction. Equilibration, as I
understand it, is thus an active process. It is a process of self-regulation.
I think that this self-regulation is a fundamental factor in development.
I use this term in the sense in which it is used in cybernetics, that is, in
the sense of processes with feedback and with feedforward, of processes
which regulate themselves by a progressive compensation of systems.
This process of equilibration takes the form of a succession of levels of
equilibrium, of levels which have a certain probability which I shall
call a sequential probability, that is, the probabilities are not established

a priori. There is a sequence of levels. It is not possible to reach the second level unless equilibrium has been reached at the first level, and the equilibrium of the third level only becomes possible when the equilibrium of the second level has been reached, and so forth. That is, each level is determined as the most probable given that the preceding level has been reached. It is not the most probable at the beginning, but it is the most probable once the preceding level has been reached.

As an example, let us take the development of the idea of conservation in the transformation of the ball of plasticene into the sausage shape. Here you can discern four levels. The most probable at the beginning is for the child to think of only one dimension. Suppose that there is a probability of 0.8, for instance, that the child will focus on the length, and that the width has a probability of 0.2. This would mean that of ten children, eight will focus on the length alone without paying any attention to the width, and two will focus on the width without paying any attention to the length. They will focus only on one dimension or the other. Since the two dimensions are independent at this stage, focusing on both at once would have a probability of only 0.16. That is less than either one of the two. In other words, the most probable in the beginning is to focus only on one dimension and in fact the child will say, "It's longer, so there's more in the sausage." Once he has reached this first level, if you continue to elongate the sausage, there comes a moment when he will say, "No, now it's too thin, so there's less." Now he is thinking about the width, but he forgets the length, so you have come to a second level which becomes the most probable after the first level, but which is not the most probable at the point of departure. Once he has focused on the width, he will come back sooner or later to focus on the length. Here you will have a third level where he will oscillate between width and length and where he will discover that the two are related. When you elongate you make it thinner, and when you make it shorter, you make it thicker. He discovers that the two are solidly related and in discovering this relationship, he will start to think in terms of transformation and not only in terms of the final configuration. Now he will say that when it gets longer it gets thinner, so it's the same thing. There is more of it in length but less of it in width. When you make it shorter it gets thicker; there's less in length and more in width, so there is compensation—compensation which defines equilibrium in the sense in which I defined it a moment ago. Consequently, you have operations and conservation. In other words, in the course of these developments you will always find a process of self-regulation which I call equilibration and which seems to me the fundamental factor in the acquisition of logical-mathematical knowledge.

I shall go on now to the second part of my lecture, that is, to deal with the topic of learning. Classicially, learning is based on the stimulus-response schema. I think the stimulus-response schema, while I won't say it is false, is in any case entirely incapable of explaining cognitive learning. Why? Because when you think of a stimulus-response schema, you think usually that first of all there is a stimulus and then a response is set off by this stimulus. For my part, I am convinced that the response was there first, if I can express myself in this way. A stimulus is a stimulus only to the extent that it is significant, and it becomes significant only to the extent that there is a structure which permits its assimilation, a structure which can integrate this stimulus but which at the same time sets off the response. In other words, I would propose that the stimulus-response schema be written in the circular form—in the form of a schema or of a structure which is not simply one way. I would propose that above all, between the stimulus and the response, there is the organism, the organism and its structures. The stimulus is really a stimulus only when it is assimilated into a structure and it is this structure which sets off the response. Consequently, it is not an exaggeration to say that the response is there first, or if you wish at the beginning there is the structure. Of course we would want to understand how this structure comes to be. I tried to do this earlier by presenting a model of equilibration or self-regulation. Once there is a structure, the stimulus will set off a response, but only by the intermediary of this structure.

I should like to present some facts. We have facts in great number. I shall choose only one or two and I shall choose some facts which our colleague, Smedslund, has gathered. (Smedslund is currently at the Harvard Center for Cognitive Studies.) Smedslund arrived in Geneva a few years ago convinced (he had published this in one of his papers) that the development of the ideas of conservation could be indefinitely accelerated through learning of a stimulus-response type. I invited Smedslund to come to spend a year in Geneva to show us this, to show us that he could accelerate the development of operational conservation. I shall relate only one of his experiments.

During the year that he spent in Geneva he chose to work on the conservation of weight. The conservation of weight is, in fact, easy to study since there is a possible external reinforcement, that is, simply weighing the ball and the sausage on a balance. Then you can study the child's reactions to these external results. Smedslund studied the conservation of weight on the one hand, and on the other hand he studied the transitivity of weights, that is, the transitivity of equalities if A = B and B = C, then A = C, or the transitivity of the inequalities if A is less than B, and B is less than C, then A is less than C.

As far as conservation is concerned, Smedslund succeeded very easily with five- and six-year-old children in getting them to generalize that weight is conserved when the ball is transformed into a sausage or into little pieces or into a pancake or into any other form, he weighs it, and he sees that it is always the same thing. He will affirm it will be the same thing, no matter what you do to it; it will come out to be the same weight. Thus Smedslund very easily achieved the conservation of weight by this sort of external reinforcement.

In contrast to this, however, the same method did not succeed in teaching transitivity. The children resisted the notion of transitivity. A child would predict correctly in certain cases but he would make his prediction as a possibility or a probability and not as a certainty. There was never this generalized certainty in the case of transitivity.

So there is the first example, which seems to me very instructive, because in this problem in the conservation of weight there are two aspects. There is the physical aspect and there is the logical-mathematical aspect. Note that Smedslund started his study by establishing that there was a correlation between conservation and transitivity. He began by making a statistical study on the relationships between the spontaneous responses to the questions about conservation and the spontaneous responses to the questions about transitivity, and he found a very significant correlation. But in the learning experiment, he obtained a learning of conservation and not of transitivity. Consequently, he successfully obtained a learning of what I called earlier physical experience (which is not surprising since it is simply a question of noting facts about objects), but he did not successfully obtain a learning in the construction of the logical structure. This doesn't surprise me either, since the logical structure is not the result of physical experience. It cannot be obtained by external reinforcement. The logical structure is reached only through internal equilibration, by self-regulation, and the external reinforcement of seeing the balance did not suffice to establish this logical structure of transitivity.

I could give many other comparable examples, but it seems useless to me to insist upon these negative examples. Now I should like to show that learning is possible in the case of these logical-mathematical structures, but on one condition—that is, that the structure which you want to teach to the subjects can be supported by simpler, more elementary, logical-mathematical structures. I shall give you an example. It is the example of the conservation of number in the case of one-to-one correspondence. If you give a child seven blue tokens and ask him to put down as many red tokens, there is a preoperational stage where he will put one red one opposite each blue one. But when you spread out the red ones, making them into a longer row, he will say to you, "Now, there are more red ones than there are blue ones."

Now how can we accelerate, if you want to accelerate, the acquisition of this conservation of number? Well, you can imagine an analogous structure but in a simpler, more elementary situation. For example, with Mlle. Inhelder, we have been studying recently the notion of one-to-one correspondence by giving the child two glasses of the same shape and a big pile of beads. The child puts a bead into one glass with one hand and at the same time a bead into the other glass with the other hand. Time after time he repeats this action, a bead into one glass with one hand and at the same time a bead into the other glass with the other hand and he sees that there is always the same amount on each side. Then you hide one of the glasses. You cover it up. He no longer sees this glass but he continues to put one bead into it while at the same time putting one bead into the other glass which he can see. Then you ask him whether the equality has been conserved, whether there is still the same amount in one glass as in the other. Now you will find that very small children, about four years old, don't want to make a prediction. They will say, "So far, it has been the same amount, but now I don't know. I can't see any more, so I don't know." They do not want to generalize. But the generalization is made from the age of about five and one-half-years.

This is in contrast to the case of the red and blue tokens with one row spread out, where it isn't until seven or eight years of age that children will say there are the same number in the two rows. As one example of this generalization, I recall a little boy of five years and nine months who had been adding the beads to the glasses for a little while. Then we asked him whether, if he continued to do this all day and all night and all the next day, there would always be the same amount in the two glasses. The little boy gave this admirable reply: "Once you know, you know for always." In other words, this was recursive reasoning. So here the child does acquire the structure in this specific case. The number is a synthesis of class inclusion and ordering. This synthesis is being favored by the child's own actions. You have set up a situation where there is an iteration of one same action which continues and which is therefore ordered while at the same time being inclusive. You have, so to speak, a localized synthesis of inclusion and ordering which facilitates the construction of the idea of number in this specific case, and there you can find, in effect, an influence of this experience on the other experience. However, this influence is not immediate. We study the generalization from this recursive situation to the other situation where the tokens are laid on the table in rows, and it is not an immediate generalization but it is made possible through intermediaries. In other words, you can find some learning of this structure if you base the learning on simpler structures.

In this same area of the development of numerical structures, the psychologist Joachim Wohlwill, who spent a year at our Institute at Geneva, has also shown that this acquisition can be accelerated through introducing additive operations, which is what we introduced also in the experiment which I just described. Wohlwill introduced them in a different way but he too was able to obtain a certain learning effect. In other words, learning is possible if you base the more complex structure on simpler structures, that is, when there is a natural relationship and development of structures and not simply an external reinforcement.

Now I would like to take a few minutes to conclude what I was saying. My first conclusion is that learning of structures seems to obey the same laws as the natural development of these structures. In other words, learning is subordinated to development and not vice-versa as I said in the introduction. No doubt you will object that some investigators have succeeded in teaching operational structures. But, when I am faced with these facts, I always have three questions which I want to have answered before I am convinced.

The first question is: "Is this learning lasting? What remains two weeks or a month later?" If a structure develops spontaneously, once it has reached a state of equilibrium, it is lasting, it will continue throughout the child's entire life. When you achieve the learning by external reinforcement, is the result lasting or not and what are the conditions necessary for it to be lasting?

The second question is: "How much generalization is possible?" What makes learning interesting is the possibility of transfer of a generalization. When you have brought about some learning, you can always ask whether this is an isolated piece in the midst of the child's mental life, or if it is really a dynamic structure which can lead to generalizations.

Then there is the third question: "In the case of each learning experience what was the operational level of the subject before the experience and what more complex structures has this learning succeeded in achieving?" In other words, we must look at each specific learning experience from the point of view of the spontaneous operations which were present at the outset and the operational level which has been achieved after the learning experience.

My second conclusion is that the fundamental relation involved in all development and all learning is not the relation of association. In the stimulus-response schema, the relation between the response and the stimulus is understood to be one of assimilation. Assimilation is not the same as association. I shall define assimilation as the integration of any sort of reality into a structure, and it is this assimilation which seems to me to be fundamental in learning, and which seems to me to be the fundamental relation from the point of view of pedagogical or didactic applications. All of my remarks today represent the child and the learning subject as active. An operation is an activity. Learning is possible only when there is active assimilation. It is this activity on the part of the subject which seems to me to be underplayed in the stimulus-response schema. The presentation which I propose puts the emphasis on the idea of self-regulation, on assimilation. All the emphasis is placed on the activity of the subject himself, and I think that without this activity there is no possible didactic or pedagogy which significantly transforms the subject.

Finally, and this will be my last concluding remark, I would like to comment on an excellent publication by the psychologist Berlyne. Berlyne spent a year with us in Geneva during which he intended to translate our results on the development of operations into stimulus-response language, specifically into Hull's learning theory. Berlyne published in our series of studies of genetic epistomology a very good article on this comparison between the results obtained in Geneva and Hull's theory. In the same volume, I published a commentary on Berlyne's results. The essence of Berlyne's results is this: Our findings can very well be translated into Hullian language, but only on condition that two modifications are introduced. Berlyne himself found these modifications quite considerable, but they seemed to him to concern more the conceptualization than the Hullian theory itself. I am not so sure about that. The two modifications are these. First of all, Berlyne wants to distinguish two sorts of response in the S-R schema: (a) responses in the ordinary, classical sense, which I shall call "copy responses"; (b) responses which Berlyne calls "transformation responses." Transformation responses consist of transforming one response of the first type into another response of the first type. These transformation responses are what I call operations, and you can see right away that this is a rather serious modification of Hull's conceptualization because here you are introducing an element of transformation and thus of assimilation and no longer the simple association of stimulus-response theory.

The second modification which Berlyne introduces into the stimulus-response language is the introduction of what he calls internal reinforcements. What are these internal reinforcements? They are what I call equilibration or self-regulation. The internal reinforcements are what enable the subject to eliminate contradictions, incompatibilities, and conflicts. All development is composed of momentary conflicts and incompatibilities which must be overcome to reach a higher level of equilibrium. Berlyne calls this elimination of incompatibilities internal reinforcements.

So you see that it is indeed a stimulus-response theory, if you will, but first you add operations and then you add equilibration. That's all we want!

Editor's note: A brief question and answer period followed Professor Piaget's presentation. The first question related to the fact that the eight-year-old child acquires conservation of weight and volume. The question asked if this didn't contradict the order of emergence of the pre-operational and operational stages. Piaget's response follows:

The conservation of weight and the conservation of volume are not due only to experience. There is also involved a logical framework which is characterized by reversibility and the system of compensations. I am only saying that in the case of weight and volume, weight corresponds to a perception. There is an empirical contact. The same is true of volume. But in the case of substance, I don't see how there can be any perception of substance independent of weight or volume. The strange thing is that this notion of substance comes before the two other notions. Note that in the history of thought we have the same thing. The first Greek physicists, the pre-Socratic philosophers, discovered conservation of substance independently of any experience. I do not believe this is contradictory to the theory of operations. This conservation of substance is simply the affirmation that something must be conserved. The children do not know specifically what is conserved. They know that since the sausage can become a ball again there must be something which is conserved, and saying "substance" is simply a way of translating this logical necessity for conservation. But this logical necessity results directly from the discovery of operations. I do not think that this is contradictory with the theory of development.

Editor's note: The second question was whether or not the development of stages in children's thinking could be accelerated by practice, training, and exercise in perception and memory. Piaget's response follows:

I am not very sure that exercise of perception and memory would be sufficient. I think that we must distinguish within the cognitive function two very different aspects which I shall call the figurative aspect and the operative aspect. The figurative aspect deals with static configurations. In physical reality there are states, and in addition to these there are transformations which lead from one state to another. In cognitive functioning one has the figurative aspects—for example, perception, imitation, mental images, etc.

The operative aspect includes operations and the actions which lead from one state to another. In children of the higher stages and in adults, the figurative aspects are subordinated to the operative aspects. Any given state is understood to be the result of some transformation and the point of departure for another transformation. But the pre-operational child does not understand transformations. He does not have the operations necessary to understand them so he puts all the emphasis on the static quality of the states. It is because of this, for example, that in the conservation experiments he simply compares the initial state and the final state without being concerned with the transformation.

In exercising perception and memory, I feel that you will reinforce the figurative aspect without touching the operative aspect. Consequently, I'm not sure that this will accelerate the development of cognitive structures. What needs to be reinforced is the operative aspect— not the analysis of states, but the understanding of transformations.

---

1. How would you define these terms: operation, equilibration, reversibility, assimilation, accommodation, conservation, logical necessity, structure, operational, schema?
2. How do Piaget's four stages of intellectual development differ from one another?
3. Can you think of any reasons why educators would want to accelerate the various stages of development in children?

13 P. C. DODWELL

Children's Understanding
of Spatial Concepts

Spatial concepts of children have been assessed by Piaget and he has written numerous articles and books about such development.[1] Many studies have been conducted that attempt to verify his results and this paper by Dodwell represents one such study. It is included as an example of how a person might go about investigating certain aspects of a child's cognitive development. The quantitative treatment of the data should be dealt with rather lightly in your reading. The description of the interviews, the qualitative treatment of the data, and the discussion are oriented more toward a nonstatistical treatment of the data collected during the interviews with children. If statistics are not a threat to you, then you might find the "Quantitative Treatment" section to be of interest.

If you have children available, it might be interesting to try to repeat the tests described under the seven subgroups. The first-hand experience of collecting data on how children think communicates aspects that words on paper, fall short of doing.

In *The Child's Conception of Space* (Piaget and Inhelder, 1956) rather extensive investigations of children's understanding of spatial concepts and relations are described, investigations based on experimental procedures which are typical of the practice of Piaget and his co-workers in their recent studies. As in many of his investigations, Piaget claims to demonstrate a fairly clear progression in spatial concept development with age, and, as in many previous instances, he can be criticized for basing his generalizations on inadequate evidence. He gives no indication of the number of children tested, of the consistency of trends from one stage to another with age, or—more important—the consistency of

Reprinted from *The Canadian Journal of Psychology*, Vol. 17, 1963, pp. 141-161, by permission of the editor and the author. Dr. Dodwell has conducted studies extensively in the area of cognitive development.

1. See: *The Child's Conception of Space* by Piaget and Inhelder, (New York: W. W. Norton, Inc., 1967.)

the steps in the progression within individual children. The investigation here reported is an attempt to verify some of Piaget's conclusions concerning spatial concepts on a fairly large sample of children, and is thus parallel to an earlier investigation of the development of number concepts (Dodwell, 1960, 1961).

Piaget's Theory

Piaget's theory of the development of spatial concepts, like his theory of number concept development, is a particuluar application of his general theory of intelligence (Piaget, 1950), which was briefly outlined in the introduction to the study on number concepts (Dodwell, 1960) and will not be repeated here. However, some important new concepts are introduced, the most important being the concept of *sub*-logical (spatio-temporal) operations, which are distinguished from logico-arithmetical operations mainly on the grounds that they involve notions of proximity and continuity. These notions are not strictly necessary for the first steps in logico-arithmetical operations (that is, the logic of classes) but are clearly required in the development of spatial concepts.

The theory of the development of spatial operations and concepts is, roughly, that the first spatial operations the child comes to understand involve primitive notions of proximity, enclosure, and boundary which are entirely non-metric in character. Piaget makes a perfectly reasonable distinction between *perceived* space and *conceived* space: whereas a quite young child may be able to distinguish perceptually between, say, a square and a circle, this does not mean that the child can conceptualize this difference, or marshal the operations which are necessary for making anything more than a perceptual distinction. *Understanding* spatial properties and relations, as opposed to perception of similarities and differences between spatially extended objects, involves operations which are thought of as "virtual" or "internalized" actions. It is interesting to note that the "psychologically primitive" operations of order, proximity, enclosure, etc. correspond quite closely to the "mathematically primitive" concepts used in that branch of geometry known as topology, which also deals with the most general, and usually non-metric, properties of space. In this there is quite a close parallel to the relations between the logical primitives on which mathematics is based, and the primitive notions the child develops before coming to understand numbers (cf. Dodwell, 1960).

One tends to think of Euclidean geometry as *the* "natural" geometry, and hence that children should easily come to understand space in terms of Euclidean concepts. According to Piaget, however, the use and under-

standing of such concepts is preceded first by the development of topological operations and concepts, as described above, and then by operations and concepts of a projective character, for example those required
for an understanding of perspective.

The stages in the development of spatial concepts in Piaget's theory
are a good deal more complex than in the case of number concepts.
However, the same sorts of stages are envisaged, starting with "global"
comparisons, proceeding through an "intuitive" stage, at which the child
starts to grasp the correct operations and the relations between them, to
a stage of "concrete operations" at which the correct operations are used
in a consistent fashion. This is complicated, however, by the simultaneous
development from topological to projective to Euclidean concepts, so
that the *sorts* of operations the child uses change at the same time as he
is learning *what* operations and groupings of operations are.

Piaget's Evidence

Piaget's study of spatial concepts is divided into three parts, corresponding to the three types of geometrical concepts outlined above. In
investigating the topological stage he made use primarily of drawings,
"haptic" perception (perception by touch, without vision), linear and
circular order (as with beads on a string), the study of knots, and
situations involving the concept of continuity—for example, the number
of points on a line, the end result of indefinitely repeated bisection of a
line, and continual reduction in size of a geometric figure.

Understanding of projective properties was investigated by such techniques as: observing children's ability to *construct* straight lines using
numbers of discrete objects, getting them to draw various perspective
figures, asking questions about the projection of the shadows of objects,
the relations between objects perceived from different points of view,
sections through solid geometric figures such as a cylinder or cone, etc.

The transition from projective to Euclidean concepts was investigated
in terms of "affine" transformations (transformations preserving parallels) with "Lazy Tongs," in terms of understanding of similarity and
proportion in figures such as the rectangle and triangle, and in terms
of the understanding of systems of horizontal and vertical reference axes.
None of Piaget's procedures have been described here in detail, since
many of them are followed fairly closely in the tests to be described
below: in general he avoids basing his conclusions on a single demonstration situation, but tends to use two or more situations both of which
require use of the same sorts of operation. However, as noted above, he
does not give any idea of the generality of his findings, either between

children at the same age or between different tests allegedly chosen to demonstrate similar or identical operations in action within the same child.

Procedure

Aim

To assess the generality of the sorts of spatial concepts and their development, as reported by Piaget and his co-workers (Piaget and Inhelder, 1956); to examine age trends, the consistency of the reported activities at different ages and stages, and to assess these factors as evidence for a theory of cognitive development based, first, on the notion of the formation of operational groupings, and secondly, on the progression from topological to Euclidean spatial concepts.

Method

Three persons took part in the investigation, two of them as testers, and all three as scorers. Ss were 194 children in Kingston public schools, ranging in age from five years and one month to eleven years and three months, and in I.Q. (measured on a group test) from 80 to 136 (no I.Q.s were available for kindergarten children). The average range of I.Q. was somewhat over-represented at the expense of the extremes, and all children were in either kindergarten or Grades I, II, or III. Age distributions with grades were similar to those reported previously (Dodwell, 1960); the children were in three different schools and were drawn from all socioeconomic levels. The test was administered individually and took in most cases about 20-30 min. per child. Thirty-four different situations or items were used in the test, which was divided into seven main subsections. The order in which the items were administered was standardized, as was the scoring procedure and, to a large extent, the use of subsidiary questioning. However, some latitude was allowed in the latter respect, since the point of such questioning is to follow up ambiguous answers and clarify the processes of thought which led to them.

The seven subgroups of the test, which follow quite closely some of the situations used by Piaget, are listed in Table 1.

Subgroup I Construction of Straight Line (Items 1-5)

In the first subsection, understanding of the *construct* "straight line" was investigated (as opposed to the *discrimination* between straight and curved lines). (1) The child was confronted with a heavy cardboard disk, about 14 in. in diameter, placed on a fairly large table, and about 12 in. from its edge. Ten colored plastic toothpicks on plasticene bases were also

Table 1
Subgroups of the Spatial Concept Test

Sub-group	Name	Materials and/or method
I	Construction of straight line	"Telegraph poles"
II	Drawing shapes	Pencil and paper, shapes to be copied.
III	Plane figures, lines, points, and continuity	Pencil and paper, demonstration by tester.
IV	Horizontal and vertical coordinates	Bottles, "boat," plumbline, pictures.
V	Geometrical sections	Plasticene solid geometrical models, sections to be drawn.
VI	Similarity and porportion	Shapes, similar shapes to be drawn around them, by parallel lines.
VII	Coordination of perspective	Table model with mountains, pictures of "points of view."

placed on the table, and the tester said: "These are telephone poles [indicating the toothpicks] and I would like you to set them up so that they will be in a straight line beside a straight road. I will put in the one that will be at the beginning of the line and the one that will be at the end and I would like you to put in the ones in between that go to make the straight line." The end-posts were placed some distance apart from each other on the circumference of the disk, at the ends of a cord parallel to the diameter of the disk sagittal to the child. The child's performance was noted down on a standard test blank, which listed the common types of response as indicated by Piaget (in this case: posts arranged in a straight line; posts follow curve of circle; posts form zigzag line; posts at random over surface; evenly spaced; bunched). Checking one or more of the items served to characterize the response in most cases, but if some substantially different response occurred, it was noted separately. The procedure was repeated using (2) a cardboard square, with end posts at the corners of the side closest to the child, (3) with the circle, placing the end points so that the cord joining them ran obliquely to the sagittal axis, (4) with the square, so that the end points were on the base and on the left side of the square. Lastly in this subsection, the posts were placed on the square in a nonstraight line, and the child asked to straighten them (5). If the child did not spontaneously sight along the line, it was moved to various positions around the table and asked which positions would help to show if the line were straight or not.

Subgroup II Drawing Shapes (Item 6)

The child was asked to draw a picture of a man (to make sure that it had *some* drawing ability: however, this was not scored) and then was asked to copy a series of 20 shapes, ranging from the "topological" shapes shown in Figure 1 through various simple geometrical shapes (circle, square, triangle, ellipse, rectangle) to more complex shapes, such as a pair of circles intersecting, touching, and separated, an equilateral triangle enclosed in a circle, etc. The purpose here was to try to discover the extent to which children can draw the shapes with (*a*) topological, (*b*) projective, and (*c*) Euclidean properties correctly reproduced.

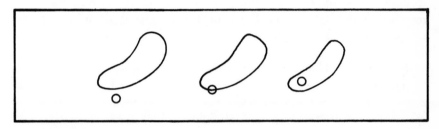

FIGURE 1.   The topological shapes used as models in subgroup II.

Subgroup III Points and Continuity (Items 7-12)

Items in this subgroup deal with understanding of the concept of point, and the ideas of continuity and limit in a very elementary sense. (7) The tester first said: "I am going to draw a box [square] on this sheet of paper. Here right beside it I would like you to draw the smallest box that can possibly be drawn, one so small that no one could make one smaller." (The common alternatives here were: draws a smaller square; draws immediately the smallest square; draws a series of squares decreasing in size; does not draw a smaller square. Distinguishing between the first two of these alternatives was almost always quite easy.) The same procedure was repeated for a *bigger* square (8): here the "biggest" square was taken as one which followed fairly closely the edges of the paper. For item 9: "Here is a straight line drawn on a sheet of paper. Under it I want you to draw a straight line just half as long as this one. . . . I want you to draw one just half as long as the one you just drew. . . ." etc. When the child had drawn his "smallest" line, the tester said (10): "You can do a lot of things in your mind, can't you? Well then, try to imagine that you are going to go on cutting up this little bit [line] without stopping. How long could you go on cutting it up like this? . . . What is going to be left in the end?"

Next (11), the tester took a fresh sheet of paper, drew a line about an inch long on it, and asked: "How many lines do you need to get a big one like this?" and then (12), drawing two points about an inch apart: "How many points are there between these two points? Draw in the points. . . . Could you get any more points in? What would you have if you drew in as many points as you could possibly draw?" Following this was an item (13) concerning the limit for the "smallest" square; in this case the child was allowed to "cut up" the square (by drawing dividing lines through it); the child was asked what the final product of this process would be. If it said "nothing at all," it was asked: "What would you get just before nothing at all?" As before, all responses were recorded, either as one of the standard responses, or as a separate response where necessary.

Subgroup IV Horizontal and Vertical (Items 14-20)

This group concerns the understanding and use of systems of horizontal and vertical reference axes. The materials used consisted of two narrow-necked bottles, one with straight parallel sides and a flat base, the other spherical, each about one-quarter full of colored liquid; two other empty jars, one each of the types described; a cork with a matchstick fixed to it, and perpendicular to one of the flat faces; a plumbline with a bob shaped like a fish; a plasticine model of three mountains; and various pictures of the jars.

Item 14: "We are going to tip the straight jar over like this. . . .Will the water stay where it is, or will it move? Show with your finger on the jar where the water will be. . . . Draw on your picture of the jar (tilted) where the water will be when it is tipped. . . . Now we will see whether it is right. . . . Were you right? Now draw what you see." This was repeated with the *round* jar (15) and in both cases the tilt was about 45°.

Item 16: "Here are some pictures of jars with water in them." [Three jars, one vertical, one horizontal, one tilted at 45°.] "Take them one at a time and tip them so that the water looks right," followed by item 17: "Here are some [6] pictures of jars with water in them. Some of them are tipped so that the water looks right [4] and some are not [2]. Put all the ones that are right in one pile and all the others in another pile." So far the items in this subgroup have been concerned with a horizontal reference axis (the surface of the water). The remaining items deal with a vertical reference axis.

Item 18: With the parallel-sided jar: "Here is a cork with a match-stick in it. Let's pretend that it is a little boat. We will let the boat float on the water in the jar. Which way does the mast of the boat point now? [Jar vertical.] We are going to tip the jar, and I want you to draw the way the mast will look with the jar tipped: I will tip the *empty* jar the way this jar is going to be tipped [45°]. Now draw the little boat. . . . Now we will tip the jar with the water in it and see if you were right. Were you right? Draw it again the way it should look." This procedure was repeated with the jar tipped through 90° (Item 19).

Item 20, again with the parallel-sided jar: "Here is a line with a fish on it. We will hang it inside the empty jar. Now we will tip the jar like this [45° tip demonstrated with similar jar] and I would like you to draw the way the string would look with the jar tipped. Now let's see if you were right [tip jar with line in it]. Were you right? Now please make your drawing look right."

Item 21: "Here is a mountain, and here are some posts [9]. I would like you to plant three posts nice and straight on the top of the mountain. . . . Plant three posts on the ground nearby. . . . Plant three posts on the slopes of the mountain. . . Now *draw* the mountain with four trees nice and straight on the sides."

Subgroup V Geometrical Sections (Items 22-27)

The problems in this group concern understanding of the sections of a three-dimensional geometrical figure. The materials used were a plasticene cylinder, a rectangular parallelepiped, a cone, and a hollow rubber ball.

For item 22 the child was shown the cylinder, and a knife. The tester said: "I am going to cut this roller in the middle like this [perpendicular to the main axis, indicated by a gesture]. I would like you to draw the side you'll see where it has been cut. . . ." Then, showing a cut section: "Did you think it would look like that?" The same procedure was repeated with the cone (23), the parallelepiped (24), the hollow ball (25), a longitudinal section of the cylinder (26), and an oblique (elliptical) section of the cone (27).

Subgroup VI Similarity and Proportion (Items 28-33)

Drawings of isoceles and scalene triangles and of a rectangle were used, and a ruler provided. The items were designed to elucidate understanding of similarities and proportions.

Item 28, showing the isosceles triangle: "Do you know what we call this drawing? [Yes, it looks like a tent and is called a triangle.] I am going to draw a line just below the bottom of this triangle [actually, parallel, to its base]. I would like you to start with this line and make a bigger triangle just the same shape as this other one, around the outside of it. You may use this ruler to help you draw it, and you may turn the paper any way you like." The same procedure was repeated with the scalene triangle (29) and rectangle (30), and with the rectangle having one diagonal drawn in and produced, to see if the child would use this to help obtain a similar figure (31).

Item 32: "Here are some pictures [eight pairs of similar figures and three pairs of dissimilar ones]. Each picture has two triangles on it. The triangles may be exactly the same shape, or they may be of different shapes. Put all the pictures with triangles that are the same in this pile, and all the others over here." This was repeated, with cards showing pairs of rectangles (33).

Subgroup VIII Coordination of Perspectives (Items 34-35)

Materials. A papier mâché model of three mountains on a square base, with various identifying details, such as a truck parked on one mountain, a sheep on another, a tree on the third; in addition each mountain was a different color (green, brown, grey); a doll; and 10 pictures representing different views of the scene.

Item 34: "These pointed things are mountains, and from different sides you can see different things. I will put this little doll at different places, and then I would like you to pick out the picture that shows what the doll would see from those places." Four positions were used, one the child's own position, and opposite the three other sides of the model.

Item 35: "Here is a picture that shows what the doll would see from one side of the scene. Look at it carefully and then show me where the doll would be standing to see this picture." The same procedure was repeated for four different positions of the doll, and the child was not allowed to move around the model at any time. As with previous items in the test, boxes were provided on the test blank for common types of answers, and unusual or ambiguous responses were noted down in full.

Results

Description and analysis of the results of this test are not by any means as straightforward as in the case of the number concept test: first of all, because the range and variability of responses is greater in the present test, and the categorization of responses not so objective in all cases, and secondly because several different processes appear to be developing concurrently. As was mentioned above, according to Piaget the child develops through different stages characterized by changing concepts of space (topological, projective, Euclidean), but at the same time it is elaborating the "mental structure" of operations, and groupings of operations. Also a number of the items in the present test depend for their solution on drawing ability, and this is something which is developing rapidly during the age range under investigation (of course this development is probably dependent to some extent on the changes in spatial concepts, but it seems doubtful whether this is the only factor involved).

On the whole Piaget's assertions about the development of spatial concepts, as measured by the present types of test situations, were corroborated, although not in all respects, as will become evident in the descriptions below. It was not found possible to assign any child to a particular stage of development, either in terms of the type of spatial (geometrical) concepts the child entertained, or the correctness of its answers within a particular conceptual framework. Thus a child might get all solutions to one set of problems correct in terms of projective characteristics, yet in another set it might not grasp even the topological relations involved. Furthermore, the division of responses into "global" (perceptual), "intuitive," and "operational" categories, according to the adequacy of a response, was not in all cases as readily or reliably attainable as in the number concept study (Dodwell, 1960). However, responses were classified in this way, the labels A, B, and C stages being used, as before. So far as possible Piaget and Inhelder's classification into stages was followed, at least approximately. The relations of the A, B, and C stages to the sometimes more complex subdivisions of Piaget and Inhelder are noted in the appropriate places below.

Qualitative Observations

These qualitative observations can best be followed by referring back to Table 1 which lists the methods and materials for the various subgroups.

Subgroup I construction of straight line

This set of items is concerned with ability to construct a straight line, and Piaget's findings are borne out, to the extent that many of the younger children could place their posts between the end-posts, but did not attempt to space them evenly or in a straight line. Rather, they seemed to be satisfied with an arrangement of "linear proximity." (This Piaget calls "stage I.") Another common response among younger children was to follow the edge of the platform on which the line was to be constructed, thus forming a curved, or even two-sided "straight line" between the end-posts. (Piaget's "stage II.") Characteristically, such children did not see the advantages of viewing the line of sticks from a particular point of view to "get them straight," whereas older children, even if they did not spontaneously sight along the line, were easily convinced of the advantage of doing so, and of course were not influenced in their constructions by the contour of the platform. Division into stages A, B, and C on any one item was not difficult in this subgroup and corresponded to Piaget's stages I, II, and III: however, so many children displayed different types of behavior between the different items in the subgroup (despite their apparent similarity—see description in previous section) that a special "mixed" category was included, and proved to be the largest single category.[2] Table 2 demonstrates the main characteristics of the responses in this subgroup, on the basis of age. It is evident that the age overlap of the different stages is very great, and the size of the "mixed" category strongly suggests that clear verification of the Piagetian stage of development for a particular child, even within such a homogeneous group of items, often cannot be made even approximately.

Subgroup II drawings of shapes

From the point of view of classification, this set of items was, perhaps, the most troublesome. It may seem, a priori, that it should be fairly easy

TABLE 2

CHARACTERISTICS OF RESPONSES TO ITEMS IN SUBGROUP I
(5 ITEMS) IN TERMS OF AGE

	Typical behavior	N	Mode	Range
Stage A	"Linear proximity," with no attempt to form straight line.	11	7.3	5.3 –8.3
Stage B	Follows model edge, often in two separate lines.	36	7.0	5.3–10.3
Stage C	Forms straight line, posts usually evenly spaced between end points.	66	8.8	5.8–11.3
Mixed		81	5.8	5.3– 9.8

2. The criterion for classifying a child as in the "mixed" category for a subgroup was that at least two of the responses within the subgroup should be rated differently from the remainder. Thus a child given four A's and one B in subgroup I would be rated as in category A, but a child with three A's and two B's would be rated "mixed."

to decide whether or not a shape has been drawn so that Euclidean, projective, topological, or no characteristics of the model are more or less faithfully reproduced. However, in many cases the decision is not so simple, especially as the level of drawing competence is obviously relevant. Thus, a child that has to draw an equilateral triangle inscribed in a circle may, in the attempt to get the sides of the triangle of equal length, fail to have them join on the circle, so that the result is not even topologically correct. How does one score such a drawing? After several attempts at classification, and discussion of the results, the three scorers managed to agree on just over 80 per cent of the drawings, classified independently, and no further improvement seemed likely.

As one might expect, the level of drawing competence increased with age. The youngest children frequently did not draw their shapes even topologically correctly, but were more often correct in a topological than in a projective or Euclidean sense. Older children, on the other hand, tended to make progressively more of their drawings correct in the latter two senses, but in view of the uncertainties of the scoring procedures, it seems hardly worthwhile to elaborate on these changes, except to state that even among the oldest children some non-Euclidean drawings were made.

Subgroup III points and continuity

Piaget interprets a crude notion of continuity as the end-product of elaborating operations of ordering, seriating, and enclosing, and distinguishes three stages in its development. Evidence was found for his first two stages (the third being a stage of "formal understanding" occuring only at about 11-12 years of age): in the first stage children are held to be unable to draw "largest" and "smallest" figures since, as Piaget puts it, "they lack an operational schema of seriation (Piaget and Inhelder, 1956, p. 128), are unable to subdivide a line or figure more than a very few times, and consider the ultimate elements of indefinitely repeated division to have the same shapes as the original figures. Also, a line cannot be understood as a collection of points.

Table 3 shows some characteristics of age levels in this subgroup: there was only one child that could be characterized as "pure A," that is, that had no concept of continuity at all, and the most striking feature of the table is the enormous preponderance of the "mixed" category. This very large "mixed" category suggests that the development of the operations concerned may proceed in a rather haphazard fashion. The question of whether or not there is a discernible pattern in the "mixed" response group is taken up below. In the second stage subdivision leads to a "point," but the point is still thought of as having extension, its shape

Table 3

Characteristics of Responses to Items in Subgroup III
(6 items) in Terms of Age

	Typical behavior	N	Mode	Range
Stage A	Inability to draw "largest" and smallest," inability to subdivide line, or "construct" line out of points.	1	6.8	—
Stage B	Draws series, to find smallest, or largest figure. Subdivision of line not completed.	23	7.3	5.3– 9.8
Stage C	"Largest" and "smallest" found immediately. Subdivision of line, and composition of line from points understood.	6	8.3	5.8– 9.8
Mixed		164	8.3	5.3–11.3

depending on the mode of subdivision and the process as having a finite number of steps. The "building up" of a line or surface is understood, in an elementary sense, as the reverse of the process of subdivision. A third stage was identified (stage C, which is not the same as Piaget's final, formal, stage) in which a "point" is understood as being without spatial extension, and the number of points in a line or surface as being unlimited. Naturally these notions are only entertained by children in a very elementary and crude way.

Here is a typical "mixed" set of responses, made by a boy aged eight years and ten months, of average intelligence: (7) To the "smallest box" instruction, the boy responded by drawing a *series* of squares of decreasing size, one beside the other (rated B). (8) To the "largest box" instruction he responded also by drawing a series, one outside the other (B). (9) Asked to draw a series of lines of decreasing size, he did so, ending up with a point (C). (10) Asked how much further his point could be cut up, he said "about three more times" (rated B, since the response was not entirely determined by perceptual properties—the line had already been reduced to a point). Asked what would be left, after a final division, he said "a little bit" (B). (11) Asked how many lines go to make a longer line, he said "about seven" (A), and (12) that a given line would be made up of about 12 points [some of which he drew— spaced apart (A)]. Asked what one would have when all the dots had been drawn in, he said "a jumble of little dots" (A). (13) The final product of dividing up a square was said to be "a tiny bit of the square" (not "a square") (B). Evidently this boy has the beginnings of an understanding of "continuity," in an elementary way, but is not able to apply his ideas too consistently.

Subgroup IV horizontal and vertical axes

Again, all the substages and stages described by Piaget were observed, and the results were divided into three stages corresponding to Piaget's stages I, II, and III. At stage A, the child has no conception of horizontal and vertical, cannot draw the water levels or plumblines, nor relate movements of the jars to different pictures of the water levels, etc. At stage B, the rudimentary concepts of horizontal and vertical appear, but cannot be maintained with respect to an external reference point, or line: that is, when the jar is tilted, the water level or plumbline tends to tilt with it. At the third stage, C, the levels are correctly predicted and drawn, as are the directions of plumblines. Table 4 shows distributions of these stages over age: Piaget mentions ages four to five as typical for stage A, and "after seven to eight" for stage C. The present findings suggest that the age limits cannot be so precisely identified, and the enor-

TABLE 4

CHARACTERISTICS OF RESPONSES TO ITEMS IN SUBGROUP IV
(8 ITEMS) IN TERMS OF AGE

	Typical behavior	N	Mode	Range
Stage A	No idea of horizontal and vertical axes, either in prediction, drawing or recognition of pictures.	15	6.3	5.8–10.3
Stage B	Some recognition of axes, but not maintained when jar tipped.	9	8.8	5.3–10.3
Stage C	Correct prediction, drawing and recognition of axes.	12	8.3 and 9.3	7.3– 9.8
Mixed		158	8.3	5.3–11.3

mously preponderant "mixed" category again suggests very little regularity in the developmental pattern.

As an example from the "mixed" category, the boy whose responses were described under subgroup III above was able to predict the direction of the mast and water level perfectly well when the cork was tilted in the bottle (stage C) but placed sticks on the mountain, and drew them, perpendicular to the mountain sides (stage B). He was also unable to predict the water levels for the initial items in the subgroup. There is possibly a learning effect here, since responses to the bottle problems improved: however, a number of other children gave more adequate answers to the early items in the subgroup than to the later ones, so it is certain that not all children in the "mixed" category are there because they learned how to answer this type of question while the test was in progress.

Subgroup V geometric sections

Three main stages in developing the ability to predict the results of sectioning a geometrical solid are described by Piaget, and all three were observed in the present study. First stage responses are characterized by inability to reproduce even an approximation to the section, and are frequently characterized by a "medley of viewpoints;" that is, the child may draw part of the solid object, with perhaps one or more smaller figures inside it to represent the section. Evidently it cannot "abstract" the section from the object and the operation of cutting. The second stage is characterized by progressively greater ability to imagine the section and to draw it, although imperfectly. In the third stage the problem is solved at once and the section drawn correctly. Piaget mentions ages four to six years as characteristic of the first stage, about five and a half to seven years for the second. The age ranges found in this study are shown in Table 5. Again, the "mixed" category is very large, indi-

TABLE 5

CHARACTERISTICS OF RESPONSES TO ITEMS IN SUBGROUP V
(6 ITEMS) IN TERMS OF AGE

	Typical behavior	N	Mode	Range
Stage A	No reproduction of cross-section; often a "medley of viewpoints."	82	7.3	5.3–11.3
Stage B	Partially correct drawings of sections.	1	9.8	—
Stage C	Fully correct drawings, and correct predictions of cross-sections.	12	9.3	5.8–11.3
Mixed		99	—[a]	5.3–10.3

[a] No clear mode.

cating that the "mental construction" of a section is not an "all-or-nothing" affair; that is, consistency from one situation or object to another is comparatively exceptional. Moreover, only one child was consistently in stage B, and very few consistently in stage C. The age overlap for the stages is again enormous.

Subgroup VI similarities and proportions

The results are quite straightforward in this group. In the first stage, "drawing a similar figure" means simply "drawing another figure around the given model"—usually with more or less straight sides, and usually the right number of sides, but with no attempt to make corresponding sides in model and drawing parallel. The second stage is characterized by fairly careful drawing, but inconsistency in achieving parallels. In the third stage, a similar enlarged figure is correctly produced, with all sides parallel to the corresponding sides of the model. Piaget distinguishes a number of substages in this development, but since the evidence in Table 6 indicates that it is not possible to assign most children to a category, even when just three categories are employed, further refinements were not attempted.

TABLE 6

CHARACTERISTICS OF RESPONSES TO ITEMS IN SUBGROUP VI
(6 ITEMS) IN TERMS OF AGE

	Typical behavior	*N*	*Mode*	*Range*
Stage A	No idea of drawing parallels to produce similar figures.	8	6.3	5.6– 9.3
Stage B	Inconsistency in drawing sides parallel to model to produce similar figures.	14	7.3	5.3– 9.3
Stage C	All sides drawn parallel to those of model.	10	—[a]	7.3–10.3
Mixed		162	—[a]	5.3–11.3

[a] No clear mode.

Subgroup VII coordination of perspectives

Only two of Piaget's stages are relevant here, each one divided into two substages. In practice it seems impossible to distinguish between the middle pair of these substages (IIB and IIIA), both of which are "transitional," and have been labeled B in the present classification.[3]

The behavior characteristic of stage A (Piaget's stage IIA) is a lack of ability to coordinate position of the doll ("point of view") with a particular view of the model, the child either always choosing the picture of the model as seen from his own position, or choosing a picture at

3. The division into stages does not always correspond very closely with the division used by Piaget, who tends to distinguish a number of substages. In general the system used here is to distinguish the (usually easily recognizable) stages A and C, and to lump together all "transitional" responses as stage B.

random. Stage C again is the stage characterized by ability to coordinate position and perspective view of model perfectly, and stage B includes various partly correct transitional types of response. Again, responses were observed in all three stages, A, B, and C, but there was a preponderance of "mixed" responses. Table 7 gives the relevant data. Rather exceptionally, Piaget mentions the number of children observed in this

TABLE 7

CHARACTERISTICS OF RESPONSES TO ITEMS IN SUBGROUP VII
(2 ITEMS) IN TERMS OF AGE

	Typical behavior	*N*	*Mode*	*Range*
Stage A	No coordination of position and "point of view" of doll. Chooses view from *own* position, or at random.	44	5.8	5.3– 9.3[a]
Stage B	Partially correct, transitional responses.	30	8.3	5.3–10.3[a]
Stage C	Complete coordination of position and perspective view of model.	11	9.8	8.3–10.3
Mixed		109	7.3	5.3–11.3

[a] Plus a "straggler" at 11.3.

case (Piaget and Inhelder, 1956, p. 212), namely, one hundred, between the ages of four and twelve years. However, he fails to give any indication of age ranges, except to mention that stage C is usually found after about seven to eight years of age. As a matter of fact, the separation into stages is here rather clearer than in most of the other subgroups, despite the large mixed category, and the age ranges and modes are approximately what one might expect from Piaget's thory, except that the upper limits for stages A and B are rather high.

Quantitative Treatment of Results

A point score was devised, points being awarded for correct answers and solutions to problems. Also, an A score was computed, which consisted simply of a count of the number of responses classified as in group A. It should be noted that A responses are those which show no evidence of grasping spatial concepts of widely different types; for instance, in subgroup I an A response indicates inability to arrange a set of posts in a straight line, except in the topological sense of making the posts neighbors, whereas in subgroup VII it indicates inability to understand the coordination of position and perspective. However, the A score can be considered a rather general measure of primitiveness in grasping spatial concepts, and it is not surprising that it has a fairly high negative correlation with the point score, as shown in Table 8. This table also shows a number of other test characteristics: as one would expect, there is a considerable correlation with age, and an even more marked correlation with mental age. The partial correlations indicate that mental age is a source of variation at least as important as chronologoical age alone. This result is in conformity with other findings on the relation of Piage-

TABLE 8
TEST CHARACTERISTICS[a]

Items correlated	r	N
Total score, A score	−.69	194
Total score, M.A.	.69	152
Total score, C.A.	.56	194
Total score, M.A. (C.A. constant)	.52	152
Total score, C.A. (M.A. constant)	.22	152
Total score, I.Q.	.31	152
Total score (test-retest)	.95	20

[a] Test mean = 91.6; standard deviation = 20.45; error of measurement = 4.8.

tian stages to mental and chronological age (Dodwell, 1961; Harker, 1960; Carpenter, 1955). A group of 20 children was re-tested with the test approximately one week after the first administration, and the test-retest correlation demonstrates that the test is satisfactorily reliable. This may be an overestimate of reliability, since the children were drawn from a fairly wide age range. However, calculation of r from the actual differences between scores on first and second administrations of the test, according to Gulliksen's formula (Gulliksen, 1950, formula (5), chap. 4, p. 40) yielded a value of .92 indicating a genuinely high reliability.

Table 9 shows the intercorrelations between the scores on items in the various subgroups. The "battery" is too small to make a factor analysis worthwhile, but a cluster analysis (Harman, 1960) was performed to determine which, if any, of the tests could be considered as forming well-defined clusters. The analysis was entirely inconclusive: there is no evidence to suggest clustering. Inspection of the intercorrelations does not suggest any striking hypotheses or obvious points of confirmation

Table 9

Intercorrelations of Subgroup Scores

Subgroup	Subgroup						
	I	II	III	IV	V	VI	VII
I		.37	.40	.38	.20	.07	.40
II			.46	.50	.25	.43	.38
III				.64	.34	.05	.30
IV					.24	.49	.52
V						.10	.35
VI							.37
VII							

for Piaget's theory; the fact that all the correlations are positive is not surprising, and probably is due simply to the fact that all the types of geometrical conceptualization tested tend to improve with age. On the basis of Piagetian theory, one might expect high correlations between groups of items apparently requiring use of similar or identical operations, but in the absence of any evidence for clustering, there is no point in pursuing speculations on this point.

It has been noted already that, within subgroups of the test, a mixed category of responses is generally far more common than any one of the pure categories, and usually the mixed category is larger than all the others put together. It is possible that, within the mixed category of a subgroup, meaningful patterns of response can be discerned. On the other hand, it may be that the "mixed" answers are fairly irregular in their patterns of occurrence. To attempt to resolve this question, all responses to items in subgroup III were analyzed in the following way:[4]

There are seven items in the subgroup, and the response to each one could be classified as an A, B, or C response, in terms of its adequacy, as defined above.

The record of every child that had at least one fully correct (type C) response in the subgroup was examined.[5] In order to discover what pattern, if any, there might be among the various responses given by these children, the frequency of occurrence of correct responses to *both*

4. Subgroup III was chosen for this analysis partly because it seemed to be one of the most interesting subgroups, partly because the sorts of operation required to answer questions correctly seemed to be fairly easily recognizable.

5. This choice of response type is arbitrary, but serves to keep the figures down to a reasonable size. Also, it emphasizes the distinction between correct and incorrect responses, which is probably the most reliable of the possible partitions of the responses.

of all possible pairs of items in the subgroup was computed, as was frequency of occurrence of all the various possible combinations of pairs of correct and incorrect answers. These are shown in Table 10. It is immediately evident from this table that consistent type-C responses are the exception rather than the rule: in only one case (items 9-12) does the

TABLE 10

RELATIONS BETWEEN STAGES IN SUBGROUP III

Stages[b]	Items[a]										
	7-8	7-9	7-10	7-11	7-12	7-13	8-9	8-10	8-11	8-12	8-13
C-C	14	10	1	4	13	4	28	2	14	25	8
C-B	5	8	14	5	0	12	17	33	14	1	23
C-A	0	1	5	11	6	1	4	14	20	24	19
B-C	25	60	4	29	65	18	47	3	19	48	15
A-C	0	0	0	0	0	0	2	0	0	2	1

	9-10	9-11	9-12	9-13	10-11	10-12	10-13	11-12	11-13	12-13
C-C	4	23	55	15	4	4	0	21	11	13
C-B	51	15	3	34	1	1	2	3	14	33
C-A	23	37	17	28	2	0	3	5	8	29
B-C	2	11	11	8	22	41	15	13	2	2
A-C	0	0	9	2	8	29	8	42	10	7

[a] The items are: 7, draw smallest box; 8, draw largest box; 9, subdivide line; 10, imaginary end product of subdivision; 11, number of lines in longer line; 12, number of points in a line; 13, subdivide box.
[b] The stages (rows) are interpreted as follows: C-C means that, for the pair of items at the column head (items 7 and 8 in the first column), type C responses were made to both—in this case by 14 children. C-B means that the first of the pair (item 7, in the first column) was answered with a C response, but the record of the pair (item 8, in the first column) with a B response. There were five children in this category, for the first column. The remaining row symbols are interpreted in a similar way.

number of consistent type-C responses exceed every other type. This is hardly surprising, since it has already been noted that a mixed category (for children rather than test items) is the single largest category. Of more interest is the question of the relations which hold among the various sorts of mixed-type responses. The important ones appear to be the following:

(i) Starting with the last line in the table, one observes that a child that answers items 7, 8, or 9 with an A response has almost no likelihood of giving any C responses. On the other hand, type A responses to items 10, 11, and 12 are quite frequently associated with C responses to other (later) items. This is quite consistent with what one would expect on the basis of Piaget's theory: items 7 and 8 are concerned with the operations of seriation (according to Piaget) and an A response indicates no understanding of this operation. Without this understanding, one could hardly expect correct solutions to other problems about points, limits, and so on to be given. Similarly, item 9 is concerned with subdivision of a line, and some understanding of this operation would seem to be a prerequisite of correct solutions to the later items.

(ii) On the other hand, it is quite clear, from inspection of the fourth line in the table, that B responses to the first two items (7 and 8) are readily compatible with correct solutions to later items, but this is again consistent with Piaget's theory, since the B response in this case (described earlier) involves drawing a *series* of squares, rather than the smallest or largest square immediately, that is, an understanding of seriation, but not one that is applied immediately to the problem of "largest" and "smallest."

(iii) It is clear that the marked difference between lines four and five has disappeared, and even possibly been reversed, in the last few columns of the table, although it is difficult to see why such a reversal should occur.

(iv) The interpretation of the difference between lines four and five for the lefthand columns of the table given is supported to some extent by the frequencies in lines two and three. There are no consistent differences between these two rows, and of course neither one represents any possible "learning" effect. Rather they give an estimate of what might be termed "random" moves between stages.

(v) A rather striking fact emerges when one compares, within a column, the sum of the frequencies of rows two and three with the sum of the frequencies for rows four and five. There is an inverse relationship; a rank order correlation yields a highly significant negative value of $\rho = -.75$. This might be interpreted in the following way: if an item is one which can be solved on the basis of learning within the test situation, there is a low probability that it will be answered wrongly when earlier items have been answered correctly. On the other hand, if the solution is not so learnable, there is a greater chance of the items being answered incorrectly following earlier correct solutions. This is only an interpretation, and it is clear that the evidence is far from conclusive on this point.

(vi) By inspection, the most "learnable" responses are to questions 9, 11, and 12, and the least "learnable" are correct responses to items 10 and 13. It may be noted that these last two are questions to which the child had to answer in terms of what he could *imagine* rather than what he could *do*.

The sorts of relation found among the answers to questions in subgroup III were not common to all subgroups. Similar analyses were undertaken for subgroups I and IV which showed, in the first place, that subgroup I is much more homogeneous than the others, in the sense that the frequency of "both correct" was always higher than for any other response pair. Secondly, for subgroup I the lines corresponding to lines 2-5 of Table 9 showed none of the patterns described above for subgroup III. Subgroup IV, on the other hand, showed the same pattern of negative correlation between lines 2 and 3 on the one hand, and lines 4 and 5 on the other. Inspection of these four lines in Table 11 seems to indicate that while "learnability" is higher in this group than in subgroup III, items 16 and 17 are especially high in this characteristic. Interestingly enough, these two items involve sorting and identifying pictures, whereas the remaining items in the subgroup concern actual manipulation of the jars and their contents.

Thus, some of the points that emerge in the detailed breakdown of the mixed responses appear to be compatible with Piaget's theory, and

TABLE 11

RELATIONS BETWEEN STAGES IN SUBGROUP IV

Items[a]

Stages	14-15	14-16	14-17	14-18	14-19	14-20	14-21	15-16	15-17
C-C	26	38	43	19	31	25	10	38	37
C-B	18	4	1	16	9	9	33	5	6
C-A	1	1	0	8	4	12	3	1	0
B-C	18	26	31	14	18	18	7	27	38
A-C	0	44	87	9	18	37	20	43	86

	15-18	15-19	15-20	15-21	16-17	16-18	16-19	16-20	16-21
C-C	18	28	25	11	102	41	59	59	29
C-B	15	13	6	32	5	60	44	12	79
C-A	8	1	9	1	1	14	12	38	4
B-C	15	18	20	7	44	7	9	19	10
A-C	8	17	34	27	11	1	4	2	1

	17-18	17-19	17-20	17-21	18-19	18-20	18-21	19-20	19-21	20-21
C-C	36	62	73	35	28	31	10	39	16	19
C-B	89	70	25	120	9	6	30	9	48	58
C-A	33	27	64	6	3	6	3	16	2	2
B-C	6	5	8	2	30	36	16	33	17	6
A-C	0	0	1	0	6	14	11	7	5	12

[a] The items are: 14, predict water level in tilted straight jar; 15, predict water level in tilted round jar; 16, tilt pictures to show correct levels; 17, sort pictures showing level; 18, draw boat and mast 45°; 19, draw boat and mast 90°; 20, draw plumbline 45°; 21, put posts on mountain.

even to some degree tend to confirm it [for example, points (i), (ii), and (iii)]. Others are neutral with respect to the theory.

Discussion

No doubt more elaborate analyses of the relations between single items both in the same and in different subgroups might be attempted, but it appears to me that a sufficiently detailed exposition has been given to show, as has been shown before (for example, Dodwell, 1960, 1962), that the patterns which emerge in this sort of study of cognitive development are complex, and certainly not completely compatible with Piaget's statements about the topic. However, it should also be noted that further examination within mixed categories (as in the latter part of the results section) might reveal further factors which are consonant with the theory.

Since the sorts of behavior which Piaget describes as characteristic for certain ages and stages of development have been observed, and since his theoretical account is a satisfying, coherent one (see, for instance, Hunt, 1961), it seems sensible to look for possible reasons why the pattern of development should be blurred rather than clear, rather than to reject the theory out of hand, especially if one has no better substitute to offer. I have suggested elsewhere (Dodwell, 1960, 1962) that the obvious factors which might tend to disrupt the clear pattern of stages Piaget describes, are things such as special interests and training, amount of formal instruction, and the difficulties of learning to apply a set of rules or operations learned in one context to a new situation. Part of Piaget's theory is that, once an operation or grouping of operations has been acquired, its deployment in novel situations should present few, if any, difficulties: however, this is not a logical requirement of the theory, and it seems entirely reasonable to assume that such response generalization is halting and inadequate at first, but improves with practice. Any school boy who has learned (and understood) Newton's laws, for example, and has subsequently had to apply them to problems in mechanics, would no doubt agree that this can happen. It would certainly be interesting to study more intensively the possibilities of teaching children to apply operations already used correctly in one situation to a second situation in which the operations are not applied spontaneously, and to compare such ability to learn with that of children who do not apply the operations correctly in any situation. If Piaget is close to being correct, rapid learning would be expected in the first instance, virtually no learning in the second.

No attempt was made to validate the test described. No obvious external criterion is available, since geometry is not taught in school to children of the age range under consideration. The content validity of the test seems to be high; however, probably the best way to validate a test of this sort would be through a factorial study, using established measures of spatial aptitude and understanding. Such a study was beyond the scope of the present investigation.

It has been pointed out before, and is worth emphasizing again, that an adequate understanding of the development and attainment of concepts in children will not be reached through the type of rather general investigation here reported. Such investigations should be supplemented by more intensive longitudinal studies which attempt to unravel some of the threads out of which the fabric of intellectual growth is woven.

REFERENCES

Carpenter, T. E. (1955). A pilot study for a quantitative investigation of Jean Piaget's original work on concept formation. *Educ. Rev.*, 7, 142-149.

Dodwell, P. C. (1960). Children's understanding of number and related concepts. *Canad. J. Psychol.*, 14, 191-205.

Dodwell, P. C. (1961). Children's understanding of number concepts: characteristics of an individual and of a group test. *Canad. J. Psychol.*, 15, 29-36.

Dodwell, P. C. (1962). Relations between the understanding of the logic of classes and of cardinal number in children. *Canad. J. Psychol.*, 16, 152-60.

Gulliksen, Harold (1950). *Theory of mental tests.* New York: Wiley.

Harker, Wilda H. (1960). Children's number concepts: ordination and cardination. Unpublished Master's thesis, Queen's University.

Harman, H. H. (1960). *Modern factor analysis.* Chicago: University of Chicago Press.

Hunt, J. McV. (1961). *Intelligence and experience.* New York: Ronald.

Piaget, J. (1950). *The psychology of intelligence.* London: Routledge.

Piaget, J., and B. Inhelder (1956). *The child's conception of space.* London: Routledge.

---

1. Can you identify any specific kinds of preschool learning that would fall into the category of spatial concepts or relations?
2. Can you identify any specific kinds of "formal" learning in school that would involve spatial relations?
3. Do the qualitative observations have any implications for elementary schools?

14 JOACHIM F. WOHLWILL

From Perception to Inference: A Dimension of Cognitive Development

Wohlwill presents a theoretical discussion of the relationship between sensory perception and conceptualization as related to cognitive development. In Piaget's "formal operational" stage of development, the individual is capable of dealing logically with variables, combinations, etc., in the abstract. That is, he is not tied to perceptual cues in order to engage in thought processes about some object or event.

Parts of this paper by Wohlwill may be somewhat specialized for the reader who is just beginning to study cognitive development. The overall analysis of perceptual activity and conceptual thinking, however, should offer some insight into how a child thinks.

Introduction

How shall we conceptualize the changes which the child's mental processes undergo during the course of development? This question has been answered most frequently in terms that emphasize an increase in powers of abstraction or an increased intervention of symbolic processes. More generally, one might say that there is a decreasing dependence of behavior on information in the immediate stimulus field. For instance, in the delayed reaction experiment we find that the maximum delay that may intervene between the presentation of a stimulus and a discriminatory response increases with age (Munn, 1955, pp. 306ff.). Similarly, much of Piaget's work on the development of concepts—particularly that on the conservation of length, weight, volume, number, and so forth —is interpretable in terms of the increasing stability of concepts in the face of (irrelevant) changes in the stimulus field.

We have here, then, the makings of a significant dimension along which to analyze the course of cognitive development. The eventual aim of this paper is to suggest a more systematic approach for such an analy-

Reprinted from *Monographs of the Society for Research in Child Development*, Vol. 27, No. 2, 1962, pp. 87-112, by permission of the editor and the author. Dr. Wohlwill, from Clark University, is an authority on cognitive development and continues to research this field.

sis, based on certain principles relating to the ways in which the organism utilizes sensory information. However, the realization of this aim presupposes an adequate understanding of the interrelation between perception and thinking; it should therefore prove valuable to undertake a prior examination, in some detail, of the various ways in which this relation has been conceptualized, and more particularly of the developmental aspects of this problem.

A prefatory note of caution—given the notoriously elusive and ill-defined nature of such concepts as perception and thinking, no single, uniformly acceptable characterization of their relation is to be expected. For the same reason, the analysis of the developmental changes in the relationship between these two functions is beset with obvious difficulties. Nevertheless we shall find that the alternative formulations that have been proposed to deal with this problem, and especially Piaget's illuminating comparison between perceptual and conceptual development, are not only of great interest in their own right, but contribute materially to the dimensional analysis of mental development.

Three Views of the Perception-Conception Relation

Let us start by reviewing three different ways in which theorists have conceptualized the relationship between perception and conception. These three clearly do not exhaust all the different positions that have been taken on this question, but they probably represent the major trends of thought; of greater importance, they define three sharply differentiated foci from which this problem may be approached, so that their consideration should bring out some major theoretical issues. It should be noted at the outset that all three of these viewpoints are essentially nongenetic, at least insofar as any explicit treatment of development is concerned.

The gestalt position

One of the solutions to the problem at hand is to take a model of perception and to attempt to fit it intact to the area of thinking, thus reducing these two functions to a common set of basic processes. This appears to be in large measure the course followed by the Gestalt school in its efforts to interpret phenomena in the field of the thought processes —as seen in Köhler's (1925) classical work on the problem solving behavior of his chimpanzees or Wertheimer's (1959) analysis of "productive thinking" in the solution of mathematical and other conceptual problems. In these works we find a heavy emphasis on such quasiperceptual terms as "insight," "restructuring of the field," "closure," and the like, which seem to represent the sum, if not the substance, of the repertoire of concepts used by the Gestaltists to handle the processes of human reasoning. This point is expressed quite explicitly by Koffka in *The Growth of the Mind*. After paying lip service to the increasing importance in the development of thinking of psychological processes affecting a delay between a stimulus and a consequent reaction of the individual Koffka (1924), states that:

> . . . the ideational field depends most intimately upon the sensory, and any means that enable us to become independent of immediate perception are rooted in perception, and, in truth, only lead us from one perception to another.

This formulation, quite apart from its rather meager empirical yield, does not seem to have proved overly successful in its theoretical power. Not only has a major portion of problems in the field of thinking been left aside (e.g., concept formation, the nature of symbolic processes, and so forth), but even when applied to the situations with which the Gestaltists have concerned themselves, the explanatory worth of their concepts appears quite limited.[1] Thus, interpretations of problem solving in terms of restructuring of the field have a somewhat hollow ring in the absence of attention to the question of how a Gestalt may be restructured and of what keeps it from being appropriately structured at the outset. In fact, the whole problem of the ways in which conceptual activity may *transform* an immediate percept is ignored. Paraphrasing Guthrie's dictum about Tolman, whom he accused of "leaving the rat buried in thought," one might therefore be justified in criticizing the Gestaltists for leaving the organism too readily short-circuited in closure to permit him to think.

Last, but by no means least, the a prioristic and thus inherently nongenetic bias of the Gestalt school should be noted. In their work, even when it deals with the behavior of children, as in the books by Koffka and Wertheimer cited earlier, there is little interest in matters relating to developmental changes underlying such behavior—a limitation for which Piaget (1946, 1954), among others, has repeatedly taken them to task.

Bruner's position

Let us examine next a point of view diametrically opposed to the Gestaltists, one which regards perception as basically an inferential pro-

---

1. The work of such investigators as Duncker and Maier might be cited in refutation of this statement. But these psychologists really fall outside the classical Gestalt tradition, utilizing concepts that bear little direct relationship to the principles of this school of thought—cf. Maier's "functional fixedness" and the general attention given to problems of set.

cess, in which the perceiver plays a maximal—and maximally idiosyncratic—role in interpreting, categorizing, or transforming the stimulus
input. This view is represented generally by the latter-day functionalist
school of perception, particularly that of the transactionalist variety. Its
most explicit statement has, however, come from Bruner (1957), according to whom:

> Perception involves an act of categorization . . . the nature of the in-
> ference from cue to identity in perception is . . . in no sense different
> from other kinds of categorical inferences based on defining attributes
> . . . are discontinuous as one moves from perceptual to more concep-
> tual activities. (pp. 123f)

While Bruner claims neither that all perception processes can be en-
compassed in such a theory nor that it precludes a distinction between
perceptual and conceptual inference, he does argue that the theory
covers a wide variety of perceptual phenomena which conform in many
essential respects to principles akin to those observed in the conceptual
sphere.

Bruner's formulation raises a number of difficult questions. What is
the implicit definition of perception on which it is based? What is the
role assigned to structural aspects of the stimulus in such a model of
perception? Most importantly, perhaps, to what extent does the operation of conceptual mechanisms in perception depend on conditions of
inadequate or impoverished stimulation? Bruner has not ignored this
latter problem, but he is inclined to dismiss its importance; for example,
he reduces the difference between ordinary and tachistoscopic perception
to a matter of degree—inferential mechanisms are always at work, but
categorizations vary in the univocality of their coding of stimulus cues
in proportion to the amount of stimulus information provided. Thus, for
Bruner (1957), vertical perception is a joint function of redundancy in
the stimulus and the accessibility of appropriate categorizing systems,
in the following sense:

> Where accessibility of categories reflects environmental probabilities,
> the organism is in the position of requiring less stimulus input, less re-
> dundancy of cues for the appropriate categorization of objects . . . the
> more inappropriate the readiness, the greater the input or redundancy
> of cues required for appropriate categorization to occur. (p. 133)

We will find this notion of some interest in connection with one of
the dimensions to be proposed later for tracing the development from
a perceptual to an inferential level of cognitive functioning. For the
present, it may suffice to point out, as Piaget and Morf (1958a) have,
that Bruner's model of perception presupposes an adult perceiver; it
would be difficult to apply it to the perceptions of a very young child,

whose conceptual categories were still in the process of formation. Not surprisingly, under the circumstances, we find that Bruner has thus far failed, as much as the Gestaltists, to consider the developmental aspects of perception and thinking, either in the paper discussed here or in his monograph on thinking (Bruner, Goodnow, and Austin, 1956).

Brunswik's position

The third viewpoint to be considered is that of Brunswik, who occupies a place somewhere between the two poles just discussed, emphasizing as he does the differences between perception and thinking, rather than attempting to explain one in terms of the other. While his untimely death kept him from pursuing this question beyond the sketchy treatment of it in his last work (Brunswik, 1956), his ideas still may contribute significantly to a workable distinction between perception and thinking—a point which we shall have occasion to acknowledge in the last portion of this paper.

Brunswik starts out by drawing a comparison—based on an actual empirical study—between the achievements of perceptual size judgments in a constancy situation and those of arithmetic reasoning where the equivalent task is presented in symbolic form. The perceptual task yielded the typical clustering of settings within a fairly narrow range of the point of objective equality; in contrast, a majority of the answers given to the arithmetic reasoning task coincided exactly with the correct value, but several subsidiary clusters of answers were found which were quite discretely separated from this mode and which corresponded to false solutions of the problem.

Generalizing from this example—the significance of which is obviously purely demonstrational—Brunswik (1956) contrasts the machinelike precision of the reasoning processes with the more approximate achievements of perception.

> The entire pattern of the reasoning solutions . . . resembles the switching of trains at a multiple junction, with each of the possible courses being well organized and of machinelike precision, yet leading to drastically different destinations . . . the combination of channelled mediation, on the one hand, with precision or else grotesquely scattered error in the results, on the other, may well be symptomatic of what appears to be the pure case of explicit intellectual fact-finding.
>
> On the other hand, . . . perception must simultaneously integrate many different avenues of approach, or cues. . . . The various rivalries and compromises that characterize the dynamics of check and balance in perception must be seen as chiefly responsible for the above noted relative infrequency of precision. On the other hand, the organic multiplicity of factors entering the process constitutes an effective safeguard against drastic error. (pp. 91f)

This conception of the difference between perception and thinking, while hardly exhaustive, is a fairly intriguing as well as plausible one. It has, moreover, definite implications for the analysis of the development of reasoning, although Brunswik has not given these explicit consideration. It is pertinent, however, to note his suggestion in regard to the developmental changes in color and shape constancy which he studied in his early work; he attributed the decline in constancy found in adolescence to the intervention of cognitive mechanisms which lessened the *need* for precise veridical perceptual achievements (cf. Brunswik, 1956, p. 91).

Developmental Approaches to the Interrelationship Between Perception and Conception

The three contrasting positions just discussed serve to sketch out the boundaries within which one can trace the course of cognitive development from perception to thinking. As noted above, of the three positions, Brunswik's embodies the sharpest differentiation between these two functions and will be found the most useful for our purposes; in fact, we will presently see a striking similarity between Brunswik's view and Piaget's conception of this problem.

The views of Piaget

The Two Piagets

Let us turn, then, to the work of Piaget, who has given us by far the most explicit and formalized comparison between perception and thought and between their respective developmental patterns. We should note at the outset that there appear to be at least two altogether different Piagets. On the one hand, we have Piaget, the psychologist of the development of intelligence, author of a long and impressive series of books covering an array of cognitive functions (language, reasoning, judgment) and of dimensions of experience (time, number, quantity, space, and so forth). On the other hand, there is Piaget, the psychologist of perception, author or sponsor of an equally impressive and even longer series of studies on a variety of perceptual phenomena, published in the *Archives de Psychologie*.

To these two divergent areas of interest correspond two sharply differentiated modes of approach to research. The "clinical" method which Piaget has followed in his study of the development of intelligence, with its deliberate avoidance of standardized procedures and quantitative analysis, stands in marked contrast to the more traditional experimental approach which he has favored in his perception research. Furthermore, while Piaget's aim in his work on thinking is essentially a genetic one, his purpose in tracing developmental changes in perception appears to be rather different. The developmental dimension in the perception research represents primarily an additional variable, coordinate with other situational, experimentally manipulated variables through which basic perceptual processes are exhibited. In this connection it is worth pointing to Piaget's (1956, p. 33) view that developmental stages exist in the realm of intellectual, but not of perceptual, development. We will consider later the possible grounds for such a position.

In view of these various symptoms of a double personality, it is hardly surprising to find Piaget attempting to divorce thinking from perception and to minimize their mutual interrelatedness. Like East and West, "ne'er the twain shall meet"—or hardly ever. One of the very few instances where they do meet, i.e., where Piaget confronts perception and thinking in the context of the same experimental situation, provides an illuminating picture of his basic position. This is a study by Piaget and Taponier (1956), devoted in part to the investigation of a constant error arising in the comparison of the length of two parallel horizontal lines, drawn to form the top and bottom of a parallelogram (without the sides). In this situation the top line tends to be slightly overestimated; this illusion increases, however, from a zero-order effect at the age of 5 years to a maximum at about 8 years; for adults the extent of the error is intermediate. Piaget contrasts this developmental pattern with that obtained when the same judgment is made in the context of a cognitive task: The two equal lines are presented initially in direct visual superposition, so as to be perceived as equal; the top one is then displaced horizontally, the arrangement of the two lines corresponding to that of the previous problem. In this cognitive task, it is the 5-year-old children who show a pronounced bias in their judgment, which leads them to pronounce the two lines as unequal following the displacement. In other words, there is an absence of "conservation of length" in the face of configurational changes. By the age of 8, however, the equality of the lines is maintained fairly uniformly—conservation of length has been acquired. On the strength of these findings Piaget argues against a simple perceptual explanation for the young children's lack of conservation; since their error of perceptual judgment is at a minimum, their failure to maintain the equality of the two lines in the cognitive task must be due to other factors.

This example illustrates well the independence, in Piaget's thinking, between perception and conception or inference—even at the stage of "intuitive thought" where the child's responses appear to be governed by particular aspects of the stimulus field. In fact, as we shall note, Piaget (1946, 1957) has repeatedly stressed that these two functions follow very different paths and arrive at different ends during the course of development. With Brunswik, although on somewhat different grounds, he has been impressed by the statistical, probabilistic nature of perceptual judgments, as opposed to the precise, determinate, and phenomenologically certain results achieved through conceptual inference.

The Concept of "Partial Isomorphisms"

Piaget's most recent and most systematic treatment of this question is contained in an article (Piaget and Morf, 1958a) the title of which states his position succinctly: "The partial isomorphisms between logical structures and perceptual structures." In spite of his characteristic reification of such concepts as "structures" and "schemata," Piaget is concerned here with the correspondence between the achievements or end products of perceptual as against conceptual mechanisms, the mechanisms themselves being left largely out of the picture.

In this paper Piaget and Morf discuss a number of phenomena which Werner (1957) has considered as illustrative of "analogous functions," i.e., functions serving similar ends but operating at different levels of cognitive organization. Like Werner, Piaget and Morf draw parallels between perceptual groupings and conceptual classes, between invariance in perception (the constancies) and in conception (the conservations); between the perception of stimulus relationships and the conceptual representation of relationships at the symbolic level. For these authors however, these analogies, or isomorphisms, are only partial; they emphasize, rather, the ways in which perceptual mechanisms differ from the corresponding inferential ones. They point out that perceptual phenomena generally do not meet the requirements of the fundamental operations of logic (reversibility, additivity, transitivity, inversion) except in a limited and approximate sense. For example, with respect to additivity, a line divided into a number of equal segments is actually perceived as slightly longer than its undivided counterpart (the Oppel-Kundt illusion); similarly, in the case of figure-ground reversals the perceptual inversion fails to satisfy the logical criterion of inversion insofar as the boundary line always remains part of the figure. To these examples relating to the logic of classes are added several others involving the logic of relationships. Thus, lack of additivity is illustrated in threshold phenomena, where two subthreshold differences when added together may yield a suprathreshold difference (i.e., $= + = \rightarrow \neq$ is possible in perception). Again, a person's difficulty in judging projective size is considered a case of lack of inversion of the relationship between retinal size, distance and perceived size ($r \times d = p$): given r and d jointly, the subject may "solve" for p, but he cannot obtain r by "dividing through" by d—i.e., by abstracting size from distance.

Finally, Piaget and Morf argue that there are "pre-inferences" in perception which are partially isomorphic to the inferential mechanisms of logical reasoning. Indeed, all perceptual judgment *qua* judgment is thought to involve a decision-process partaking to a greater or lesser extent of the character of an inference from the sensory information given. The extent to which it does so depends on the level of complexity (mediation?) of the judgment, ranging from the simple, direct judgments found in psychophysical thresholds to judgments dependent on "perceptual activity" as in size constancy. Here the difference between these perceptual pre-inferences and conceptual inferences can be found not only in the certainty or univocality of the outcome of the conceptual inference, but also in the subjects' lack of awareness of the separate steps in the inferential chain in the perceptual pre-inferences.[2]

The Perception-Conception Relationship in the Development of the Child

Despite the semblance of a link between perception and inference represented in Piaget's concept of "perceptual pre-inferences," the overall impression one obtains from his treatment of partial isomorphisms, as well as from other discussions of the differences between these two functions, is of a parallelistic conception—perception and thinking represent two sharply differentiated processes which display certain structural similarities, but even more important differences. Developmentally, too, he considers perception and thinking as following two separate and independent courses, as may be seen in his comparison of the development of the "conservations" from the conceptual realm with that of the perceptual constancies (Piaget, 1957).

Conservation may be exemplified by the invariance of the volume of a liquid under changes in its container, as when water is poured from a narrow glass into a shallow bowl. Piaget invokes here a gradual process of "equilibration," leading the child from an initial stage at which he focuses only on one biasing aspect of the stimulus (e.g., the height of the container) through an oscillatory stage where he shifts back and forth between this aspect and a competing one (here the width of the

2. This specification of lack of awareness as a characteristic of pre-inferential processes in perception clearly brings to mind Helmholtz's "unconscious inference." Piaget is careful, however, to dissociate himself from those (e.g., Cassirer) who have read into this concept implications of a ratiomorphic process.

container), to a third stage in which the compensatory role of these two aspects begins to be suspected, and then to the final realization, with perfect certitude on the part of the child, of absolute, exact conservation, despite the perceptual changes. In the perceptual constancies, on the other hand, all aspects of the stimulus field, and notably the two stimuli to be compared, are always included in the individual's perceptual exploration of the situation, at least from a very early level of development. The only developmental change is in the extent and efficacy of this exploration or, conversely, in the potency of distorting factors present in this situation. These factors (e.g., a favored attention to the near object) bring about a relative lack of constancy in younger children, which is reduced in later childhood due to more intensive and complete perceptual exploration of the stimuli. But in the domain of perception the exact compensations achieved in the fourth stage of the development of conservation are not realized; instead, the compensations either fall short, as in most illusions, or actually lead to overcompensation, as in size constancy where overconstancy is the rule for adults.

We are now in a position to appreciate the reasons that probably motivated Piaget's denial of the existence of stages in perception, while affirming it for mental development. This distinction would be warranted, not in the sense that ontogenetic change in perception is necessarily more gradual, but rather in the sense that no meaningful structural criteria can be found in the area of quantitative perceptual judgments for distinguishing among different stages. The differences between successive perceptual achievements are necessarily only quantitative, whereas structural differences of a qualitative type, as in the above-mentioned sequence of stages, can be specified for conceptual development.

Some critical comments on Piaget's views

The foregoing presentation is a highly condensed distillation of Piaget's ideas in which many and frequently subtle lines of reasoning —not to mention a number of obscure points—have been omitted. It would therefore be somewhat inappropriate to base an evaluation of the merits of his argument on the picture of it given here. Nevertheless there are several criticisms of Piaget which can safely be anticipated; let us consider three of these points in particular. This will lead us to a somewhat more general question regarding Piaget's approach and will pave the way to a reformulation in the final portion of this paper.

The first objection that is bound to be raised concerns the nonoperational, and at times frankly mentalistic, terms used by Piaget which may seem to leave his analysis devoid of empirical, and perhaps even of theoretical, significance. For example, the criteria which he proposes for a diagnosis of inferential and pre-inferential processes are anything but unambiguous; indeed, his whole conceptual apparatus of schemata, operations, centrations, and so forth appears to lack direct empirical reference. Admittedly, Piaget does little to dispel this impression; concrete illustrations or applications are at best sporadic, and rigorous, systematic efforts at tying the empirical phenomena to his constructs are generally eschewed in favor of ad hoc and post hoc arguments.

It is important to remember, however, that Piaget's ideas on the interrelation between perceptual and conceptual development are not in themselves intended as a theoretical system; they serve rather to explicate, in formal terms, the different models underlying Piaget's theories of perception and intelligence, respectively. Furthermore, a few empirical studies relevant to this discussion can actually be cited (e.g., Piaget and Lambercier, 1946; Piaget and Taponier, 1956; Piaget and Morf, 1958b), and, while the first two of these are mainly demonstrational in character, Piaget and Morf's investigation of "perceptual pre-inferences" represents a step toward a more systematic empirical approach in this area through the manipulation of stimulus cues which change the nature of the task from a perceptual to a more nearly judgmental one. Unfortunately, the experimental design of this study leaves much to be desired, and the rather elaborate interpretations of the results seem unconvincing, if not unwarranted.

A second criticism might well be directed at Piaget's highly idealized conception of adult thought and, at the same time, at his insistence on the distorting and probabilistic character of the processes of immediate perception. In regard to the first point, Piaget has of course been repeatedly taken to ask for his inclination to see nothing but perfect logic and rationality in adult intelligence. His reliance on the principles of abstract logic as a model for human thinking has blinded him to the question of the breadth and stability of logic as *used* by the individual. In actual fact, of course, it is little more than a truism that logical principles understood in the abstract may not be applied in particular contexts (as in the atmosphere effects in syllogistic reasoning); likewise, even in the thinking of adults we find frequent instances of failures to apply or generalize a concept or principle when it is presented in unfamiliar ways or extended to novel situations. Differential generalization in the realm of thinking, furthermore, may have all the earmarks of the generalization *gradient* familiar from sensory phenomena.

Conversely, one may argue that Piaget overstates the case for the statistical, approximative, and generally biasing aspects of perceptual achievements. For quantitative judgments, to be sure, Piaget's probabilistic model seems quite appropriate and, indeed, seductively appealing in its simplicity and generality (cf. Piaget, 1955).[3] If we deal, on the other hand, with qualitative judgments and more particularly with judgments of identity or difference among discrete categories of stimuli, we typically find something closely approaching the reliability and specificity of conceptual classifications. Parenthetically, it may be noted that for Bruner it is precisely this type of perceptual judgment which serves as his model of perception, a fact which presumably accounts for some of the ratiomorphic flavor of this model.

If Piaget, then, even more than Brunswik, overestimates the discrepancy between the respective achievements of perception and thinking, he seems also to exaggerate their functional independence. The very fact that the conceptual processes of adults can be characterized along such dimensions as concrete-abstract testifies to the continual interplay between these two functions in much of conceptual activity. Pointing in the same direction are the results from one of Piaget's own experiments (Piaget and Lambercier, 1946) involving size-at-a-distance judgments in which the correct matches could be arrived at inferentially by the intermediary of a reference stimulus. At a certain age level (in middle childhood) there is clear evidence of a "perceptual compromise," showing the mutual interaction, rather than absolute separation, between perception and thinking. We shall attempt to show below how the conceptualization of the development of the symbolic processes in general can be furthered by assigning to perception a differential role in conceptual tasks at different age levels.

Piaget's Structural Approach

If one examines Piaget's thinking further in order to account for his espousal of some of the views just discussed, as well as for the somewhat unsatisfactory explanatory status of the constructs of his system, one finds a ready answer in the structural approach which he has consistently favored in his theory of intelligence. What he seems in fact to have done is to specify the *formal* properties of the products of the thought processes at different stages of development. This has led him inescapably to a picture of successive metamorphoses in the mental development of the child. From this structural point of view, the differences between the reasoning processes of a child lacking "reversibility" and "conservation" and an adult whose thinking does conform to these principles will in fact appear comparable to the differences between

3. An interesting feature of this model is its ability to account for the instances of nondeforming shape perception represented by the Gestaltists' "good figures" as a special case in which the relationships among the component parts are such as to yield, on the average, zero-order errors due to complete mutual compensation among the various possible distortions arising in such stimuli.

a caterpillar and a butterfly—or, to suggest a rather more pertinent analogy, between the pattern of locomotion of the 6-month infant and that of the child who has learned to walk. At the same time, this process of conceptual development will emerge as quite incommensurate with the much less dramatic and seemingly more continuous changes in the area of perception. However, it may be that the structural differences between the *products* of perceptual and conceptual processes obscure the continual interplay between the two in most, if not all, cognitive activity and therefore detract from a true appreciation of the differential involvement of perception in conceptual activity at varying developmental levels.

This interdependence between perception and thinking is the major premise for an alternative conception of intellectual development to be offered presently—a conception built around the person's dependence on various aspects of the information contained in the stimulus field. Such a conception, it is hoped, will contribute to a more truly experimental attack on the phenomena of mental development and their determinants, and thereby serve to supplement the structural analysis which Piaget has given us.

Three Dimensions of the Transition from Perception to Conception

If we ask ourselves how one might operationally distinguish between a purely perceptual and a purely inferential task, one criterion for inference would be the opportunity for the subject to supplement or replace the sensory data with information or knowledge not contained in the immediate stimulus field. As a matter of fact, this criterion differentiates the two portions of the study by Piaget and Taponier (1956) referred to earlier in which perception was contrasted to conception within the same stimulus context. The only difference between the two tasks was that in the conservation task the subjects were in effect informed beforehand of the equality of the two lines; this knowledge could take precedence over the lines themselves, and provide a basis for the subsequent judgment under altered stimulus conditions.

It seems possible, however, to formulate this criterion in quantitative, rather than all-or-none terms; that is, the relative amount of information which the subject needs from the stimulus field in order to make the judgment may vary over a wide range. The precise sense in which this quantitative criterion permits us to place perception and conception at opposite ends of a single dimension will be more fully explained below. For the moment, let us simply grant the possibility of doing so and propose this dimension, along with two others that are closely related, as a skeleton for the construction of an experimentally useful conceptual framework within which the cognitive development of the child may be traced.

The three dimensions along which perception and conception can be related may be specified as follows:

1. *Redundancy:* As one proceeds from perception to conception, the amount of redundant information required decreases.
2. *Selectivity:* As one proceeds from perception to conception, the amount of irrelevant information that can be tolerated without affecting the response increases.
3. *Contiguity:* As one proceeds from perception to conception, the spatial and temporal separation over which the total information contained in the stimulus field can be integrated increases.

It should be noted that these dimensions are stated in such a way as to be applicable either to intertask differences or to intersubject differences. Let us examine these three dimensions in some detail from the double standpoint of their relevance to the differentiation of perceptual from conceptual tasks on the one hand and to the analysis of changes during the course of development from a perceptual level of functioning to a conceptual level on the other hand—bearing in mind that these two terms are to be regarded as the poles of a continuum.

The dimension of redundancy

The dependence of perceptual functions on a high degree of redundancy in the stimulus input is rather easily demonstrated. Redundancy is basic to the differentiation of figure from ground; similarly it is a requisite for shape perception, the perception of speech, and to some extent for perceptual constancy (as shown in the multiplicity of overlapping cues involved in size constancy). In contrast, at the conceptual end we find redundancy reduced to an absolute minimum—typically zero—in the symbolic representation of mathematical or logical relationships. Whether the average adult is capable of operating consistently at this rarefied level is another question; the difficulty which most people experience in dealing with such nonredundant material, and the fact that a considerable amount of redundancy is built into our language, suggests that there are definite limitations in this respect. This conclusion is supported by work on concept formation, such as that of Bruner, Goodnow, and Austin (1956).

A developmental trend in the direction of decreasing reliance on redundant stimulation can be found in a variety of contexts. First of all, within the area of perception as such, the writer found considerable relevant evidence in a recent survey of the literature on perceptual development (Wohlwill, 1960). The clearest example of this point comes from studies on the identification of geometric or familiar-object stimuli on the basis of partial cues (e.g., Gollin, 1956), where the degree of completion of the figure necessary for its identification gradually decreases during the course of development. It seems justifiable, in fact, to regard such a task as becoming increasingly inferential as the amount of information which the subject has to "fill in" increases.[4] Indeed, this appears to be in part the import of Piaget and Morf's study of "perceptual pre-inference," in which the importance of continuity of lines serving as cues in a perceptual judgment was found to decrease with age.

Looking at redundancy in temporal sequences of events, furthermore, one might conceptualize the formation of Harlow's learning sets in terms of the reduction of redundant information to a minimum; it is of interest, therefore, that the rapidity of formation of such learning sets is strongly correlated with mental age (cf. Stevenson and Swartz, 1958).

This conception is relevant, incidentally, to Bruner's (1957) view of perception as an "act of categorization;" as we noted earlier, he has postulated that the amount of redundant information required for veridical identification is inversely proportional to the availability or accessibility of the particular category in the individual's repertoire of perceptual categories. While the intervention of a specific perceptual category cannot be equated to the operation of general symbolic processes, the fact that the action of both can in some sense compensate for lack of redundancy in the stimulus suggests that Bruner, too, is dealing essentially with a dimension running from immediate perception to conceptually mediated judgment.

The dimension of selectivity

The ubiquitous interaction between sensory dimensions in virtually every area of perception (psychophysical judgments and illusions, for example) bears ample testimony to the organism's very limited ability to dissociate relevant from irrelevant information at the perceptual level. At the level of thinking, on the other hand, this discussion represents a *sine qua non* of conceptual functions; the formation of conceptual classes clearly requires the systematic, selective abstraction of relevant (i.e., criterial) from irrelevant information. The same is true in the realm of

---

4. The view proposed here offers a resolution to a rather ticklish question which confronted Attneave (1954) in his attempt to analyze form perception in informational terms. Should a task in which the subject has to predict the "state" of a visual field at a point, on the basis of information obtained at preceding points of a contour, be considered a perceptual or a conceptual one?

logical inference, deductive reasoning, mathematical problem solving, and other such manifestations of symbolically mediated behavior.

It is thus noteworthy that one of the major developmental changes that seems to take place in the development of abstract concepts is precisely the differentiation of relevant from irrelevant, but more readily discriminable, attributes. This development is shown in various studies of concept formation (e.g., Vurpillot, 1960): it may also lie at the heart of a problem which Piaget has studied intensively—the development of conservation. Here one aspect of the stimulus, such as number, weight, volume, or quantity, has to be conceived as invariant, in the face of highly visible changes in some other irrelevant attribute with which it is typically correlated. Similar phenomena are involved in the development of the concepts of time, velocity, and movement, as studied by Piaget.

The dimension of contiguity

The third dimension is perhaps the most obvious one. Indeed, the major role which spatial and temporal contiguity plays in perception hardly needs detailed discussion. Spatially, we find it illustrated in the Gestalt law of proximity, as well as in the variation of illusions, figural aftereffects, and other perceptual phenomena as a function of the distance between the central stimulus and contextual portions of a field; similarly, figural aftereffects, among other phenomena, demonstrate the relatively limited temporal span over which two stimulus events separated in time interact.

It is characteristic of conceptual processes, on the other hand, that they enable the individual to deal with stimulus information whose components are widely separated in space or time. To give just one example, conceptual groupings can be achieved where the objects to be grouped are not in close spatial relationship and may not even be exposed simultaneously. Here again absolute independence of contiguity represents an ideal which is scarcely, if ever, realized even by adults. Thus, Davidon (1952) has shown that the opportunity for the subject to manipulate the stimulus materials in an object-classification task so as to provide spatial contiguity for the groupings made improves performance significantly; yet the results are perhaps more remarkable for the small size of the effect which manipulation produced.

Davidon's problem would be an ideal one in which to explore developmental changes; it would be hypothesized that with increasing age this factor of spatial proximity in conceptual grouping would steadily decrease in importance. While there is no evidence on this specific point, a variety of related findings can be mentioned. In the realm of perception, first of all, the writer's review of the literature on perceptual development (Wohlwill, 1960) uncovered various examples of developmental changes in the direction of an increasing ability or tendency to relate objects in the stimulus field, independently of their spatial or temporal contiguity. Such a trend appeared, for instance, in studies of size constancy, which for young children deteriorates much more rapidly with increasing distance between the stimuli than for adults, and in the perception of causality, which for children, but not for adults, requires a perceived contact between the objects in order for them to appear as causally related. With increasing age, furthermore, relatively remote visual frameworks exert an increasing influence on perception in diverse situations.[5]

With respect to tasks of reasoning or concept formation, we unfortunately have much less direct evidence of developmental changes indicating a decrease in the role of this factor of contiguity, although what we know of the thinking and problem solving behavior of children is consistent with the assumption of such an age trend. One experimental study that might be mentioned in this connection is that by Kendler and Kendler (1956), who found that the ability of 3- to 4-year-old children to respond inferentially in a Maier-type reasoning task was closely dependent on the temporal sequence in which the steps in the inferential chain were presented. Thus, if children were shown that *A* leads to *B*, *X* leads to *Y* and *B* leads to *G* (the main goal object), and if they were then presented with a choice of *A* or *X*, the frequency of inferential responses (choice of *A*) was considerably higher if the *B-G* exprience had immediately followed or preceded the *A-B* experience, than it was where the *X-Y* experience intervened between these two. Inferential choices likewise depended on the *direction* of the temporal sequence, being significantly more frequent when *B-G* followed *A-B* *t*han when it preceded it—pointing to a rather obvious fact—that the temporal order between two events is of importance quite independently of the interval separating them. It would be of interest to determine whether this ordinal factor also decreases in importance with age.

The resultant of the three dimensions: specificity

Taken together, these three dimensions yield responses of varying specificity, ranging from those of perceptual judgment, in which accuracy is always relative and error is the rule, to the absolute precision and

---

5. Certain perceptual phenomena appear, however, to be exceptions to this developmental trend, notably the role played by the factor of proximity in grouping and the role of spatial and temporal separation between stimuli in apparent movement. Thus, there appear to be definite limitations to the applicability of the principles outlined here.

accuracy of the products of conceptual processes. To this extent they do not represent a departure from Brunswik's and Piaget's conceptions of the problem but rather an extension in the direction of continuity of process from perception to conception.

To illustrate the relevance of our dimensions to this specificity criterion, let us compare the assessment of the relative size of two objects through direct perceptual judgment with that achieved by the conceptual process of measurement, i.e., by the intermediary of a ruler. In the former case, the results will be affected by spatial or temporal separation by variation in irrelevant aspects and by lack of redundancy, i.e., one-dimensional stimuli yield larger thresholds than two- or three-dimensional ones (Werner, 1957, p. 118)—all of these factors interfering with accuracy and precision of judgment. None of these aspects, on the other hand, influences the results obtained through measurement, the precision of which is limited only by the accuracy of the instrument and the observer's visual acuity in reading it. A very similar kind of comparison could have been made between the assessment of quantity by estimation and by counting. It is thus of no little significance that, in the case of length and in the case of number, perceptual discrimination and conceptual measurement appear to develop in close interdependence (Braine, 1959; Long and Welch, 1941).

Conclusions

Granting for the moment the validity of the dimensions suggested earlier for the representation of important components of developmental change in cognitive functioning,[6] the question of their conceptual fruitfulness arises. Insofar as they do appear to encompass a wide array of phenomena, their status presumably transcends the level of pure description. It is suggested, moreover, that they provide the basis for the construction of a higher-order theoretical framework within which a more systematic and a more generalized approach to problems in this area may be realized.

The major argument in support of this seemingly pious hope is the built-in potential of these dimensions for leading to a set of constructs which can be securely anchored on the stimulus and response sides and which will also facilitate the integration of developmental changes with principles derived from the experimental study of perception and thinking. To give just one example, the conception should prove of heuristic value in the analysis of the perceptual constancies in terms of the role

---

6. For an empirical demonstration of the heuristic value of these dimensions in the study of abstraction see the Appendix to this paper.

of stimulus variables such as amount of surplus cues, or redundant information, in interaction with organismic variables such as age.

Admittedly, the actual mechanisms mediating the effects of our dimensions of cognitive activity remain quite obscure as yet. Possibly, neurophysiological or cybernetic models of cognitive activity related to the internal activity of the organism in transforming the stimulus input so as to allow for varying degrees of stimulus determination of behavior may provide us with fruitful leads in our quest for such mechanisms. Thus, one might suggest the operation of scanning mechanisms as characteristic of perception, as against digital mechanisms intervening in reasoning. The process of developmental change could then be conceptualized in terms of varying forms of interaction between these two.

It would undoubtedly be sheer pretentiousness to elaborate further upon these highly speculative questions at this point, but one may point to certain empirical hypotheses that appear to be implicit in the postulated dimensions of developmental change themselves. For instance, in the previous discussion of selectivity, it was suggested that the problem of the development of conservation might be handled in terms of the dissociation of a particular concept (e.g., number) from irrelevant, though typically correlated and highly visible, perceptual cues (e.g., length over which a row of elements extends). If this dissociation does in fact represent a factor relevant to the psychological process involved in the development of conservation (as opposed to a mere description of the results of this process), it seems to follow that systematically arranged experiences aimed at untying these two variables for the child should at least facilitate the appearance of conservation.[7]

This brings us, lastly, to the more general question of the bearing of the formulation outlined in this paper on Piaget's work in this area. At first sight, it may seem that the two are at variance in several respects, notably in our postulation of essentially continuous dimensions, as opposed to Piaget's discontinuous stages of development, and in the emphasis here on modes of utilizing stimulus information as against Piaget's system of internal structures, operations, and mental actions. Much of this apparent contradiction disappears, however, if one recog-

7. With respect to the development of number conservation, the writer is currently investigating the role of such experience experimentally, alongside other experimental effects pertinent to the alternative theoretical formulations of Piaget (involving the activation of relevant mental operations, e.g., those of addition and subtraction) and of learning theory (focusing on the role of reinforcement, through direct confrontation with the *fact* of number invariance).

A very similar research project, dealing with experiential effects in the realm of the conservation of weight (under changes in shape) is being conducted in Norway by Smedslund (1959). As regards the effects of dissociating irrelevant perceptual cues, the preliminary report of this author indicates mainly negative results thus far.

nizes that Piaget's concern is with changes in the structural characteristics of the products of intellectual activity, whereas the interest here is in the specification of the dimensions and processes of developmental change.

The distinction between these two essentially complementary approaches may be clarified by reference to their respective handling of the role of external environmental factors. Piaget, as is well known, tends to ignore the effects of antecedent conditions and environmental variables in development, relegating them to a place definitely subsidiary in importance to the unfolding of internal structures. This does not mean that he advocates a strict nativist position, for he has frequently emphasized the continual interaction between external and internal forces. Nevertheless, his biological orientation and interest in structure leads him to take external factors for granted and to regard the form which this interaction takes as largely predetermined from the start. The only problem, then, is that of specifying the successive stages through which the organism passes; little leeway is left for differential manifestations of external conditions. It is not surprising therefore that his treatment of learning effects in the development of logical processes (Piaget, 1959) is limited almost exclusively to the activation of previously formed structures bearing a logical relationship to the particular structure under investigation. In comparison, the approach advocated here probably is less adequate to the task of analyzing the structural complexities of intellectual activity and its development; in compensation, however, it allows for a more thorough exploration of functional relationships between antecedent condition and developmental change and should contribute thereby to a more explicit understanding of the processes at work in the interaction between environmental and organismic forces.

Appendix

An illustrative experiment

By way of introducing some substance into the argument developed in this paper, let us consider an experiment specifically designed to show the applicability and usefulness of the first two of the dimensions discussed, namely, redundancy and selectivity. Since the purpose of this study is primarily illustrative, it should not be surprising if the results appear to some extent trivial.

The task was a very simple one—to pick out the odd one from among three stimuli. The stimuli were simple geometric figures, varying along one or more of the following four attributes: shape (square, triangle, pentagon); color (red, green, blue); shading (outline, dotted, solid), and size (large, medium, small). Five different sheets, each containing eight such triplets of figures, were constructed, according to the design outlined in Table 1 (the terminology in this table is taken from Bruner

TABLE 1

SCHEMA FOR STUDY ON THE ROLE OF IRRELEVANT AND
REDUNDANT INFORMATION

| | Number of Attributes that are: | | |
Sheet	Criterial	Quiet	Noisy
a	3	0	1
b	2	1	1
c	1	2	1
d	1	1	2
e	1	0	3

et al., 1956). Samples of each type of stimulus set are shown in Figure 1 and the appropriate colors are indicated under each stimulus.

"Critical" attributes in this study were those on which two of the three figures were alike, the third being the odd one. Where more than one attribute was criterial, they were perfectly correlated; thus, sheets *a* to *c* may be said to vary on the dimension of redundancy. Sheets *c* to *e*, on the other hand, vary with respect to the amount of noise or irrelevant information contained, i.e., the number of attributes on which all three figures of a triplet differed. It will be noted that redundancy was varied while keeping irrelevant information constant, and vice versa, this being accomplished by concomitant variation of number of "quiet" attributes —attributes on which all three figures of a triplet were identical. Each attribute was noisy twice on sheets *a* to *c* and criterial twice on sheets *c* to *e*, thus accounting for eight sets of triplets per sheet.

The hypothesis was that, as relevant information decreased or irrelevant information increased, there would be a gradual shift from a perceptual mode to a conceptual mode of functioning, reflected in three different ways. In children errors would increase, and younger subjects would show a larger effect in this respect than older subjects; for adults, time taken to complete each sheet would be directly related to degree of irrelevant or redundant information.

Table 2 presents the means for preliminary results obtained from 15 subjects from a third grade, 15 subjects from a fifth grade, and 15 college students.

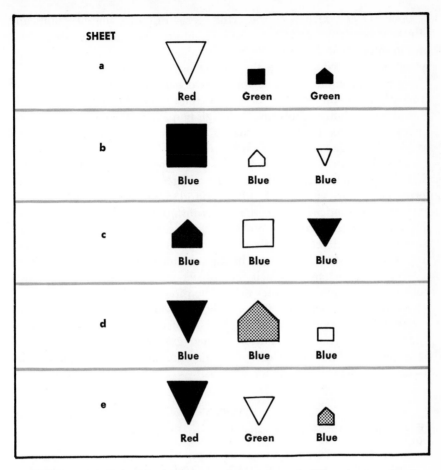

FIGURE 1. Sample stimulus sets used to represent different amounts of redundant and irrelevant information.

TABLE 2
MEAN NUMBER OF ERRORS AND MEAN TIME (FOR ADULTS) PER SHEET

Sheet	Mean Number of Errors			Mean Time (Adults)
	3rd Grade	5th Grade	Adults	
a	.6	.5	.1	17.0 sec.
b	.8	.3	.4	19.8
c	1.2	1.2	.4	19.5
d	3.4	3.0	1.2	32.2
e	3.8	3.9	1.9	31.0

Analysis of variance of the error scores discloses highly significant effects of age (third and fifth grades vs. adults), both as a main variable, and in interaction with the stimulus variable. In view of this interaction, which is in accordance with the second hypothesis, no test of the main effect of the stimulus variable was carried out, though the over-all trend is clearly as predicted. For the adults' time scores the effect of stimuli was likewise highly significant, although here, as in the case of the error scores as well, the major difference is between sheets *a, b,* and *c* on the one hand, as against *d* and *e* on the other.

This sharp rise in time and errors between sheets *c* and *d* suggests that the function relating the amount of *irrelevant* information to performance in this type of task differs considerably from that applying to amount of *redundant* information. This difference probably reflects the differences in the processes involved; whereas changes in the amount of redundancy affect primarily the perceptual differentiation of the odd from the even stimuli, changes in the amount of irrelevant information determine the extent to which the subject must try out successive hypotheses with regard to the critical dimension.

As for the age variable, it is clearly represented in this study in only a very perfunctory fashion. It might be noted, incidentally, that for a small group of younger children (second graders), there was a strong indication that the amount of redundant information played a more important role than for the older subjects.[8]

REFERENCES

Attneave, F. (1954). Some informational aspects of visual perception. *Psychol. Rev.,* 61, 183-193.

Braine, M. D. S. (1959). The ontogeny of certain logical operations: Piaget's formulation examined by nonverbal methods. *Psychol. Monogr.,* 73 (5), Whole No. 475.

Bruner, J. S. (1957). On perceptual readiness. *Psychol. Rev.,* 64, 123-152.

Bruner, J. S.; J. Goodnow; and G. A. Austin (1956). *A study of thinking.* New York: Wiley.

Brunswik, E. (1956). *Perception and the representative design of psychological experiments,* second ed. Berkeley, Calif.: University of California Press.

Davidon, R. S. (1952). The effects of symbols, shift, and manipulation upon the number of concepts attained. *J. exp. Psychol.,* 44, 70-79.

Gollin, E. S. (1956). Some research problems for developmental psychology. *Child Develpm.,* 27, 223-235

Kendler, H. H., and T. S. Kendler (1956). Inferential behavior in preschool children. *J. exp. Psychol.,* 51, 311-314.

Koffka, K. (1924). *The growth of the mind.* New York: Harcourt.

Köhler, W. (1925). *The mentality of apes.* London: Routledge.

8. A more extensive investigation of these developmental changes has recently been carried out by Lavoie (1961) with results substantially in agreement with those reported here.

Lavoie, G. (1961). Contribution à l'étude des relations entre la perception et l'intelligence. Unpublished L. Ps. thesis, Université de Montreal.

Long, L., and L. Welch (1941). The development of the ability to discriminate and match numbers. *J. genet. Psychol.*, 59, 377-387.

Munn, N. L. (1955). *The evolution and growth of human behavior.* Boston: Houghton Mifflin.

Piaget, J. (1946). *La psychologie de l'intelligence.* Paris: Presses Universitaires. (Trans. from second French ed. as *The psychology of intelligence.* London: Routledge, 1950.)

———. (1954). ce qui subsiste de la théorie de la Gestalt dans la psychologie contemporaine de l'intelligence et de la perception. *Schweiz. Z. Psychol. Anwend.,* 13, 72-83. (Also in J. de Ajuriaguerre *et al., Aktuelle Probleme der Gestalttheorie.* Bern: Hans Huber, 1954. Pp. 72-83.

———. (1955). Essai d'une nouvelle interpretation probabiliste des effets de centration, de la loi de Weber et de celle des contrations relatives. *Arch. Psychol. Genève,* 35, 1-24.

———. (1956). Les stades du dévelopement intellectuel de l'enfant et de l'adolescent. In P. Osterrieth *et al., Le Problème des stades en psychologie de l'enfant.* Paris: Presses Universitaires. Pp. 33-49.

———. (1957). Logique et équilibre dans les comportements du sujet. In L. Apostel *et al.,* Logique et équilibre. *Etudes d'épistémologie génétique,* Vol. 2. Paris: Presses Universitaires. Pp. 27-117.

———. (1959). Apprentissage et connaissance. In M. Goustard *et al.,* La logique des apprentissages. *Etude d'épistémologie génétique,* Vol. 2. Paris: Presses Universitaires. Pp. 159-188.

Piaget, J., and M. Lambercier (1946). Transpositions perceptives et transitivité opératorie dans les comparaisons en profondeur. *Arch. Psychol., Genève,* 31, 325-368.

Piaget, J., and A. Morf (1958a). Les isomorphismes partiels entre les structures logiques et les structures perceptives. In J. S. Bruner *et al.,* Logique et perception. *Etudes d'épistémologie génétique,* Vol. 6. Paris: Presses Universitaires. Pp. 49-116.

——— (1958b). Les préinférences perceptives et leurs relations avec les schèmes sensorimoteurs et opératories. In J. S. Bruner *et al.,* Logique et perception. *Etudes d'épistémologie génétique,* Vol. 6. Paris: Presses Universitaires. Pp. 117-155.

Piaget, J., and S. Taponier (1956). L'estimation des longueurs de deux droites horizontales et parallèles extrémités décalées. *Arch. Psychol., Genève,* 35, 369-400.

Smedslund, J. (1959). Learning and equilibration: a study of the acquisition of concrete logical structures. Pre-publication draft, Oslo.

Stevenson, Harold W., and Jon D. Swartz (1958). Learning set in children as a function of intellectual level. *J. comp. Physiol. Psychol.,* 51, 755-757.

Vurpillot, E. (1960). Etude génétique sur la formation d'un concept: role données perceptives. *Psychol. Franc.,* 5, 135-152.

Werner, H. (1957). *Comparative psychology of mental development,* revised ed. New York: International Universities.

Wertheimer, M. (1959). *Productive thinking,* enlarged ed. New York: Harper & Row.

Wohlwill, J. F. (1960). Developmental studies of perception. *Psychol. Bull.,* 57, 249-288.

---

1. Can you compare perceptual and conceptual development?

15 JOACHIM F. WOHLWILL

Cognitive Development and the
Learning of Elementary Concepts

In this paper, Wohlwill looks at the "mystery" of development and the measure of such. He raises questions regarding the nature and causes of a child's continued intellectual development. How is it that a child is a nonconserver of number in July and a conserver of the same a year later? What aspects of experience, maturation, etc., effect this particular change? Without any specific attempts to provide a child with experiences related to, say, conservation of number, he develops "into" a conserver from a nonconserver.

The central question is, what experiences, if any, can be provided for children that will maximize certain kinds of intellectual development?

What I would like to talk about briefly concerns some general thoughts relating to the discussion inspired by Professor Piaget's remarks, and to the controversy that followed it. This will bring us to a topic brought up by Professor Piaget, the topic of measurement, which I feel is of general interest with respect to some of the concepts that Piaget has dealt with.

There was some feeling expressed in the discussion that we didn't have to invoke any mystical force to account for the development that one observes in the acquisition of conservation and certain other kinds of problems. Piaget rejoined that he did not feel any particular mysticism involved here and that the phenomena could be accounted for consistently in terms of his model. I certainly wouldn't want to argue here for a position of mysticism, but I do want to suggest that there is a mystery here nevertheless. (I don't think you have to be a mystic to enjoy a mystery, and I do enjoy this one.) The mystery for me has to do with the nature of the change that takes place in the child's mode

Reprinted from *The Journal of Research in Science Teaching*, Vol. 2, issue 3, 1964, pp. 222-226 by permission of the editor.

of reasoning. Let us consider a child, say a five-year-old child, who is responding in a perfectly self-assured manner in a nonconservation sense; that is, he feels that once we stretch out the ball of clay, then there is more clay. This same child, maybe a year later, will make a complete turnabout and declare that obviously you haven't changed anything, it is still the same amount of clay.

The forcefulness of this point is somewhat diluted, I think, if you simply look at one group of children at one age as opposed to another group at an older age and simply compare these two groups of children. Then it looks a little like just two different breeds of cats, and you tend to ignore the fact that one child actually changes to become a member of the other group. I might simply refer you, in this connection, to some films that I have always felt are among the most convincing and dramatic illustrations of the reality of the phenomenon which takes place in the area of conservation, for instance. These films were made by Dr. Inhelder at Geneva showing a single child at successively different levels of reasoning with respect to the conservation problem, spanning about a period of a year or a year and a half at the most. (In part this is just a plug that I would like to make for more intensive longitudinal analysis of this sort to trace the change in the nature of the reasoning processes of a particular child.) These are longitudinal studies that don't have to encompass generations, with all the difficult problems that arise in such projects; they can be quite limited and self-contained and easy to manage. But I do think we stand to gain a good deal by looking at what actually goes on during the period in which this change must take place.

Meanwhile, although we don't have a good sequential analysis of this problem as yet, I would still like to address myself to the general question, "Just what is it that's going on here? How can you account for this change in the reasoning process?" Let me simply state that I don't think, with respect to most problems of this type, that you can really account for it in terms of the acquisition of a specific response. The child typically does not have very much direct experience during such an early period in judging the relative weight of things while the shape is altered, for instance. This doesn't mean that I'm ruling out the role of the experience that the child may be exposed to in this period. I do think that experience has something to do with it, but it is not a matter of acquisition of specific responses. The question then arises, what kind of experience or what aspects of experience are important here, and in what manner does it act to effect this particular change?

Professor Piaget has given us a general answer as to how to approach this problem in his equilibration model. That is, he suggests that there are certain modes of response that tend to satisfy the child for a while, but later he will be led to explore other possibilities or be confronted with contradictions arising from his mode of reasoning that will compel him to move on to the following level. In general terms this is undoubtedly a useful way of looking at the matter, but it still leaves open a variety of specific alternatives as to the exact nature of the processes at work here. Or, if you ask the question, how one might manipulate experience in such a way as to induce the child to change his level of reasoning, the equilibrium model still allows for a variety of possible solutions to this question.

One particular approach is the one which Dr. Smedslund talked about, having to do with the notion of cognitive conflict. That is, you actually put the child in a bind, as it were, as the result of a particular preoperational type of reasoning. You confront him with inconsistencies in his judgment without giving him any answer as to the way out, and simply expose him to this presumably somewhat stressful situation—not necessarily stress in the negative sense, but one which impels him to move on, as it were. You get him to resolve this conflict by changing his mode of conceptual functioning. Dr. Smedslund has indeed succeeded in illustrating the possible role of this type of process in some of his experiments quite convincingly. But a question arises here as to the place of this kind of cognitive conflict in the normal process of cognitive development.

A former student of Piaget's, Hans Aebli, now at the Free University of Berlin, has actually gone one step further. Essentially following this position of Smedslund's, he has suggested that we should look for the locus of the cognitive change in the experimental situation itself. Outside of the experimental situation there is just a general diffuse maturation going on and if you actually get a child to change his mode of reasoning it is as a function of his exposure to questioning of the type that you normally find in a conservation study or the like. Now, for me at least, the problem with regard to this position—and I would be inclined to make the same argument against the generality of the answer that Dr. Smedslund has given us—is that if this were the case it would be just too bad for the 99.99 per cent of the children who never find their way into a Piaget-type experiment. How would they ever come to function in the way you expect? There must be something in the normal process of development that takes the place of this experience, or makes up for their lack of good fortune in this respect. In general it seems to me implausible to suppose that a child is normally exposed to that much cognitive dissonance, let's say in the kindergarten or first grade period during which these things seem to develop "spontaneously."

I don't really have a terribly good specific answer to propose to solve this mystery. However, I would like to suggest one alternative here, and that is that the child comes to develop a different attitude or a different type of set in responding to a conceptual problem. The preconservation child, the child at the age of intuitive thought, is responding mainly on the basis of particular perceptual cues which to him dominate the situation. Thus, if you stretch out the piece of clay, this leads him to assume a change in the weight of the piece, based on the obviously visible change in the shape or the length of the piece. In other words he is operating on the basis of a perceptual set in his handling of the concept of weight.

You could describe in similar terms the child's problem with respect to the conservation of number: if you stretch out the row of buttons, he is responding to this immediately visible increase in length. What seems to me to happen, then, is that a different kind of set emerges during this period, which has to do more with the symbolic operations that relate to that particular concept. In the case of number this would of course involve such operations as adding, subtracting, counting—although I think that has to be qualified, because simple rote counting does not seem to be very effective here. But given a particular quantity of objects, a child looks at number as something that has to do with adding pieces or taking pieces away. Similarly, in regard to the conservation of weight the notion would be that the amount of weight has to do not with the object's looks but with such things as comparing weight on a balance, for instance. Or the quantity of liquid has to do with measuring the relative amount of water through some kind of a measuring instrument. It seems to me the whole notion of measurement is essential to all of these kinds of phenomena. What I am suggesting, in other words, is that this different type of set in responding to these concepts supplants the earlier one, and that the perceptual approach is gradually sloughed off, as it were, as the child develops. He isn't aware that he is giving anything up; it simply becomes a kind of vestigial form of reasoning.

As you can see, at some point both of these tendencies may be in some sort of balance, since one is going down as the other one is going up. Presumably if you catch a child at the point when both of these tendencies are present to almost equal strength, then exposing them to a cognitive-conflict type of situation may be effective in getting him over the hump. But I don't think you have to argue that this is a necessary condition for the change; it will simply speed it up if you happen to catch him at that particular moment.

Well, now you might ask, "How does this new type of attitude or set develop?" Some might argue that this is a matter of learning experiences that a child ordinarily gets exposed to in our culture, through school, through the kinds of toys he has, etc. One point to be made first of all, however, is that you have a situation here where one type of response set supplants another. It is not simply the acquisition of a *new* response, in the sense that a child might learn about somthing that he did not know before. It is not the acquisition of facts or knowledge generally, but it is a matter of giving up one type of response, which is extinguished while another one is being developed. I think that when a learning interpretation is advanced, this has to be borne in mind.

Secondly, while undoubtedly experience in the general sense is quite important here, one has to look at the timing of these processes. I would argue that it is probably impossible to devise experiences that would develop this kind of a conceptual attitude while the child is at the height of the perceptual-dominance stage. I suspect that one of the factors involved here is the development of language and of other mediational processes, such as observing responses, in this transition period. I am not putting the stress on language as such. I think it is more of a correlational situation where the development of language serves as a symptom of the same process reflected in the changes in the development of the child's reasoning. These go hand in hand. In the same way it would probably be futile to try to teach a three-year-old child the use of words that relate to a set of concepts such as equilibrium, for instance. I am sure you could teach a child to use these words but they would have highly limited meaning. In other words, I think one has to look at the role of experience in relation to the level of the development of the child.

Finally, in a more positive sense, what type of experience is likely to be relevant with regard to these kinds of processes? The kind of conception I have suggested here would indicate that it should be an experience which gets the child involved with the conceptual aspects of the situation. This might consist of activities which involve adding things together, or measuring by comparing things quantitatively. More particularly, it seems to me that the experience ideally should have a built-in feedback possibility for the child. I believe that externally administered reinforcement, or information as to the correctness or incorrectness of the child's response is not going to be very fruitful. On the other hand, there is a variety of actions that the child can do which provide him with feedback in regard to the effect of his actions. A particularly good illustration of this point was contained in the example that Professor Piaget cited of the mathematician who discovered conservation by rearranging a group of stones and beads in order of size and counting them forwards and backwards. The process of counting itself in this particular situation provides built-in feedback, since one finds out by counting that the total number is always the same.

I would be somewhat reluctant to put too much stress on counting as such in relation to the conservation of number, however, in that some work that I have done in this area suggests very definite limits as to how far the child will go on the basis of simple counting. Let us suppose you put the child in a conservation situation where there are two equally-spaced rows of beads and he agrees that the two rows have the same number. Then you stretch one row out and you ask, "Who has more beads, you or I, or are they the same?" He may give a nonconservation answer. "You have more because you have stretched it out." Now I have had children in whom I had previously built up a definite set to respond to number (so you can reasonably assume that for them "more" had reference to "greater number;" they had gone through a long series of number responses). After these children gave such a nonconservation response, I had them count both of the rows. Occasionally you find a child who seems deliberately to make it come out wrong, in accordance with his hypothesis. He'll count one row, let's say to seven and so he'll count the other, "one, two, three, four, five, (skipping a bead) six—see, you have more!" Most of them won't be quite that smart, and they find that they have seven and you have seven. Then you repeat the question: "Well, who had more, you or I?" They still persist: "You have more, because it's longer." So, simply confronting himself with the equality of these rows isn't necessarily the answer here. The aspect of th previous example of Professor Piaget's that struck me at once was the fact that the child did engage in some action with the material. Perhaps this spontaneous action had something to do with the success of this particular case.

In any event I would say that getting children involved in manipulating the material in the conceptual sense, rearranging the objects, counting them and balancing them—this does strike me as a useful way of looking at what normally happens in the development of the kind of concepts which we have been discussing. The notion of measurement, as we have seen from Professor Piaget's paper, is, of course, itself subject to a very definite developmental process. But I think that if you work on that and follow it step by step, trying to develop the concepts and skills involved in that particular sequence by relevant types of experience, this would be likely to yield a good deal of transfer with regard to such notions as conservation, transitivity and other concrete-operation concepts.

In closing, let me say one word concerning the question of acceleration. I think, first of all, one might ask the question, why do we want to accelerate development? What is so desirable about getting a child who normally would acquire a certain kind of reasoning at six to show it at the kindergarten level, and continuing from there on, to find that you can perhaps cut two years off his normal schooling period? The net result of this is that you throw him into the labor force that many years earlier, and that creates an employment problem. Maybe we should work on the opposite premise and try to *extend* the curriculum for several years to ease up the employment situation. But, more seriously, I think you have to ask the question, what exactly are you doing when you do this? Is it possible that you are accelerating the process of cognitive development with respect to one particular concept at the expense of breadth or generality of learning or transfer to other later concepts? I can conceive of the possibility of considerably accelerating the child's appreciation of the conservation of weight, for instance. But it may be that the other things which normally would develop at the same time, such as notions about transitivity, would be left behind, as it were, and as a result you have a particular pattern of conceptual responses that may not be such a useful one.

I would throw out a tentative hypothesis here, to the effect that the more generalized the experience that a child gets at an earlier point is, the less specific teaching instruction will be necessary later. An implication of this is that if we do manipulate experience at these early levels, we should make provision for a variety of types of experiences, including perhaps some rather unstructured ones, so as to be sure that one is not depriving the child of learnings which he would normally pick up in a more incidental fashion.

To conclude, then, I would place the emphasis in the teaching of scientific and mathematical subjects to young children on a focused enrichment of their experience, aimed at generalization and transfer, rather than at acceleration per se. Get them actively involved in measuring the sizes, shapes, weights, temperatures, etc., of the objects around them, in many different and even novel ways; set them problems to solve and operations to perform, giving them an opportunity to apply their measurement skills and the concepts embodied in them. If the child is thus provided with a broad base of experience, assuring him of extensive practice in abstracting structural similarities and common principles from diverse material contents or specific tasks, this may surely be expected to influence the development of his cognitive skills in a very fashionable sense.

---

1. Apart from manners, values and attitudes (affective domain), how do you think a child learns what he does (cognitive domain) before he gets to school?
2. What effect do you think one's environment has on his intellectual development?
3. "The more generalized the experience that a child gets at an earlier point is, the less specific teaching instruction will be necessary later." How can this be interpreted?

16 RONALD G. GOOD

Conversations with Children: Their Interpretation of Causality

An early book by Piaget, The Child's Interpretation of Physical Causality *contains many conversations with children about objects and events in their environment. The following paper represents some recent (1971) conversations with children that include but a few topics because of the space required to present a comprehensive view of the wide variation of children's conceptions of causality. You are encouraged to pursue the technique with children.*

Talking with children can be a fascinating and rewarding process, especially when the objective is to find out how they think. Adults are usually so preoccupied trying to teach, they seldom really listen to children. This paper contains some conversations with children about physical causality. What they think about the world around them obviously influences what they are capable of understanding in science investigations. If children are available to you, perhaps you might want to talk with some of them to find out what they think about such things as: airplanes, cars, birds, clouds, air, trees, television, names, refrigerators, light, fire, rain, snow, telephones, etc. The art of talking with children to find out about their thinking abilities takes practice and a perceptiveness that requires real concentration on the part of the questioner. The following interviews were conducted by preservice elementary school teachers.

1. Jim, five years:
   Q: Do you think it's going to rain? A: Yes, because I brought my raincoat.
   Q: Is there any other way you know it is going to rain? A: Yes, when the clouds move away.

This paper was written for use in the science education program for prospective elementary school teachers at Florida State University. Dr. Good is Assistant Professor of Science Education at Florida State University.

Q: How do the clouds make it rain when they move away? A: Because if it doesn't rain it will snow.

Q: What is snow? A: Hard water.

Q: How does it get hard? A: It freezes, water and snow are the same.

Q: How does it get cold? A: You can put water in the refrigerator.

2. Kathy, six years:

Q: How does a television work? A: You have to plug it in and it works.

Q: Is that all? A: Something comes in through the wall to make it go.

Q: How does it go? A: The picture is made by people inside the set. They don't live in there, they only come out at special times. They make sound when you turn the knob. When you turn the knob it tells them to be quieter or louder.

3. Regina, six years:

Q: How does a television work? A: you have to plug it in the wall.

Q: And then how does it work? A: The picture is made by people inside the set. They change costumes for each show.

4. Tom, seven years:

Q: Where does the sun come from? A: Up in the sky.

Q: Does the sun move? A: No, it looks like it but we are moving.

Q: What about at night, what happens? A: It goes behind the mountains.

Q: Does it move? A: Yes.

Q: How? A: Well, the sun gets too hot on some glasses and it is pushed, but sometimes it goes by itself.

Q: Where is the sun today? (overcast day) A: Behind the mountains (there are no mountains)

Q: Why? A: Cause it didn't want to come out today, it was tired.

Q: Does the sun rest very often? A: Just at night and on days like this.

5. Tina, seven years:

Q: What makes the rain come down? A: God makes the rain. I think he's up there and he pours the water down.

Q: Where does the rain come from? A: The sky.

Q: Why do we need rain? A: Grass, flowers and some people drink it.

Q: Can it rain while the sun shines? A: No, cause the sun dries it up.

Q: Can it rain at night? A: Yes, cause there's a hole over my bed and the rain comes down and tickles me.

6. Pat, seven years:
   Q: When do you think the first airplane was made? A: A real long time ago, before I was born.
   Q: What makes it fly? A: The wind.
   Q: How does the wind do that? It lifts the plane up.
   Q: Why doesn't the wind lift you up? A: I'm too heavy.
   Q: Are you heavier than the plane? A: No, but it's meant to fly, I'm not.

7. Pat, seven years:
   Q: How do clouds get in the sky? A: God made them.
   Q: Why did he do that? A: So it could rain.
   Q: What do they do when it rains? A: They turn black and blue.
   Q: Why do they turn colors? A: God makes them change colors so that people know when it's going to rain.
   Q: What does a cloud feel like? A: Like smoke.
   Q: Could you walk on one? A: No.
   Q: Why not? A: They're up too high.
   Q: You wouldn't fall through? A: No.

8. Cecelia, eight years:
   Q: Is the sun far away? A: Yes.
   Q: Would you say it was farther than that tree? A: Yes, you can't touch it.
   Q: Where does the sun go at night? A: In the clouds. It stays in the sky but the moon comes out and it's not bright.
   Q: What makes the sun move? A: The clouds.
   Q: How? A: They push it.
   Q: How did the sun get its name? A: It named itself and it shines and then everyone knew to call it sun.

9. Paul, eight years:
   Q: Where do trees come from? A: The ground.
   Q: Why do they have branches and leaves? A: Birds wouldn't have anyplace to build their nests.
   Q: Why do some trees lose their leaves? A: So new ones can grow.

10. Debbie, nine years:
    Q: Where did the sky come from? A: God.
    Q: Can you touch it? A: If you go way over there you could.
    Q: Have you ever touched it? A: No.
    Q: Why is it blue sometimes and gray at other times? A: The sun makes it blue and the clouds make it gray.
    Q: Why do we have a sky? A: So clouds can float somewhere.

11. Charles, twelve years:

> Q: Where do stars come from? A: From the light in the moon.
> Q: Why do you think they are in the sky? A: Cause they are.
> Q: What are they made of? A: Light.
> Q: What happens to them during the day? A: They go under the clouds and go away.
> Q: Do you think they move? A: Yes, if they would stay in one place, it would be too crowded.
> Q: How far away are they? A: 1,000 miles.
> Q: Why does a star "twinkle" at night? A: Because of the light.
> Q: Where do you think they got their name? A: Baby Jesus.

12. Norma, eleven years:

> Q: Where do stars come from? A: From the moon.
> Q: Why do you think they are in the sky? A: Cause they come out every night.
> Q: What are they made of? A: Silver.
> Q: What happens to them during the day? A: They go away to the moon.
> Q: Do you think they move? A: Yes, they go away in the daytime.
> Q: How far away do you think they are? A: 60 miles.
> Q: Why does a star twinkle at night? A: Cause they get darker.
> Q: Where do you think they got their name? A: The moon gave it to them.

The majority of these conversations were with children who were from families in the lower socio-economic bracket in the community. It is interesting to look at science textbooks for elementary schools and see such concepts as energy changes, conservation, work, atoms and molecules and other equally abstract things that are supposed to be "learned" by children in first grade. What nonsense this must be for children who attribute causality to God or some equally mysterious entity. The children in the previous interviews were not capable of logical thought. Their explanations reflected pre-logical thinking that was not concerned with internal consistency or other thought strategies required for logical thought. Reality is in the mind of the individual and it cannot be superimposed from the outside by those who hold a different conception of reality.

———————

1. Can you talk with children for the purpose of finding out some things about their thinking?

17 JONAS LANGER

Implications of Piaget's Talks for Curriculum

What is knowledge? This question and others are considered by Dr. Langer in the light of Piaget's theories. Conceptual knowledge is differentiated from "copying" knowledge. Cognition and non-cognition are likewise compared using Piaget's ideas. This paper generally addresses itself to an epistemological problem: What is knowledge?

For the interested reader, an excellent book by Furth, entitled Piaget and Knowledge *probes the nature of knowledge in much greater detail, with Piaget's theory of cognitive development as the reference point. The somewhat philosophical nature of this topic of the nature of knowledge should be carefully considered, since it can be argued that all of life is a matter of values and philosophical orientation. What knowledge is of most worth and how does one decide?*

I have had one major impression throughout this conference, namely, that there is a gap between what the developmental psychologist of cognition is talking about and what the people responsible for the teaching of knowledge are doing. Piaget's and much work of its kind is primarily directed towards studying the development of cognitive functioning, i.e., the cognitive operations which emerge in the course of ontogenesis. These operations determine the forms of knowledge which the organism may construct at a given stage of development.

There is, however, the other side to the problem which has been relatively neglected in the psychology of cognitive development and particularly in this conference, namely, the operations whereby the community communicates the forms of knowledge which it has accumulated to the individual and vice versa. The means of expression utilized determine the forms of knowledge which may be communicated. This is particularly important to curriculum development since the goal must

Reprinted from The Journal of Research in Science Teaching, Vol. 2, issue 3, 1964, pp. 208-213, by permission of the editor. Dr. Langer, from the University of California at Berkeley, is well-known for his work related to cognitive development in children.

involve the creation of means of communication which increasingly facilitate the task of teacher and student, i.e., learning from each other.

In this connection it becomes necessary to review what is meant by development. Professor Piaget characterizes cognitive development as equilibration rather than maturation, experience or social transmission (cf. Piaget, *The origins of intelligence in children*; Inhelder and Piaget, *The growth of logical thinking from childhood to adolescence*). Equilibration is defined as progressive interior organization of knowledge in step-wise fashion. Progressive development is the resultant of the interaction between the functions of assimilation and accommodation.

Now, I have noticed that very little has been said in this conference about accommodation. But it has always been my understanding that it is the relationship between these two functions which makes for either disequilibrium or equilibrium and, consequently, developmental change and stabilization of knowledge. I wonder if one may not suggest that the focus upon the formation of knowledge comes from an emphasis upon assimilation, i.e., with how things can become meaningful and interiorized in the first place, so that they can be dealt with. But if one is also concerned with the exterior fitting of oneself to the community and the community to oneself, then it becomes necessary to focus, in addition, upon organismic accommodation. Accommodation involves adapting to what is there and reorganizing it in such a fashion that it may be integrated with present schemata.

In attempting to understand, on the one hand, what it means to assert that a child is achieving knowledge and, on the other hand, that knowledge is being communicated to him and by him, in the course of development, it is necessary to make certain distinctions. These distinctions will permit me to raise several issues for your consideration with respect to (1) the growth of knowledge, about other things and oneself, and (2) the process whereby knowledge is interiorized and exteriorized, i.e., communicated to oneself and to others.

The first distinction which we must make is between what is knowledge and what is not knowledge. Professor Piaget seems to reserve true, or at least the highest, forms of knowledge to those concepts which arise as a consequence of formal operations. He distinguishes conceptual knowledge, and even that which results from developmentally earlier operations, from those experiences which arise as a result of imaging, perceiving and copying the environment. The development of this latter set of behaviors, according to Piaget, is independent of cognitive development.

A problem which we may raise in passing, and which requires much further empirical investigation, is whether other developmental relationships do not obtain between cognitive and non-cognitive operations, such as imaging. It is particularly likely that relationships such as subordination may obtain where functions such as imagery subserve those of thought. For example, visual imagery of spatial dimensions has often been used in the service of formal theory construction.

The distinction between cognition and non-cognition hinges upon the operations involved. What is taken on in a passive fashion, as Professor Smedslund argued, what is *impressed* upon the child is not cognition. It is merely that experience which mirrors the environment. What is *acted upon,* what is created is cognition.

A further distinction has to be made between the means of achieving knowledge and the objects of knowledge. The means towards the formation of knowledge are always acts and they are always *constructive* acts. The assumption is that the organism is always involved in constructive schematization *via* the functional interaction of assimilation and accommodation. Piaget has characterized five stages of cognitive development and the functionally analogous operations which emerge at each stage. The first three are relatively external actions upon or with actualities. There are sensori-motor actions *upon* things; preoperational actions *upon* things; and intuitive operations, but now *with* things.

The first truly internal actions are concrete operations *with* things. Only at the highest stage of cognitive development do formal operations appear which involve contemplation *about* things. The last stage permits operating upon operations or the transcendent activity of being conscious of one's consciousness. It becomes possible to reason deductively, formulate hypotheses, and deal with possibilities in addition to mere actualities.

As a consequence of these various schematizing operations different forms of knowledge arise, in the course of development. The objects of knowledge, which are constituted via different schematizing operations, are *qualitatively* different in addition to possible quantitative changes.

Now it may be argued that these constructed objects of knowledge will always be intuited in spatial, temporal, numerical and/or causal form. These categorical forms of intuition provide the *continuity* of cognitive organization even though it is constantly changing in the course of developmental growth.

Nevertheless, the various schematizing operations which emerge at different stages insure the *discontinuity* of cognitive development. For example, sensori-motor means result in different organizations of space than do formal operations. The forms of spatial knowledge, as a consequence of sensori-motor operations, are the resultants of actual manipulations by the organism within his environment. In this sense the organization of space is relatively egocentric, i.e., the intuition of space is not differentiated from the actions involved in its apprehension. It is grasped in an immediate, *external* fashion such that the spatial group achieved is that described by the action itself. Consequently, it will be a buccal space, a prehensile space, a visual space, etc. These spatial schemata are not even coordinated with each other in the earliest substages of sensori-motor activity (cf. Piaget, *Construction of Reality in the Child*). They are radically discontinuous from those constituted in the highest stage of cognitive development. The spatial knowledge is differentiated from the operations involved and is the result of *internal* operations. Consequently, it becomes feasible to construct possible spatial systems in addition to those which are actually intuited, e.g., the conception that the earth revolves around the sun in addition to the immediate external intuition of the sun revolving around the earth.

I believe that this formulation of functional (sensori-motor actions through formal operational) discontinuity and organizational (spatial, temporal, etc.) continuity consistently complements the picture of functional (assimilatory: accommodatory) continuity and organizational (cognitive) discontinuity presented by Professor Piaget in his *Psychology of Intelligence*. It raises the major problem, however, of the processes whereby external forms of knowledge become *interiorized* as schemata. We shall return to this issue after briefly making certain distinctions with respect to the process of *expressing* and *communicating knowledge*. This should permit a fuller understanding of the ramifications of the problem of interiorizing and exteriorizing knowledge.

In order to communicate knowledge, whether to oneself as in inner speech or to others as in external speech, it is necessary to make reference to some object(s) of cognition. This requires the embodiment of the referent in some vehicle of expression. The process of depicting referents is representation. Now, the stages of schematizing operations involved in forming symbolic representations of knowledge are not well delineated. Much ontogenetic research analogous to that provided by Piaget on the development of knowledge is required. However, it is clear that the earliest representations are bodily gestures. Professor Piaget himself has provided us with many examples of postural-gestural representation by pre-verbal children in *Play, Dreams and Imitation*. To cite but one example:

> At 1; 4(0) L. tried to get a watch chain out of a matchbox when the box was not more than an eighth of an inch open. She gazed at the box with great attention, then opened and closed her mouth several times in succession, at first only slightly and then wider and wider. It is clear that the child, in her effort to picture to herself the means of enlarging the opening, was using as "signifier" her own mouth, with the movements of which she was familiar tactually and kinaesthetically as well as by analogy with the visual image of the mouths of others.

As can be seen from this example, the symbolizing operation involves making reference to a cognitive problem, i.e., getting the chain out of the box, by gesturally representing it. The gesture schematically depicts the dynamics of the situation. There are at least two components to this schematic depiction, namely, pretending and imitating the dynamics of opening a box.

It is clear that the symbol, in this instance, is relatively little differentiated from the object of knowledge which it represents. It is a relatively natural form of expression since it closely mimics the object of reference. This is also characteristic of those vocal-gestural representations usually referred to as onomatopoesis.

At the opposite end of the developmental continuum the forms of schematizing expression are relatively conventional and artificial. The symbol is well differentiated from the referent which it represents. The name 'cow' is arbitrarily assigned to a schema of knowledge. This makes it possible for me to communicate with you now about that object of our knowledge, cow, without any actual exemplar being present.

There must, of course, be transitional stages between these extremes. For a more comprehensive treatment I refer you to a recent work by Werner and Kaplan, *Symbol Formation.* I might just suggest that these transitional stages are partially natural and partially conventional. For example, when the child yells "mama" much of the meaning is represented by the vocal-gestural qualities of excitement. This is also an important quality, but to a less degree, of adult representation. Gestural expression may serve as a conjunction of substitutive function in adult verbal-linguistic communication.

Communication—exteriorizing and interiorizing knowledge—must be looked at not only from the viewpoint of the organism's representational activity. It must also be looked at from the viewpoint of the community. The knowledge of a community is its scientific, ethico-religious, aesthetic, etc., cognitive systems. This knowledge is symbolized in its mythical, linguistic, mathematical, etc., codes (cf. Cassirer, E. *The Philosophy of Symbolic Forms*). The problem of communication, then, becomes how the community's and the organism's symbolic codes match up. It cannot be emphasized too strongly that the problem is twofold. It is both a question of how the organism interiorizes knowledge, and how cognition is exteriorized by the organism and the community.

This is particularly interesting if we maintain, and I for one would, with Professor Piaget that the spatial, temporal, etc., categories of knowledge are already being constructed by pre-verbal, sensori-motor operations. (One might note that Professor Piaget has reserved the title of *The Construction of Reality in the Child* for his study on the sensori-motor bases of cognition.) Then it is necessary to argue that both the basic forms and functions of cognition are interior as well as exterior in the first stages of development. In this respect sensori-motor actions are particularly suited to the simultaneous role of interiorizing and exteriorizing forms and operations of knowledge. Because of their bodily yet graphic nature they are little differentiated from the internal organization of knowledge and the external environment.

We may now directly face the question of what is becoming interiorized and what is becoming exteriorized in the course of development? While the forms of knowledge are progressively becoming interiorized schemata, the forms of expression are increasingly becoming exteriorized symbols. It is this dual process which insures progressive communication. After all, if knowledge were merely interiorized how could any exterior correspondence, and consequently comprehension, occur between communicants. Yet we know that the course of development is characterized by progressive understanding between communicants.

It is, then, the exterior means of expression which facilitate increasing communicative correspondence between individuals whose knowledge is, at the same time, becoming progressively interiorized. Progressive development is characterized by (1) the increasing differentiation of these exterior forms of expression from the interior forms of knowledge, yet (2) their increasing integration by the establishment of arbitrary representational relationships rather than the fused relationships (as exemplified by gestural representation, word realism, etc.) which obtain in the early stages. It is this process of differentiation and integration between interior and exterior forms within the cognitive organization of individuals which is the necessary condition for correspondence between the exterior expressions of different individuals. That is, it is the condition whereby individuals may employ exterior forms to communicate their interior knowledge and achieve increasing understanding.

I should like to turn briefly to another issue with respect to the development of cognition. When one characterizes development as progressive it becomes necessary to speak about an organizing force. I believe one may use the analogy of embryogenesis in speaking of an organizer which serves to direct the course of developmental organization (cf. Ludwig von Bertalanffy, *Modern Theories of Development*). I have the distinct impression from Professor Piaget's works that the end stage to which development is directed is that of perfect equilibration. This stage is characterized by formal operations. It involves operations upon operations and is consequently the highest possible stage of cognitive activity: dynamic equilibrium has been reached. The theoretical conception of cognitive development, then, is that of a closed system.

If development is truly a closed system, with formal operations as the last stage, then what happens in development when the last stage is achieved (at about 15 years of age, according to Piaget)? What happens to cognitive development— is that the end? I believe that the initial answer to this problem must come from a characterization of development which goes beyond the formulation of analogous functions at different stages. Although Professor Piaget has described cognitive development in terms of functionally analogous intellectual operations, I do not believe that he would deny that other relationships between these operations may obtain which further characterize development.

I would suggest that in order to conceive of cognitive development as an open rather than a closed system, it is necessary to speak of other relationships between cognitive operations. This should permit the theoretical conception of stages beyond formal operations. For example, one might have to consider exclusiveness, that is, functionally independent operations: when one achieves a new set of operations, in the course of development, the earlier ones are no longer available. More interesting, however, would be a consideration of subsumption or the hierarchization of operations which emerge at different stages. This would mean the integration of the earlier, more rudimentary operations by the later more sophisticated operations, such as formal operations. The resultant cognitive organization may be radically different and require the emergence of new cognitive operations. This theoretical issue takes on practical significance if we extend our consideration of curriculum development to higher education, at the undergraduate, graduate and post-graduate levels.

Finally, I should like to raise a major problem which has been totally ignored at this conference, namely, the relationship of person-emotional development to that of cognitive development. Let us briefly consider some of the genetic relationships between the organization of affect and intellect which are not typically dealt with. The organization of personality is largely a matter of identification. It is similar to the problem of the identification of any other object of knowledge in the course of development. In that sense one may draw very interesting genetic parallels for longitudinal study. This would involve the investigation of the development of permanence, conservation, etc. of personal identity in the course of the life cycle (cf. Erik H. Erikson, Identity and the Life Cycle, *Psychol. Issues*, 1959, *1*, 1-171). To put it plainly, we have yet to study the mechanisms of integration which insure developmental coherence of identity (e.g., that I am the same person now as when I was a child even though I have changed). On the other hand, we still have much to learn about the disintegration of identity in pathology, e.g., in dissociation, amnesia, etc.

There are also some striking differences between the operations involved in the formation of personal identity and that of other objects of cognition. In conceptualizing the organization of objects of knowledge, one recognizes that in the course of development the individual gives different cognitive status to objects (cf. V. Aldrich, *Philosophy of Art*). In particular, the self takes on the cognitive status of a relatively subjective (i.e., internal, psychological, spiritual) object; while other things are made into relatively objective (i.e., external, physical, material,) objects of knowledge. This is why, for example, scientists come to distrust their personal assessment of phenomena and place so much trust in "objective" analysis.

Professor Piaget's distinction between efficacy and phenomenalism is particularly relevant in this regard (cf. Piaget, *The Child's Conception of Physical Causality*). These are the two basic causal relationships which are formed. In the sensori-motor stage of development no differentiation is made between efficacious and phenomenalistic relationships, just as no distinction is made between objects as subjective or objective. With development, efficacious and phenomenalistic relationships progressively differentiate. Efficacy becomes the intentional mode and phenomenalism the physical-causal mode. The cognitive status of subjectivity is given to intentionality—the inner state or reason for doing something (cf. Peters, *The Concept of Motivation*). If for example, I make a noise by hitting the table, then the cause of the noise may be asked. If we mean by this what is the reason for the occurrence of the noise we are asking a question of intention. That is, we are asking about the purpose for making the noise. On the other hand, if we are asking how the noise happened, then we are concerned with the physical relationships between objects which produce noise. The cognitive status of objectivity is given to the establishment of such physical-causal, external relationships.

At this point I should merely like to add that my comments have been directed towards some of the implications of Professor Piaget's powerful theoretical-empirical model of cognitive development for curriculum development. It is with this purpose in mind that I have taken this occasion to raise some problems. I hope they will serve to stimulate consideration of the relationship of communication and personal development to cognitive development.

---

1. How is knowledge in science different from knowledge in history? Music? Art? On what bases do you make your decisions?

2. "The assumption is that the organism is always involved in constructive schematization *via* the functional interaction of assimilation and accommodation." What do these words mean to you?
3. What part does language play in conceptual learning? Could language ever be a detriment to conceptual learning?

18 ARTHUR W. COMBS

Intelligence from a
Perceptual Point of View

Perceptual psychology has received increased attention from psychologists and educators alike. Carl Rogers is probably the best known spokesman for the group of people who believe that behavior is a function of perception. Self-concept is central to the perceptual psychologist and intelligence is viewed in this paper by Combs as a problem of perception. Although the ideas in this paper are a sharp departure in many ways from the development psychology of Piaget, significant relationships can be drawn that have direct bearing on curriculum and instruction endeavors. From Combs' observation that intelligence is dependent upon the nature of past experiences, it is easy to see how this is directly related to Piaget's experience factor in development. It is left to you to make up other relationships between these two theories whenever it seems logical.

There is a growing trend in psychology toward viewing behavior as a function of perception. More and more we have come to understand that the individual's behavior is not so much a function of the physical stimulus as it is a function of his perceptions of the events to which he is exposed. It is the meaning of events to the individual rather than the externally observed nature of events which seems crucial in behavior. As a result, psychologists in increasing numbers are turning their attention to the problems of human perception and are attempting to observe behavior, not from an external point of view, but from the point of view of the individual who is behaving. This paper is an attempt to relate this method of observation to the problem of intelligence. The question we wish to explore in this paper is: "What is the nature of intelligence viewed from a perceptual or phenomenological frame of reference?"

Reprinted from *The Journal of Abnormal and Social Psychology*, Vol. 47, 1952, pp. 662-673, by permission of the editor and the author. Dr. Combs has been a leader in the field of perceptual psychology as related to education and continues his work at the University of Florida.

Intelligence as a Problem of Perception

By the term *intelligence* we ordinarily refer to the effectiveness of the individual's behavior. In a personal frame of reference the individual's behavior is described in terms of the perceptions that he can make his own unique perceptive field. This perceptive field has been called by Snygg and Combs *The Phenomenal Field* and has been defined by them as "the universe of experience open to the individual at the moment of his behavior." In other words, the behavior of the individual will be dependent upon the perceptions that the individual makes in his phenomenal field at the moment of action. The effectiveness of his behavior will necessarily be a function of the adequacy of those perceptions.

If an entity in the perceptive field is vague and ill defined, the behavior of the individual will be correspondingly vague and lacking in precision. Until the child has clearly differentiated that 2 plus 2 equals 4, this function is comparatively meaningless and his behavior in arithmetic is correspondingly inaccurate and ineffective. Thus, the precision and effectiveness of the individual's behavior will be dependent upon the scope and clarity of his personal field of awareness. Intelligence, then, from a perceptual point of view becomes a function of the factors which limit the scope and clarity of an individual's phenomenal field.

The perceptions that could be made of any given situation, such as looking at a stone wall, for example, are, theoretically, practically infinite in number and quality. As a matter of fact, however, we are strictly limited in our perceptions of a stone wall to those which we, as human beings, can make. The perceptions possible to us are only those that people can make. We cannot, for instance, perceive the wall as it would appear to a man from Mars, or from the interior of an atom, or as it would appear to a centipede. What is more, we cannot even perceive it as it would appear to all people. Different people will perceive different aspects of the wall differently, even at the same instant. I can only perceive the wall, and hence behave toward it, in terms of the perceptions that I, as an individual, can make regarding it. I may, for instance, perceive it as a fine, sturdy fence enclosing my property, while a stone mason friend might perceive it as having been poorly designed or as having been built with too little cement in the mortar mixture. The perceptions open to my mason friend are the result of his unique experience. I, not having such experience, am incapable of those perceptions at this moment.

Potential and Functional Perceptions

Before proceeding further with our discussion of the limiting factors in perception, it is necessary for us to pause for a moment to distinguish between potential and functional perceptions. By potential perceptions I mean those perceptions that exist in the individual's unique field of awareness and that, given the right circumstances at any particular moment, *could* occur. The fact that a perception is potentially possible to any individual, by no means, however, means that it will occur at the moment of action. Even those perceptions that I can make potentially may not be active for me at any given moment. Potentially, I might be able, for instance, to perceive the wall that we have just been using as an example as a barrier to be gotten over, as an eyesore to be beautified, as composed of 687 bricks costing me $80.27, or as providing pleasant shade on a hot day. These are all potential perceptions I am capable of making about the wall. They will affect my behavior, however, only when they are active or functioning in my field of perceptions. When I am beating a hasty retreat pursued by a neighbor's angry dog, perceptions about the shade, beauty, or cost of the wall, though potential, are not functional in affecting my behavior. I behave only in terms of my functioning perception of the wall as something to get over—and quickly. The fact that particular perceptions may exist potentially in the phenomenal field of an individual is by no means a guarantee that they may exist functionally at the moment of action.

While the potential intelligence of the individual is of interest in judging his capacities, it is practically always a matter impossible to measure with any degree of accuracy. We can only sample those parts of a phenomenal field that *we* happen to feel are important. Obviously the measurement of a person's potential perceptions in these terms is open to extremely grave sampling error and improves in accuracy only as the individuals tested have common experience in the materials chosen for testing. It seems probable that an intelligence test cannot accurately measure the potential differentiations that the individual can make in his phenomenal field. Rather, what we usually measure are the subject's functional perceptions. That is, we measure what differentiations he can make when confronted with the necessity to do so for one reason or another. We may define these functional perceptions as: those perceptions in the field experienced by the individual at the moment of behaving.

From a perceptual viewpoint, if intelligence is the capacity for effective behavior, *the intelligence of an individual will be dependent upon the richness and variety of perceptions possible to him at a given moment*. To understand and effectively to foster intelligent behavior, it will be necessary for us to be concerned with the limiting factors upon the perceptions of an individual. We need to know not only what the individual *could* perceive, but what he *would* perceive at a given moment of behaving.

Some Limiting Factors Upon Perception

Physiologic limitations upon perception

Certainly the physical limitations upon the organism affect the differentiations possible in the phenomenal field. Some forms of prenatal anomalies, like mongolism, microcephalia, and similar disorders, indubitably reduce the level of operation at which the individual can function and seriously impair the abiltiy of the organism to make adequate perceptions. Similarly, there seems good reason to believe that some types of mechanical or disease injury to the central nervous system may result in impaired functioning, such as occurs in cerebral palsy, birth injuries, prefontal lobotomy, the aftermath of such diseases as encephalitis or, even, in common childhood diseases accompanied by prolonged fever. Various forms of endocrinopathies, particularly cretinism, also appear to have limiting effects upon differentiational capacity for some individuals. Such physical or biological limitations upon the organism have been widely studied but account for only a small proportion of those persons operating at impaired intelligence levels.

Other less dramatic forms of physical handicaps may also have important effects upon the perceptions possible to the individual, however. This is particularly true of individuals suffering impairment of various sense modalities which may inhibit the clarity or even the existence of some perceptions. We need to remind ourselves, however, that such persons may have as rich and varied a perceptive field within their own limitations as we have within ours. Testing persons living in one frame of reference with tests based on those of another can easily lead us astray, a fact well known to the makers of some tests for the handicapped. The limitations imposed upon perception by such physical handicaps as the loss or impairment of locomotion or the use of arms or hands are also important in limiting certain kinds of perceptions. These people experience different, but not necessarily fewer or poorer, perceptions of events than so-called "normals."

Perhaps less well recognized in their effects upon perception are such factors as malnutrition, focal infections, and chronic fatigue, which may reduce both the need for and the ability to make adequate perceptions. It is well known in industrial psychology, for example, that fatigued workers are more likely to have accidents, perhaps because of failure to make the right differentiations at the right time. It is conceivable that persons suffering from chronic fatigue over long periods similarly fail to make differentiations useful to them on later occasions.

Certainly such physical factors as these have important effects upon the ability of the individual to make adequate differentiations in his perceptive field. The more dramatic of these have often been recognized and studied. Others, such as the effects of malnutrition, fatigue, and the like, have been less adequately explored. In spite of the lack of research in respect to some of the physical limitations upon intelligence, far more work has been done in this area, however, than in some of those to be discussed below.

Environment and opportunity as a limitation upon perception

The differentiations in the phenomenal field that an individual can make will, of course, be affected by the opportunities for perception to which he has been exposed. To appear in the perceptive field an event must have been, in some manner, experienced by the person who perceives it. Environmental effects upon perception appear to be of two types, actual or concrete and symbolic or vicarious.

Exposure to Actual Environmental Events

In the first place the perceptions possible to any individual will be limited, in part, by the actual environmental factors to which he has been exposed. Eskimos ordinarily do not comprehend bananas, nor African Bushmen, snow, since neither has had the opportunity to experience these events in their respective environments. It is not necessary to go so far afield for illustration, however. In our own country our experience with the testing of children in various parts of the nation has shown that perceptions are highly limited by the environmental conditions surrounding the individual. Mountain children, for example, often give bizarre responses on intelligence tests. Sherman and Henry found intelligence test results on such children arranged themselves in order of the opportunities provided by their environment.

There are differences also between the perceptions of rural and urban children, children from the North and children from the South, mountain and valley, seaboard and plains. Nor are such differences confined only to children. Adults, too, are limited in their perceptions by environmental factors. During the war I worked for a time in an induction station receiving men from the mountains of Kentucky, West Virginia, and southern Ohio. An intelligence test in use at this station was composed of a series of five pictures with instructions to the subject to cross out that one of each series of five objects that did not belong with the others. One set of five pictures showed four stringed instruments, a guitar, harp, violin, bass fiddle, and a trumpet. Large numbers of these back country men crossed out the harp because they had never seen one or because "all the others are things in our band." We cannot assume that these men were less able to make differentiations or had perceptive fields less rich than their examiner on the basis of these tests. We can only suggest that their perceptions are different from those who made the test. Presumably, had they made the test and administered it to the psychologist, the psychologist would have appeared rather dull!

Exposure to Symbolic or Vicarious Events

Differentiations may occur in the perceptive field upon a symbolic basis as well as from exposure to an actual event. That is, perceptions may occur in the individual's field through indirect exposure to experience as in reading, conversation, movies, and other means of communication. Although I cannot directly perceive that it is dangerous to expose myself to rays from an atomic pile, for example, I can differentiate this notion through what others whom I respect have told me. Ideas and concepts are largely differentiations of this sort, and it is probable that many of our perceptions are acquired through a symbolic rather than an actual exposure. Certainly most of our formal schooling falls in this category which may explain, in part, why so little of it is effective in our behavior.

It will be recognized at once that exposure to events in no sense completely determines the perceptions that the individual will make. Exposure to events is only one of the factors involved in determining whether or not an event will be differentiated. Even with equivalent exposure, the perceptions we make are not alike. Perception is not an all or none proposition but a selective process. The same person in the same situation at different times may perceive quite different aspects of the situation and behave accordingly. The provisions of opportunity to perceive is by no means a guarantee that a particular perception will occur, a phenomenon of which teachers are only too aware. The personal field of the individual is always organized and meaningful and, even with individual in his own unique economy will be differentiated with exposure to events, only those aspects that have meaning for the permanence.

The individual in a particular culture perceives those aspects of his environment that, from his point of view, he needs to perceive to maintain and enhance his self in the world in which he lives. This does not mean he makes fewer perceptions than an individual in another culture; he makes only *different* perceptions. Thus, intelligence tests made in one culture and applied in another do not measure the ability to differentiate, nor do they measure the richness of the individual's field. Perhaps what they really measure is no more than the difference between cultures. American-made intelligence tests applied to other cultures generally show the following arrangement of nationality groups in decreasing order: British Isles, Germany, France, Italy, the Balkans,

Asiatic countries. It will be noted that these nationality groups are also roughly arranged in order of the degree of commonality with our own culture.

Time as a limitation upon perception

Differentiation requires time. The richness of perception, therefore, will be in part a function of how long the individual has been in touch with experiences. While it is true that a perception is possible only when confronted by an experience, it is also true that this exposure must be long enough to make differentiation possible. This principle is familiar to anyone who has looked at a painting for a period of time. The perceptions which can be made are almost limitless if one looks long enough.

In thinking of the effect of time upon differentiation, it is necessary for us to keep in mind that we are speaking of the duration of the individual's experience with an event and not of the observer's experience. Thus, while it may appear to an outside observer that an individual is confronted by an experience, from the individual's own point of view, he may have no contact with it whatever. A child may sit in school all day, apparently exposed to the curriculum, but may actually be experiencing and perceiving quite different aspects of the situation. Perception is an internal, individual phenomenon and may be quite different from that of another person, even in the same situation.

Most perceptions that the individual makes are functions of previous differentiations he has made in his phenomenal field. For example, before one can perceive the mechanics of multiplication, he must have perceived addition. In the same way, before he can perceive the function of a sand dome on top of the locomotive, he must differentiate the fact that locomotive wheels sometimes slip. Clearly this process of differentiation takes time. It seems axiomatic that to make differentiations an individual must have lived long enough to do so, a fact we recognize in the construction of intelligence tests calibrated for various age levels, and which teachers recognize in the concept of readiness.

Differentiations in the phenomenal field seem to be occurring continuously as the organism seeks to satisfy its needs in the myriad situations of life. In this sense, intelligence never ceases to develop but is continuously increasing so long as the individual remains alive and operating. That intelligence seems to level off at age sixteen or later is probably a mere artifact of our method of observation. So long as the individual remains in school we have at least a modicum of comparable experience which can be tested in different persons. After the school years, when individuals are free to go their separate ways, this modicum of comparable experience rapidly disappears. The older one gets, the more diverse is his experience. Intelligence tests based upon comparability of experience may thus fail to evaluate properly the effectiveness of adults.

The individual's goals and values as a limiting factor upon perception

Up to this point in our discussion we have been dealing with factors affecting perception that are widely discussed in the literature and for the most part are well understood. In the remainder of this paper let us turn our attention to several factors less well explored as they appear in a phenomenological setting. The first of these has to do with the effects of the individual's own goals and values as a limiting factor on perception.

From a phenomenological view the individual is forever engaged in a ceaseless attempt to achieve satisfaction of his need through goals and values he has differentiated as leading to that end. These goals and values may be explicit or implicit, simple or complex, but they are always unique to the personality itself. The goals of an individual will vary in another respect as well. The individual's goals and values may be either positive or negative. That is, in the course of his experience, the person may differentiate some things as matters to be sought, while other things may be differentiated as matters to be avoided. What is more, although there is a considerable degree of stability in the major goals and values of a particular individual, there may be great fluctuations in how some goals are perceived from time to time, depending upon the total organization of the perceptual field at any moment.

The goals and values an individual seeks have a most important effect upon the perceptions he can make. Once goals have been established by the individual they continue to affect his every experience. Thus, the person who has differentiated good music as a goal to be sought perceives music more frequently. His entire experience with music is likely to be affected. Certainly his experience will differ markedly from the person who has formulated a goal to avoid music at all costs. In the same way the experiences of children who perceive schooling as something to be sought are vastly different from those of children who try to avoid all aspects of schooling. If the fundamental thesis of this paper is accurate, that intelligence is a function of the variety and richness of the perceptive field, then the individual's goals must have a most important effect upon intelligence. A considerable body of research has been accumulating over the past several years, demonstrating this controlling effect of goals and values on the individual's perceptive experience. Such studies as those of J. M. Levine, R. Levine, Postman, and Bruner are fascinating cases in point.

This effect of goals on perception is by no means limited to the subject whose intelligence we wish to measure. It is equally true of the intelligence test constructor. It leads to the very confusing situation wherein the test constructor with one organization of goals perceives certain experiences to be marks of intelligence for another person who may or may not have similar goals. Indeed, the likelihood is that he, almost certainly, does not have similar goals. Intelligence tests thus become highly selected samplings of perception in terms of what the testers consider important. Low scores do not necessarily mean less rich and varied fields of perception; they may mean only fields of perception more widely divergent from those of the examiner. A young man whom the writer tested at an induction center during the war illustrates the point very well. This young man was a newsboy on the streets of a West Virginia city. Although he had failed repeatedly in grammar school and was generally regarded as "not bright," he appeared on a national radio hook-up as "The Human Adding Machine." He was a wizard at figures. He could correctly multiply such figures as 6235941×397 almost as fast as the problem could be written down. He astounded our induction center for half a day with his numerical feats. Yet, on the Binet Test given by the writer he achieved an IQ of less than 60! People in his home town, who bought his papers, amused themselves by giving him problems to figure constantly. When not so occupied this young man entertained himself by adding up the license numbers of cars that passed his corner. He was a specialist in numbers. Apparently as a result of some early success in this field, he had been led to practice numbers constantly, eventually to the exclusion of all else. This was one area in which a poor colored boy could succeed and he made the most of it. His number perceptions were certainly rich and varied but other things were not. Although he was capable of arithmetic feats not achieved by one in millions, he was classified as dull! I do not mean to argue that variety of perception is unimportant in effective behavior. I do mean to suggest the importance of goals in determining perception.

Cultural effects on goals and perceptions
We have stated here that the richness of the individual's perceptive field is in part a function of the goals he has differentiated as important or threatening to him. But, clearly these goals are themselves the results of the individual's experience. The culture one grows up in deeply affects the goals one holds. Cultures both restrict and encourage, approve and disapprove the formulation of goals in the individual. This selective effect of the culture in large measure determines the goals sought and avoided by the individual. These goals in turn must exert

important effects upon the perceptions that become part of the individual's perceptive field.

I remember the Kentucky moonshiner to whom I once administered the Wechsler-Bellevue. This man could not tell me "how many pints in a quart" although he had certainly been taught this fact in his early schooling. Knowing that my client did a considerable business in bootleg liquor, I framed the question differently and asked "Well, how do you sell your liquor?" He smiled tolerantly and replied, "Oh Boss, I just sell it by the jug full!" In his community to have done otherwise would have been to risk bankruptcy. In a culture where a jug is standard container for spirits, what need to know about quarts?

It is conceivable that low intelligence may be, at least in part, no more than a function of the goals an individual is striving to reach in achieving his need satisfaction. The well-known phenomenon in which intelligence tests give best results in the school years, when experience and goals have a degree of commonality, and break down badly following those years would seem to corroborate this point. Perhaps by concerning ourselves with human goals we can affect perception, and thus intelligence, much more than we believed possible. Can it be that the child of low apparent intelligence is not so much a problem of an unfortunate heredity as an unfortunate constellation of goals or values? We could do a great deal about intelligence if that were true.

The self-concept as a factor limiting perception

We are just beginning to understand the tremendous effects of the individual's concept of self upon his perceptions and behavior. Lecky, for instance, reports the effect of a change in self-concept in improving the ability of children to spell. Other researches have reported similar effects of the self-concept upon the perceptions which the individual may make. Clinical experience would tend to bear out such observations. Any clinician is familiar with numerous instances in which a child's conception of his abilities severely limited his achievement, even though his real abilities may have been superior to his perception of them. One needs but to go shopping with one's spouse to discover again how one's conception of himself as a male or female affects the things he sees and the things he hears.

Perception is a selective process, and the conception one holds of himself is a vital factor in determining the richness and the variety of perception selected. It makes a great deal of difference, for example, how one perceives the president of our country if one conceives of himself as a Democrat, a Republican, or a Communist. One needs but to observe a group of children to become aware that little boys perceive things quite differently from little girls. Professors do not perceive like truck drivers, although when I have had to ride with professor automobile-drivers, I have often wished they did. Thousands of people in our society avoid perceptions having to do with mathematical functions by their firm concept of themselves as people who "cannot do mathematics." The self-concepts we hold have a very vital effect in selecting the perceptions which become part of our perceptive fields. If the effectiveness of behavior is dependent on our perceptive fields, it follows that the self-concepts we hold must affect the "intelligence" of our behavior.

There is another factor in the effect of the self-concept upon perception that makes it even more important as a selector of experience. That factor is the circular effect of a given concept of self. Let us take, as an example, the child who has developed a concept of himself as "unable to read." Such a child is likely to avoid reading, and thus the very experience which might change his concept of self is bypassed. Worse still, the child who believes himself unable to read, confronted with the necessity for reading, is more likely than not to do badly. The external evaluation of his teachers and fellow pupils, as well as his own observations of his performance, all provide proof to the child of how right he was in the first place! The possession of a particular concept of self tends to produce behavior that corroborates the self-concept with which the behavior originated.

Every clinician has had experience with children of ability who conceive of themselves as unable, unliked, unwanted, or unacceptable and perceive and behave in accordance with their perceptions. And this effect is not limited to children alone. It seems to me one of the great tragedies of our society that millions of people in our society perceiving themselves as able to produce only X amount, behave in these terms. Society, in turn, evaluates them in terms of this behavior and so lends proof to what is already conceived by the individual. Compared to this waste of human potential in our society, our losses in automobile accidents seem like a mere drop in the bucket. It is even conceivable in these terms that we create losses in intelligence. If, in our schools, we teach a child that he is unable and if he believes us and behaves in these terms, we need not be surprised when we test his intelligence to discover that he produces at the level at which we taught him!

It is conceivable that psychology has unwittingly contributed to this situation by the widespread publication of a static conception of intelligence and human capacities. The concept of severe limits upon the capacities of the organism simply corroborates the self-concept of the man in the street and decreases the likelihood of change in his concept of self. Even more important must be the effect upon our educational system. Teachers who believe in an unchanging character of child capacities provide the attitudes and experiences that produce and maintain a child's conception of self and his abilities. It is notorious that children's grades vary very little from year to year through the course of schooling. This continuous and little-changing evaluation must have important effects on the self-concept of the child. If the school system in which the child lives is thoroughly imbued with the notion that a child's capacities are comparatively fixed, it is even conceivable that the system may in large measure produce a child's intellignce level by the circular effect we have mentioned above.

Threat as a Factor in Perception

The last of the factors I should like to discuss as a possible factor in intelligence is the effect of threat upon the perceptive field. If our fundamental assumption that intelligence is a function of the richness and breadth of the phenomenal field is correct, the effect of threat on this field becomes a most important consideration. Although these effects have been so widely understood by the layman that they have been made a part of his everyday speech, it is interesting that until very recently the phenomenon has been given little attention by psychologists. The perception by the individual of threat to himself seems to have at least two major effects upon the perceptive field.

Restriction of the perceptive field under threat

The first of these effects is the restrictive effect that the perception of threat to self seems to have on the individual's perception. When he feels himself threatened, there appears to be a narrowing of the perceptive field to the object of threat. This has often been described in the psychology of vision as "tunnel vision." The phenomenon is extremely common, and almost everyone has experienced it at some moment of crisis in his lifetime. One hears it described in such comments as "All I could see was the truck coming at us," or, "I was so scared I couldn't think of a thing." There seems reason to believe that this effect is not limited to traumatic experiences alone, but exists in lesser degree in response to milder threats as well. Combs and Taylor, for example, have demonstrated the effect under extremely mild forms of threat.

Such limiting effects on perception must certainly have a bearing upon perceptions available to the individual in his phenomenal field. Subjects who have participated in food deprivation experiments report uniformly that when threatened by hunger, food becomes an obsession. Recently, at the dinner table, I asked my young daughter what she had learned at school that day. "Oh nothing," said she with much feeling, "but was our teacher mad! Wow!" It would appear from her remarks that, feeling threatened by an angry teacher, it was difficult for her to perceive much else. Her perceptions of the day were apparently entirely concerned with the nature of anger. No doubt these are valuable perceptions to possess, but I know of no intelligence test which measures them.

I recall, too, the behavior of two little girls whose mother was taken to a mental hospital at the beginning of the summer. The matter was kept a deep secret from these two children for fear they "would not understand." The children spent most of the summer with the writer's daughter in an incessant game of "hospital." From morning to night this game went on outside our living-room window. Apparently, this preoccupation was the direct outcome of the threat they felt in the loss of their mother, for with the mother's return the game ceased as suddenly as it had begun. To the best of my knowledge it has not occurred since. Under threat there seem to be severe limits imposed upon the breadth and character of perception.

Defense of the perceptive field under threat

There is a second effect of threat upon the individual's perceptions. This effect has to do with the defense reactions induced in the individual on perceiving himself to be threatened. The perception of threat not only narrows the field and reduces the possibility of wide perceptions, but causes the individual to protect and cling to the perceptions he already holds. Thus, the possibility of perceptual changes is reduced, and the opportunities for new perceptions or learning are decreased. Under threat, behavior becomes rigid. The fluidity and adaptation which we generally associate with intelligent behavior is vastly decreased. A number of interesting experiments in the past few years have demonstrated this phenomenon. Cowen, for example, illustrated this effect in problem solving.

Our own experiment previously mentioned also demonstrated this effect with even very mild forms of threat. This rigidity or resistance of perception to change under threat is well known to the layman and is well illustrated in some of the sayings of our culture. Such aphorisms as "Nobody ever wins an argument" or "You can lead a horse to water but you cannot make him drink" seem to be illustrations of a vague understanding of the phenomenon in the public mind. It is surprising that this principle has been so long overlooked.

I think it will be generally agreed that intelligent behavior is quite the antithesis of rigidity. In the terms we have used in this article, intelligent behavior is a function of the variety and richness of perception in the phenomenal field. Whatever produces narrowness and rigidity of perception becomes an important factor in limiting intelligence. If this reasoning is accurate, or even partly so, one is led to wonder about the effects of long-continued threat upon the development of intelligence. What of the child who has suffered serious threats to himself for long periods of his life, as in the case of the delinquent, for example? Or what of the child who has been seriously deprived of affection and warmth from those who surround him over a period of years? Is it possible that we have created low intelligence in such children? Axline has reported a number of cases in which intelligence scores improved considerably under therapy. We have observed similar changes in our own clinical practice.

It may be argued that, although threat seems to reduce perception, some people under threat apparently produce more effectively. I think, however, it is necessary for us to distinguish between "threat" and "challenge." In threat, the individual perceives himself in jeopardy and feels, in addition, a degree of inadequacy to deal effectively with the threat perceived. In challenge, the individual perceives himself threatened but feels at the same time a degree of adequacy to deal with the threat. It would appear that whether an event is perceived as threatening or challenging is a function of the individual's feeling of competence to deal with it. If this analysis is correct, it would explain why a situation that appears threatening to a person, from the viewpoint of an outside observer, might one time produce rigidity and another highly effective behavior. This description of events seems characteristic of the history of civilization as well as of individuals, if Toynbee's explanation can be given credence. He points out that the most productive (more intelligent?) societies are those in which the society faces some crisis within its capacities to cope with the situation (challenge), while societies without crisis or in which the crisis is overwhelming produce very little or collapse entirely.

Some Implications of this Conception of Intelligent Behavior

If the conception of intelligence we have been discussing in this paper should prove accurate, it seems to me to raise serious questions about some of our common assumptions with respect to intelligence and, at the same time, opens some exciting new possibilities for the treatment or education of persons we have often assumed to be beyond help. It implies that our conception of the limiting factors of intelligence may have been too narrow. It would suggest perhaps that our very point of view with respect to intelligence may have resulted in our own tunnel vision, such that we have not been able to perceive other factors given little attention to this point. Perhaps we have been too impressed with the limitations upon growth and development which we observe in physical maturation. We may, for instance, have jumped too quickly to the assumption that intelligent behavior was limited as severely as physical growth and that we have explored to exhaustion other factors that may limit intelligence.

I am not suggesting that physiologic limits do not exist in respect to intelligence. I am suggesting that we may have conceded too early that we had approached those limits. There is no doubt that we can demonstrate in some cases, such as mongolism, cretinism, and the like, that physical factors severely limit intelligence. But these cases are comparatively few compared to the so-called "familial" cases of low intelligence that we often assume are hereditary in origin. What evidence do we really possess that would lead us to the position that an individual of "normal" physical condition and vigor may be limited in his capacity for effective behavior by some physical condition? We assume there must be such factors operating because we cannot explain his handicap otherwise. That biological science has not yet been able to demonstrate such physical bases has not deterred us in this. On the contrary, we have simply deplored the lack of sufficient advance in that discipline to demonstrate our conclusion! I should like to suggest that this may not be their failure but ours. Until it can be definitely established that limitations exist as biological functions, our task as psychologists is to assume that they may just as well be social or psychological in character and to work just as hard exploring the matter in our discipline as we expect the biologist to work in his.

Let us, for example, explore to the very fullest the possibility that in those cases where we cannot demonstrate biologic impairment, the limitations upon intelligence may be psychological. If it turns out not to be true, we shall find out in time. I do not believe we can afford to limit the places were we look by the preperceptions we have about the matter. Our responsibility here is too great. Education, to name but the most obvious of our social institutions, has in large measure predicated its goals and methods on a concept of humanity with certain static limitations on intelligence. If these limitations are not static, it is up to us as psychologists to find out. The task of the scientist is to question, not to be content with answers. We cannot afford to accept an undemonstrated point of view that prevents us from asking questions.

Some Implications for Intelligence Testing

If the concepts of intelligence we have been discussing prove accurate, another area of psychological thought toward which we must cast a quizzical eye is the area of intelligence testing. This is particularly important at a time when our culture has come to accept these instruments as trustingly as the family doctor's prescription. If our approach to intelligent behavior as a function of the variety and richness of the perceptual field is a valid consideration, we need to ask regarding these tests at least the following questions:

1. Is our sampling of the perceptive field truly adequate? If I lived for years in a prison cell, I presume I should become expert in perceptions about that cell. Unfortunately, they would be of little value outside the prison walls, but can it truthfully be said that my perceptions are less rich or varied, or only that they are less rich and varied about things I have not had opportunity to experience? Is the delinquent, with rich and varied perceptions on how to elude the police, less intelligent or has he simply not perceived things society wishes he had?

2. Since perceptions are always closely affected by need, by whose need shall we sample perceptions—yours, mine, society's, the subject's own? I suspect that in terms of his own needs and perceptions the subject might be deemed quite brilliant, though he might or might not appear so from the point of view of society. For the most part our tests are based on the assumption that academic, upper middle-class, intellectual perceptions are important. But are they? Can we assume that the expert machinist, who can perceive things "out of this world" for most of the rest of us about a piece of stock on his lathe, is less intelligent than a diplomat who perceives many things about foreign affairs? Can we be so sure of our values as to call one bright and the other dull? Can we blame the machinist for his lack of perception about foreign affairs without asking the diplomat to be equally skilled in the machinist's field of perceptions?

3. Finally, if perceptions are affected by the factors we have discussed in this paper, is it fair to sample intelligence irrespective of the control of such factors? Shall we, for example, examine the child who has lacked opportunity to perceive, has possessed a concept of self or been so threatened over a long period of time so as to have been unable to perceive what we wish to sample without consideration of those factors? Shall we overlook such factors and be satisfied that the perceptions important to us are not there, or shall we seek for ways to make it possible for the child to have them? Shall we assume that our failure to discover a particular perception present in the field is, *ipso facto*, evidence of lack of capacity; or seek to discover why it is not? On the positive side of the picture, if the concepts we have here been discussing are sound, there is reason to believe that intelligence may be far less immutable than we have thought. It may be that we can do far more than we have dreamed we could. Perhaps we may even be able to create intelligence!

Implications for Constructive Action

Who can say, for example, what results we might be able to achieve by a systematic effort to remove or decrease the effectiveness of the limitations on perception discussed in this paper? It is fascinating to speculate on the possibilities one might try in constructing a situation for a child, or adult, consciously designed to minimize the limitations imposed on perception by physical condition, environment, goals, the individual's self-concept, and the effects of perceived personal threat.

If the position we have taken is accurate, it would suggest that there is much we can do (a) to free individuals from the restraints upon perception and (b) to provide the opportunities for perception to occur.

1. First and most obviously, we should be able to discover and make available to far more people the means to achieve better physical condition. We have already done a good deal in this area but much needs yet to be done. Who can say, for instance, what completely adequate medical care for all our people might mean a generation hence?

2. If this discussion has merit, there lies the possibility of providing experiences for people that will make adequate perceptions possible. We have tried to do this in our schools, but have not always accomplished it. We have succeeded very well in gathering information and in making it available to students. We have not succeeded too well in making such information meaningful. Can it be that the decreases in school success with advance through the school years is more a function of lack of meaning for students than lack of intelligence? Is it enough to assume that experience provided by us to the student is truly provided when he is free to experience it? Has the child in school, who is so worried about his relationship with his peers that he cannot perceive what his book is saying, truly been provided opportunity to perceive?

In our training of children of "low intelligence," we often provide situations wherein they are carefully taught to perform repeatedly a simple act. Is it possible that in so doing we may be further narrowing their fields of perception and building self-concepts that produce even narrower perceptive fields?

What kinds of environments could we construct that might more effectively result in increased perception? Such experiments as Lippitt and White have carried on with democratic and autocratic environments suggest some possibilities, but we need to know much more. Perhaps we could learn to build such environments from observing with greater care and understanding the methods of good teachers.

3. Who can say what possible effects might occur from a systematic release of the individual's perceptions by the satisfaction of his most pressing needs or goals? We college professors insist we can produce

more, which is another way of saying perceive more, when we have the leisure time to do so, when we are freed from the necessity of spending our time satisfying our needs for sheer existence. Can this be less true of others? It is possible that the child with needs of love, affection, status, prestige, or a girl friend might also be freed to perceive more widely and richly, if we could but find ways of helping him satisfy his needs. Ordinarily, we pay a good deal of attention to the physical needs of a child, understanding that with these needs unfulfilled, he makes a poor student. Is there any good reason to suppose his psychological needs are less pressing or less important in freeing him to perceive widely and accurately? We spend much time and energy trying to find ways of "motivating" people or blaming them for not being motivated to do what we need them to do. We assume that if permitted to seek their own needs, people will not satisfy ours. Perhaps we should get further by helping them satisfy their needs; they might then be free to satisfy ours.

4. Most of our educational methods are directed at the provision of perceptions for the student. He is lectured, required, shown, exhorted, and coerced to perceive what someone thinks he should. It seems possible that with equal energy devoted to the matter of creating needs, goals, and values in students, rich and varied perceptions might be more efficiently produced.

What effects might we be able to produce by providing experiences that build adequate concepts of self in children and adults? What differences in the richness and variety of perception might result from a generation of people with "I can" rather than "I can't" conceptions of themselves? What possibilities of increased perceptions and hence of increased intelligence might accrue to such a program? Clinical experience has demonstrated frequently how a changed perception of self as a more adequate personality can free children for improved school performance, for example.

What would happen if we were consciously and carefully to set about the task of providing experiences that would lead people to conceptions of themselves as adequate, worthy, self-respecting people? If freedom to perceive is a function of adequate perceptions of self, it should not surprise us that the child who perceives himself as unwanted, unacceptable, unable, or unliked behaves in rigid fashion. It should be possible, too, to reverse this process and produce more adequate perceptions by systematic efforts at producing more adequate definitions of self. The possibilities seem tremendous but we have scarcely scratched the surface of this problem.

Finally, if threat to the individual has as important effects as seem indicated in this discussion, the removal of threat would seem a most important factor to consider in the release of the individual to perceive more adequately. The work of Rogers and his students in client-centered therapy has already illustrated to some degree what possibilities freeing the individual to perceive more adequately may accomplish through the provision of a permissive nonthreatening relationship between counselor and client. We have already mentioned the effects Axline has reported following a permissive, nonthreatening form of play therapy.

Such effects do not seem limited to the therapeutic situation, however. A number of workers have applied this principle of permissiveness to the classroom situation with equally gratifying results. Experiments in student-centered teaching at Syracuse have led many of us to believe in the tremendous educational possibilities in the removal of threat.

This paper has asked many questions. Indeed, it has asked far more questions than it has presumed to answer. That, it seems to me, is the function of theory. The picture of intelligence presented here as it seems from a phenomenological viewpoint may be accurate or false or, more likely, partly true and partly false. Only time and the industry of many observers can check its adequacy or inadequacy. It seems to me to pose problems that are both exciting and challenging. If it proves as stimulating to the reader as it has to the author, I shall rest content that a theory has achieved its purpose.

---

1. How is intelligence as defined by an I.Q. test related to intelligence as viewed by the perceptual psychologist?
2. How does "threat" affect one's perceptions?
3. Do you see any relationships between developmental psychology (Piaget) and perceptual psychology (Combs)?

PART THREE

Instructional Strategies: Research and Development

If *evidence* is to be used in making decisions about elementary school science, then what a child is capable of thinking about should be a major determining factor. The nature of science and the developmental nature of children's thinking have been considered so it seems reasonable to include a look at the nature of teaching at this point. In his recent book, *Crisis in the Classroom*, (1971), Silberman refers to *mindless* education as the major problem confronting our schools today. *Why* do we do what we do in our classrooms? Is it because the needs, interests, and abilities of children logically suggest such schooling or are there other reasons?

What goes on in a classroom is usually determined to a large extent by the teacher. So in the long run, each teacher should feel the responsibility of providing a *mindful* environment that is carefully thought out.

It is hoped that some of the positions and research presented by the various authors in this section will help to stimulate worthwhile thinking and discussion among those individuals who are interested in the education of children.

19 LEE S. SHULMAN

Psychological Controversies in the Teaching of Science and Mathematics

By which mode do educators decide what and how to teach? Should the structure of the various fields of science determine the manner in which education should proceed for elementary school science? The nature of current controversies in the teaching of science are examined by Dr. Shulman in this paper. "Guided" learning is compared with "discovery" learning with the two positions being represented by two well known educators, Robert Gagne and Jerome Bruner, respectively. Each position is analyzed in terms of instructional objectives, instructional styles, readiness, and transfer.

As you read this paper, try to decide what it is that might cause each of these men to hold such differing views with respect to learning. Papers which deal with thinking in children follow this particular article and may help to provide some evidence for one position over another.

The popular press has discovered the discovery method of teaching. It is by now, for example, an annual ritual for the Education section of *Time* magazine to sound a peal of praise for learning by discovery (e.g., *Time*, December 8, 1967(7). *Time's* hosannas for discovery are by no means unique, reflecting as they do the educational establishment's general tendency to make good things seem better than they are. Since even the soundest of methods can be brought to premature mortality through an overdose of unremitting praise, it becomes periodically necessary even for advocates of discovery, such as I, to temper enthusiasm with considered judgment.

The learning by discovery controversy is a complex issue which can easily be over-simplified. A recent volume has dealt with many aspects of the issue in great detail(8). The controversy seems to center essen-

Reprinted from *The Science Teacher*, Vol. 35, No. 6, 1968, pp. 34-38, by permission of the editor. Dr. Shulman is a professor of Educational Psychology and Medical Education at Michigan State University.

tially about the question of how much and what kind of guidance ought
to be provided to students in the learning situation. Those favoring learning by discovery advocate the teaching of broad principles and problem-
solving through minimal teacher guidance and maximal opportunity for
exploration and trial-and-error on the part of the student. Those pre-
ferring guided learning emphasize the importance of carefully sequencing instructional experiences through maximum guidance and stress the
importance of basic associations or facts in the service of the eventual
mastering of principles and problem-solving.

Needless to say, there is considerable ambiguity over the use of the
term *discovery*. One man's discovery approach can easily be confused
with another's guided learning curriculum if the unwary observer is not
alerted to the preferred labels ahead of time. For this reason I have
decided to contrast the two positions by carefully examining the work
of two men, each of whom is considered a leader of one of these general
schools of thought.

Professor Jerome S. Bruner of Harvard University is undoubtedly the
single person most closely identified with the learning-by-discovery position. His book, *The Process of Education*(1), captured the spirit of discovery in the new mathematics and science curricula and communicated
it effectively to professionals and laymen. His thinking will be examined
as representative of the advocates of discovery learning.

Professor Robert M. Gagné of the University of California is a major
force in the guided learning approach. His analysis of *The Conditions of
Learning*(3) is one of the finest contemporary statements of the principles of guided learning and instruction.

I recognize the potential danger inherent in any explicit attempt to
polarize the position of two eminent scholars. My purpose is to clarify
the dimensions of a complex problem, not to consign Bruner and Gagné
to irrevocable extremes. Their published writings are employed merely
to characterize two possible positions on the role of discovery in learning, which each has expressed eloquently at some time in the recent
past.

In this paper I will first discuss the manner in which Bruner and
Gagné, respectively, describe the teaching of some particular topic. Using
these two examples as starting points, we will then compare their positions with respect to instructional objectives, instructional styles, readiness for learning, and transfer of training. We will then examine the
implications of this controversy for the process of instruction in science and mathematics and the conduct of research relevant to that
process.

Instructional Example: Discovery Learning

In a number of his papers, Jerome Bruner uses an instructional example from mathematics that derives from his collaboration with the mathematics educator, Z. P. Dienes(2).

A class is composed of eight-year-old children who are there to learn some mathematics. In one of the instructional units, children are first introduced to three kinds of flat pieces of wood or "flats." The first one, they are told, is to be called either the "unknown square" or "X square." The second flat, which is rectangular, is called "1 X" or just X, since it is X long on one side and 1 long on the other. The third flat is a small square which is 1 by 1, and is called 1.

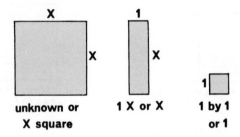

unknown or   1 X or X   1 by 1

X square   or 1

After allowing the children many opportunities simply to play with these materials and to get a feel for them, Bruner gives the children a problem. He asks them, "Can you make larger squares than this X square by using as many of these flats as you want?" This is not a difficult task for most children and they readily make another square such as the one illustrated below.

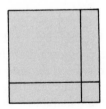

Bruner then asks them if they can describe what they have done. They might reply, "We have one square X, with two X's and a 1." He then asks them to keep a record of what they have done. He may even suggest a notational system to use. The symbol $X^=$ could represent the square X, and a + for "and." Thus, the pieces used could be described as $X^2 + 2X = 1$.

Another way to describe their new square, he points out, is simply to describe each side. With an X and a 1 on each side, the side can be described as $X + 1$ and the square as $(X + 1)$ $(X + 1)$ after some work with parentheses. Since these are two basic ways of describing the same square, they can be written in this way: $X^2 + 2X + 1 = (X + 1)$ $(X + 1)$. This description, of course, far oversimplifies the procedures used.

The children continue making squares and generating the notation for them.

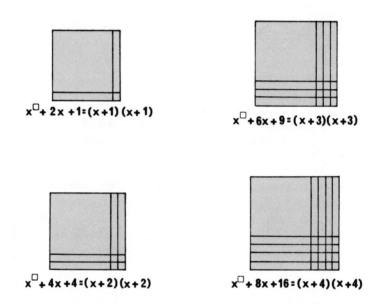

$x^{\square} + 2x + 1 = (x+1)(x+1)$

$x^{\square} + 6x + 9 = (x+3)(x+3)$

$x^{\square} + 4x + 4 = (x+2)(x+2)$

$x^{\square} + 8x + 16 = (x+4)(x+4)$

At some point Bruner hypothesizes that they will begin to discern a pattern. While the X's are progressing at the rate of 2, 4, 6, 8, the ones are going 1, 4, 9, 16, and on the right side of the equation the pattern is 1, 2, 3, 4. Provocative or leading questions are often used Socratically to elicit this discovery. Bruner maintains that, even if the children are initially unable to break the code, they will sense that there is a pattern and try to discover it. Bruner then illustrates how the pupils transfer what they have learned to working with a balance beam. The youngsters are ostensibly learning not only something about quadratic equations, but more important, something about the discovery of mathematical regularities.

The general learning process described by Bruner occurs in the following manner: First, the child finds regularities in his manipulation of the materials that correspond with intuitive regularities he has already come to understand. Notice that what the child does for Bruner is to find some sort of match between what he is doing in the outside world and some models or templates that he already has in his mind. For Bruner, it is rarely something *outside* the learner that is discovered. Instead the discovery involves an internal reorganization of previously known ideas in order to establish a better fit between those ideas and the regularities of an encounter to which the learner has had to accommodate. Remember the lovely dialogue of the *Meno* by Plato, in which the young slave boy is brought to an understanding of what is involved in doubling the area of a square. Socrates maintains throughout this dialogue that he is not teaching the boy anything new; he is simply helping the boy reorganize and bring to the fore what he has always known.

Bruner almost always begins with a focus on the production and manipulation of materials. He describes the child as moving through three levels of representation. The first level is the *enactive level*, where the child manipulates materials directly. He then progresses to the *ikonic level*, where he deals with mental images of objects but does not manipulate them directly. Finally he moves to the *symbolic level*, where he is strictly manipulating symbols and no longer mental images of objects. This sequence is an outgrowth of the developmental work of Jean Piaget. The synthesis of these concepts of manipulation of actual materials as part of a developmental model and the Socratic notion of learning as internal reorganization into a learning-by-discovery approach is the unique contribution of Jerome Bruner.

The Process of Education was written in 1959, after most mathematics innovations that use discovery as a core had already begun. It is an error to say that Bruner initiated the learning-by-discovery approach. It is far more accurate to say that, more than any one man, he managed to capture its spirit, provide it with a theoretical foundation, and disseminate it. Bruner is not the discoverer of discovery; he is its prophet.

Instructional Example: Guided Learning

Robert Gagné takes a very different approach to instruction. He begins with a task analysis of the instructional objectives. He always asks the question, "What is it you want the learner to be able to do?" This *capability* he insists, must be stated *specifically* and *behaviorally.*

By capability, he means the ability to perform certain specific functions under specified conditions. A capability could be the ability to solve a number series. It might be the ability to solve some problems in non-metric geometry.

This capability can be conceived of as a terminal behavior and placed at the top of what will eventually be a complex pyramid. After analyzing the task, Gagné asks, "What would you need to know in order to do that?" Let us say that one could not complete the task unless he could first perform prerequisite tasks *a* and *b*. So a pyramid begins.

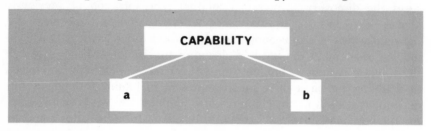

But in order to perform task *a*, one must be able to perform tasks *c* and *d* and for task *b*, one must know *e, f,* and *g*.

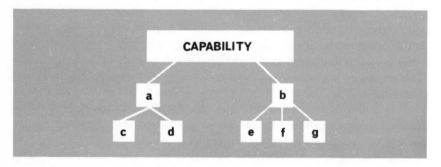

So one builds a very complex pyramid of prerequisites to the objective which is the desired capability.

Gagné has developed a model for discussing the different levels of such a hierarchy. If the final capability desired is a *problem-solving* capability, the learner first must know certain *principles*. But to understand those principles, he must know specific *concepts,* and prerequisite to these are particular *simple associations* or *facts* discriminated from each other in a distinctive manner. He continues the analysis until he ends up with the fundamental building blocks of learning—classically or operantly conditioned responses.

Gagné, upon completing the whole map of prerequisites, would administer pretests to determine which have already been mastered. Upon completing the diagnostic testing, the resulting pattern identifies precisely what must be taught. This model is particularly conductive to subsequent programming of materials and programmed instruction. When prerequisites are established, a very tight teaching program or package develops.

Earlier, we discussed the influences on Bruner. What influenced Gagné? This approach to teaching comes essentially from a combination of the neo-behaviorist psychological tradition and the task analysis model that dominates the fields of military and industrial training. It was precisely this kind of task analysis that contributed to successful programs of pilot training in World War II. Gagné was trained in the neo-behaviorist tradition and spent the major portion of his early carreer as an Air Force psychologist.

Nature of Objectives

The positions of Bruner and Gagné take very different points of view with respect to the objectives of education. This is one of the major reasons why most attempts at evaluating the relative effectiveness of these two approaches have come to naught. They really cannot agree on the same set of objectives. Any attempt to ask which is better—Michigan State's football team or the Chicago White Sox—will never succeed. The criteria for success are different, and it would be absurd to have them both on the same field competing against each other.

For Gagné, or the programmed-instruction position which can be derived from him, the objectives of instruction are capabilities. They are behavioral products that can be specified in operational terms. Subsequently they can be task-analyzed; then they can be taught. Gagné would subscribe to the position that psychology has been successful in suggesting ways of teaching only when objectives have been made operationally clear. When objectives are not clearly stated, the psychologist can be of little assistance. He insists on objectives clearly stated in behavioral terms. They are the cornerstones of his position.

For Bruner, the emphasis is quite different. The emphasis is not on the *products* of learning but on the *processes*. One paragraph from *Toward a Theory of Instruction* captures the spirit of educational objectives for Bruner. After discussing the mathematics example previously mentioned, he concludes,

> Finally, a theory of instruction seeks to take account of the fact that a curriculum reflects not only the nature of knowledge itself—the specific capabilities—but also the nature of the knower and of the knowledge-getting process. It is the enterprise par excellence where the line between the subject matter and the method grows necessarily indistinct. A body of knowledge, enshrined in a university faculty, and embodied in a series of authoritative volumes is the result of much prior

intellectual activity. To instruct someone in these disciplines is not a matter of getting him to commit the results to mind; rather, it is to teach him to participate in the process that makes possible the establishment of knowledge. We teach a subject, not to produce little living libraries from that subject, but rather to get a student to think mathematically for himself, to consider matters as a historian does, *to take part in the process of knowledge-getting. Knowing is a process, not a product.* (2, p. 72)

Speaking to the same issue, Gagné's position is clearly different.

Obviously, strategies are important for problem-solving, regardless of the content of the problem. The suggestion from some writings is that they are of overriding importance as a goal of education. After all, should not formal instruction in the schools have the aim of teaching the student "how to think?" If strategies were deliberately taught, would not this produce people who could then bring to bear superior problem-solving capabilities to any new situation? Although no one would disagree with the aims expressed, it is exceedingly doubtful that they can be brought about by teaching students "strategies" or "styles" of thinking. Even if these could be taught (and it is possible that they could), they would not provide the individual with the basic firmament of thought, which is subject-matter knowledge. Knowing a set of strategies is not all that is required for thinking; it is not even a substantial part of what is needed. *To be an effective problem solver, the individual must somehow have acquired masses of structurally organized knowledge. Such knowledge is made up of content principles not heuristic ones.* (3, p. 170) (Italics mine)

While for Bruner "knowing a process, not a product," for Gagné, "knowledge is made up of content principles, not heuristic ones." Thus, though both espouse the acquisition of knowledge as the major objective of education, their definitions of *knowledge* and *knowing* are so disparate that the educational objectives sought by each scarcely overlap. The philosophical and psychological sources of these differences will be discussed later in this paper. For the moment, let it be noted that when two conflicting approaches seek such contrasting objectives, the conduct of comparative educational studies becomes extremely difficult.[1]

Instructional Styles

Implicit in this contrast is a difference in what is meant by the very words *learning by discovery.* For Gagné, *learning* is the goal. How a be-

1. Gagné has modified his own position somewhat since 1965. He would now tend to agree, more or less, with Bruner on the importance of processes or strategies as objectives of education. He has not, however, changed his position regarding the role of sequence in instruction, the nature of readiness, or any of the remaining topics in this paper. (5) The point of view concerning specific behavioral products as objectives is still espoused by many educational theorists and Gagné's earlier arguments are thus still relevant as reflections of that position.

havior or capability is learned is a function of the task. It may be by discovery, by guided teaching, by practice, by drill, or by review. The focus is on *learning* and discovery is but one way to learn something. For Bruner, it is learning by *discovery*. The method of learning is the significant aspect.

For Gagné, in an instructional program the child is carefully guided. He may work with programmed materials or a programmed teacher (one who follows quite explicitly a step-by-step guide). The child may be quite active. He is not necessarily passive; he is doing things, he is working exercises, he is solving problems. But the sequence is determined entirely by the program. (Here the term "program" is used in a broad sense, not necessarily simply a series of frames.)

For Bruner much less system or order is necessary for the package, although such order is not precluded. In general Bruner insists on the child manipulating materials and dealing with incongruities or contrasts. He will always try to build potential or emergent incongruities into the materials. Robert Davis calls this operation "torpedoing" when it is initiated by the teacher. He teaches a child something until he is certain the child knows it. Then he provides him with a whopper of a counter-example. This is what Bruner does constantly—providing contrasts and incongruities in order to get the child, because of his discomfort, to try to resolve this disequilibrium by making some discovery (cognitive restructuring). This discovery can take the form of a new synthesis or a new distinction. Piaget, too, maintains that cognitive development is a process of successive disequilibria and equilibria. The child, confronted by a new situation, gets out of balance and must accommodate to achieve a new balance by modifying the previous cognitive structure.

Thus, for Gagné, instruction is a smoothly guided tour up a carefully constructed hierarchy of objectives; for Bruner, instruction is a roller-coaster ride of successive disequilibria and equilibria until the desired cognitive state is reached or discovered.

Readiness

The guided learning point of view, represented by Gagné maintains that readiness is essentially a function of the presence or absence of prerequisite learning.

When the child is capable of *d* and *e* above, he is by definition ready to learn *b*. Until then he is not ready. Gagné is not concerned with genetically developmental considerations. If the child at age five does not have the concept of the conservation of liquid volume, it is not because of an unfolding in his mind; he just has not had the necessary

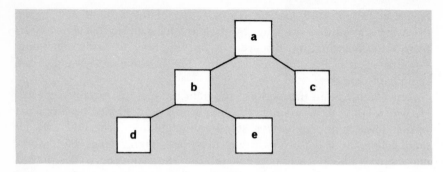

prior experiences. Ensure that he has acquired the prerequisite behaviors, and he will be able to conserve(4).

For Piaget (and Bruner) the child is a developing organism, passing
through cognitive stages that are biologically determined. These stages
are more or less age-related, although in different cultures certain stages
may come earlier than others. To identify whether the child is ready to
learn a particular concept or principle, one analyzes the structure of
that to be taught and compares it with what is already known about the
cognitive structure of the child at that age. If they are consonant, it can
be taught; if they are dissonant, it cannot.

Given this characterization of the two positions on readiness, to
which one would you attribute the following statement? ". . . any subject can be taught effectively in some intellectually honest form to any
child at any stage of development." While it sounds like Gagné, you
recognize that it isn't—it's Bruner! (2, p. 33) And in this same chapter
he includes an extensive discussion of Piaget's position. Essentially he is
attempting to translate Piaget's theories into a psychology of instruction.

Many are puzzled by this stand, including Piaget. In a recent paper
delivered in the United States, he admitted that he did not understand
how Bruner could make such a statement in the light of Piaget's experiments. If Bruner meant the statement literally; i.e., *any* child can learn
*any*thing, then it just is not true! There are always things a child cannot
learn, especially not in an intellectually honest way. If he means it
homiletically, i.e., we can take almost anything and somehow resay it,
restructure it so it now has a parallel at the child's level of cognitive
functioning, then it may be a truism.

I believe that what Bruner is saying, and it is neither trivial nor
absurd, is that our older conceptions of readiness have tended to apply
Piagetian theory in the same way as some have for generations applied
Rousseau's. The old thesis was, "There is the child—he is a developing
organism, with invariant order, invariant schedule. Here, too, is the subject matter, equally hallowed by time and unchanging. We take the sub-

ject matter as our starting point, watch the child develop, and feed it in at appropriate times as he reaches readiness." Let's face it; that has been our general conception of readiness. We gave reading readiness tests and hesitated to teach the pupil reading until he was "ready." The notion is quite new that the reading readiness tests tell not when to begin teaching the child, but rather what has to be done to get him more ready. We used to just wait until he got ready. What Bruner is suggesting is that we must modify our conception of readiness so that it includes not only the child but the subject matter. Subject matter, too, goes through stages of readiness. The same subject matter can be represented at a manipulative or enactive level, at an ikonic level, and finally at a symbolic or formal level. The resulting model is Bruner's concept of a spiral curriculum.

Piaget himself seems quite dubious over the attempts to accelerate cognitive development that are reflected in many modern math and science curricula. On a recent trip to the United States, Piaget commented,

> . . . we know that it takes nine to twelve months before babies develop the notion that an object is still there even when a screen is placed in front of it. Now kittens go through the same stages as children, all the same sub-stages, but they do it in three months so they're six months ahead of babies. Is this an advantage or isn't it? We can certainly see our answer in one sense. The kitten is not going to go much further. The child has taken longer, but he is capable of going further, so it seems to me that the nine months probably were not for nothing.
>
> It's probably possible to accelerate, but maximal acceleration is not desirable. There seems to be an optimal time. What this optimal time is will surely depend upon each individual and on the subject matter. We still need a great deal of research to know what the optimal time would be. (6, p. 82)

The question that has not been answered, and which Piaget whimsically calls the "American question," is the empirical experimental question: To what extent is it possible through a Gagnéan approach to accelerate what Piaget maintains is the invariant clock-work of the order? Studies being conducted in Scandinavia by Smedslund and in this country by Irving Sigel, Egon Mermelstein, and others are attempting to identify the degree to which such processes as the principle of conservation of volume can be accelerated. If I had to make a broad generalization , I would have to conclude that at this point, in general, the score for those who say you cannot accelerate is somewhat higher than the score for those who say that you can. But the question is far from resolved; we need many more inventive attempts to accelerate cognitive development than we have had thus far. There remains the question of whether such attempts at experimental acceleration are strictly of interest for psychological theory, or have important pedagogical implications as well—a question we do not have space to examine here.

Sequence of the Curriculum

The implications for the sequence of the curriculum growing from these two positions are quite different. For Gagné, the highest level of learning is problem-solving; lower levels involve facts, concepts, principles, etc. Clearly, for Gagné, the appropriate sequence in learning is, in terms of the diagram below, from the bottom up. One begins with simple prerequisites and works up, pyramid fashion, to the complex capability sought.

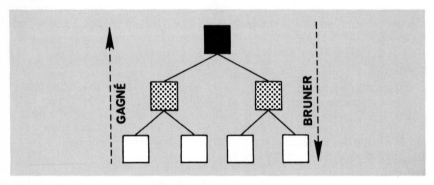

For Bruner, the same diagram may be appropriate, but the direction of the arrow would be changed. He has a pupil begin with *problem-solving*. This process is analogous to teaching someone to swim by throwing him into deep water. The theory is that he will learn the fundamentals because he needs them. The analogy is not totally misbegotten. In some of the extreme discovery approaches we lose a lot of pupils by mathematical or scientific frowning. As one goes to the extreme of this position, he runs the risk of some drownings. For Gagné, the sequence is from the simple to the complex; for Bruner one starts with the complex and plans to learn the simple components in the context of working with the complex.

It is unclear whether Bruner subscribes to his position because of his concept of the nature of learning or for strictly motivation reasons. Children may be motivated more quickly when given a problem they cannot solve, than they are when given some little things to learn on the premise that if they learn these well, three weeks from now they will be able to solve an exciting problem. Yet, Bruner clearly maintains that learning things in this fashion also improves the transferability of what is learned. It is to a consideration of the issue of transfer of training that we now turn.

Transfer of Training

To examine the psychologies of learning of these two positions in any kind of comprehensive form would require greater attention than can be devoted here, but we shall consider one concept—that of transfer of training. This is probably the central concept, or should be, in any educationally relevant psychology of learning.

Gagné considers himself a conservative on matters of transfer. He states that "transfer occurs because of the occurrence of specific identical (or highly similar) elements within developmental sequence" (4, p. 20). To the extent that an element which has been learned, be it association, concept, or principle, can be directly employed in a new situation, transfer will occur. If the new context requires a behavior substantially different from the specific capability mastered earlier, there will be no transfer.

Bruner, on the other hand, subscribes to the broadest theories of transfer of training. Bruner believes that we can have massive transfer from one learning situation to another. Broad transfer of training occurs when one can identify in the structures of subject matters basic, fundamentally simple concepts or principles which, if learned well, can be transferred both to other subject matters within that discipline and to other disciplines as well. He gives examples such as the concept of conservation or balance. Is it not possible to teach balance of trade in economics in such a way that when ecological balance is considered, pupils see the parallel? This could then be extended to balance of power in political science, or to balancing equations.

Even more important, for Bruner, is the broad transferability of the knowledge-getting processes—strategies, heuristics, and the like—a transfer whose viability leaves Gagné with deep feelings of doubt. This is the question of whether learning discovery leads to the ability *to* discover, that is, the development of broad inquiry competencies in students.

What does the evidence from empirical studies of this issue seem to demonstrate? The findings are not all that consistent. I would generalize them by saying that most often guided learning or expository sequences seem to be superior methods for achieving learning. With regard to long-term retention, the results seem equivocal, with neither approach consistently better. Discovery learning approaches appear to be superior when the criterion of transfer of principles to new situations is employed(9). Notably absent are studies which deal with the question of whether general techniques, strategies, and heuristics of discovery can be learned—by discovery or in any other manner—which will transfer across grossly different kinds of tasks.

Why is transfer of training superior in the discovery situation when the learning of principles is involved? There are two kinds of transfer—positive transfer and negative transfer. We call something positive transfer when mastery of task X facilitates mastery of task Y. Negative transfer occurs when mastery of task X inhibits mastery of task Y. Positive transfer is a familiar notion for us. Negative transfer can be exemplified by a piece of advice baseball coaches often give their players. They tell them not to play golf during the baseball season because the baseball swing and the golf swing involve totally different muscles and body movements. Becoming a better golf swinger interferes with the baseball swing. In psychological terms there is negative transfer between golf and baseball.

What is needed for positive transfer is to minimize all possible interference. In transfer of training, there are some ways in which the tasks transferred to are like the ones learned first, but in other ways they are different. So transfer always involves striking a balance between these conflicting potentials for both positive and negative transfer. In discovery methods, learners may transfer more easily because they learn *the immediate things less well*. They may thus learn the broad strokes of a principle, which is the aspect most critical for remote transfer, while not learning well the detailed application of that specific principle, which could interfere somewhat with successful remote transfer.

If this formulation is correct, we are never going to find a method that will both allow for tremendous specific learning of products and broad transfer, because we are dealing in a closed system in which one must make a choice. To the extent that initial learning is well done, transfer is restricted. The instructor may have to decide which is more important—an immediate specific product or broad transfer—and choose his subsequent teaching method on the basis of that decision. This is a pessimistic view, and I hope that future studies might find it flawed.

Synthesis or Selection

Need we eternally code these as two alternatives—discovery versus expository teaching—or can we, without being heretical, manage to keep both of these in our methodological repertories as mathematics and science educators?

John Dewey was always very suspicious whenever he approached a controversy between two strongly stated positions, each of which insisted that the other was totally in error. The classic example of this is in his monograph *Experience and Education,* in which he examines the controversy of traditional versus progressive education, Dewey teaches us that whenever we confront this kind of controversy, we must look for the possibility that each position is massively buttressed by a brilliant half-truth from which is extrapolated the whole cloth of an educational philosophy. That is, too often a good idea wears thin as its advocates insist that it be applied outside its appropriate domain.

As educators, we find it extremely important to identify the conditions under which each of these theories can be applied most fruitfully. First, one must examine the nature of the objectives. More than half of this controversy can be resolved not at the level of which is the better psychology, but at the level of evaluative philosophical judgments. Given one set of goals, clearly the position Gagné advocates presently has more evidence in its favor; given another set of goals, there is no question but that Bruner's position is preferable to Gagné's.

But there are other questions. The age and personality of the learner must be taken into account. All things being equal, there are some kinds of children who cannot tolerate the ambiguity of a discovery experience. We all know this; some of us prefer to hear lectures that are well-organized so that we can take notes in a systematic manner. Others of us like nothing better than a free-flowing bull session; and each of us is convinced that we learn more in our preferred mode than the others learn in theirs. Individual differences in learning styles are major determinants of the kinds of approaches that work best with different children.

Yet this is something we have in general not taken into consideration at all in planning curricula—and for very good reasons. As yet, we do not have any really valid ways of measuring these styles. Once we do, we will have a powerful diagnostic tool. Subject matter, objectives, characteristics of children, and characteristics of the teacher are all involved in this educational decision. Some teachers are no more likely to conduct a discovery learning sequence than they are to go frugging at a local nightclub.

There appear to be middle routes as well. In many of the experimental studies of discovery learning, an experimental treatment labeled *guided discovery* is used. In guided discovery, the subjects are carefully directed down a particular path along which they are called upon to discover regularities and solutions on their own. They are provided with cues in a carefully programmed manner, but the actual statement of the principle or problem solution is left up to them. Many of the well-planned Socratic dialogues of our fine teachers are forms of guided discovery. The teacher carefully leads the pupils into a series of traps from which they must now rescue themselves.

In the published studies, guided discovery treatments generally have done quite well both at the level of immediate learning and later transfer. Perhaps this approach allows us to put the Bruner roller-coaster of discovery on the well-laid track of a Gagné hierarchy.

Thus, the earlier question of which is better, learning by discovery or guided learning, now can be restated in more functional and pragmatic terms. Under what conditions are each of these instructional approaches, some sequence or combination of the two, of some synthesis of them, most likely to be appropriate? The answers to such questions ought to grow out of quite comprehensive principles of human learning. Where are we to find such principles?

Theories of Learning and the Science and Mathematics Curriculum

There is a growing psychology of learning that is finally becoming meaningful to curriculum construction and educational practice. Children are being studied as often as rats, and classrooms as often as mazes. Research with lower animals has been extremely useful in identifying some principles of learning that are so basic, so fundamental, so universal that they apply to any fairly well-organized blob of protoplasm. But there is a diminishing return in this approach insofar as transfer to educational practice is concerned. Today, a developing, empirically based psychology of learning for *homo sapiens* offers tremendous promise. But it can never be immediately translatable into a psychology of the teaching of mathematics or science. Mathematics and science educators must not make the mistake that the reading people have made and continue to make. The reason that the psychology of the teaching of reading has made such meager progress in the last 25 years is that the reading people have insisted on being borrowers. Something new happens in linguistics and within three years a linguistic reading series is off the press. It is an attempt to bootleg an idea from one field and put it directly into another without the necessary intervening steps of empirical testing and research.

Mathematics and science education are in grave danger of making that same error, especially with the work of Piaget and Bruner. What is needed now are well-developed empirically based psychologies of mathematics and science learning. Surely they will grow out of what is already known about the psychology of learning in general, but they must necessarily depend upon people like yourselves, your students, and your colleagues who are interested in mathematics and science conducting empirical studies of how certain specific concepts are learned under certain specific conditions with certain specific kinds of pupils. If anything is true about the field of mathematics and science education, it is that rarely have any disciplines been so rich in theory and brilliant ideas. But we must seriously consider the admonition of Ivan Pavlov, the great Russian psychologist, who is said to have told his students the following:

> Ideas and theories are like the wings of birds; they allow man to soar and to climb to the heavens. But facts are like the atmosphere against which those wings must beat, and without which the soaring bird will surely plummet back to earth.

REFERENCES

1. Bruner, Jerome S., *The Process of Education,* Cambridge, Massachusetts: Harvard University Press, 1960.
2. Bruner, Jerome S., *Toward a Theory of Instruction,* Cambridge, Massachusetts: Belknap Press, 1966.
3. Gagné, Robert M., *The Conditions of Learning,* New York: Holt, Rinehart & Winston, 1965.
4. Gagné, Robert M., "Contributions of Learning to Human Development," Address of the Vice-President, Section 1 (Psychology), American Association for the Advancement of Science, Washington, D. C., December, 1966.
5. Gagné, Robert M., "Personal-Communication," May, 1968.
6. Jennings, Frank G., "Jean Piaget: Notes on Learning." *Saturday Review,* May 20, 1967, p. 82.
7. "Pain & Progress in Discovery." *Time,* December 8, 1967, pp. 110 ff.
8. Shulman, Lee S. and Keislar, Evan R., Editors, *Learning by Discovery: A Critical Appraisal,* Chicago: Rand McNally, 1966.
9. Worthen, Blaine R., "Discovery and Expository Task Presentation in Elementary Mathematics," *Journal of Educational Psychology Monograph Supplement 59*: 1. Part 2; February 1968.

---

1. Which position in this paper best represents your past educational experiences?
2. Try to identify a few strong points and weak points in each position.
3. Do you think discovery learning or guided learning would be more appropriate for the teaching of reading? Why?
4. How can we decide when a child is *ready* to understand something?

20 JEROME S. BRUNER

The Act of Discovery

Discovery! Few people that I have had the occasion to talk with about this topic disagree that it is important. Incorporating opportunities for such activity for children in classrooms, however, becomes a stumbling block. Professor Bruner has championed the cause of discovery as a major instructional strategy, particularly in the area of science. This paper contains a rather comprehensive look at discovery along with certain outcomes that might be expected as a result of such an approach. It might be interesting to compare Bruner's own ideas about discovery with those presented in the previous paper where Shulman analyzes Bruner's position.

Maimonides, in his *Guide for the Perplexed*,[1] speaks of four forms of perfection that men might seek. The first and lowest form is perfection in the acquisition of worldly goods. The great philosopher dismisses such perfection on the ground that the possessions one acquires bear no meaningful relation to the possessor: "A great king may one morning find that there is no difference between him and the lowest person." A second perfection is of the body, its conformation and skills. Its failing is that it does not reflect on what is uniquely human about man: "he could [in any case] not be as strong as a mule." Moral perfection is the third, "the highest degree of excellency in man's character." Of this perfection Maimonides says: "Imagine a person being alone, and having no connection whatever with any other person; all his good moral principles are at rest, they are not required and give man no perfection whatever. These principles are only necessary and useful when man comes in contact with others." "The fourth kind of perfection is the true perfection of man; the possession of the highest intellectual faculties.

Reprinted from *Harvard Educational Review*, Vol. 31, No. 1, 1961, pp. 21-32, by permission of the editor and the author. Copyright © 1961 by President and Fellows of Harvard College. Dr. Bruner is Professor of Psychology and Co-Director of the Center for Cognitive Studies at Harvard University.

1. Maimonides, *Guide for the Perplexed* (New York: Dover Publications, 1956).

. . . " In justification of his assertion, this extraordinary Spanish-Judaic philosopher urges: "Examine the first three kinds of perfection; you will find that if you possess them, they are not your property, but the property of others. . . . But the last kind of perfection is exclusively yours; no one else owns any part of it."

It is a conjecture much like that of Maimonides that leads me to examine the act of discovery in man's intellectual life. For if man's intellectual excellence is the most his own among his perfections, it is also the case that the most uniquely personal of all that he knows is that which he has discovered for himself. What difference does it make, then, that we encourage discovery in the learning of the young? Does it, as Maimonides would say, create a special and unique relation between knowledge possessed and the possessor? And what may such a unique relation do for a man—or for a child, if you will, for our concern is with the education of the young?

The immediate occasion for my concern with discovery—and I do not restrict discovery to the act of finding out something that before was unknown to mankind, but rather include all forms of obtaining knowledge for oneself by the use of one's own mind—the immediate occasion is the work of the various new curriculum projects that have grown up in America during the last six or seven years. For whether one speaks to mathematicians or physicists or historians, one encounters repeatedly an expression of faith in the powerful effects that come from permitting the student to put things together for himself, to be his own discoverer.

First, let it be clear what the act of discovery entails. It is rarely, on the frontier of knowledge or elsewhere, that new facts are "discovered" in the sense of being encountered as Newton suggested in the form of islands of truth in an uncharted sea of ignorance. Or if they appear to be discovered in this way, it is almost always thanks to some happy hypotheses about where to navigate. Discovery, like surprise, favors the well prepared mind. In playing bridge, one is surprised by a hand with no honors in it at all and also by hands that are all in one suit. Yet all hands in bridge are equiprobable: one must know to be surprised. So too in discovery. The history of science is studded with examples of men "finding out" something and not knowing it. I shall operate on the assumption that discovery, whether by a schoolboy going it on his own or by a scientist cultivating the growing edge of his field, is in its essence a matter of rearranging or transforming evidence in such a way that one is enabled to go beyond the evidence so reassembled to additional new insights. It may well be that an additional fact or shred of evidence makes this larger transformation of evidence possible. But it is often not even dependent on new information.

It goes without saying that, left to himself, the child will go about discovering things for himself within limits. It also goes without saying that there are certain forms of child rearing, certain home atmospheres that lead some children to be their own discoverers more than other children. These are both topics of great interest, but I shall not be discussing them. Rather, I should like to confine myself to the consideration of discovery and "finding-out-for-oneself" within an educational setting—specifically the school. Our aim as teachers is to give our student as firm a grasp of a subject as we can, and to make him as autonomous and self-propelled a thinker as we can—one who will go along on his own after formal schooling has ended. I shall return in the end to the question of the kind of classroom and the style of teaching that encourages an attitude of wanting to discover. For purposes of orienting the discussion, however, I would like to make an overly simplified distinction between teaching that takes place in the *expository mode* and teaching that utilizes the *hypothetical mode*. In the former, the decisions concerning the mode and pace and style of exposition are principally determined by the teacher as expositor; the student is the listener. If I can put the matter in terms of structural linguistics, the speaker has a quite different set of decisions to make than the listener: the former has a wide choice of alternatives for structuring, he is anticipating paragraph content while the listener is still intent on the words, he is manipulating the content of the material by various transformations, while the listener is quite unaware of these internal manipulations. In the hypothetical mode, the teacher and the student are in a more cooperative position with respect to what in linguistics would be called "speaker's decisions." The student is not a bench-bound listener, but is taking a part in the formulation and at times may play the principal role in it. He will be aware of alternatives and may even have an "as if" attitude toward these and, as he receives information he may evaluate it as it comes. One cannot describe the process in either mode with great precision as to detail, but I think the foregoing may serve to illustrate what is meant.

Consider now what benefit might be derived from the experience of learning through discoveries that one makes for oneself. I should like to discuss these under four headings: (1) the increase in intellectual potency, (2) the shift from extrinsic to intrinsic rewards, (3) learning the heuristics of discovering, and (4) the aid to memory processing.

Intellectual Potency

If you will permit me, I would like to consider the difference between subjects in a highly constrained psychological experiment involving a two-choice apparatus. In order to win chips, they must depress a key either on the right or the left side of the machine. A pattern of payoff is designed such that, say, they will be paid off on the right side 70 per cent of the time, on the left 30 per cent, although this detail is not important. What is important is that the payoff sequence is arranged at random, and there is no pattern. I should like to contrast the behavior of subjects who think that there *is* some pattern to be found in the sequence—who think that regularities are discoverable—in contrast to subjects who think that things are happening quite by *chance*. The former group adopts what is called an "event-matching" strategy in which the number of responses given to each side is roughly equal to the proportion of times it pays off: in the present case R70: L30. The group that believes there is no pattern very soon reverts to a much more primitive strategy wherein *all* responses are allocated to the side that has the greater payoff. A little arithmetic will show you that the lazy all-and-none strategy pays off more if indeed the environment is random: namely, they win seventy per cent of the time. The event-matching subjects win about 70% on the 70% payoff side (or 49% of the time there) and 30% of the time on the side that pays off 30% of the time (another 9% for a total take-home wage of 58% in return for their labors of decision). But the world is not always or not even frequently random, and if one analyzes carefully what the event-matchers are doing, it turns out that they are trying out hypotheses one after the other, all of them containing a term such that they distribute bets on the two sides with a frequency to match the actual occurrence of events. If it should turn out that there is a pattern to be discovered, their payoff would become 100%. The other group would go on at the middling rate of 70%.

What has this to do with the subject at hand? For the person to search out and find regularities and relationships in his environment, he must be armed with an expectancy that there will be something to find and, once aroused by expectancy, he must devise ways of searching and finding. One of the chief enemies of such expectancy is the assumption that there is nothing one can find in the environment by way of regularity or relationship. In the experiment just cited, subjects often fall into a habitual attitude that there is either nothing to be found or that they can find a pattern by looking. There is an important sequel in behavior to the two attitudes, and to this I should like to turn now.

We have been conducting a series of experimental studies on a group of some seventy school children over the last four years. The studies have led us to distinguish an interesting dimension of cognitive activity that can be described as ranging from *episodic empiricism* at one end to *cumulative constructionism* at the other. The two attitudes in the choice experiments just cited are illustrative of the extremes of the dimension. I might mention some other illustrations. One of the experiments employs the game of Twenty Questions. A child—in this case he is between 10 and 12—is told that a car has gone off the road and hit a tree. He is to ask questions that can be answered by "yes" or "no" to discover the cause of the accident. After completing the problem, the same task is given him again, though he is told that the accident had a different cause this time. In all, the procedure is repeated four times. Children enjoy playing the game. They also differ quite markedly in the approach or strategy they bring to the task. There are various elements in the strategies employed. In the first place, one may distinguish clearly between two types of questions asked: the one is designed for locating constraints in the problem, constraints that will eventually give shape to an hypothesis; the other is the hypothesis as question. It is the difference between, "Was there anything wrong with the driver?" and "Was the driver rushing to the doctor's office for an appointment and the car got out of control?" There are children who precede hypotheses with efforts to locate constraint and there are those who, to use our local slang, are "pot-shotters," who string out hypotheses non-cumulatively one after the other. A second element of strategy is its connectivity of information gathering: the extent to which questions asked utilize or ignore or violate information previously obtained. The questions asked by children tend to be organized in cycles, each cycle of questions usually being given over to the pursuit of some particular notion. Both within cycles and between cycles one can discern a marked difference on the connectivity of the child's performance. Needless to say, children who employ constraint location as a technique preliminary to the formulation of hypotheses tend to be far more connected in their harvesting of information. Persistence is another feature of strategy, a characteristic compounded of what appear to be two components: a sheer doggedness component, and a persistence that stems from the sequential organization that a child brings to the task. Doggedness is probably just animal spirits or the need for achievement—what has come to be called *n-ach*. Organized persistence is a maneuver for protecting our fragile cognitive apparatus from overload. The child who has flooded himself with disorganized information from uncovered hypotheses will become discouraged and confused sooner than the child who has shown a certain cunning in his strategy of getting information—a cunning whose principal component is the recognition that the value of information is not simply in getting it but in being able to carry it. The persistence of the organized child stems from his knowledge of how to organize questions in cycles, how to summarize things to himself, and the like.

Episodic empiricism is illustrated by information gathering that is unbound by prior constraints, that lacks connectivity, and that is deficient in organizational persistence. The opposite extreme is illustrated by an approach that is characterized by constraint sensitivity, by connective maneuvers, and by organized persistence. Brute persistence seems to be one of those gifts from the gods that make people more exaggeratedly what they are.[2]

Before returning to the issue of discovery and its role in the development of thinking, let me say a word more about the ways in which information may get transformed when the problem solver has actively processed it. There is first of all a pragmatic question: what does it take to get information processed into a form best designed to fit some future use? Take an experiment by Zajonc[3] as a case in point. He gives groups of subjects information of a controlled kind, some groups being told that their task is to transmit the information to others, others that it is merely to be kept in mind. In general, he finds more differentiation and organization of the information received with the intention of being transmitted than there is for information received passively. An active set leads to a transformation related to a task to be performed. The risk, to be sure, is in possible overspecialization of information processing that may lead to such a high degree of specific organization that information is lost for general use.

I would urge now in the spirit of an hypothesis that emphasis upon discovery in learning has precisely the effect upon the learner of leading him to be a constructionist, to organize what he is encountering in a manner not only designed to discover regularity and relatedness, but also to avoid the kind of information drift that fails to keep account of the uses to which information might have to be put. It is, if you will, a necessary condition for learning the variety of techniques of problem solving, of transforming information for better use, indeed for learning how to go about the very task of learning. Practice in discovering for oneself teaches one to acquire information in a way that makes that information more readily viable in problem solving. So goes the hypothesis. It is still in need of testing. But is an hypothesis of such important human implications that we cannot afford not to test it—and testing will have to be in the schools.

Intrinsic and Extrinsic Motives

Much of the problem in leading a child to effective cognitive activity is to free him from the immediate control of environmental rewards and

---

2. I should also remark in passing that the two extremes also characterize concept attainment strategies as reported in *A Study of Thinking* by J. S. Bruner *et al.* (New York: J. Wiley, 1956). Successive scanning illustrates well what is meant here by episodic empiricism; conservative focussing is an example of cumulative constructionism.

3. R. B. Zajonc (Personal communication, 1957).

punishments. That is to say, learning that starts in response to the rewards of parental or teacher approval or the avoidance of failure can too readily develop a pattern in which the child is seeking cues as to how to conform to what is expected of him. We know from studies of children who tend to be early over-achievers in school that they are likely to be seekers after the "right way to do it" and that their capacity for transforming their learning into viable thought structures tends to be lower than children merely achieving at levels predicted by intelligence tests. Our tests on such children show them to be lower in analytic ability than those who are not conspicuous in overachievement.[4] As we shall see later, they develop rote abilities and depend upon being able to "give back" what is expected rather than to make it into something that relates to the rest of their cognitive life. As Maimonides would say, their learning is not their own.

The hypothesis that I would propose here is that to the degree that one is able to approach learning as a task of discovering something rather than "learning about" it, to that degree will there be a tendency for the child to carry out his learning activities with the autonomy of self-reward or, more properly by reward that is discovery itself.

To those of you familiar with the battles of the last half-century in the field of motivation, the above hypothesis will be recognized as controversial. For the classic view of motivation in learning has been, until very recently, couched in terms of a theory of drives and reinforcement: that learning occurred by virtue of the fact that a response produced by a stimulus was followed by the reduction in a primary drive state. The doctrine is greatly extended by the idea of secondary reinforcement: any state associated even remotely with the reduction of a primary drive could also have the effect of producing learning. There has recently appeared a most searching and important criticism of this position, written by Professor Robert White,[5] reviewing the evidence of recently published animal studies, of work in the field of psychoanalysis, and of research on the development of cognitive processes in children. Professor White comes to the conclusion, quite rightly I think, that the drive-reduction model of learning runs counter to too many important phenomena of learning and development to be either regarded as general in its applicability or even correct in its general approach. Let me summarize some of his principal conclusions and explore their applicability to the hypothesis stated above.

4. J. S. Bruner and A. J. Caron, "Cognition, Anxiety, and Achievement in the Preadolescent." *Journal of Educational Psychology.*
5. R. W. White, "Motivation Reconsidered: The Concept of Competence," *Psychological Review* 66 (1959): 297-333.

I now propose that we gather the various kinds of behavior just mentioned, all of which have to do with effective interaction with the environment, under the general heading of competence. According to Webster, competence means fitness or ability, and the suggested synonyms include capability, capacity, efficiency, proficiency, and skill. It is therefore a suitable word to describe such things as grasping and exploring, crawling and walking, attention and perception, language and thinking, manipulating and changing the surroundings, all of which promote an effective—a competent—interaction with the environment. It is true of course, that maturation plays a part in all these developments, but this part is heavily overshadowed by learning in all the more complex accomplishments like speech or skilled manipulation. I shall argue that it is necessary to make competence a motivational concept; there is *competence motivation* as well as competence in its more familiar sense of achieved capacity. The behavior that leads to the building up of effective grasping, handling, and letting go of objects, to take one example, is not random behavior that is produced by an overflow of energy. It is directed, selective, and persistent, and it continues not because it serves primary drives, which indeed it cannot serve until it is almost perfected, but because it satisfies an intrinsic need to deal with the environment.[6]

I am suggesting that there are forms of activity that serve to enlist and develop the competence motive, that serve to make it the driving force behind behavior. I should like to add to White's general premise that the *exercise* of competence motives has the effect of strengthening the degree to which they gain control over behavior and thereby reduce the effects of extrinsic rewards or drive gratification.

The brilliant Russian psychologist Vigotsky[7] characterizes the growth of thought processes as starting with a dialogue of speech and gesture between child and parent; autonomous thinking begins at the stage when the child is first able to internalize these conversations and "run them off" himself. This is a typical sequence in the development of competence. So too in instruction. The narrative of teaching is of the order of the conversation. The next move in the development of competence is the internalization of the narrative and its "rules of generation" so that the child is now capable of running off the narrative on his own. The hypothetical mode in teaching by encouraging the child to participate in "speaker's decisions" speeds this process along. Once internalization has occurred, the child is in a vastly improved position from several obvious points of view—notably that he is able to go beyond the information he has been given to generate additional ideas that can either be checked immediately from experience or can, at least, be used as a basis for formulating reasonable hypotheses. But over and beyond that, the child is now in a position to experience success and failure not as reward and

6. *Ibid.,* pp. 317-18.
7. L. S. Vigotsky, *Thinking and Speech* (Moscow, 1934).

punishment, but as information. For when the task is his own rather than a matter of matching environmental demands, he becomes his own paymaster in a certain measure. Seeking to gain control over his environment, he can now treat success as indicating that he is on the right track, failure as indicating he is on the wrong one.

In the end, this development has the effect of freeing learning from immediate stimulus control. When learning in the short run leads only to pellets of this or that rather than to mastery in the long run, then behavior can be readily "shaped" by extrinsic rewards. When behavior becomes more long-range and competence-oriented, it comes under the control of more complex cognitive structures, plans and the like, and operates more from the inside out. It is interesting that even Pavlov, whose early account of the learning process was based entirely on a notion of stimulus control of behavior through the conditioning mechanism in which, through contiguity a new conditioned stimulus was substituted for an old unconditioned stimulus by the mechanism of stimulus substitution, recognized by his account as insufficient to deal with higher forms of learning. To supplement the account, he introduced the idea of the "second signalling system," with central importance placed on symbolic systems such as language in mediating and giving shape to mental life. Or as Luria[8] has put it, "the first signal system [is] concerned with directly perceived stimuli, the second with systems of verbal elaboration." Luria, commenting on the importance of the transition from first to second signal system, says: "It would be mistaken to suppose that verbal intercourse with adults merely changes the contents of the child's conscious activity without changing its form. . . . The word has a basic function not only because it indicates a corresponding object in the external world, but also because it abstracts, isolates the necessary signal, generalizes perceived signals and relates them to certain categories; it is this systematization of direct experience that makes the role of the word in the formation of mental processes so exceptionally important."[9, 10]

It is interesting that the final rejection of the universality of the doctrine of reinforcement in direct conditioning came from some of Pavlov's own students. Ivanov-Smolensky[11] and Krasnogorsky[12] published

8. A. L. Luria, "The Directive Function of Speech in Development and Dissolution," *Word* 15 (1959): 341-464.

9. *Ibid.,* p. 12.

10. For an elaboration of the view expressed by Luria, the reader is referred to the forthcoming translation of L. S. Vigotsky's 1934 book being published by John Wiley and Sons and the Technology Press.

11. A. G. Ivanov-Smolensky, "Concerning the Study of the Joint Activity of the First and Second Signal Systems," *Journal of Higher Nervous Activity,* I (1951): 1.

12. N. D. Krasnogorsky, *Studies of Higher Nervous Activity in Animals and in Man,* Vol. I (Moscow, 1954).

papers showing the manner in which symbolized linguistic messages could take over the place of the unconditioned stimulus and of the unconditioned response (gratification of hunger) in children. In all instances, they speak of these as *replacements* of lower, first-system mental or neural processes by higher order or second-system controls. A strange irony, then, that Russian psychology that gave us the notion of the conditioned response and the assumption that higher order activities are built up out of colligations or structurings of such primitive units, rejected this notion while much of American learning psychology has stayed until quite recently within the early Pavlovian fold (see, for example, a recent article by Spence[13] in the *Harvard Educational Review* or Skinner's treatment of language[14] and the attacks that have been made upon it by linguists such as Chomsky[15] who have become concerned with the relation of language and cognitive activity). What is the more interesting is that Russian pedagogical theory has become deeply influenced by this new trend and is now placing much stress upon the importance of building up a more active symbolical approach to problem solving among children.

To sum up the matter of the control of learning, then, I am proposing that the degree to which competence or mastery motives come to control behavior, to that degree the role of reinforcement or "extrinsic pleasure" wanes in shaping behavior. The child comes to manipulate his environment more actively and achieves his gratification from coping with problems. Symbolic modes of representing and transforming the environment arise and the importance of stimulus-response-reward sequences declines. To use the metaphor that David Riesman developed in a quite different context, mental life moves from a state of outer-directedness in which the fortuity of stimuli and reinforcement are crucial to a state of inner-directedness in which the growth and maintenance of mastery become central and dominant.

Learning the Heuristics of Discovery

Lincoln Steffens,[16] reflecting in his *Autobiography* on his under graduate education at Berkeley, comments that his schooling was overly specialized on learning about the known and that too little attention was given to the task of finding out about what was not known. But how

13. K. W. Spence, "The Relation of Learning Theory to the Technique of Education," *Harvard Educational Review* 29 (1959): 84-95.

14. B. F. Skinner, *Verbal Behavior* (New York: Appleton-Century-Crofts, 1957).

15. N. Chomsky, *Syntactic Structure* (The Hague, The Netherlands: Mouton & Co., 1957).

16. L. Steffens, *Autobiography of Lincoln Steffens* (New York: Harcourt, Brace, 1931).

does one train a student in the techniques of discovery? Again I would like to offer some hypotheses. There are many ways of coming to the arts of inquiry. One of them is by careful study of its formalization in logic, statistics, mathematics, and the like. If a person is going to pursue inquiry as a way of life, particularly in the sciences, certainly such study is essential. Yet, whoever has taught kindergarten and the early primary grades or has had graduate students working with him on their theses— I choose the two extremes for they are both periods of intense inquiry —knows that an understanding of the formal aspect of inquiry is not sufficient. There appear to be, rather, a series of activities and attitudes, some directly related to a particular subject and some of them fairly generalized, that go with inquiry and research. These have to do with the *process* of trying to find out something and while they provide no guarantee that the *product* will be any *great* discovery, their absence is likely to lead to awkwardness or aridity or confusion. How difficult it is to describe these matters—the heuristics of inquiry. There is one set of attitudes or ways of doing that has to do with sensing the relevance of variables—how to avoid getting stuck with edge effects and getting instead to the big sources of variance. Partly this gift comes from intuitive familiarity with a range of phenomena, sheer "knowing the stuff." But it also comes out of a sense of what things among an ensemble of things "smell right" in the sense of being of the right order of magnitude or scope of severity.

The English philosopher Weldon describes problem solving in an interesting and picturesque way. He distinguishes between difficulties, puzzles, and problems. We solve a problem or make a discovery when we impose a puzzle form on to a difficulty that converts it into a problem that can be solved in such a way that it gets us where we want to be. That is to say, we recast the difficulty into a form that we know how to work with, then work it. Much of what we speak of as discovery consists of knowing how to impose what kind of form on various kinds of difficulties. A small part but a crucial part of discovery of the highest order is to invent and develop models or "puzzle forms" that can be imposed on difficulties with good effect. It is in this area that the truly powerful mind shines. But it is interesting to what degree perfectly ordinary people can, given the benefit of instruction, construct quite interesting and what, a century ago, would have been considered greatly original models.

Now to the hypothesis. It is my hunch that it is only through the exercise of problem solving and the effort of discovery that one learns the working heuristic of discovery, and the more one has practice, the more likely is one to generalize what one has learned into a style of problem solving or inquiry that serves for any kind of task one may encounter—or almost any kind of task. I think the matter is self-evident, but what is unclear is what kinds of training and teaching produce the best effects. How do we teach a child to, say, cut his losses but at the same time be persistent in trying out an idea; to risk forming an early hunch without at the same time formulating one *so* early and with so little evidence as to be stuck with it waiting for appropriate evidence to materialize; to pose good testable guesses that are neither too brittle nor too sinuously incorrigible; etc., etc. Practice in inquiry, in trying to figure out things for oneself is indeed what is needed, but in what form? Of only one thing I am convinced. I have never seen anybody improve in the art and technique of inquiry by any means other than engaging in inquiry.

Conservation of Memory

I should like to take what some psychologists might consider a rather drastic view of the memory process. It is a view that in large measure derives from the work of my colleague, Professor George Miller.[17] Its first premise is that the principal problem of human memory is not storage, but retrieval. In spite of the biological unlikeliness of it, we seem to be able to store a huge quantity of information—perhaps not a full tape recording, though at times it seems we even do that, but a great sufficiency of impressions. We may infer this from the fact that recognition (i.e., recall with the aid of maximum prompts) is so extraordinarily good in human beings—particularly in comparison with spontaneous recall where, so to speak, we must get out stored information without external aids or prompts. The key to retrieval is organization or, in even simpler terms, knowing where to find information and how to get there.

Let me illustrate the point with a simple experiment. We present pairs of words to twelve-year-old children. One group is simply told to remember the pairs, that they will be asked to repeat them later. Another is told to remember them by producing a word or idea that will tie the pair together in a way that will make sense to them. A third group is given the mediators used by the second group when presented with the pairs to aid them in tying the pairs into working units. The word pairs include such juxtapositions as "chair-forest," "sidewalk-square," and the like. One can distinguish three styles of mediators and children can be scaled in terms of their relative preference for each: *generic mediation* in which a pair is tied together by a superordinary idea: "chair and

17. G. A. Miller, "The Magical Number Seven, Plus or Minus Two," *Psychological Review*, 63 (1956): 81-97.

forest are both made of wood;" *thematic mediation* in which the two terms are inbedded in a theme or little story: "the lost child sat on a chair in the middle of the forest;" and *part-whole mediation* where "chairs are made from trees in the forest" is typical. Now, the chief result, as you would all predict, is that children who provide their own mediators do best—indeed, one time through a set of thirty pairs, they recover up to 95% of the second words when presented with the first ones of the pairs, whereas the uninstructed children reach a maximum of less than 50% recovered. Interestingly enough, children do best in recovering materials tied together by the form of mediator they most often use.

One can cite a myriad of findings to indicate that any organization of information that reduces the aggregate complexity of material by imbedding it into a cognitive structure a person has constructed will make the material more accessible for retrieval. In short, we may say that the process of memory, looked at from the retrieval side, is also a process of problem solving: how can material be "placed" in memory so that it can be got on demand?

We can take as a point of departure the example of the children who developed their own technique for relating the members of each word pair. You will recall that they did better than the children who were given by exposition the mediators they had developed. Let me suggest that in general, material that is organized in terms of a person's own interests and cognitive structures is material that has the best chance of being accessible in memory. That is to say, it is more likely to be placed along routes that are connected to one's own ways of intellectual travel.

In sum, the very attitudes and activities that characterize "figuring out" or "discovering" things for oneself also seems to have the effect of making material more readily accessible in memory.

---

1. Are there things that children should learn in elementary school science that cannot be left for them to discover? Identify a few and explain why you think it would be impossible or impractical to employ such an instructional strategy.
2. Some research findings suggest that certain children seem to "learn better" when they are directed closely about what to do and how to do it. Do you think teachers have the moral right to try to help that type of child become better able to cope with more open, discovery-type learning?

21 GREGOR A. RAMSEY AND ROBERT W. HOWE

An Analysis of Research: Related to Instructional Procedures in Elementary School Science

Research on instructional procedures in education is usually used sparingly, if at all, by the elementary school teachers in making decisions about what will happen in their classrooms. This paper includes an extensive bibliography that makes reference to research and various issues of interest in elementary science education. Conflicting results among research studies in education are common, so do not expect to find clear-cut answers to all of your questions. Most of the results of the studies are shortened to such an extent that little definitive information is really available. Hopefully, this brief introduction to instructional research will encourage you to pursue, in greater detail, evidence for certain classroom procedures.

There is little doubt that science has a place in the elementary school. This position has become more firmly established in recent years; however, what that place is seems not at all clear from the research studies which have been undertaken and are reviewed in this article. If science were removed from the elementary school ciurriculum, it is difficult to know what would be lost because there is a lack of adequate and appropriate research which examines the actual outcomes of science instruction. Instructional procedures selected for study by researchers seem to be chosen on the basis of whim or tradition rather than from a firmly established proposition that if a certain procedure is used then definite, specifiable, and desirable outcomes will be the end result.

The authors found it necessary, while reviewing the available research literature, to sketch a working model of the complete instructional process. It was then possible to match any given research study to that part of the model being investigated, and also relate its relevance to the total instructional picture. The reviewers are aware that this

Reprinted from *Science and Children*, Vol. 6, No. 7, 1969, pp. 25-36, by permission of the editor. Dr.'s Howe and Ramsey are Acting Director and Information Analyst, respectively, for The Education Resources Information Center (ERIC) for Science Education at Ohio State University.

practice may impose a model on a researcher to which he may not subscribe. However, very few researchers established clearly which part of the instructional process they were attempting to investigate.

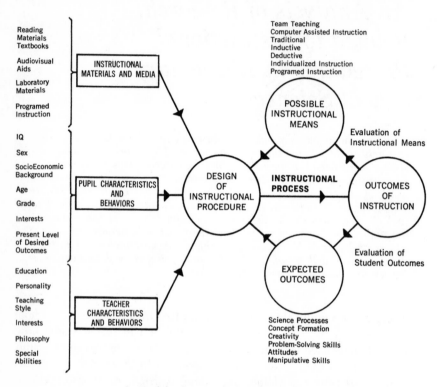

A Model of Instructional Sequence.*

*At the end of any instructional sequence, the inputs, e.g., student or teacher characteristics and behaviors have been changed by the sequence and this will have to be taken into account when planning the next.

The fact that there seemed to be no common model among researchers as to what constitutes instruction made it difficult for the authors to draw together a number of studies and make common generalizations regarding them. Also, there was some confusion over terminology used by investigators to describe the instructional process, and there seems to be an urgent need for a common set of terms to describe both the instructional procedure and the expected outcomes of the instructional sequence. More basically perhaps, what is required is a viable instructional theory which can act as a common springboard for research; however, until this is achieved, a common set of terms based on a functional model of instruction would help greatly in bringing order to the field of educational research.

Science is taught in the elementary school presumably because it is expected to bring about pupil growth in the cognitive, affective, and psychomotor domains of knowledge—a growth not as easily achieved through another content area. Evidence of such growth can only be observed through desirable changes in pupil behavior—so before embarking on any instructional sequence, it should be possible to define what behavior changes to expect, and after the sequence, be able to measure if they occur. Any learning experience will provide unexpected and unmeasurable (at least for the present) changes in behavior; however, this is not sufficient reason to neglect all attempts at measuring expected pupil growth. Only rarely did the authors review studies which paid close attention to the dual problems of devising a procedure to produce certain specified outcomes, and then measuring to see whether the outcomes have been attained.

The working model of the instructional process against which the research studies were reviewed is shown in the accompanying chart. This chart is provided for the reader not because it is complete, nor even completely accurate, but because it was useful to the reviewers for pinpointing those aspects of instruction being researched, and helped them in deciding quickly whether the researcher had accounted for all the variables which could influence instruction and its outcomes.

The boxes on the left represent three important inputs which help decide which instructional procedure should be used. The instructional materials and media available, the characteristics of the pupils to be taught, and the personalities and other traits of the teachers are relatively constant factors in any given instructional situation. The two major variables are the possible instructional means and the expected outcomes. For example, if an outcome like creativity is desired, then it is unlikely that a conventional class—teacher-didactic situation—will produce the greatest gains. So, if expected outcomes are defined, they help determine the instructional procedure to be used within the constraints imposed by the characteristics and behaviors of both the teachers and pupils, and the instructional materials and media available.

Once an instructional procedure has been established and used to teach children, then certain outcomes are attained. These outcomes are evaluated, usually by some form of testing, against the outcomes expected when the procedure was designed. How closely the outcomes attained match the outcomes expected will give some indication of what changes are needed in the instructional procedure chosen.

In reviewing the research, the model was used in the following way: There are four major sets of variables which may affect the outcomes of instruction—the instructional materials and media used, pupil characteristics and behaviors, teacher characteristics and behaviors, and the instructional means chosen. To know whether a particular instructional means (e.g., a problem-solving method) does produce the change in behavior indicating the desired outcome, then all the other factors must be held constant or allowed for in the research design before one can be reasonably certain that it was the instruction and not some other variable which produced the change. Any one of the components of each of the four areas could be investigated in this way. If, in a comparative study, one wanted to investigate the effect of pupil socioeconomic background on the outcomes of a particular instructional sequence, then all *other* student characteristics must be controlled, the teachers should have essentially the same characteristics and philosophies, and the materials used must be identical in all classes taught the method.

This complex arrangement of variables which can develop may help the elementary school teacher understand some of the problems of research in this area. In fairness, it must be pointed out that most researchers coped very well with all the variables. Randomization of pupil populations is a much more effective way of controlling student characteristics than identifying matched pairs, and was used in many studies. Major objections to many of the designs were in terms of teacher characteristics not being fully controlled, and the instructional sequence not used for a long enough time in many cases for marked gains to be noted. No doubt these weaknesses are partly due to the problem that much of the research reviewed was done for doctoral dissertation purposes, where the rush to "get finished" was a contributing factor.

The reviewers found it necessary to place arbitrary limits on the studies reviewed so that the field could be contained in manageable form. In general, only studies reported after 1960 were examined, and from these only those studies which attempted some objective evaluation of the outcomes of an instructional sequence are discussed in detail in this article. Likewise, studies which were designed to test various aspects of learning theory, although they may have used a novel instructional procedure to do this, were ignored. Learning theory forms an important basis for designing an instructional procedure, but it has only an indirect effect on classroom teaching.

A number of classification systems could have been chosen in terms of the model to systematize the widely divergent research studies encountered. Four variables seemed to stand out, namely: the instructional procedure used, the outcomes evaluated, the subject matter taught, and the grade level of instruction. In practice only the first two remained relevant. The choice of subject matter in most cases seemed quite arbitrary, and when grade level was considered, more than 95 per cent of the studies involved grades 4-6 and the bulk of this attention was directed at grade 6.

The studies are reviewed in terms of whether they focused on the instructional procedure, e.g., inductive or deductive, individualized instruction, programed instruction, or whether the studies focused on outcomes, e.g., development of concepts, attitudes, problem-solving skills, creativity, or understanding content. It was surprising to find the outcome category "development of psychomotor skills" void, since it might be expected that this would be an important area to be developed in elementary school science. No information was obtained concerning what manipulative skills in science can be developed in elementary school children, nor whether a hierarchy of such skills can be identified. This area requires much more basic research.

A number of "status" studies were identified. School systems were surveyed for procedures used, e.g., Snoble(113) and Swan(120), or wider surveys of national practices were made, e.g., those by McCloskey (79), Moorehead(83), Smith and Cooper (111), Blackwood(13), Stokes (116), and Melis(81).

These status studies are in a sense reviews themselves and provided sound statements of the position in the areas mentioned. They are not discussed further in this article, but are cited as useful sources for the interested reader.

Only one study was identified which attempted evaluation of one of the newer course improvement projects in elementary science. This study was undertaken by Walbesser *et al.*, (126) and the American Association for the Advancement of Science in their comprehensive study of *Science—A Process Approach.* An evaluation model was posed which described expected learner behaviors and established what might be accepted as evidence of learner accomplishments. Evaluation in these terms allows for objective comparisons of courses, gives objective evidence that learning has occurred, and makes independent replication of the findings possible.

The behavioral objectives of each instructional sequence were clearly identified, and they were evaluated by determining the percentage of pupils acquiring a certain standard percentage of specified behaviors, and comparing this to an established level of expectation. From this information, feedback to improve the instructional sequence was constantly available. For example, an arbitrary 90/90 (90 per cent of students acquire 90 per cent of the prescribed behaviors) was chosen as the standard. If the standard attained by pupils were lower than this, then modifications were made to the instructional sequence.

Specific findings of the evaluation were too varied and far reaching to be described in a review of this nature; however, it is the model provided by the evaluation, rather than the results which are important. Much has been said and written about the efficacy of stating objectives in behavioral terms. This study gives concrete evidence that this is so.

Comparative Studies: Traditional vs. Nontraditional

In this section are reviewed those studies which compared outcomes obtained when the same body of content is taught by two methods. A "conventional" or "traditional" method was the usual standard of comparison, although what researchers meant by these terms was not always clear. Methods investigated included "inductive," "directed self-discovery," a "field method," "democratic," and "problem solving." It was in this area of comparison studies that the reviewers had the most concern regarding the research design. It is extremely difficult in such circumstances to control all the variables which may affect instruction. A study by Brudzynski(16) illustrates this point. He compared an inductive method where pupils learned concepts by "directed self-discovery" in a pupil-centered atmosphere to a "lecture-demonstration" teacher-centered one. The "inductive" method favored above-average students while the "lecture-demonstration" method favored average and below average students in the fifth- and sixth-grade population studied. These differences need not be ascribed to the particular instructional method. Teacher expectation may have been far more important. The less able students may not be "expected" by the teacher, perhaps subconsciously, to perform as well in a self-directed situation. He may act in the classroom accordingly and this subconscious expectation could affect the outcomes of the students more than the instructional procedure used.

Anklam(5) identified the teachers who liked to use "democratic" instructional methods and those who preferred a more "autocratic" approach. No significant differences in achievement motivation existed between the groups of pupils taught in each of these environments. This finding points clearly to the importance of teacher characteristics and behaviors to the whole instructional procedure, and the danger of imposing a particular procedure upon teachers who do not have the personal characteristics to teach it. In this study, the teachers investigated had adopted a style of teaching which suited them. Even though the simplicity of the democratic-autocratic dichotomy may be doubted, the study did show that teachers performing within a frame of reference which they have built for themselves, motivated students equally. What is needed is research into determining instructional procedures which suit different personality types, rather than research directed to finding one procedure "best" for all teachers.

Other studies where no significant differences were found between methods used included Gerne(51) who compared a traditional textbook method with a method utilizing a specially designed board to teach electricity and magnetism, and one by Bennett(10) who compared a field method with a classroom method for teaching ecology. Smith(110) compared a lecture-demonstrated style of teaching carried out in a classroom to teaching in a planetarium for presenting a lesson on astronomy concepts to sixth-grade pupils. Children in the classroom achieved significantly higher than those taught in the planetarium. These studies suggest that the use of any visual aid or direct experience will not necessarily of itself produce significant outcome gains in children.

Carpenter(24) used fourth-grade pupils to compare a "textbook recitation method" with a "problem method." In effect, the textbook method included no demonstrations while the problem method was based on classroom demonstration and experimentation of the problem-solving method for teaching units on "magnetism" and "adaption of animals." This finding was even more definite for the slower learners—who were, in general, poor readers.

Pershern(91) investigated student achievment outcomes obtained by integrating industrial-arts activities with science instruction in grades 4, 5, 6. He used electricity and machines as his content vehicles and found significant gains in favor of integration for the electricity unit, but no significant differences for the machines unit. Integration seems to add an important dimension to instruction, and may prove a useful approach for further research.

It is difficult to generalize from comparison studies, however, it seems that pupil activity and pupil-performed experiments are important prerequisites to the effective learning of science concepts. Instructional procedures where the responsibility for the conceptual leap is placed upon the child, as in problem solving and inductive methods, do seem to bring about more significant achievement gains than do those methods where the teacher or the text material provides the concept. It appears that for these inductive methods to be fully effective, the teacher must have a certain teaching philosophy and a certain set of personal characteristics.

Audiovisual Aids

The bulk of the research in this area involved the use of television and movie film in the classroom. How these aids can best be used in an instructional situation, what their effect is on student achievement and attitudes, and how they can improve classroom instruction are all questions to which research has been directed. Much of the research was of the "direct-comparison" type where control of all variables is extremely difficult. Conclusions based on such studies should be viewed with some caution.

Bickel(12), Decker(36), and Skinner(109) investigated changes in attitude, achievement, and interest in children following television instruction. Bickel(12) found no significant differences in the learning outcomes of his fourth-, fifth-, and sixth-grade pupils taught science by closed-circuit television incorporating a "talk-back" facility and teacher follow-up, when compared with students taught science without the aid of television.

Skinner(109) compared two television presentations for two separate groups of fifth graders. In one presentation a problem was identified, and many questions were posed which were not answered in the lesson. In this way, it was hoped that pupils' curiosity and interest in science would be aroused. The other presentation included the same materials, but used a direct expository teaching style with very few questions. Teacher follow-up of these lessons was either a modified inquiry session where the teacher answered only pupils' questions or a typical discussion session with teacher and pupils participating fully. Skinner found that pupils who experienced the television presentation with unanswered questions, regardless of teacher follow-up, achieved significantly higher than pupils who viewed "explanation" on television.

Decker(36), like Skinner, also worked with fifth graders and followed a somewhat similar procedure. He prepared two sets of ten half-hour television programs using the same materials for each. One set stressed providing information, concepts, and generalizations while the other stressed the posing of problems. No significant differences in pupil achievement were detected, so Decker concluded that the problem-solving method was as effective as the information-giving method in teaching natural science.

These conflicting results of Skinner and Decker, where one finds a significant difference in one and no significant difference in the other, point clearly to the difficulties associated with these direct-comparison type studies. They oversimplify the learning process and do not take into account how individual student needs, interests, and abilities interact with instruction. An instructional method which may be in tune with the profile of characteristics of one group of students in the class may be out of tune with another, so any gains obtained with one group will be offset by the losses in the other, and no significant differences are detected. Research on instructional procedures must be increasingly multi-dimensional, since no one method of instruction can be considered "best" for all students.

Bornhorst and Hosford(15) investigated television instruction at the third-grade level by comparing the achievement of a group of television-taught pupils with a group who had only classroom instruction. The television group achieved significantly higher results on tests than the control group, and it was felt that the "wonder-box" where children placed questions arising from the television lessons for future discussion was an important factor.

Allison(3) investigated the influence of three methods of using motivational films[1] on the attitudes of fourth-, fifth-, and sixth-grade students toward science, scientists, and scientific careers. He adapted the Allen attitude inventory[2] for use with these elementary school children. Allison concluded that the films did change the attitudes of the students favorably toward science, scientists, and scientific careers, and that these changes in attitude were not related to mental ability, science achievement scores, sex, science training, or the economic status of parents. This study suggests that film sequences can be devised which will effectively bring about a desired attitude change. More research in this area is needed particularly in the development and evaluation of material.

Novak(87) describes the development and use of audiotape programed instruction for teaching first- and third-grade elementary science. Cartridge tape recorders and projectors with simple "on-off" switches were used. Some of the problems associated with setting up such a program included vocabulary difficulty, pace of audio instruction, difficulty of task to be performed, density of information to be presented, inadequacies of filmloops, and unexpected distractions. Four to eight revisions of each program sequence were necessary to be sure that students could proceed with very few apparent difficulties.

Evaluation of the program was highly experimental. Individual interview using loop films, display materials, and appropriate questioning was found too time consuming. Pencil and paper tests using drawings, administered orally to the whole class, were then tried. Also, several suggestions as to future possible avenues of evaluation were developed along with other ways the materials may be used. The study leaves little doubt that audio-tutorial instruction is feasible in grades one, two, and three, and should be looked on as a useful way to individualize instruction.

1. "Horizons of Science." Films produced by Educational Testing Service, Princeton, New Jersey.
2. Allen Hugh Jr. "Attitudes of Certain High School Seniors Toward Science and Scientific Careers." Teachers College, Columbia University, New York City, 1960.

Programed Instruction

The role of programed instruction in the elementary school has had some attention from researchers. This is understandable since such programs encourage individual student work, and free the teacher from direct instruction to perform other tasks.

Hedges and MacDougall(61) investigated the effectiveness of teaching fourth-grade science using programed science materials and laboratory experiences. The study had three phases. In phase one, the purpose was to establish the possibility of programed instruction as a teaching method. This was done by observing students using the materials, and determining student and teacher attitudes. The information was used to revise and rewrite the programs as part of phase two of the study. The final report on the evaluative phase (phase three) has not yet come to the reviewers' attention; however, the intention was to compare innovative ways of using the materials with a more traditional approach under the headings: achievement, interest, problem-solving ability, ability to generalize, and retention. This three-phase method of determining feasibility, refining materials and methods, and evaluating student and teacher outcomes outlines a promising sequence for the development of instructional procedures.

Blank(14) investigated developing inquiry skills through programed-instruction techniques. The programs trained children to ask questions about the relative dimensions of problems before attempting to solve them. He found that the children given inquiry training asked significantly more questions (as well as a lower proportion of irrelevant ones) on oral and written criterion tests than did students in control groups. This improvement in inquiry skills was not at the expense of other achievement criteria, so it was found possible to introduce inquiry training without affecting progress in regular course work.

Dutton(41) investigated pupil achievement using programed materials on heat, light, and sound with fourth graders. He found that children did proceed at different rates and that they could perform simple science experiments with little teacher supervision. Pupils using the programed materials learned concepts more efficiently than did those in class taught in a conventional way.

Crabtree(30) studied the relationships between score, time, IQ, and reading level for fourth-grade students by structuring programed science materials in different ways. Linear programs seemed preferable to branched versions since the same amount of material was learned in less time. Other findings were of the "no significant difference" type, although there was some evidence that multiple choice type response requires a higher reading ability than other response forms.

Taylor(122) investigated the effect of pupil behavior and characteristics and teacher attitudes on achievement when programed science materials are used at the fourth-grade level. Teacher attitudes, combinations of pupil and teacher attitudes, pupil intelligence, interest, and initial knowledge of science, along with other selected personality and performance factors all contribute significantly to pupil final achievement. The study indicates that any given set of programed science materials cannot meet the needs of all the students at any given grade level.

Individualized Instruction

Instruction may be classified as individualized if experiences are specifically designed for each individual child, taking into account such factors as background, knowledge and experience, reading level, interests, and intelligence. There have been several attempts at individualizing which have tried to allow for the individual needs of children in the instructional design.

Baum(8) prepared materials to test the feasibility of individualizing science experiences for fifth-grade pupils. He devised a series of pretests of skills and knowledge so that pupil deficiencies could be identified. Each pupil was then assigned a kit specially designed to help him acquire the skill or competency shown to be deficient on the tests. This method was found suitable for helping pupils achieve curricular goals in the area of science. Evaluation was carried out by observing pupil reactions to this instruction, and though the evaluation was subjective, the strengths of the program in terms of desired outcomes clearly emerged.

O'Toole(89) compared an individualized method with a teacher-centered approach in the teaching of science to fifth graders. He found no significant differences between his groups in achievement, problem-solving ability, or science interest. The teacher-centered program stressing problem solving as a major objective was more effective in developing the ability to identify valid conclusions while the individualized program was more effective in developing ability to recognize hypotheses and problems.

It is likely that group methods of instruction will develop some outcomes more effectively than individualized methods, while other outcomes will develop more effectively in an individualized situation. This study was the only one which attempted to identify what some of these outcome differences might be.

Schiller(102) used activity booklets and data sheets to individualize instruction for sixth-grade pupils. The materials were designed to give children an opportunity to complete some science experiments and other activities which were in addition to the formal instructional program. Much of the evaluation was subjective, but students were eager to participate in the activities and seemed to gain from them.

Other attempts at individualizing instruction were undertaken by LaCava(69) who used the tape recorder as an aid in individualizing, Carter(25) who developed a science experience center, and Lipson(74) who developed an individualized program by coordinating audio-tapes to simple science kits. These studies, in general, support the contention that individualizing instruction is possible and educationally desirable at the elementary level. To date, however, evaluation has been highly subjective.

A more rigorous evaluation of an individualized program was undertaken by Gleason(54). He measured pupil growth in areas of general science knowledge, liking for science, and learning to generalize. Although he found no specific advantages in favor of individualized self-study activity in science, pupils learned as much content by themselves as they did when taught by a teacher.

An important project related to individualizing instruction is the Oakleaf Project for Individuality Prescribed Instruction discussed by Lindvall and Bolvin(72). Here, the Oakleaf Elementary School is used as a laboratory for testing the feasibility of individualizing instruction, developing suitable programs, and evaluating the effects of such instruction.

Ability Grouping—Socioeconomic Status of Students

Three studies investigated the effects of socio-economic status on achievement in elementary school science. Some of the findings have clear implications for instruction.

Rowland(98) compared the science achievement of sixth-grade pupils of high socio-economic status with those of generally low status. He found that given equal intelligence and equal science background experiences, higher socio-economic status pupils show greater science achievement than do lower groups, and these differences carry over to all the various types of science achievement measured. He found that it is of great importance that lower socio-economic status pupils have opportunities to manipulate and study simple science materials, and this should precede experience with more complex types of commercial science aids. Also these students should engage in concrete science experiences before being expected to learn from reading or discussing science material.

Wagner(124) compared the responses of economically advantaged and disadvantaged sixth-grade pupils to science demonstrations. Pupil responses to the demonstrations were obtained by getting them to either write about, tell about, or construct pictorially, using predesigned plastic templates, suitable applications of the demonstrations. Advantaged pupils were significantly superior in written and oral responses, but no differences were detected in the construction responses. This finding suggests that disadvantaged pupils understand and can communicate their understandings of science concepts when placed in situations requiring limited language response.

Becker(9) investigated the achievement of gifted sixth-grade students when segregated from, partly segregated from, or homogeneously mixed with students of lower ability. No significant differences were detected between the groups, and no special advantages accrued when gifted children were placed in special groups. Unfortunately, the description of the design of the study did not mention some important aspects, one of which was the length of time students were placed in these various arrangements. This time factor is likely to be highly significant in such a study.

These studies point to the great importance which must be placed on student characteristics in the design of instructional procedures. Selecting one factor, e.g., ability, from the whole range of factors which influence learning, and then separating instructional groups on the basis of it, is unlikely to significantly improve student outcomes. The factors involved in determining the outcomes of instruction are much more subtle than this.

Use of Reading Materials

Little research was detected on investigating ways reading materials may be used in an instructional situation. Some very interesting studies, however, were identified.

Fryback(48) evaluated some elementary science curriculum materials which had been written to accommodate five different reading levels in a fifth-grade class. Other variables in the design included whether the students performed experiments or not, and the extent of class discussion. He found that the provision for different reading ability levels and class discussion did not show any significant influence on achievement. Only when pupils worked experiments were significant achievement gains noted. The provision of different reading levels and class discussion may have a motivational effect for later work and may affect other outcomes, but these data indicate that the provision of experiments to be performed individually by pupils is important.

Bennett and Clodfelter(11) investigated student learning of earth-science concepts when the science unit was integrated within the reading program of second-grade children. For the integration, a "word-analysis" approach was used. In this method, the child was given a basic list of words to be used in the new resource unit on earth science, and then introduced to their meanings before presentation of the unit. The "word-analysis" group showed greater achievement gains than the control groups where the science was taught in the traditional way. The study demonstrated that certain earth-science concepts can be learned at the second-grade level.

Williams(128) rewrote sixth-grade science materials to a third-grade level of readability, and used them with his sixth-grade pupils. Gains in reading speed and comprehension seemed to occur when the materials were used, but the duration of the study was far too short for differences in learning outcomes to be evaluated.

Research in the area of the use of reading materials is indeed thin. More and more textbooks and other materials directed to the elementary pupil are coming onto the market, yet the role of reading materials in science instruction has had little recent evaluation.

Critical Thinking

Over the period of review, only one study was identified which investigated the development of critical thinking in children. Mason(78), in a two-year study, developed materials for teaching critical thinking in grades K-6. The first year was devoted to developing materials and providing inservice seminars for the teachers who would eventually teach the course. Basic assumptions were that children should have planned experiences in science rather than incidental ones, they should have direct experience with both content and methods of science, and that experiences can be identified to give students direct training in the acquisition of scientific skills and attitudes. Evaluation of the course was subjective for grades K-3 because of the lack of suitable instruments; but, in grades 4-6 significant gains in critical thinking were made over the period of a year. The materials were particularly effective at the fifth-grade level where maximum gains were made.

It seems quite clear that instructional sequences can be devised which will develop pupils' powers of critical thinking. Only by evaluating the outcomes of the experiences can the effectiveness of these materials be assessed. There is a lack of activity in this area, particularly in grades K-3.

Process: Inquiry in Science

Much emphasis has been placed on the development of science process skills and the use of inquiry methods to develop certain cognitive abilities by the new elementary science course improvement projects. Less research has been reported in this area than might have been expected if one judges from the significant sums of money spent on developing these programs.

Raun(95) investigated the interaction between curriculum variables and selected classroom-student characteristics using the AAAS *Science —A Process Approach* materials. He was interested in the changes in cognitive and affective behavior brought about by children using some of the strategies of science. Some of the factors investigated included problem solving, perceptual closure, verbal fluency, ideation fluency, tested intelligence, achievement, and attitudes toward science and scientists. The strategies of inquiry selected for performance evaluation after five months instruction were classifying, observing, using number relations, and recognizing space-time relations. He found limited evidence of significant grade differences between behaviors and performance in the strategies of inquiry in science, and that there was no consistent pattern of behavioral change among grades. In fact, on many of the factors investigated, grades 5 and 6 showed regressive tendencies which support the argument that there is rather slow development of science process skills beyond grade 5.

Price(93) investigated whether students who had manipulated objects and materials to gather empirical data in an elementary classroom would transfer this manipulative process behavior to a test situation outside the classroom. It was found that children rarely sought data by overt manipulative processes in the test situations, even though verbal responses to them indicated high motivational interest. Also gifted children showed no greater tendency to empirically gather data to solve problems than students in the normal range of intelligence.

Scott and Sigel(106) used grades 4-6 to investigate the effects of inquiry training in physical science on creativity and cognitive style. Pupils receiving inquiry training learned science concepts as well or better than children in conventional classes, and no significant differences were found between boys and girls. Cognitive styles did seem to be influenced by the inquiry process, and some differences in the developmental trends of cognitive styles of boys compared to girls were apparent.

More studies like the above are needed if instructional procedures are to be developed which meet the individual needs of students at each stage in their development. Inquiry methods and methods designed to have children working with the processes of science are likely to produce different outcomes than conventional procedures. These new procedures are becoming more carefully controlled, and with the development of more sensitive evaluative instruments, a clearer idea of what these differences may be is starting to emerge. Increased research on ways the new materials may be used and the outcomes obtained seems essential.

Problem Solving

A number of studies investigated problem solving in elementary children. Dyrli(42), Gunnels(55), and Harris(59) all made some analysis of the problem-solving behavior of children at various grade levels. Only Schippers(103) extended what is known about problem solving into a suggested instructional sequence.

Dyrli(42) wished to discover whether instruction had any effect on the length of transition period from the stage of concrete operations to more formal patterns of thought in the Piagetian developmental sequence. Gunnels(55) also investigated cognitive devlopment based on the Piagetian stages of intuitive, conrete, and formal thought. He used an interview technique to study the development of logical judgments in science of successful and unsuccessful problem solvers in grades 4-9. In general, the Piagetian order of development was confirmed that suc cessful problem solvers operate at a higher level of operational thought than do unsuccessful problem solvers; however, even though a child is at a given chronological age, this does not guarantee a definite level of thought process skills.

Harris(59) used sixth graders and investigated the usefulness of pupil drawings in developing a problem-solving approach to learning science concepts. He identified two kinds of problem-solving behavior: verificational and insightful, but his study concentrated on the verificational aspects which seem most often encountered in school. He made an intensive individual analysis of the problem-solving processes of eighteen children. Some of his findings are pertinent to the development of instructional procedures. He found that children do not use consistent patterns of thinking in different problem situations, and that the confidence of the child in his ability to solve problems is an important factor in his success. Also instruction in science, which includes drawing of concepts in a tangible form by the learner, was not significantly related to growth in the ability of the learner to use these concepts in problem-solving situations. A particularly significant finding relating to the evaluation of an instructional sequence was that pencil and paper tests did not provide an adequate means for evaluating problem-solving processes in individual children.

Schippers(103) designed materials and a procedure to teach sixth graders a problem-solving instructional method using a multi-reference activity base. Three steps in the instructional process were identified:

first, establish the background situation; second, understand the problem; and third, work out a solution. Supervision and the use of illustrative lessons were found important if inexperienced teachers were to use the method effectively. Evaluation of student outcomes was largely subjective.

Creativity

Only two studies were identified which made an attempt to develop materials and procedures for encouraging creativity and creative thinking in students.

DeRoche(37) used creative exercises with sixth-grade pupils to see if these produced any gains in creative thinking and achievement not seen in classes doing more traditional work. The experimental group had creative exercises in 26 space science lessons and four "brain-storming" sessions, while control classes either had 30 space science lessons without the exercises or no space science instruction at all. The *Minnesota Tests of Creative Thinking* and specially prepared content achievement tests were used to evaluate outcomes. For high intelligence students, the experimental method was significantly superior to the control in developing creative factors like verbal fluency, flexibility, originality, and elaboration. This trend was less marked for average and low ability students. No significant differences on the achievement tests were found between the "creative" group and the "traditional" group taught space science.

Tating(121) studied ways of developing creative thinking in elementary school science. Creative thinking was defined operationally as divergent and original thinking measured in terms of questions asked and hypotheses given. More divergent responses were obtained with the trained groups than with the control, but the number of divergent responses decreased if pupils were given instructions to be original. Tating "primed" creative thinking by getting pupils to write down as many questions as they could about a particular demonstration, which, if given a "yes-no" answer by the teacher, would help the child understand why a given event occurred. Another method of priming used was to get students to write down a number of words in response to a given word.

Although the asking of questions could be primed, the development of hypotheses was not as responsive to training. The formulation of hypotheses in science is a highly complicated mental process, and the formation of an original hypothesis probably requires more time than is needed to think of questions.

The evidence is mounting that creative exercises can be designed to increase creative responses in children without any losses in content achievement. Teachers are constantly being urged to teach science creatively, and more research needs to be done to estimate the effectiveness of various forms of instruction.

Concept Development

Many of the studies in this area were concerned with concept development as part of research into learning theory, rather than evaluating different instructional procedures for their efficiency in developing concepts.

Voelker(123) gives an example of pertinent research on the development of concepts within the field of science education. He compared two instructional methods for teaching the concepts of physical and chemical change in grades 2-6. Using essentially similar lesson procedures and materials in both cases, he found that formulation and statement by the teacher of the generalization to be learned was not superior to a procedure in which the pupil individually formulated the generalization concerning physical and chemical change. An interesting sidelight of the study was that although sixth-grade pupils were significantly better verbalizers of the concepts, if the criterion of understanding was simply to classify observed phenomena, no significant differences could be detected among grades 2-6. In this study, where teaching method and materials were carefully controlled, there did not seem to be any significant advantages of an "inductive-discovery" approach over a "deductive" one on the outcomes selected. Unfortunately, the concept of physical and chemical change appeared rather difficult except for pupils in grade 6.

Salstrom(100) compared concepts learned by sixth-grade pupils in two types of guided discovery lessons. The same experimental lessons were presented as a science game to each of his groups. Following this, one group had an oral inquiry session while the other received a battery of cards which on one side had printed questions a pupil might ask in an inquiry session and on the other, the answers to those questions were printed. In the card group, each pupil could draw only cards that would yield information needed to solve the problem. They were then ordered by the pupil to give a solution to the problem posed in the lesson. The card treatment group showed greater gains in concept development than the oral inquiry group, supporting the contention that more guidance than can be given each pupil in an oral inquiry session helps concept development.

Three studies were directed at finding the relationship between the child's level of maturity and the understanding of a particular concept.

Carey(21) investigated the particle nature of matter in grades 2-5, Haddad(56) investigated the concept of relativity in grades 4-8, and Helgeson(62) investigated the concept of force. Maturity studies like these are extremely useful in helping course developers decide the level to which a particular concept may be unfolded with pupils at a particular stage in development. The studies suggested that there was almost as much variation in maturity within a grade level as there was between grade levels. These data question the grouping of children by grades if the aim is to provide a group of children at the same stage of mental development.

Kolb(66) investigated integrating mathematics and science instruction with fifth-grade pupils to determine if such integration would facilitate the acquisition of quantitative science behaviors. He used *Science— A Process Approach* materials and found that such integration with mathematics did significantly increase achievement. Integration seems a promising way to reduce the time spent in developing concepts which have elements common to both mathematics and science, and this aspect should be pursued further.

Ziegler(132) investigated the use of mechanical models in teaching theoretical concepts regarding the particle nature of matter to pupils in grades 2-6. They found that children who had not previously learned to use such a model could learn to do so with suitable instruction, and those who had some knowledge of such models improved their ability to use them. These concrete experiences with mechanical models helped pupils form theoretical concepts to explain expansion, contraction, change of phase, and mixtures by the time they completed grade 4.

Studies like this and those of Carey(21), Haddad(56), Voelker(123), and Helgeson(62) should be extended into other concept areas so that a more complete picture of the concepts which may be developed at any given level may emerge. From this, suitable instructional procedures using mechanical models and other devices can be developed. Until this is done, courses of instruction in elementary schools will be based on subjective opinion and feeling about what can be accomplished at any given grade level or stage of development, rather than on a soundly researched experimental base.

Summary and Conclusions

Reviewing the available research into the outcomes of instruction in elementary science has revealed a number of areas where little in the way of a planned attack on the problems has been initiated. Such areas include the development of psychomotor skills, critical thinking skills, creativity, and work in the affective domain on the development of attitudes toward science and scientists. Only in the field of understanding concepts can one see steady progress being made.

The tentative nature of the findings of much educational research and the massive qualifications which surround any generalizations made by researchers often appear confusing to the classroom teacher. The feeling is sometimes expressed that research "has nothing to say to the classroom teacher." In light of this, the reviewers have decided to outline a number of tentative conclusions which seem to emerge from the research reviewed. They are stated without qualification so that they may be readily grasped by teachers. The purists may assume that they are surrounded by the usual modifiers demanded by the idiosyncrasies of educational research.

1. *Instructional procedures, whether in the classroom or in the research situation, should be based on some clearly defined model of what constitutes the instructional process.* The major criteria for such a model should be that it is useful in helping understand the components of instruction and that the instruction develops desired behavior changes in pupils.

2. *For teachers skilled in handling them, problem-solving or inductive methods or instructional procedures designed to improve creativity can bring about gains in outcome areas which are greater than if more traditional approaches are used.* This is not achieved at the expense of knowledge of content.

3. *Audiovisual aids and reading materials should be carefully integrated into the instructional sequence for a definite instructional purpose, otherwise little effect on achievment outcomes will be noted.*

4. *Pupil activity and pupil performed experiments are important prerequisits for the effective learning of science concepts.* This seems true for all levels of ability.

5. *Instructional procedures can be devised to bring about specific outcomes, provided these are clearly defined.* Both problem-solving skills and creativity can be developed.

6. *Individualized instruction is a satisfactory alternative to total class instruction.* Even very young children can work alone on preplanned experiences using quite sophisticated aids with minimal teacher help.

7. *Elementary children can learn by using programed-instruction materials.* Outcomes from these are enhanced if they are integrated with laboratory experiences.

8. *Each child should have the opportunity to develop science concepts and process skills in both individual and group situations.* The out-

comes of one kind of instruction will complement rather than parallel the other.

9. *Verbalization of a concept is the last step in a child's understanding of it.* He can demonstrate aspects of his understanding in concrete situations long before he can verbalize them.

10. *Any given class in elementary school is likely to contain children who are in at least two stages of cognitive development—that of concrete operations and formal thought.* These two groups require quite different instructional strategies.

11. *Ability grouping has little effect on the achievement of high ability students.* Other student characteristics are just as significant as intelligence in the learning process.

12. *Educationally disadvantaged students can communicate their understanding of science concepts if the response mode is by a means other than language; e.g., pictorial representation.*

13. *Integration of mathematics and science saves time.* Where common concepts are being developed, achievement in both areas seems to be enhanced.

14. *Educationally disadvantaged children need even greater recourse to simple materials and individual experiments if they are to develop the desired science concepts to the level of other children.*

15. *Teachers should decide on instructional procedures which suit their own personal characteristics and philosophy.* Modification of firmly established patterns of teaching can only occur if there is a corresponding modification of personal characteristics and behaviors.

These conclusions are given in this way so that the classroom teacher may be encouraged to try something new or do something different and the educational researcher to assemble evidence either to support or reject them. If both these aims are met, then this review may have sparked some improvement both in classroom instruction per se, and in its enigmatic research.

REFERENCES

1. Ainslie, D. S. "Simple Equipment and Procedures in Elementary Laboratories." *The Physics Teacher.* September 1967.
2. Allen, Leslie Robert. "An Examination of the Classificatory Ability of Children Who Have Been Exposed to One of the 'New' Elementary Science Programs." (M)*. 1967.
3. Allison, Roy W. "The Effect of Three Methods of Treating Motivational Films Upon the Attitudes of Fourth-, Fifth-, and Sixth-Grade Students Toward Science, Scientists, and Scientific Careers." Pennsylvania State University, 1967.

*(M) denotes University Microfilms, Ann Arbor, Michigan.

4. Anderson, Ronald D. "Children's Ability to Formulate Mental Models to Explain Natural Phenomena." *Journal of Research in Science Teaching.* December 1965.

5. Anklam, Phoebe Anne. "A Study of the Relationship between Two Divergent Instructional Methods and Achievement Motivation of Elementary School Children." (M). 1962.

6. Barker, D. "Primary School Science—An Attempt to Investigate the Effects of the Informal Use of a Discovery Table on the Scientific Knowledge of Primary School Children." *Educational Research.* February 1965.

7. Barrett, Raymond E. "Field Trip Tips." *Science and Children.* October 1965.

8. Baum, Ernest A. "Report of the Individualization of the Teaching of Selected Science Skills and Knowledges in an Elementary School Classroom with Materials Prepared by the Teacher." (M). 1965.

9. Becker, Leonard John. "An Analysis of the Science and Mathematics Achievement of Gifted Sixth-Grade Children Enrolled in Segregated Classes." (M). 1963.

10. Bennett, Lloyd M. "A Study of the Comparison of Two Instructional Methods, the Experimental-Field Method and the Traditional Classroom Method, Involving Science Content in Ecology for the Seventh Grade." *Science Education.* December 1965.

11. Bennett, Lloyd M. and Cherie Clodfelter. "A Study of the Integration of an Earth Science Unit Within the Reading Program of a Second Grade by Utilizing the Word Analysis Approach." *School Science and Mathematics.* November 1966.

12. Bickel, Robert F. "A Study of the Effect of Television Instruction on the Science Achievement and Attitudes of Children in Grades 4, 5, and 6." (M). 1964.

13. Blackwood, Paul E. "Science Teaching in the Elementary School: A Survey of Practices." *Journal of Research in Science Teaching.* September 1965.

14. Blank, Stanley Solomon. "Inquiry Training Through Programed Instruction." (M). 1963.

15. Bornhorst, Ben A., and Prentiss M. Hosford. "Basing Instruction in Science on Children's Questions: Using a Wonder Box in the Third Grade." *Science Education.* March 1960.

16. Brudzynski, Alfred John. "A Comparative Study of Two Methods for Teaching Electricity and Magnetism with Fifth- and Sixth-Grade Children." (M). 1966.

17. Brusini, Joseph Anthony. "An Experimental Study of the Development of Science Continua Concepts in Upper Elementary and Junior High School Children." (M). 1966.

18. Buell, Robert R. "Inquiry Training in the School's Science Laboratories." *School Science and Mathematics.* April 1965.

19. Butts,• David P. "The Degree to which Children Conceptualize from Science Experiences." *Journal of Research in Science Teaching.* June 1962.

20. Butts, David P. "The Relationship Between Classroom Experiences and Certain Student Characteristics." University of Texas, February 1967.

21. Carey, Russell LeRoy. "Relationship Between Levels of Maturity and Levels of Understanding of Selected Concepts of the Particle Nature of Matter." (M). 1967.

22. Carlson, Jerry S. "Effects of Instruction on the Concepts of Conservation of Substance." *Science Education.* March 1967.

23. Carpenter, Finley. "Toward a Systematic Construction of a Classroom Taxonomy." *Science Education.* April 1965.

24. Carpenter, Regan. "A Reading Method and an Activity Method in Elementary Science Instruction." *Science Education.* April 1963.

25. Carter, Neal. "Science Experience Center." *Science and Children.* February 1967.

26. Caruthers, Bertram, Sr. "Teacher Preparation and Experience Related to Achievement of Fifth-Grade Pupils in Science." (M). 1967.

27. Chinnis, Robert Jennings. "The Development of Physical Science Principles in Elementary-School Science Textbooks." (M). 1962.

28. Cobun, Ted Charles. "The Relative Effectiveness of Three Levels of Pictorial Presentation of Biological Subject Matter on the Associative Learning of Nomenclature by Sixth-Grade Students." (M). 1961.

29. Cox, Louis T. "Working with Science in the Kindergarten." *Science Education*. March 1963.

30. Crabtree, J. F. "A Study of the Relationships Between 'Score,' 'Time,' 'IQ,' and 'Reading level' for Fourth-Grade Students Using Programed Science Materials." *Science Education*. April 1967.

31. Crabtree, Charlotte Antoinette. "Effects of Structuring on Productiveness in Children's Thinking: Study of Second-Grade Dramatic Play Patterns Centered on Harbor and Airport Activities under Two Types of Teacher Structuring." (M). 1962.

32. Cunningham, Roger. "Implementing Nongraded Advancement with Laboratory Activities as a Vehicle—An Experiment in Elementary School Science." *School Science and Mathematics*. February 1967.

33. Cunningham, John D. "On Curiosity and Science Education." *School Science and Mathematics*. December 1966.

34. Dart, Francis E., and Panna Lal Pradham. "Cross-Cultural Teaching of Science." *Science*. February 1967.

35. Davis, Joseph E., Jr. "Ice Calorimetry in the Upper Elementary Grades." *Science and Children*. December 1966.

36. Decker, Martin George. "The Differential Effects Upon the Learning of the Natural Sciences by Fifth Graders of Two Modes of Teaching over Television and in the Classroom." (M). 1965.

37. DeRoche, Edward Francis. "A Study of the Effectiveness of Selected Creative Exercises on Creative Thinking and the Mastery of a Unit in Elementary Science." (M). 1966.

38. Dietmeier, Homer J. "The Effect of Integration of Science Teaching by Television on the Development of Scientific Reasoning in the Fifth-Grade Student." (M). 1962.

39. Downing, Carl Edward. "A Statistical Examination of the Relationship Among Elementary Science Achievement Gains, Interest Level Changes, and Time Allotment for Instructional Purposes." (M). 1963.

40. Drenchko, Elizabeth K. "The Comparative Effectiveness of Two Methods of Teaching Grade School Science." (M). 1966.

41. Dutton, Sherman S. "An Experimental Study in the Programing of Science Instruction for the Fourth Grade." (M). 1963.

42. Dyrli, Odvard Egil. "An Investigation into the Development of Combinational Mechanisms Characteristic of Formal Reasoning, through Experimental Problem Situations with Sixth-Grade Students." (M). 1967.

43. Eccles, Priscilla J. "Research Reports—Teacher Behavior and Knowledge of Subject Matter in Sixth-Grade Science." *Journal of Research in Science Teaching*. December 1965.

44. Elashhab, Gamal A. "A Model for the Development of Science Curricula in the Preparatory and Secondary Schools of the United Arab Republic." (M). 1966.

45. Engelmann, Siegfried, and James J. Gallagher. "A Study of How a Child Learns Concepts about Characteristics of Liquid Materials." EDRS, National Cash Register Company, 1966.

46. Fischler, Abraham S. "Science, Process, The Learner—A Synthesis." *Science Education*. December 1965.

47. Fish, Alphoretta S., and Bernice Goldmark. "Inquiry Method—Three Interpretations." *The Science Teacher.* February 1966.

48. Fryback, William H. "Evaluation of Multi-Level Reading Materials, Intra-Class Discussion Techniques and Student Experimentations on Achievement in Fifth-Grade Elementary Science." (M). 1965.

49. Garone, John Edward. "Acquiring Knowledge and Attaining Understanding of Children's Scientific Concept Development." *Science Education.* March 1960.

50. Gehrman, Joseph Leo. "A Study of the Impact of Authoritative Communication of Expected Achievement in Elementary School Science." (M). 1965.

51. Gerne, Timothy A., Jr. "A Comparative Study of Two Types of Science Teaching on the Competence of Sixth-Grade Students to Understand Selected Topics in Electricity and Magnetism." (M). 1967.

52. Glaser, Robert. "Concept Learning and Concept Teaching." University of Pittsburgh, Learning Research and Development Center. 1967.

53. Glaser, Robert. "The Design of Instruction." National Society for the Study of Education Yearbook, 1966.

54. Gleason, Walter Patterson. "An Examination of Some Effects of Pupil Self-Instruction Methods Compared with the Effects of Teacher-Led Classes in Elementary Science of Fifth-Grade Pupils." (M). 1965.

55. Gunnels, Frances Goodrich. "A Study of the Development in Logical Judgments in Science of Successful and Unsuccessful Problem Solvers in Grades Four Through Nine." (M). 1967.

56. Haddad, Wadi Dahir. "Relationship Between Mental Maturity and the Level of Understanding of Concepts of Relativity in Grades 4-8." (M). 1968.

57. Harris, William, and Verlin Lee. "Mental Age and Science Concepts—A Pilot Study." *Journal of Research in Science Teaching.* December 1966.

58. Harris, William. "A Technique for Grade Placement in Elementary Science." *Journal of Research in Science Teaching.* March 1964.

59. Harris, William Ned. "An Analysis of Problem-Solving Behavior in Sixth-Grade Children, and of the Usefulness of Drawings by the Pupil in Learning Science Concepts." (M). 1962.

60. Haugerud, Albert Ralph. "The Development of a Conceptual Framework for the Construction of a Multi-Media Learning Laboratory and its Utilization for Elementary School Science." (M). 1966.

61. Hedges, William D., and Mary Ann MacDougall. "Teaching Fourth-Grade Science by Means of Programed Science Materials with Laboratory Experiences." *Science Education.* February 1964.

62. Helgeson, Stanley Leon. "An Investigation into the Relationships between Concepts of Force Attained and Maturity as indicated by Grade Levels." (M). 1967.

63. Hinmon, Dean E. "Problem Solving." *Science and Children.* April 1966.

64. Johnson, Mervin LeRoy. "A Determination of Aerospace Principles Desirable for Inclusion in Fifth- or Sixth-Grade Science Programs." (M). 1966.

65. Karplus, Robert. "Science Curriculum Improvement Study." *Journal of Research in Science Teaching.* December 1964.

66. Kolb, John R. "Effects of Relating Mathematics to Science Instruction on the Acquisition of Quantitative Science Behaviors." *Journal of Research in Science Teaching.* 1968.

67. Korey, Ruth Anne. "Contributions of Planetariums to Elementary Education." (M). 1963.

68. Kraft, Mary Elizabeth. "A Study of Information and Vocabulary Achievement from the Teaching of Natural Science by Television in the Fifth Grade." (M). 1961.

69. LaCava, George. "An Experiment Via Tape." *Science and Children.* October 1965.

70. Languis, Marlin, and Loren L. Stull. "Science Problems—Vehicles to Develop Measurement Principles." *Science Education.* February 1966.
71. Lansdown, Brenda, and Thomas S. Dietz. "Free Versus Guided Experimentation." *Science Education.* April 1965.
72. Lindvall, C. Mauritz, and John D. Bolvin. "Individually Prescribed Instruction—The Oakleaf Project." University of Pittsburgh, Learning Research and Development Center, February 1966.
73. Lipson, Joseph I. "Light Test—Comparison Between Elementary School Children and College Freshman." University of Pittsburgh, Learning Research and Development Center. February 1966.
74. Lipson, Joseph I. "An Individualized Science Laboratory." *Science and Children.* December 1966.
75. Livermore, Arthur H. "The Process Approach of the AAAS Commission on Science Education." *Journal of Research in Science Teaching.* December 1964.
76. Lowery, Lawrence F. "An Experimental Investigation into the Attitudes of Fifth-Grade Students Toward Science." *School Science and Mathematics.* June 1967.
77. Los Angeles City Schools. "The Art of Questioning in Science—Summary and Implications." Los Angeles City Schools. 1967.
78. Mason, John M. "The Direct Teaching of Critical Thinking in Grades Four Through Six." *Journal of Research in Science Teaching.* December 1963.
79. McCloskey, James. "The Development of the Role of Science in General Education for Elementary and Secondary Schools." (M). 1963.
80. McKeon, Joseph E. "A Process Lesson in Density." *Science and Children.* December 1966.
81. Melis, Lloyd Henry. "The Nature and Extent of Reading Instruction in Science and Social Studies in the Intermediate Grades of Selected School Districts." (M). 1964.
82. Mermelstein, Egon; Edwina Carr; Dorothy Mills; and Jeanne Schwartz. "The Effects of Various Training Techniques on the Acquisition of the Concept of Conservation of Substance." U. S. Department of Health, Education, and Welfare, February 1967.
83. Moorehead, William D. "The Status of Elementary School Science and How it is Taught." (M). 1965.
84. Nasca, Donald. "Effect of Varied Presentations of Laboratory Exercises within Programed Materials on Specific Intellectual Factors of Science Problem-Solving Behavior." *Science Education.* December 1966.
85. Neal, Louise A. "Techniques for Developing Methods of Scientific Inquiry in Children in Grades One Through Six." *Science Education.* October 1961.
86. New York State Department of Education. "Tips and Techniques in Elementary Science." Bureau of Elementary Curriculum Development. 1966.
87. Novak, Joseph D. "Development and Use of Audio-Tape Programed Instruction for Elementary Science." Purdue University, February 1967.
88. O'Toole, Raymond J. "A Review of Attempts to Individualize Elementary School Science." *School Science and Mathematics.* May 1968.
89. O'Toole, Raymond J. "A Study to Determine Whether Fifth-Grade Children Can Learn Certain Selected Problem-Solving Abilities Through Individualized Instruction (Research Study Number 1)." (M). 1966.
90. Perkins, William D. "The Field Study as a Technique in Elementary School Science." *Science Education.* December 1963.
91. Pershern, Frank Richard. "The Effect of Industrial Arts Activities on Science Achievements and Pupil Attitudes in the Upper Elementary Grades." (M). 1967.
92. Pollach, Samuel. "Individual Differences in the Development of Certain Science Concepts." (M). 1963.
93. Price, LaMar. "An Investigation of the Transfer of an Elementary Science Process." (M). 1968.

94. Ramsey, Irvin L., and Sandra Lee Wiandt. "Individualizing Elementary School Science." *School Science and Mathematics.* May 1967.
95. Raun, Chester Eugene. "The Interaction Between Curriculum Variables and Selected Classroom Student Characteristics." (M). 1967.
96. Reese, Willard Francis. "A Comparison of Interest Level and Problem-Solving Accuracy Generated by Single Concept Inductive and Deductive Science Films (Research Study Number 1)." (M). 1966.
97. Riessman, Frank. "Education of the Culturally Deprived Child." *The Science Teacher.* November 1965.
98. Rowland, George William. "A Study of the Relationship Between Socio-Economic Status and Elementary School Science Achievement." (M). 1965.
99. St. John, Clinton. "Can Science Education be Scientific? Notes Toward a Viable Theory of Science Teaching." *Journal of Research in Science Teaching.* December, 1966.
100. Salstrom, David. "A Comparison of Conceptualization in Two Types of Guided Discovery Science Lesson." (M). 1966.
101. Sands, Theodore; Robert E. Rumery; and Richard C. Youngs. "Concept Development Materials for Gifted Elementary Pupils—Final Report of Field Testing." Illinois State University. 1966.
102. Schiller, LeRoy. "A Study of the Effect of Individualized Activities on Understanding in Elementary School Science." (M). 1964.
103. Schippers, John Vernon. "An Investigation of the Problem Method of Instruction in Sixth-Grade Science Classes." (M). 1962.
104. Shulz, Richard William. "The Role of Cognitive Organizers in the Facilitation of Concept Learning in Elementary School Science." (M). 1966.
105. Scott, Lloyd. "An Experiment in Teaching Basic Science in the Elementary School." *Science Education.* March 1962.
106. Scott, Norval C., Jr., and I. E. Sigel. "Effects of Inquiry Training in Physical Science on Creativity and Cognitive Styles of Elementary School Children." U. S. Office of Education, Cooperative Research Branch, 1965.
107. Scott, Norval, C., Jr., "Science Concept Achievement and Cognitive Functions." *Journal of Research in Science Teaching.* December 1964.
108. Scott, Norval, C., Jr. "The Strategy of Inquiry and Styles of Categorization." *Journal of Research in Science Teaching.* September 1966.
109. Skinner, Ray, Jr. "An Experimental Study of the Effects of Different Combinations of Television Presentations and Classroom Teacher Follow-up on the Achievement and Interest in Science of Fifth Graders." (M). 1966.
110. Smith, Billy Arthur. "An Experimental Comparison of Two Techniques (Planetarium Lecture-Demonstration and Classroom Lecture-Demonstration) of Teaching Selected Astronomical Concepts to Sixth-Grade Students." (M). 1966.
111. Smith, Doyne M. and Bernice Cooper. "A Study of the Use of Various Techniques in Teaching Science in the Elementary School." *School Science and Mathematics.* June 1967.
112. Smith, Robert Frank. "An Analysis and Classification of Children's Explanations of Natural Phenomena." (M). 1963.
113. Snoble, Joseph Jerry. "Status and Trends of Elementary School Science in Iowa Public Schools, 1963-1966." (M). 1967.
114. Stapp, William Beebe. "Developing a Conservation Education Program for the Ann Arbor Public School System, and Integrating It into the Existing Curriculum (K-12)." (M). 1963.
115. Stauss, Nyles George. "An Investigation into the Relationship between Concept Attainment and Level of Maturity." (M). 1967.
116. Stokes, William Woods. "An Analysis and Evaluation of Current Efforts to Improve the Curriculum by Emphasis on Disciplinary Structure and Learning by Discovery." (M). 1963.

117. Stone, Ruth Muriel. "A Comparison of the Patterns of Criteria Which Elementary and Secondary School Teachers Use in Judging the Relative Effectiveness of Selected Learning Experiences in Elementary Science." (M). 1963.
118. Suchman, J. Richard. "Idea Book—Inquiry Development Program in Physical Science." Science Research Associates, Inc., Chicago. 1966.
119. Suchman, J. Richard. "Inquiry Training: Building Skills for Autonomous Discovery." *Merrill-Palmer Quarterly.* 1961.
120. Swan, Malcolm D. "Science Achievement as it Relates to Science Curricula and Programs at the Sixth-Grade Level in Montana Public Schools." *Journal of Research in Science Teaching.* June 1966.
121. Tating, Marcela Tionko. "Printing Creative Thinking in Elementary School Science." (M). 1965.
122. Taylor, Alton L. "The Influence of Teacher Attitudes on Pupil Achievement with Programed Science Materials." *Journal of Research in Science Teaching.* March 1960.
123. Voelker, Alan Morris. "The Relative Effectiveness of Two Methods of Instruction in Teaching the Classification Concepts of Physical and Chemical Change to Elementary School Children." (M). 1967.
124. Wagner, Bartlett Adam. "The Responses of Economically Advantaged and Economically Disadvantaged Sixth-Grade Pupils to Science Demonstrations." (M). 1967.
125. Walbesser, Henry H. "Science Curriculum Evaluation—Observations on a Position." *The Science Teacher.* February 1966.
126. Walbesser, Henry H., *et al.* "Science—A Process Approach, An Evaluation Model and Its Application—Second Report." American Association for the Advancement of Science, AAAS Miscellaneous Publication 68-4. 1968.
127. Washton, Nathan S. "Teaching Science for Creativity." *Science Education.* February 1966.
128. Williams, David Lee. "The Effect of Rewritten Science Textbook Materials on the Reading Ability of Sixth-Grade Pupils." (M). 1964.
129. Wilson, John Harold. "Differences Between the Inquiry-Discovery and the Traditional Approaches to Teaching Science in Elementary Schools." (M). 1967.
130. Wolinsky, Gloria F. "Science Education and the Severely Handicapped Child." *Science Education.* October 1965.
131. Zafforoni, Joseph. "A Study of Pupil-Teacher Interaction in Planning Science Experiences." *Science Education.* March 1963.
132. Ziegler, Robert Edward. "The Relative Effectiveness of the Use of Static and Dynamic Mechanical Models in Teaching Elementary School Children the Theoretical Concept—The Particle Nature of Matter." (M). 1967.

---

1. Can you "link up" each of the fifteen concluding statements with the research studies reviewed in this paper?
2. If conclusion 9 is supported by evidence, what are some implications for teaching science?
3. Are there any conclusions reached in the paper that disagree with your own beliefs? What evidence can you give to substantiate your beliefs?

22 LEE CRONBACH

Learning Research and Curriculum Development

Just as the work of B. F. Skinner helped to inspire programmed learning in education, the work of Piaget has inspired numerous approaches to learning in science. Piaget is not an educator, however, so he seldom concerns himself with specific implications of his research for curriculum and instructional developments. Cronbach tries to identify certain questions that need serious consideration such as the one of discovery. Do we know enough about learning in children to make definitive statements about how and where discovery should be incorporated as an instructional strategy? For the science curriculum in particular, the questions raised in this paper are highly significant and point up the large gap that always seems to exist between so-called "evidence" that is gathered from research and its implementation in the classroom.

My role is to provide some sort of bridge between the psychologist and the curriculum reformer. I do not propose to talk about learning theory in any formal sense. It is, I hope, useful to talk about the sorts of assumptions that underlie current curriculum experiments in this country as I gather them from various investigators, and to talk about the gap that exists between learning research and curriculum development.

The learning theory that has been the preoccupation of the American psychologist since the days of Thorndike—SR theory—seems not to have had much impact on the curriculum work that has been going on. The strongest connection between SR theory and current educational experimentation is the work that Skinner has inspired in programming. This certainly has a considerable significance for education, but it has not been closely tied to curriculum studies. While some of those who prepared new curricula have recently asked programmers if programming

Reprinted from *The Journal of Research in Science Teaching*, Vol. 2, issue 3, 1964, pp. 204-207, by permission. Dr. Cronbach is presently at the Center for Advanced Studies of the Behavioral Sciences at Stanford University.

could be applied to their materials, one would not say that the work of Skinner inspired the curriculum development itself.

A large number of curricula, in science and mathematics particularly, have started on the road since 1958; indeed, a few of them date back to 1952. Some of the innovations and reforms have had nothing to do with the psychology of learning; they have essentially been changes of content. Sometimes the change of content has been purely for the sake of getting up to date. If schools were teaching the wrong theory of physics, they were advised to teach the right theory, to bring the textbook in line with more recent experimental knowledge. Sometimes there has been a shift from subject matter the scientist or mathematician regards as trivial to something he regards as having greater significance. The introduction in the elementary school, for example, of computation on bases other than ten has come not out of any special theory of learning but out of the view that this is a more fundamental way of comprehending arithmetic; i.e., it is better mathematical subject matter. All of these innovations have been approached with the same principles of pedagogy that we have been using for a long time: emphasizing exactly what you want the student to do, teaching him to do it, providing him opportunities for practice, and rewarding him when he does the job right.

But there are some other things going on, rather far removed from what psychologists typically have investigated. These not only embody some new pedagogical or psychological assumptions but are tangential to notions that Piaget has been presenting out of his own investigations. Generally, these ideas arise under cognitive theories of learning, which are less theories than points of view or emphases. It is difficult if not impossible to find any systematic theoretical point of view uniting the concerns of the psychologists in the cognitive camp.

One of our long-standing tenets has been that in any instruction you get better results if the pupil understands what is being presented. "Understanding" has never been elaborated as a concept in SR theory. We saw one form of elaboration of it in Professor Piaget's remarks when he talked about the necessity to capitalize upon the operations that the child has already mastered. Since the operations are in part cognitive, this is saying something about one meaning the term "understanding" might have. But there has been very little theoretical explication of that term.

Prominent in American curriculum development has been a stress on pushing topics downward. As Professor Piaget has said, whenever you tell Americans about some process of development, their first question is "How can you accelerate it?" It has been the spirit of many of the curriculum innovations to say "If this is worth teaching at the ninth grade level, why can't we teach it in the kindergarten?" Many experiments seem to have done precisely that. In the first grade can we teach set theory? coordinate geometry? the force concept? Very often, at least at some level of understanding, that teaching has been successful. It does appear that things can be taught much earlier than we have been teaching them. But in most of these curriculum experiments, the chunks that have been brought down to lower grades have been isolated chunks. We have seen very little yet in the way of a sequential plan that says: We want to teach this topic at this point in the elementary school so that it will be available for use a little later on. (The high school innovations have been much more sequential.)

The notion that you can teach things early obviously is threatened by Professor Piaget's statement about the child's moving through stages, not necessarily with a fixed timing, but with a timing that is very difficult to accelerate. His remark that if you teach something early it may be learned in a false way carries a strong hint that appears to pose considerable problems for both the evaluation of the new curricula and for the theory of instruction that we use. Right now I know of very little information that we could bring to bear on such questions. We may know that after a certain unit, by certain tests, results were rather good; but of the long-term effects of any procedure on the child's structured outlook on mathematics or science we know practically nothing.

In many of the curricula—not the ones I talked about a few moments ago as merely introducing new topics, but the ones that are more radical —there is an emphasis that may be summed up in a phrase such as: "We want to teach the child to think like a scientist" or "like a mathematician." Such notions have been adopted as slogans. They haven't been closely examined, yet they pose some of the most important questions for the educational psychologist. Implicitly they say that we are more interested in indirect learning than in direct learning. It would be easy to understand a proposal to introduce base-two numbers on the grounds that they will be used practically when these pupils as adults get to wiring up computers. This is a direct vocational use. But that is not the proposal of these curriculum makers. Nor does it cover their objective to say that they want to teach the nature of the number system. Behind even that broad objective is the further objective of enabling pupils to cope with mathematical reasoning generally.

This is most obvious in some of the lessons developed by David Page and others, where the child is introduced to a mathematical topic for which there is no mathematical theory. The topic is used for the purpose of the instruction and then abandoned, but through it Page is able to give the children certain types of experiences, for example, the experiences of developing their own technical terms, of beginning to establish their own preliminary assumptions or axioms and seeing what consequences follow. The emphasis is not on the lesson itself, not on the responses practiced during the lesson and reinforced. Rather, the aim is some development of a superstructure of attitudes and intellectual skill. This must have some relation to the development of logical structure that Piaget speaks of, yet so far we have found the connection unclear. Most of the instruction in this vein has been done artistically, without much guidance from theory, because the theory has been far from explicit. The most pertinent American research on learning is the various studies on learning how to learn, learning sets, and the like. Through learning of responses to a number of problems one can also somehow learn to be a better problem solver.

Research on transfer originally emphasized the possibility of learning a solution and then carrying that solution over into a new problem. This is an identical-element transfer of a rather obvious sort, with which many earlier curriculum reforms were concerned. Recent studies point to a second type of transfer in which, as a result of doing a number of problems, you become more competent to understand, to learn about, or to cope with a problem that—on its surface or perhaps in its structure—is different from the types of problems you practiced.

This sort of development of mental structure, if you will, or a way of using the brain—I think none of us knows what it is—seems to be very much the sort of thing Piaget was referring to under the heading of "development." Most of us would be uncomfortable with his separation of "development" from "learning," being convinced that intellectual development does involve learning. Piaget does not deny this. I am only saying that for us this is a somewhat forced distinction because if development involves learning, then in principle it ought to involve instruction. I think all of us would say that there must be experiences we can give at the age of two or seven or 13 that would be suitable to promote this type of development—this second-order transfer. But we are empty of suggestions as to what is most useful.

There is consensus on the necessity of starting with a thorough, concrete familiarity with and operation upon the materials that are to be understood. Hence, there is consistency between American views on teaching math and science and Professor Piaget's theory about the importance of the child's developing, through hundreds of trials, the ability to anticipate what may happen under this or that configuration of events. The risk of teaching the child some concept verbally before he has stored up appropriate images of the relevant objects in motion is a lesson every educator feels he has now learned.

Where one should introduce discovery in this process is more debated. The importance of the child's learning for himself, through discovery, has been much discussed recently in American pedagogy. But investigation on the point has been very limited and most of it untrustworthy. What research seems to say is that leaving the child to discover is not nearly so good as providing him with a guided sequence to maximize the possibility of early discovery. I am convinced that in some cases, the guided sequence will consist simply of telling him what the answer is. But which subject matter should be taught this way, and which through extensive trial and error is an unanswered question.

It is unclear how much one ought to structure the concrete experiences used for instruction. There is a big difference between having a large amount of manipulative experience in some situation, and being in the same situation with a job to be done and a means of deciding when you have done it right. We saw a demonstration a couple of weeks ago of some of the work of Zoltan Deanes, another of the innovators in the elementary classroom. His methodology seems to consist of giving the children logical and mathematical forms to play with. He has a large number of games. They can play with these an hour a day forever and presumably with luck will get insight. Some of the games involve —as their outlined mathematical structure—the powers of two. Some involve comparison of form. Some involve multiplication. But there is no course of study; no sequence of paths through which the pupil moves.

Psychologists would tend to say, "Surely there is some definite accomplishment to be achieved here, therefore there must be some best sequence of moving through these activities. There must be some criterion of when the child has had enough experience with this particular activity and is ready to go on." Somewhere between the drill approaches —demonstrate, exercise, reinforce—and the exploratory approaches— enrich the environment and let development occur—there would seem logically to be some optimal curriculum of experiences arranged in some predetermined sequence with intervention and instruction by the teacher systematically regulated. But we do not know nearly enough about such questions. On these questions I, at least, have not seen American learning theories as very helpful.

Now Piaget poses almost the same questions for us. I am not at this point able to say how to go from his position to telling the curriculum maker what he is to do with the seven-year-old. The curriculum maker is concerned with this second type of instruction—the type of instruction that somehow develops mental structures and facilitates the assimilation of new and different material. Here is the objective; on the other hand, here is Piaget's cognitive theory about assimilation. The two seem quite compatible and yet the pedagogical bridge is today quite obscure.

---

1. How can we find out when a child "understands" a concept or principle?

23 DAVID WEBSTER

How to Help Children Make Mistakes

> *The paper by Shulman analyzed a guided learning approach where a hierarchy of skills was usually involved. Task "Z" must precede "Y," and "Y" precedes "X," and "X" precedes "W," etc., until the learner arrives at the desired end point. In this process, mistakes on the part of the learner are discouraged somewhat because of the "inefficiency" connected with such "nonproductive" excursions. When a predetermined path is laid out for the learner, it seems logical to assume that the "Experts" who design the path, will try to make it as efficient as possible. Helping children make mistakes seems almost anti-educational. Such a concept is certainly thought-provoking and might be an important part of a more comprehensive instructional strategy. The brevity of this paper by Webster has little to do with the importance of the message.*

To err, and realize it, is to learn. When teaching science, we often structure the work so highly that opportunities for making mistakes are eliminated. A most significant form of learning comes from the process of making a mistake, realizing it, and then attempting to correct it. Children should be allowed to make errors on their own. There is a place in the educational pattern to devise situations which lead children into making errors.

A sequence from an Elementary Science Study (ESS) unit being developed on melting ice cubes provides several examples of teaching by having students make mistakes. The children (fourth-graders) were asked to determine the melting time for ice "cubes," of various shapes, placed in water.

The first problem became one of inventing ways to make unusual shaped ice cubes in the freezer at home. Making a spherical one was

Reprinted from *Science and Children*, Vol. 1, No. 8, 1964, pp. 13-14 by permission of the editor. The author has been a staff member of The Elementary Science Study (ESS) of Educational Services, Inc.

particularly difficult. How would you make a round ice cube? When attempting to do this, the children made numerous false starts but were able to invent some satisfactory techniques. One child froze a snowball that had been dipped in water. Another blew out the inside of an egg through two small holes and used the egg shell to form an egg-shaped ice cube. Balloons filled with water produced ice spheres when frozen. When two teacups are placed with their open ends together, a somewhat spherical space is formed inside. Some students thought of making an ice ball this way, but had some trouble getting water to stay in the top cup which was upside down. One student reported using the teacup method successfully, and others who tried were curious to learn how he filled the top cup. The teacher wondered too. "That was easy," he said, "I froze the water in one cup and then turned it upside down on a second cup of water and froze it again."

The next step was to determine how long it took for the various ice shapes to melt in water. Which will melt fastest—ice in the shape of a cube, a cylinder, a cone, a pancake, or a sphere? The children made the observations at home. When the results were compared, it was obvious that there was no consistency at all. Some children found their pancake melted faster, while others reported that their cube or sphere had disappeared first. Also, the melting times for a particular shape ranged from a few minutes to over an hour. What was wrong? The students developed several ideas when they discussed this question.

"Maybe the ice was not frozen all the way through."

"Maybe some children stirred and others did not."

The class decided that there should be no stirring.

Several of the students thought that the temperature of the water should be controlled.

"Let's all use cold water."

"I think warm water would be better."

When asked by the teacher how they would tell the proper temperature, it was generally agreed that *feeling* would suffice. Several groups of children were then asked to prepare samples of what they considered to be warm water. When these were tested by hand, it was found that the water temperatures were quite different. A thermometer seemed necessary, so each child was provided with an inexpensive one (21 cents) to use at home for his melting experiment. It was decided that everyone would use water at 70° F. Students presented several different methods of obtaining water of this specific temperature.

Another factor considered was the size of the ice "cube" that was melted. There was general agreement that the amount of ice used should be the same, but there was some problem of deciding how this could be accomplished. The children were familiar with the use of a table-spoon and a cup for measuring when cooking. A uniform amount of water for making ice could be measured in this way.

The importance of the volume of water used to melt the ice was not apparent to the children. An experiment was performed in class to help the children see that some of the variation in their results had un-doubtedly been caused by the different amounts of water in which the ice had melted. The problem was to compare the time for the ice to melt in water with its melting time in air. A previous experiment had shown, much to the surprise of all, that ice cubes in air take about an hour and a half to melt. The paper cups which were provided for melt-ing the ice in water ranged in size from 4 ounces to 32 ounces. This would insure that the children would unsuspectingly use varying amounts of water. When it was noticed that the ice cubes in the largest cups melted faster, it seemed that the speed of melting depended upon the size of the cup. The children could guess roughly how much ice was left in various sized cups without looking. A little additional thought indicated that the melting rate was related to the amount of water rather than the size of the cup.

Now, armed with considerable knowledge of the factors which affect melting, the children repeated the original experiment of melting ice of various shapes at home. They attempted to use uniform pieces of ice, melted in identical volumes of water, and at the same temperature. Even so, their results were not consistent, but they were better.

One should not be disappointed by the children's failure to obtain meaningful results. What they find out about the techniques for con-ducting an investigation is of great value. In the lessons described above, the children had practice in designing equipment, devising tech-niques for experimentation, measuring, keeping records of their results, and analyzing the data which was collected. It is also important that they had many chances to make mistakes. By so doing, children learn much about the nature of scientific inquiry.

1. Can you define a "mistake"?
2. What is the relationship between "failure" and "mistake" as identi-fied in this paper?
3. Is this strategy of helping children make mistakes more compatible with discovery learning or guided learning?

24 DAVID HAWKINS

Messing About in Science

Different "phases" in science instruction are proposed by Hawkins. The title of the paper identifies one phase, where children are encouraged to "do their own thing" in finding out some things about a system being studied. Other phases of instruction include guidance, of sorts, and attempts to interpret results. Developing instructional strategies that are defensible and consistent with stated goals requires a great deal of thought in addition to trial and error within the classroom. Continuing to experiment with an open mind will insure an instructional program that is of maximum benefit to children. The ideas in this paper merely offer one person's thinking on the subject.

"Nice? It's the *only* thing," said the Water Rat solemnly, as he leant forward for his stroke. "Believe me, my young friend, there is *nothing*—absolutely nothing—half so much worth doing as simply messing about in boats. Simply messing," he went on dreamily, "messing—about—in—boats—messing—"

Kenneth Grahame,
The Wind in the Willows

As a college teacher, I have long suspected that my students' difficulties with the intellectual process comes not from the complexity of college work itself, but mainly from their home background and the first years of their formal education. A student who cannot seem to understand the workings of the Ptolemaic astronomy, for example, turns out to have no evident acquaintance with the simple and "obvious" relativity of motion, or the simple geometrical relations of light and shadow. Sometimes for these students a style of laboratory work which might be called "Kindergarten Revisited" has dramatically liberated their

Reprinted from *Science and Children*, Vol. 2, No. 5, 1965, pp. 5-9, by permission of the editor. The author is a former Director of The Elementary Science Study from 1962 to 1964, and is presently Professor of Philosophy at The University of Colorado.

intellectual powers. Turn on your heel with your head back until you *see* the ceiling—turn the other way—and don't fall over!

In the past two years, working in the Elementary Science Study, I have had the experience, marvelous for a naive college teacher, of studying young children's learning in science. I am now convinced that my earlier suspicions were correct. In writing about these convictions, I must acknowledge the strong influence on me by other staff members in the Study. We came together from a variety of backgrounds—college, high school, and elementary school teachers—and with a variety of dispositions toward science and toward teaching. In the course of trial teaching and of inventing new curricular materials, our shop talks brought us toward some consensus but we still had disagreements. The outline of ideas I wish to present here is my own, therefore, and not that of the group which has so much influenced my thinking. The formulation I want to make is only a beginning. Even if it is right, it leaves many questions unanswered, and therefore much room for further disagreement. In so complex a matter as education, this is as it should be. What I am going to say applies, I believe, to all aspects of elementary education. However, let me stick to science teaching.

My outline is divided into three patterns or phases of school work in science. These phases are different from each other in the relations they induce between children, materials of study, and teachers. Another way of putting it is that they differ in the way they make a classroom look and sound. My claim is that good science teaching moves from one phase to the other in a pattern which, though it will not follow mechanical rules or ever be twice the same, will evolve according to simple principles. There is no necessary order among these phases, and for this reason, I avoid calling them I, II, and III, and use instead some mnemonic signs which have, perhaps, a certain suggestiveness: O, Δ, and □ .

O Phase

There is a time, much greater in amount than commonly allowed, which should be devoted to free and unguided exploratory work (call it play if you wish; I call it work). Children are given materials and equipment—things—and are allowed to construct, test, probe, and experiment without superimposed questions or instructions. I call this O phase "Messing About," honoring the philosophy of the Water Rat, who absentmindedly ran his boat into the bank, picked himself up, and went on without interrupting the joyous train of thought:

> —about in boats—or *with* boats. . . . In or out of 'em, it doesn't matter, nothing seems really to matter, that's the charm of it. Whether

you get away, or whether you don't; whether you arrive at your desti-
nation or whether you reach somewhere else, or whether you never
get anywhere at all, you're always busy, and you never do anything in
particular; and when you've done it there's always something else to
do, and you can do it if you like, but you'd much better not.

In some jargon, this kind of situation is called "unstructured," which
is misleading; some doubters call it chaotic, which it need never be.
"Unstructured" is misleading because there is always a kind of structure
to *what* is presented in a class, as there was to the world of boats and
the river, with its rushes and weeds and mud that smelled like plumcake.
Structure in this sense is of the utmost importance, depending on the
children, the teacher, and the backgrounds of all concerned.

Let me cite an example from my own recent experiences. Simple
frames, each designed to support two or three weights on strings, were
handed out one morning in a fifth-grade class. There was one such
frame for each pair of children. In two earlier trial classes, we had introduced the same equipment with a much more "structured" beginning,
demonstrating the striking phenomenon of coupled pendula and raising
questions about it before the laboratory work was allowed to begin.
If there was guidance this time, however, it came only from the apparatus—a pendulum is to swing! In starting this way I, for one, naively
assumed that a couple of hours of "Messing About" would suffice. After
two hours, instead, we allowed two more and, in the end, a stretch of
several weeks. In all this time, there was little evidence or no evidence
of boredom or confusion. Most of the questions we might have planned
for came up unscheduled.

Why did we permit this length of time? First, because in our previous
classes we had noticed that things went well when we veered toward
"Messing About" and not as well when we held too tight a rein on what
we wanted the children to do. It was clear that these children had had
insufficient acquaintance with the sheer phenomena of pendulum motion and needed to build an apperceptive background, against which a
more analytical sort of knowledge could take form and make sense.
Second, we allowed things to develop this way because we decided we
were getting a new kind of feedback from the children and were eager
to see where and by what paths their interests would evolve and carry
them. We were rewarded with a higher level of involvement and a much
greater diversity of experiments. Our role was only to move from spot
to spot, being helpful but never consciously prompting or directing. In
spite of—because of!—this lack of direction, these fifth-graders became
very familiar with pendula. They varied the conditions of motion in
many ways, exploring differences of length and amplitude, using different sorts of bobs, bobs in clusters, and strings, etc. And have *you* tried

the underwater pendulum? They did! There were many sorts of discoveries made, but we let them slip by without much adult resonance, beyond our spontaneous and manifest enjoyment of the phenomena. So discoveries were made, noted, lost, and made again. I think this is why the slightly pontifical phrase "discovery method" bothers me. When learning is at the most fundamental level, as it is here, with all the abstractions of Newtonian mechanics just around the corner, don't rush! When the mind is evolving the abstractions which will lead to physical comprehension, all of us must cross the line between ignorance and insight many times before we truly understand. Little facts, "discoveries" without the growth of insight, are *not* what we should seek to harvest. Such facts are only seedlings and should sometimes be let alone to grow into. . . .

I have illustrated the phase of "Messing About" with a constrained and inherently very elegant topic from physics. In other fields, the pattern will be different in detail, but the essential justification is the same. "Messing About" with what can be found in pond water looks much more like the Water Rat's own chosen field of study. Here, the implicit structure is that of nature in a very different mood from what is manifest in the auterities of things like pendular motion or planet orbits. And here, the need for sheer acquaintance with the variety of things and phenomena is more obvious, before one can embark on any of the roads toward the big generalizations or the big open questions of biology. Regardless of differences, there is a generic justification of "Messing About" that I would like, briefly, to touch upon.

Preschool Influences

This phase is important, above all, because it carries over into school that which is the source of most of what children have already learned, the roots of their moral, intellectual, and esthetic development. If education were defined, for the moment, to include everything that children have learned since birth, everything that has come to them from living in the natural and the human world, then by any sensible measure what has come before age five or six would outweigh all the rest. When we narrow the scope of education to what goes on in schools, we throw out the method of that early and spectacular progress at our peril. We know that five-year-olds are very unequal in their mastery of this or that. We also know that their histories are responsible for most of this inequality, utterly masking the congenital differences except in special cases. This is the immediate fact confronting us as educators in a society committed, morally and now by sheer economic necessity, to universal education.

To continue the cultivation of earlier ways of learning, therefore; to find *in school* the good beginnings, the liberating involvements that will make the kindergarten seem a garden to the child and not a dry and frightening desert, this is a need that requires much emphasis on the style of work I have called O, or "Messing About." Nor does the garden in this sense end with a child's first school year, or his tenth, as though one could then put away childish things. As time goes on, through a good mixture of this with other phases of work, "Messing About" evolves with the child and thus changes its quality. It becomes a way of working that is no longer childish, though it remains always childlike, the kind of self-disciplined probing and exploring that is the essence of creativity.

The variety of the learning—and of inhibition against learning—that children bring from home when school begins is great, even within the limited range of a common culture with common economic background (or, for that matter, within a single family). Admitting this, then if you cast your mind over the whole range of abilities and backgrounds that children bring to kindergarten, you see the folly of standardized and formalized beginnings. We are profoundly ignorant about the subtleties of learning but one principle ought to be asserted dogmatically: That there must be provided some continuity in the content, direction, and style of learning. Good schools begin with what children have *in fact* mastered, probe next to see what *in fact* they are learning, continue with what *in fact* sustains their involvement.

Δ Phase

When children are led along a common path, there are always the advanced ones and always the stragglers. Generalized over the years of school routine, this lends apparent support to the still widespread belief in some fixed, inherent levels of "ability," and to the curious notions of "under-" and "over-achievement." Now, if you introduce a topic with a good deal of "Messing About," this means the situation gets worse, not better. But I say it gets better, not worse. If after such a beginning you pull in the reins and "get down to business," some children have happened to go your way already, and you will believe that you are leading these successfully. Others will have begun, however, to travel along quite different paths, and you have to tug hard to get them back on to yours. Through the eyes of these children you will see yourself as a dragger, not a leader. We saw this clearly in the pendulum class I referred to; the pendulum being a thing which seems deceptively simple but which raises many questions in no particular necessary order. So the path which each child chooses is his best path.

The result is obvious, but it took me time to see it. If you once let children evolve their own learning along paths of their choosing, you then must see it through and *maintain* the individuality of their work.

You cannot begin that way and then say, in effect, " That was only a teaser," thus using your adult authority to devalue what the children themselves, in the meantime, have found most valuable. So if "Messing About" is to be followed by, or evolve into, a stage where work is more externally guided and disciplined, there must be at hand what I call "Multiply Programmed" material; material that contains written and pictorial guidance of some sort for the student, but which is designed for the greatest possible variety of topics, ordering of topics, etc., so that for almost any given way into a subject that a child may evolve on his own, there is material available which he will recognize as helping him farther along that very way. Heroic teachers have sometimes done this on their own, but it is obviously one of the places where designers of curriculum materials can be of enormous help, designing those materials with a rich variety of choices for teacher and child, and freeing the teacher from the role of "leader-dragger" along a single preconceived path, giving the teacher encouragement and real logistical help in diversifying the activities of a group. Such material includes good equipment, but above all, it suggests many beginnings, paths from the familiar into the unknown. We did not have this kind of material ready for the pendulum class I spoke about earlier, and still do not have it. I intend to work at it and hope others will.

It was a special day in the history of that pendulum class that brought home to me what was needed. My teaching partner was away (I had been the observer, she the teacher). To shift gears for what I saw as a more organized phase of our work, I announced that for a change we were all going to do the same experiment. I said it firmly and the children were, of course, obliging. Yet, I saw the immediate loss of interest in part of the class as soon as my experiment was proposed. It was designed to raise questions about the *length* of a pendulum, when the bob is multiple or odd-shaped. Some had come upon the germ of that question; others had no reason to. As a college teacher I have tricks, and they worked here as well, so the class went well, in spite of the unequal readiness to look at "length." We hit common ground with rough blackboard pictures, many pendula shown hanging from a common support, differing in length and in the shape and size of bobs. Which ones will "swing together?" Because their eyes were full of real pendula, I think, they could *see* those blackboard pictures swinging! A colloquium evolved which harvested the crop of insights that had been sowed and cultivated in previous weeks. I was left with a hollow feeling, nevertheless. It went well where, and only where, the class found common ground, whereas in "Messing About" all things had gone uniformly well. In staff discussion afterward, it became clear that we had skipped an essential phase of our work, the one I am now calling Δ phase, or Multiply Programmed.

There is a common opinion, floating about, that a rich diversity of classroom work is possible only when a teacher has small classes. "Maybe *you* can do that; but you ought to try it in my class of 43!" I want to be the last person to belittle the importance of small classes. But in this particular case, the statement ought to be made that in a large class one cannot afford *not* to diversify children's work—or rather *not* to allow children to diversify, as they inevitably will, if given the chance. So-called "ability grouping" is a popular answer today, but it is no answer at all to the real questions of motivation. Groups which are lumped as equivalent with respect to the usual measures are just as diverse in their tastes and spontaneous interests as unstratified groups! The complaint that in heterogeneous classes the bright ones are likely to be bored because things go too slow for them ought to be met with another question: Does that mean that the slower students are *not* bored? When children have no autonomy in learning everyone is likely to be bored. In such situations the overworked teachers have to be "leader-draggers" always, playing the role of Fate in the old Roman proverb: "The Fates lead the willing; the unwilling they drag."

A good beginning

"Messing About" produces the early and indispensible autonomy and diversity. It is good—indispensible—for the opening game but not for long middle game, where guidance is needed; needed to lead the willing! To illustrate once more from my example of the pendulum, I want to produce a thick set of cards—illustrated cards in a central file, or single sheets in plastic envelopes—to cover the following topics among others:

1. Relations of amplitude and period.
2. Relations of period and weight of bob.
3. How long is a pendulum (odd-shaped bobs)?
4. Coupled pendula, compound pendula.
5. The decay of the motion (and the idea of half-life).
6. String pendula and stick pendula—comparisons.
7. Underwater pendula.
8. Arms and legs as pendula (dogs, people, and elephants).
9. Pendula of other kinds—springs, etc.
10. Bobs that drop sand for patterns and graphs.
11. Pendulum clocks.
12. Historical materials, with bibliography.
13. Cards relating to filmloops available, in class or library.
14. Cross-index cards to other topics, such as falling bodies, inclined planes, etc.
15-75. Blank cards to be filled in by classes and teachers for others.

This is only an illustration; each area of elementary science will have its own style of Multiply Programmed materials, of course, the ways of organizing these materials will depend on the subject. There should always be those blank cards, outnumbering the rest.

Careful!

There is one final warning. Such a file is properly a kind of programming—but it is not the base of rote or merely verbal learning, taking a child little step by little step through the adult maze. Each item is simple, pictorial, and it guides by suggesting further explorations, not by replacing them. The cards are only there to relieve the teacher from a heroic task. And they are only there because there are apparatus, film, library, and raw materials from which to improvise.

☐ Phase

In the class discussion I referred to, about the meaning of *length* applied to a pendulum, I was reverting back to the college-teacher habit of lecturing; I said it went very well in spite of the lack of Multiply Programmed background, one that would have taken more of the class through more of the basic pendulum topics. It was not, of course, a lecture in the formal sense. It was question-and-answer, with discussion between children as well. But still, I was guiding it and fishing for the good ideas that were ready to be born, and I was telling a few stories, for example, about Galileo. Others could do it better. I was a visitor, and am still only an amateur. I was successful then only because of the long build-up of latent insight, the kind of insight that the Water Rat had stored up from long afternoons of "Messing About" in boats. It was more than he could ever have been told, but it gave him much to tell. This is not all there is to learning, of course; but it is the magical part, and the part most often killed in school. The language is not yet that of the textbook, but with it even a dull-looking textbook can come alive. One boy thinks the length of a pendulum should be measured from the top to what he calls "the center of gravity." If they have not done a lot of work with balance materials, this phase is for most children only the handle of an empty pitcher, or a handle without a pitcher at all. So I did not insist on the term. Incidentally, it is not quite correct physics anyway, as those will discover who work with the stick pendulum. Although different children had specialized differently in the way they worked with pendula, there were common elements, increasing with time, which would sustain serious and extended class discussion. It is this pattern of discussion I want to emphasize by calling it a separate,

☐ phase. It includes lecturing, formal or informal. In the above situation, we were all quite ready for a short talk about Galileo, and ready to ponder the question whether there was any relation between the way unequal weights fall together and the way they swing together when hanging on strings of the same length. Here we were approaching a question—a rather deep one, not to be disposed of in fifteen minutes— of theory, going from the concrete perceptual to the abstract conceptual. I do not believe that such questions will come alive either through the early "Messing About" or through the Multiply Programmed work with guiding questions and instructions. I think they come primarily with discussion, argument, the full colloquium of children and teacher. Theorizing in a creative sense needs the content of experience and the logic of experimentation to support it. But these do not automatically lead to conscious abstract thought. Theory is square! ☐

We, of the Elementary Science Study, are probably identified in the minds of those acquainted with our work (and sometimes perhaps in our own minds) with the advocacy of laboratory work and a free, fairly O style of laboratory work at that. This may be right and justified by the fact that prevailing styles of science teaching are ☐ most of the time, much too much of the time. But what we criticize for being too much and too early, we must work to re-admit in its proper place.

I have put O, Δ, and ☐ in that order, but I do not advocate any rigid order; such phases may be mixed in many ways and ordered in many ways. Out of the colloquium comes new "Messing About." Halfway along a programmed path, new phenomena are accidently observed. In an earlier, more structured class, two girls were trying obediently to reproduce some phenomena of coupled pendula I had demonstrated. I heard one say, "Ours isn't working right." Of course, pendula never misbehave; it is not in their nature; they always do what comes naturally, and in this case, they were executing a curious dance of energy transference, promptly christened the "twist." It was a new phenomenon, which I had not seen before, nor had several physicists to whom, in my delight, I later showed it. Needless to say, this led to a good deal of "Messing About," right then and there.

What I have been concerned to say is only that there are, as I see it, three major phases of good science teaching; that no teaching is likely to be optimal which does not mix all three; and that the one most neglected is that which made the Water Rat go dreamy with joy when he talked about it. At a time when the pressures of prestige education are likely to push children to work like hungry laboratory rats in a maze, it is good to remember that their wild, watery cousin, reminiscing about the joys of his life, uttered a profound truth about education.

1. Do you think equal portions of time should be spent on all three phases during science? Why?
2. How do Hawkins' ideas about instruction compare with your own at this point?
3. Do the three phases have similar implications for all ages of children in elementary school?

25 ALLAN K. KONDO

Children Can't Think

Are children encouraged to think for themselves in school? In this paper, the author looks at the issue of independent thinking as related to practices of teachers in schools. The commentary section is a reaction to the monologue and analyzes the school situation in which dependent thinking is encouraged. What courses in your formal education would you say encouraged independent thinking?

Children can't think. You have to tell them everything. And even after you tell them, they still don't understand. Children can't think.

Some are not so bad. When I ask them a question, they can give me a right answer quickly—exactly the way I want it. I don't worry about those children. But most of the others—well, I ask them a question, wait for a second or two, and either I don't get a response or I get a wrong answer. So I ask another question to help them get the right answer and then another if necessary, each time giving them more clues. Even if I narrow the answer to two alternatives, they usually pick the wrong one. A few sometimes even cry after I ask them about five questions in a row and they don't know the answers. You'd think I was pulling teeth.

Yesterday, I demonstrated a closed circuit using a bulb, wire, and a dry cell. I asked a girl why I took the wire off the dry cell. Of course, I took it off to break the circuit, but she just looked confused. She looked more puzzled and squirmed in her seat as I gave her more chances, "Why? Why? Why?" She didn't even say, "I don't know."

I am dedicated to the teaching profession, and I try to keep up with current methods. I even made a tape of my teaching, and I found I asked 148 questions in a half-hour science lesson. (The children didn't ask me any.) Many of the questions came in bunches of three or four, show-

Reprinted from *Science and Children*, Vol. 7, No. 2, 1969, pp. 31-33 by permission of the editor. Dr. Kondo is Assistant Professor of Science Education at Indiana University.

ing how I rephrased questions and gave more clues. Still, many times children can't give me the answers I'm looking for. They can't even guess what's on the tip of my tongue after I practically pronounce the answer for them. Children can't think.

The other day I asked a first-grade boy if the pile of wood dust he made from sanding a piece of redwood was darker, or lighter, or the same color as the wood.

He said, "Darker."

So I said, "Really? Look Again."

He still said, "Darker."

So I retorted, "Darker?" (Disbelieving)

He finally said, "The same."

Now anyone with a little bit of brains would know that the dust, being from the same piece of wood, would have to be the same color. Wouldn't it?

But he couldn't see that. Children just don't make the right observations. No wonder they can't come to the right conclusions.

And these children, unless you're constantly reminding them, can't do their own work. They have to talk to their neighbors and show them their materials. It's also terrible how they depend on others and sometimes just "follow-the-leader." For example, I asked each first grader in a class what they thought was in a sealed shoe box which I held up, rattled, and had the first row smell. The first boy guessed, "Perfume." Every single child in the class said the same thing, when the box actually contained a bar of fragrant soap. I even allowed the first row to smell the box twice. Sure, I was disappointed that they didn't guess the right answer, but what distressed me is that everyone copied the first boy's reply. They can't think for themselves.

Children can't think. I've taught them many times (even with visual materials such as charts and a model of the solar system) that the earth revolves around the sun and not vice versa. After I had them repeat it several times, most finally understand that the earth really travels around the sun. They can tell me now without hesitation. But two kids still can't seem to understand. They still see the sun moving around the earth. I don't know what to do about them. I guess they just don't have the ability to make spatial relations.

Sometimes, the children's thinking gives me a few lighter moments. I did a demonstration for a group of first graders to show things that float and things that sink, and we concluded that heavy things sink and light things float. One boy started to play with some of the things we used. He attached two popsickle sticks to a piece of cork with a rubber band. I asked him if the combination would float.

He said, "No."

So I said, "It wouldn't? Why not?"

He said that while each object by itself was light, when you put them together, they were heavy and would, therefore, sink. It was so funny, I laughed and laughed. I don't think the children know what I was laughing about.

As you can see, when I have a science lesson, I do a lot with the children—a lot of experiments and things.

While the materials in kits are made for children to use, it is unfortunate that children can't be trusted with equipment that costs a little more money. For example, we have a $150 microscope in the principal's office which we purchased out of NDEA funds. It's too expensive for children to use, though. It might get broken and ruined if we brought it out to the classroom. At least, we are more fortunate than other schools which don't have such expensive equipment.

I've been hearing a lot about using the discovery method. While this method sounds fine in theory, it doesn't work. I tried it once. I gave children a balance and equal volumes of water, alcohol, and oil. They couldn't discover "density." Children can't think. You have to tell them everything.

Sex education has also been in vogue, lately. I'm all for it—in high school biology when they can understand. I've heard experts say that it should begin in kindergarten or even younger. That's silly. How can children understand the concept of birth when they can't even understand a simpler concept like death? I overheard a kindergarten child say to another, "We're all going to die."

The other replied, "I'm not going to die yet. I'm not married yet."

Children can't think.

Commentary

To be sure, the monologue above was not verbalized by one teacher; rather, it was concocted from a composite of observations and inferences from observations made over the past few years.

Children *can* think. But sometimes, teachers, without realizing it, do not give them a *fair* chance. In most of the incidents described, the teacher was not aware of his own behavior and how his behavior was received by the children. It is difficult to place ourselves in our students' shoes and look at our own teaching. But we cannot improve our own teaching without first anlyzing what we do and then trying to perceive our behavior from the viewpoint of those we are trying to teach. The purpose of the foregoing fabrication was to make us aware of certain insensitive teaching behaviors (hopefully not widespread) and to make us look at ourselves and our own methods, keeping the children's viewpoint in mind.

Many of these incidents demonstrate a narrow, one-answer-only approach to science teaching, and teachers in the new curriculum projects are not immune to this approach by any means. Some of the observations, in fact, were of teachers teaching the new projects.

The first few incidents described involve questions and questioning techniques. I have observed that the density of questions asked (number of questions per unit time) generally reflects the type of questions. A high question density usually means many memory questions, usually correctly answerable by one and only one "right" word or phrase. It seems reasonable that if higher level questions are asked, questions in which more thinking is involved and which require more than a few words to answer, there will be a lower question density.

The questions teachers ask (whether they realize it or not) generally determine the kind of thinking children are required to do in a classroom. If we agree that children should do more imaginative and critical thinking, then it stands to reason that we must not only ask questions which encourage these modes of thinking and allow the children to come to grips with problems, but also give the children more time to think before demanding answers. As Mary Budd Rowe points out,* many teachers wait just one second for answers. One second is not long enough. Children need time to think.

Can you tell me all the possible uses of a coat hanger? Quick! Quick! We need time to think also.

When children cannot answer a question, we often view this as a failure to learn on their part. Maybe it is a failure on *our* part in our teaching or in our questioning. Perhaps the children did not acquire the prerequisite knowledge to answer the question; perhaps our question was unclear. Take the example of the teacher asking the child why he (the teacher) took the wire off the dry cell. He expected the child to say, "To break the circuit and put the light out." To that particular child, however, the question of "Why?" might have had no more meaning than the question, "Why does a man cross the street?" In other words, the question concerned the intention of the teacher, which may be anybody's guess. (Maybe he got tired of holding the wire.)

Actually, the teacher wanted to point out a cause and effect relationship, i.e., when the wire is removed, the circuit is broken, and the light goes out. A more meaningful question might have been, "Do you have

---

*Mary Budd Rowe, "Science, Silence and Sanctions." *Science and Children.* 6 (March 1969): 11.

any idea why the light goes out?" With young children, "Why?" questions may be particularly confusing. It is a causal "Why?" which concerns a cause and effect relationship (in which case the answer may be very complex for young children), or is it an intentional "Why?" which asks the child to guess the teacher's intention or motive in doing something? It may even be construed as an accusing "Why?" For example, "*Why* did you do that?"

What is the purpose in asking a question? Of course, there may be many reasons. Sometimes, the teacher asks a question to see if the children can guess what is on his mind. Hence, it is not uncommon to overhear children, after someone finally comes up with the answer, to say, "So, that's what he wanted." It is also not uncommon for teachers to say, "No, that's not the answer I'm looking for." Hopefully, in science teaching we are not promoting a guessing game, but rather we are stimulating the development of science processes in children. When we ask a child to describe what he sees, hears, or feels, his answer cannot possibly be wrong unless he is lying. In the case of the wood piece and dust, the teacher, by not accepting the child's sense perception, has encouraged the child to tell him what he is *supposed* to see rather than what he actually perceives. The teacher's reaction also throws some doubt on the visual acuity and discrimination of the child. (To this observer, the pile of dust *did* look darker than the piece of wood.) If our classroom science is based on empirical evidence gained through our senses, we are not teaching very scientifically when we refuse to accept answers to questions dealing with a child's sense perceptions.

The next incident concerned children's "inability" to do their own work. How could most of the children in the class have made an inference concerning the contents of the shoe box when they did not make the firsthand observations? The teacher did the shaking, etc., allowing only the first row to smell. And yet, he expected the children to make inferences. We make inferences based on observations. Without an adequate base of observations, wild guessing is promoted. But in this case, the children preferred to play it safe and followed the leader. The teacher probably was not aware of this.

While more imaginative teaching techniques would have helped the teacher who tried to present concepts about the solar system, the basic problem was the teacher's failure to realize the contradiction and confusion confronting children when they read or are told one thing and then observe something entirely opposite. We all see the sun moving. Even scientists do. And so do children. But these ideas regarding space phenomena are complex, and ascribing the lack of understanding of these phenomena to a child's inability to make spatial relationships is absurd. We must look at our own teaching. "What can we do to promote a better understanding of these concepts?" should be our comment, not "Children can't think."

"Heavy things sink and light things float." This conclusion is as much as can be expected from a first-grade class after placing different objects in a container of water. And the teacher taking advantage of a spontaneous situation in asking the boy if the combination of cork and popsicle sticks would float is commendable. The boy's logic was beautiful. But the teacher laughed. How insensitive and cruel. How would you feel if someone laughed at what you thought was a brilliant deduction.

Some science lessons are fraught with confusion and frustration under the guise of "discovery" teaching. The example of trying to discover density was one of them. You do not discover definitions. Could you concoct one of Dr. Seuss' animals, say a Mulligatawny, given a canary, a giraffe, a bear, and a lion, without knowing what a Mulligatawny looks like? There are many things and phenomena that children can discover—things which we cannot even anticipate. But to expect them to discover a precise definition which somebody has arbitrarily invented is quite unreasonable. If you want children to know the meaning of a particular word, tell them. Define it for them. They might then discover applications of the concept once they have an understanding of it.

There is often a gap between our philosophies, objectives, and planned methods and our actual practice of them. We think we know what we are doing. Do children? Are we really doing what we think we are?

---

1. Try to identify classroom conditions (especially teacher behaviors) that could tend to discourage independent thinking in elementary science.

26 MARY BUDD ROWE

Science, Silence,
and Sanctions

The technique of interaction analysis has yielded data showing that teachers' verbal patterns influence their students' verbal patterns. In this paper, the specific verbal behavior of "waiting" after asking a question is considered. What happens if a teacher waits five or ten seconds after directing a question to a child? Will such a simple technique have any influence on the responding behavior of children? The most powerful suggestion in the paper is that the technique of waiting longer for children to respond should be tried in the classroom. Until tested in the "real world" it will remain only a compilation of words, soon to be forgotten.

When you ask a child a question, how long do you *think* you wait for an answer before you either repeat the question, ask him another question, or call on another child? If you are like many experienced teachers, you allow an *average of one second* for a child to start an answer. After a child makes a response, you apparently are still in a hurry because you generally wait slightly less than a second to repeat what he said or to rephrase it or ask another question.

In inservice training classes for experienced teachers, we have been studying such questioning-teaching techniques to discover which techniques are most effective for teaching science when utilizing some of the national experimental science programs for the elementary school, e.g., Science Curriculum Improvement Study (SCIS), Science—A Process Approach (AAAS), Elementary Science Study (ESS). We have found that when teachers change certain verbal patterns, students change their verbal patterns too. We began to experiment to test the effect of the following factors on the verbal behavior of children.

Reprinted from Science and Children, Vol. 6, No. 6, 1969, pp. 11-13, by permission of the editor. Dr. Rowe is Associate Professor of Natural Science, Teachers College, Columbia University.

1. Increasing the period of time that a teacher waits for students to construct a response to a question.
2. Increasing the period of time that a teacher waits before replying to a student move.
3. Decreasing the pattern of reward and punishment delivered to students.

"Wait-Time"

While a fast pace in questioning may be suited for instruction in some subjects, it presents some special problems for teachers who are trying to conduct inquiry-oriented science lessons. In most of the new science programs that actually give children access to materials and information, ideas that develop come largely from what children do with the materials. In any collection of objects there may be more than one possible arrangement, more than one kind of experiment, more than one kind of result. The basic notion that underlies all new science programs is the belief that in inquiry the information or relevant cues lie hidden in the materials and not in the head of the teacher. Since that is the case, children need to monitor their materials more carefully than they monitor the teacher's face. Ideas can be modified or even discarded if the evidence requires. No particular point of view in the class is more sacred than another. What counts is what happens in the system of materials. Authority rests with the idea that "works." That point of view means you and the children need time to think and to evaluate. One second may not be long enough.

What happens in science if you increase the time you wait before you ask another question or call on another child? And what happens if you increase the amount of time you wait to speak *after* a child speaks? It turns out that all kinds of surprising and sometimes puzzling things result.

If you can prolong your average "wait-time" to five seconds, or preferably longer, the length of student responses increases. When wait-time is very short, students tend to give very short answers or they are more prone to say, "I don't know." In addition, their answers often come with a question mark in the tone, as if to say, "Is that what you want?" But if you increase the wait-time, especially the period after a child has made a response, you are more likely to get whole sentences, and the confidence as expressed by tone is higher. Another bonus that results from increased wait-times is the appearance of speculative thinking (e.g., "It might be the water," . . . "but it could be too many plants.") and the use of arguments based on evidence.

If the wait-time is prolonged an average of five seconds or more, young children shift from teacher-centered show-and-tell kinds of behavior to child-child comparing of differences. Why this happens is not clear. It may be that longer wait-time allows children to trust the materials so that they shift from the teacher's face to the objects they are studying.

It is the teacher who gets the most practice asking questions in the classroom. Children rarely ask questions in class even when they have materials in front of them, yet we know they are usually curious. As you increase the wait-time, the number of questions children ask and the number of experiments they need to answer the questions multiply.

Suppose you do learn to control wait-time, what are the advantages? First, by increasing the wait-time, you buy for yourself an opportunity to hear and to think. As an example, examine a learning experience with a teaching machine. Suppose the machine begins to instruct a student by showing him some objects and saying, "Tell me how these are arranged. What does the arrangement look like?" The student might answer, "A xylophone." Now if the machine is programed to expect the student to say "steps," there is a problem. The machine either goes on with whatever is next in its program or it cycles back and asks the question again and again until the student gives the "right" answer. Teachers often behave the same way. When the wait-times are very short, teachers exhibit little flexibility in the responses they allow. Contests for control of the metaphors (e.g., steps vs. xylophone) are common, and the teacher usually prevails. A machine could do as well. Errors of this kind become less frequent as wait-time increases.

Second, wait-time can change your expectations about what some children can do. Teachers who have learned to use silence report that children who do not ordinarily say much start talking and usually have exciting ideas. In one inservice experiment, each of 50 teachers taught science to two first-grade children. The teachers knew the children had been grouped in combinations of two high verbal children, or two low verbal children, or one high and one low verbal child. At the end of the lesson, each teacher tried to decide which combination she had. To the delight of everyone in the experiment, the teachers usually misjudged the combination. Most often they classified low verbal youngsters as high verbal. The interaction of children with materials plus the protracted silences of the teachers apparently "turned on" children who usually "tuned out." When these teachers returned to their classrooms and experimented with wait-times, they reported that children who did not ordinarily contribute began to take a more active part in doing and talking about science.

Expectations teachers hold for children can have a deadly effect in terms of opportunities in which children get to practice speculative thinking. For example, on request, twelve inservice teachers each identified their five best and five poorest students. After sampling the teachers' wait-times in three lessons each of science and mathematics, it was found that the twelve teachers waited *significantly less time* in both subjects for poor students to reply to questions. That is, students rated as slow or less apt by teachers had to try to answer questions more rapidly than students rated as bright or fast. This result apparently surprised the teachers. As one of them said, "I guess we just don't expect an answer, so we go on to someone else." This group of twelve teachers then began to experiment deliberately with increasing wait-times for poorer students. Response by "slow" students increased, gradually at first, and then rapidly.

Questioning behavior also varies with wait-time. As wait-time increases, teachers begin to show much more variability in the kinds of questions they ask. Students get more opportunity to respond to thought rather than straight memory questions. When the pacing is fast, teachers often ask and answer their own questions. ("What color was it? It was green, wasn't it?"). For some reason when teachers gain control of wait-time, questioning becomes less barrage-like and more flexible in form.

Rewards and Punishments

There is another factor besides silence that seems to have something to do with how children learn science and whether or not they learn to trust evidence as a basis for making judgments.

Usually, teachers use sanctions (positive and negative rewards) in the classroom somewhat indiscriminately. Sometimes teachers seem to be rewarding effort because they commend answers or work which is incorrect. At other times they reward correct responses. In fact, sanctions constitute as much as one quarter of teacher talk in many classrooms. Since evaluative comments constitute such a large part of teacher talk, it is useful to know how they influence science instruction.

Modern sience programs for the elementary school seek to develop self-confidence in children by allowing them to work out their ideas in experiments. Children find out how good their ideas are by the results. When predictions no longer work or when new information makes a point of view untenable, then pupils are free to change their views. The point is that the authority for changing comes from the results of their experiments rather than from the teacher.

It appears that when teachers measurably reduce the amount of overt verbal rewarding they do, children seem to demand less of their time for showing what happens. Instead they do more comparing and arguing which leads to more experiments. When silence on the part of the teacher increases, and/or when sanctions decrease, the incidence of speculative thought on the part of the children increases. It is doubtful whether children can distinguish when they are being rewarded for effort and when for appropriate responses. When rewards are high, children tend to stop experimenting sooner than when the number of rewards is relatively lower. There is some reason to suspect that when children work on a complex task, rewards given by the teacher may interfere with logical thought processes. When children start attending to the reward rather than to the task, the incidence of error or the necessity to repeat steps increases.

Try It Yourself

Tape record a science lesson as you would normally teach it. Listen to what children say and how they say it. Now teach another lesson, but this time experiment with the wait-times or the rewards, but not both at once. If you try to change both factors at once, you will find it more difficult to discover the effect each has by itself. Find out whether the following statements are supported by your experiments.

1. Very short wait-times combined with high teacher rewards produce short student responses, high likelihood of inflected answers reflecting low student confidence, virtually no child-child exchanges of ideas, and a high incidence of answers unsupported by evidence.
2. Long wait-times (not less than 5 seconds) combined with low teacher rewards produce longer responses, more confidence, more exchanges between children, and more speculation supported by evidence.

The children may be inquiring about natural phenomena, but inquiry into teaching is the business of the professional teacher. Run your experiments on silence and sanctions in science enough times to be sure of how the factors act in your class. Let me know what kind of results you get.

---

1. How do teachers use positive and negative verbal rewards in the classroom?

2. "When silence on the part of the teacher increases, and/or when sanctions decrease, the incidence of speculative thought on the part of the children increases." In reference to this statement by Dr. Rowe, what might be some implications for science teaching?

27 RONALD G. GOOD

When Is a Problem, a Problem?

Learning in science can be differentiated from learning in language arts, in spelling or in various skill-oriented areas. When children are permitted to depend upon themselves for finding out about things in science investigation, the learning is a type of problem-solving. Does this type of problem differ from a situation where the students are "given" a problem to solve? This paper looks at problem-solving that originates within the learner as compared to problem-solving that originates from some outside source. Such questions as "how do children learn to solve problems before they get to school" are considered. One's ideas about problem-solving are certain to influence one's behavior in the classroom.

Problem-solving is generally agreed upon as constituting the highest type of learning in which an individual can engage. Robert Gagné has categorized very neatly the varieties of learning with problem-solving at the top of the hierarchy.(1) The process of solving problems results in the acquisition of more "principles" that will aid in further problem-solving, etc. Courses in mathematics that all of us have engaged in are generally built around "problems." Finding the solutions to these problems is usually accomplished by "learning" principles and then using them to solve the so-called problems. How quickly we forget these principles, however. In fact, this newly found knowledge tends to dissipate in a way that approximates the forgetting curves usually associated with memorization of unrelated facts. If this is true, (and most of us can attest to the fact that it is) then it is questionable whether or not any "principles" were ever really learned.

We talk in school of "giving" problems to children in order that they might solve them. To facilitate this process, they are usually *given*

Reprinted from *Science and Children*, Vol. 8, No. 8, 1971, pp. 18-19 by permission of the editor. Dr. Good is presently Assistant Professor of Science Education at Florida State University.

a method for solving the problems. This "method" would correspond to the previously mentioned "principle." After *giving* the principle needed for solving the particular type of problem, children exercise the principle by doing example "problems." In this way, principle after principle becomes a part of an individual's repertory for learning. Or is this *really* the case? To what degree has real problem solving occurred and to what degree has learning occurred that will soon approximate the forgetting curves of memorization? Personal experience tells us that very little real "learning with understanding" (principle learning) has occurred. If problem-solving truly constitutes the highest form of learning in which a person can engage, then one must question whether any real "problems" were perceived by the learner.

Before children reach the age where they are required to attend school, they are on their own, intellectually. A good deal of instruction on attitudes, manners, values, etc. is received by the child from others, but the cognitive domain develops primarily through the child's own endeavors. A physical environment is certainly structured to some extent by outside forces, but the child's intellectual involvement with this environment is his own. As suggested by Bloom, Hawkins, and others in education, the learning that occurs within an individual during the first five years of life probably *exceeds* the learning that occurs thereafter! How is it that the rate of learning before formal schooling begins is at such a relatively rapid pace? Piaget has made a very strong case (also supported by the continuing research of many others) for the position that the child must structure his learning from within(2-5). The child engages in problem-solving situations that he identifies as problems to him. At ten months of age, he may want to get an object that is under a box, so he invents a way, through his actions, of solving the problem. At three years, he may want to "swing by himself" on the outdoor gym set as he sees older children doing. The learning involved is how to solve a problem and the learned "principle" results from the act of solving the problem, not vice-versa. In other words, learning *principles* that explain relationships, result from the act of solving problems. For the young child of pre-school age, the problems are identified from within. Someone else does not identify problems *for* him. He structures the problem-solving situations and continually assesses his progress. This learner *is* an independent learner during this pre-school phase. He is not taught to be independent in his thinking, it occurs naturally.

Formal schooling changes the natural tendency to continue learning through the process of problem-solving. For the most part, "problems" are now identified in advance for the child. He merely learns the principles required to solve the problems and sure enough, he can demonstrate his facility at problem-solving (if only for a limited time in one way). But this new approach has reversed the natural sequence of problem-solving in which the child has engaged, prior to formal schooling. "Problems" are not identified from within the individual, but originate outside of his intellectual domain. Problems as used in this new sense, of course, refer to any specific work assignments, etc. that allow little or no choice on the part of the child. Children are taught the principles with which to solve the problems. It is precisely at this point that the so-called problem, may well cease to be a problem from the child's standpoint! Instead of identifying problems as he has done naturally for himself before any formal schooling, he now has problems identified *for* him. The natural learning process is abruptly reversed. The likelihood of the child encountering real problems while in school has now been drastically diminished. Problems imposed from without now supercede problems that originate from within. If useful learning does, in fact, result mainly from problem-solving processes, then the percentage of time the child can devote to true problem-solving is severely limited!

Piaget's work also suggests very strongly that children of elementary school age must interact with concrete objects during these problem-solving situations. At this "concrete operational" level of intellectual development, language plays a secondary role in thought formation.(5)

The areas of science and mathematics have great potential for providing the necessary manipulative materials required by the child during this stage of concrete operational thought, but they must be provided in a way that *allows* a child to engage in true problem-solving situations. Imposing problems on children does not insure that the children perceive the directives as problems. They must have the freedom to identify problems that are perceived as *real* problems. The environment can be structured to maximize the possibility that children will engage in certain kinds of problem-solving, but once the child confronts this environment, *he* must have the freedom to identify problems as he perceives them. Outside structure from the teacher or other sources during this process must be seen by the child as only one possibility.

When is a problem a problem? The answer, then, is provided by the behavior of pre-school children in their interaction with "things."

Problems are identified from within through interactions with "things" and "ideas." The "things" are required until the child is 11 or 12 years of age and "ideas" can be dealt with on a more formal level only afterwards. There can be no assurance that "problems" originating from outside the child's intellectual domain are perceived as problems from within.

REFERENCES

1. Gagné, Robert M. *The Conditions of Learning.* New York: Holt, Rinehart, and Winston, Inc., 1965.
2. Inhelder, Barbel and Jean Piaget. *The Early Growth of Logic in the Child.* New York: W. W. Norton, 1969.
3. Piaget, Jean and Barbel Inhelder. *The Child's Conception of Space.* New York: W. W. Norton, 1967.
4. Piaget, Jean. *The Child's Conception of Number.* New York: W. W. Norton, 1965.
5. Furth, Hans G. *Piaget and Knowledge.* Englewood Cliffs, New Jersey: Prentice-Hall, 1969.

---

1. Can you identify some examples where children are encouraged to engage in problem-solving activities during the planned school curriculum?
2. How do Piaget's four factors in development (maturation, socialization, experience, equilibration) relate to problem-solving?
3. What potential difficulties can you see in asking children in a classroom to try to solve a problem that has but one solution?

28 ROBERT E. ROGERS AND ALAN M. VOELKER

Programs for Improving Science Instruction in the Elementary School: Part I, ESS

One of the best known major curriculum projects in elementary science is the Elementary Science Study (ESS). All curriculum projects represent the particular philosophies and biases of the small group of individuals who create the ideas, and due to this fact the best way to really understand such projects is to try them out in the classroom. The feasibility of such an approach is, of course, not very great so one alternative is to read an "objective" analysis of each program. This paper and the one that follows were described in a relatively objective way and a fairly good verbal understanding of ESS and SCIS can be gained by reading the two papers. ESS is usually identified as the project less concerned with behavioral objectives and learning science content and more concerned with "turning children on" to science. The previous paper in this section by Hawkins represents the early ideas that were generally sustained throughout the decade of the 1960s during which ESS produced most of its science units.

The ERIC Center for Science Education receives numerous requests for information regarding a wide range of educational programs. One such area that is currently of major interest to teachers, teacher-trainers, school administrators, university scientists, and others interested in elementary school programs is that of science for the elementary school. Information regarding programs sponsored on the whole, or in part, by the National Science Foundation are of particular interest. In response to requests for information regarding the NSF programs, the Center has undertaken to publish a series of articles designed to answer the many questions in a more comprehensive form than would be possible through the medium of numerous individual letters.

Reprinted from *Science and Children*, Vol. 7, No. 5, 1970, pp. 35-43, by permission of the editor. Dr. Rogers is a research associate at the ERIC Information Analysis Center for Science Education, Ohio State University. Dr. Voelker is Assistant Professor of Science Education at The University of Wisconsin at Madison.

The series of articles will present a description of three programs sponsored in part or in whole by the National Science Foundation . . . the Elementary Science Study (ESS), the Science Curriculum improvement Study (SCIS), and Science—A Process Approach (AAAS). These three programs have been selected on the basis of the frequency of requests for information about them and the extent of the use of the materials on a national basis.

Information for writing the articles has come from three major sources:

1. Documents housed at the ERIC Center for Science Education.
2. Documents received from the projects' staffs and others who work with the project materials, and
3. Materials obtained by searching libraries and making special contacts (telephone, etc.) with a wide variety of people (workshop leaders, etc.) who have worked with the projects in some capacity.

Six areas are generally covered for each of the three programs: (1) nature of the program; (2) instructional materials; (3) use of materials; (4) implementation and teacher programs; (5) evaluation; and (6) the role of the teacher.

Introduction

The last decade and a half has witnessed curriculum improvement projects in a number of subjects. Not the least among these has been in the area of science. First there were projects in secondary science: physics, biology, and chemistry. Then in the early sixties efforts of a large scale were undertaken to upgrade science instruction in the elementary school. Several projects involving scientists and educators were initiated. The Elementary Science Study (ESS) is one such project.[1]

ESS is one of the many curriculum programs under preparation at the Education Development Center (EDC) in Newton, Massachusetts. EDC, a nonprofit organization incorporating the Institute for Educational Innovation and Educational Services Incorporated, began in 1958 as a parent organization to the Physical Science Study Committee. One of EDC's largest endeavors, claiming approximately 10 per cent of the total EDC budget in 1968, is the elementary science program being developed by ESS.

1. The sources of information for writing this article have consisted primarily of documents held at the ERIC Center for Science Education and unpublished information supplied by the ESS director and staff members. Some information has been obtained from other assorted sources. Most information came from ESS publications, articles written about ESS by staff members, and various other articles pertaining to the program.

In 1960, ESS began on a small scale developing materials for teaching science from kindergarten through eighth grade. Since then, more than a hundred scientists and educators have been involved in the conception and design of ESS materials. These staff developers have received considerable help from staff specialists in the design of equipment, making of films, and producing printed materials.

Nature of ESS Program

In order to understand the nature of ESS materials, it is essential to know how the ESS staff has gone about developing those materials. Significantly, the materials are not based on a specific theory of how children learn, or on the logical structure of science, or any concept of the needs of society. This is not to say, however, that what children do with ESS materials is psychologically unsound and scientifically trivial. Considering the composition of the development staff (educators and scientists) this is hardly the case. Nevertheless, ESS's approach has been largely intuitive, rather than theoretical, particularly in the beginning.

Of course, ESS personnel have some ideas about what constitutes good science for children. Philip Morrison, one of the prime movers of ESS, has provided a club to what ESS considers important when children and science meet.

> One mandate is imperative for our style of work: there must be personal involvement. The child must work with his own hands, mind and heart (20, p. 70).[2]

Indeed getting children totally involved in working with materials is what gives direction to the development of ESS materials. And this involvement criterion is determined to a large extent not by theoretical assumptions about what interests children but by how children actually respond to materials during the developmental process. If the materials fail to turn children on, affectively and cognitively, the idea under consideration is discarded and others are pursued. As is readily seen, this approach to developing instructional materials relies heavily upon feedback from teachers, classroom observers, and administrators.

The ESS Development Process

In its final form, a phenomenon dealt with by ESS staff developers becomes an instructional unit.[3] The development of a unit can be thought of as progressing in stages, as described below.

2. Numerals in parenthesis refer to references listed at the end of the article.
3. The development process described here is an abbreviated version of the process described in a communication received from ESS.

1. "Gleans" and Hunches. A staff member has an idea that he thinks has potential for being developed into a unit.
2. Early Development. Staff members work out an opening series of lessons which are taught by a staff member and observed by other staff members in a local (Newton, Massachusetts and vicinity) classroom. Classroom work is followed by evaluation. If the idea still seems workable, the development process proceeds to the next stage. If not workable, the idea is discarded.
3. Advanced Development. Local teachers try out the unit. A teacher's guide is written and prototypic equipment is perfected.
4. Trial Teaching. The unit is tested against a wide background of teachers and classrooms. Trial teaching feedback may lead to changes in the Teacher's Guide, equipment design, and, sometimes, content.
5. Preparation for Commercial Release. Feedback from trial teaching is further analyzed and on the basis of this feedback necessary changes are made in written materials and equipment. Staff members work with commercial publishers in production.

The ESS Staff is primarily concerned with developing instructional materials that are, in ESS terms, appropriate for children's science learning(8). One aspect of what is appropirate is the concrete; that is, children work with things, not ideas(2). This predilection for working with things is based partly on what motivates children to explore and partly on how children learn. Thus ESS does not teach concepts such as "living forms are orderly and complex," "matter is electrical in nature," or "energy is conserved." Rather, in the words of former ESS Director Randolph Brown:

> . . . ESS finds it more profitable to help children explore the hatching and growth of tadpoles, the habits of mealworms, and the ways of lighting bulbs with batteries. . . . ESS feels that "things" encourage children to ask great questions and find their own answers (2, p. 33).

Appropriate also means that the materials must be of such a nature that they stimulate children to raise questions, as well as being conducive to yielding answers. One of the questions that children invariably ask when they are working with the unit Behavior of Mealworms is "How do mealworms find food?" The children are encouraged to have the mealworm "answer" the question for them by designing some investigations that inquire about the mealworm's sense of smell, sight, and so on.

Furthermore, ESS has some definite ideas about how its materials should be used in the classroom. Eleanor Duckworth has described ESS's approach in the following manner:

> There are two main characteristics which we keep in mind. One is that children use materials themselves, individually or in small groups, often

raising the question themselves, answering them in their own way, using the materials in ways the teacher had not anticipated, and coming to their own conclusions. . . . The other is that we try to create situations where the children are called upon to talk to each other (8, p. 242).

David Hawkins(10), a former director of ESS, has emphasized the importance of allowing children to "mess about" with materials in the early phase of a unit, the rationale being that preliminary free and unstructured experience (messing about) with the materials "produces the early and indispensable autonomy and diversity" that serves to give meaning and direction to children's questions and activities. This approach permits children to learn different things and to learn at different rates.

The ESS Approach and Psychology of Learning

Although no specific efforts have been made by ESS to base its approach on a particular psychology of learning, resulting materials do turn out to have a sound psychological basis, as Eleanor Duckworth, a psychologist who has worked with ESS, has observed(8). Two important aspects of ESS materials, using concrete things and children's active involvement in learning, are supported by Piaget's ideas on intellectual development(21). The notion that children should have free and unhurried periods of exploration during the early phases of learning has been stressed by Bruner(3), Hunt(14), Berlyne(1), Dewey(7), and John Holt(12). Moreover, Susan Isaacs(15), an outstanding leader in child growth and development in England, and Robert Sears(24), an American psychologist, have emphasized that children derive the greatest pleasure from those things (either animate or inanimate objects) that respond to their manipulations.

Allowing children to follow their own inclinations as they explore materials is obviously important to ESS's approach to children's learning. The thinking behind this is that children learn more when they are doing what they want to do instead of what someone else wants them to do. Furthermore, such self-directed learning has more meaning for them. Hunt(14), Hull(13), Hein(11), Hawkins(10), Dewey(7), Holt(12), and Isaacs(15) have emphasized the importance of allowing children to follow their own bent as they interact with their environment.[4]

4. According to the Plowden Report (Her Majesty's Stationery Office, London 1967), one-third of the primary schools in England happily and successfully operate from this rationale.

Motivation

While the wide variety of units developed by ESS allow all combinations of formal and informal, sequenced and unsequenced, large-group and small-group instruction, all units are designed to motivate children to explore, speculate, and try things, for as Philip Morrison and Charles Walcott have observed:

> . . . a major aim of a project such as this one (ESS) is to encourage children to examine the world around them and to acquire the desire, interest, and ability to continue to analyze, relate, and understand it as they go through life (18, p. 49).

According to Morrison, when speaking of the work of ESS:

> The complex thing we call motivation or attitude, the affective side of learning, is perhaps above all the human attribute which we hope to evoke (19, p. 65).

If these remarks are representative of the views of other ESS personnel, and the authors have no reason to believe that they are not, then one is led to conclude that above all else ESS materials are intended to motivate children to explore the world around them.

Scope and Sequence

Scope and sequence of content are factors that frequently draw considerable attention from curriculum makers. Nevertheless, ESS does not seem at all concerned about these factors believing that there is no way of knowing whether in fact the content of science that is important now will be important in the first half of the twenty-first century, the period in which our present elementary school children are to live most of their lives(22). ESS has given two reasons for not developing a sequential science program for the elementary school. First, since learning theorists do not fully understand just which sequences of experiences lead to the kind of changes in children ESS would like to see, it would indeed be presumptuous to develop a sequential program(18). Secondly, ESS believes in any case that it is both the prerogative and responsibility of each school system to work out its own sequence with its own objective in mind(22). While ESS is willing to consult with school systems on such matters, it does not wish to dictate a certain sequential order in which its materials are to be used. This, in ESS's view, would be tantamount to making its materials a textbook or textbook series, a curriculum pitfall it wishes to avoid. Although, as has been indicated, ESS units are not designed in a way that requires that they be taught in a certain order, many schools have constructed a complete science program around them including a locally determined sequential order in which the units are to be taught.

Instructional Materials

As of the fall of 1969, ESS has in commercial form 50 units for use in grades K-8. The majority of the units are concentrated in grades four, five, and six. There are, however, at least sixteen units that are suitable for K-3 and twelve for grades seven and eight. The variety of units produced by ESS can be used to provide a wide range of learning experiences. Some units are designed to develop fundamental skills in graphing, weighing, and measuring. Other units are oriented more toward content development; still others are concerned primarily with developing thinking skills. Most units, in fact, provide a combination of all these experiences. The Growing Seeds Unit, for example, includes activities that call upon the children to graph, to measure, and to seek ways of finding answers to their questions. At the same time pupils learn something about the conditions favorable to germination and growth of plants, about rates of growth of different plants, and about the structures of seeds and plants.

The basic instructional materials for a unit consist of a teacher's guide and a pupil kit. The teacher's guide contains background information about the content of the unit, as well as suggestions for its use, and is not written as a prescription to be followed blindly by the teacher. Rather it respects the judgment, imagination, and individuality of the teacher and encourages him to exercise these qualities. The pupil kit contains all the equipment that the children will need to carry out the ideas suggested in the teacher's guide. If encouraged to do so, the children will find other ways to use the equipment as they explore their own ideas.

In addition to the basic materials, worksheets, pictures, supplementary booklets, film loops, and 8mm films accompany some units. The film loops are each three or four minutes long and are designed to provide children with learning experiences that could not be readily obtained directly, yet contribute to children's understanding of important phenomena related to a unit. An example of such a film loop is one entitled the "Black Swallowtail Butterfly: Egg, Hatching, and Larvae." It is very difficult to raise butterflies through the stages of their life cycle in the classroom.[5] Direct observation being impractical, ESS

---

5. ESS staff has spent considerable time and money on this problem and has succeeded in rearing the "carrot" butterfly, but commercial production has not been worked out. ESS Newsletter, No. 11.

developed a film in order that children can nevertheless have an "experience" with the life cycle of a butterfly.

It should be noted that ESS worksheets are not the traditional fill-in-the blank variety. Some are designed to facilitate keeping of records and are usually based on children's observations of their own manipulations of materials. Others may be in the form of "prediction sheets" that call upon the children to make predictions on the basis of previous experiences in the unit. Frequently, these prediction problems are in the form of diagrams, as is the case with a prediction sheet in the Batteries and Bulbs unit. On this sheet several diagrams of wire connections between bulbs and batteries are shown and the child is asked to predict in which arrangements the bulb would light.

Some units are designed to be used by an entire class at the same time. These units frequently consist of student worksheets and film loops as well as teacher's guides and pupil kits. Such units can be accommodated in a typical classroom without major alternations of schedules or class organization. Units that fall in this category are listed below:

Gases and "Airs"
Batteries and Bulbs
Microgardening
Balancing
Growing Seeds
Heating and Cooling
Ice Cubes
Pendulums
Balloons
Kitchen Physics
Colored Solutions
Optics
Slips and Slides
Sink or Float
Rocks and Charts
Small Things

Other units are less definitive and may include only a teacher's guide which suggests activities and simple materials that are obtainable locally or are available from equipment-supply houses. Units of this type may involve the whole class or part of the class and may or may not be taught in a series of connected lessons. The teachers' guides for these units are less structured, more open-ended, and require more teacher initiative. A list of units in this category follows:

Bones
Mealworms
Mystery Powders
Eggs and Tadpoles
Pond Water
Mosquitoes
Brine Shrimp
Structures
Where Is The Moon?
Animal Book
Light and Shadows
Changes

Mapping
Match and Measure
Musical Instrument
    Recipe Book
Clay Boats
Starting From Seeds
Life of Beans and Peas
Butterflies
Daytime Astronomy
Tracks
Peas and Particles
Mobiles

A third category of units is designed for individual or small group work. These units lend themselves well to meeting individual needs and interests of different children. The design of these units demand an informal and flexible classroom organization where individuals or groups of students can work at different units at the same time. Working with these units can, in an organizational sense, be thought of as project work. Units in this category are listed below:

Attribute Games and Problems
Geo Blocks
Pattern Blocks
Tangrams
Sand
Animal Activity
Batteries and Bulbs II

Spinning Tables
Mirror Cards
Balance Book
Mobiles
Printing Press
Drops, Streams,
    and containers

All ESS units have gone through trial stages during the course of their development. One of the reasons for testing the materials is to determine the grade levels at which the units are most appropriate. Frequently, in trial classrooms a unit is found to work well with children in several grades. For example, Batteries and Bulbs has been used successfully with grades four, five, and six. The unit Changes has been used with children K-4. Perhaps the unstructured nature of the ESS program accounts for the appropriateness of the materials for children in different stages of intellectual development. While one child explores the materials in one direction, another child explores the same phenomenon in another direction and at a different level of understanding. Children work at their own level and pace.

From its inception one of the requisites established for ESS materials was that they should be inexpensive(8). This requisite has been met with the materials of many but not all units. For the unit Growing Seeds, for example, the cost of materials, including teacher's guide, for a class of 30 children comes to only $16.50. On the other hand the cost of materials, excluding films, for Small Things amounts to $171. It is worth noting that much of the equipment for the more expensive units can be used with other science topics. Moreover, with some effort a teacher, or school, can develop a basic supply of equipment that could be used with a number of units, and which would preclude the necessity of purchasing packaged equipment whenever a new unit is introduced to the classroom.[6] Furthermore, when ordering from the publisher, it is not necessary that one order the whole packaged kit. The components of a kit are itemized in the publisher's catalog.

It has been roughly estimated that a government-supported program, such as ESS, will cost at least three times as much to introduce in an elementary school as it does to introduce a traditional program that is essentially textbook centered(4). (No estimations have been made on cost comparison over the long run.) But a school or teacher need not make a commitment to the whole ESS program. If one had to be extremely cost-conscious, the less expensive, yet successful units such as Behavior of Mealworms, Peas and Particles, Crayfish, Starting from Seeds, Mirror Cards, and Changes could be utilized at minimal cost.

Use of Materials

According to the Sixth Report of the International Clearinghouse on Science and Mathematics Curricular Developments(25) over 7,500 teachers and 225,000 children were using ESS materials as of January, 1968. These estimates were arrived at by using sales figures received from McGraw-Hill Book Company, the chief commercial distributor of ESS materials. In a recent communication to the writers, ESS stated that approximately 40,000 teachers used ESS materials during the school year 1968-69. The ESS staff further predicts that approximately 53,000 teachers and 1,300,000 children will be using ESS materials during the school year 1969-70. All these figures were calculated from commercial sales information and from trial editions distributed by ESS. The numbers for children are calculated on the basis of 25 children per class.

There are a number of school systems throughout the country that use ESS materials almost exclusively for their science program. However, the largest number of schools using ESS materials use them with a few

6. The Elementary Science Advisory Center at the University of Colorado in Boulder has prepared a booklet entitled Science Equipment in the Elementary School that may offer considerable assistance to those who wish to establish a basic supply of science equipment in their school.

teachers who are by "disposition and inclination" attracted to the ESS approach.

ESS materials are also being used in some foreign countries. The Republic of South Korea and the province of British Columbia have adopted ESS materials and mandated their use throughout their respective elementary schools. ESS has worked with Peace Corps trainees who later adapted the materials for use in places such as Ethiopia, the Philippines, and Colombia, South America. Some of the units developed by the African Primary Science Program (an EDC project) are adapted versions of ESS units.

ESS materials are also used in preservice methods courses and in-service workshops for elementary teachers. This appears to be done for one or both of the following reasons: In the first place, course instructors and workshop leaders consider it important that elementary teachers become acquainted with some of the new elementary science projects, such as ESS. Secondly ESS materials provide a vehicle for conveying concepts of teaching (e.g., children learn science from their own exploration of concrete materials) central to science education today.

Implementation and Teacher Programs

For a number of years ESS has held workshops for a variety of educational personnel, including teachers, supervisors, consultants, team-teaching leaders, master teachers, school administrators, and personnel from colleges and universities. The duration of these workshops varies considerably, from a day for school administrators to six weeks for college students.

A significant part of the ESS implementation program is conducting workshops at Newton to prepare participants for leadership positions in regional workshops. In this workshop program, the participants usually spend about four weeks at Newton before going out to conduct regional workshops for teachers and to assist schools within the region in the implementation process. During the summer of 1968, 32 educators attended the workshop at Newton. After the Newton workshop, these 32 implementation specialists conducted six regional workshops,[7] which involved a total of 283 teachers and administrators.

It is interesting to note that the Newton workshop included a four-day intensive sensitivity training session involving workshop staff and participants. As used in education, sensitivity training refers to a range of laboratory and workshop efforts that are designed to help teachers

---

7. Regional centers were: Rochester, N.Y.; Philadelphia, Pa.; Minneapolis, Minn.; Long Island, New York; Waco, Texas.

reconceive their role in working with children. Cultivation of the heightened awareness of children as growing, self-actualizing (fulfilling one's potentialities) individuals is the focus of such training. Sensitivity training has received much of its impetus from the work of perceptual psychologists such as Combs(6), Kelly(16), Rogers(23), and Maslow(17). It is the contention of ESS that viewing children as growing, self-actualizing individuals is consonant with its approach to children's learning science. At the end of the Newton workshop, many participants indicated that the sensitivity training had caused them to "change their procedures" during the workshop. Two of the regional teams also included sensitivity training in their area workshops.

Another important aspect of both the Newton and regional workshops is the opportunity for participants to teach with ESS materials and methods by working with small groups of children. ESS imposes two conditions of participation upon each school district that sends a teacher to the regional workshops. These conditions are: (1) the district must commit $400 to the teacher for the purpose of purchasing materials, and (2) the teacher must be released at least part time during the school year to work with teachers in his district. ESS feels that these conditions are essential in order that each school district benefit fully from the teacher's workshop experience.

During the summer of 1969, ESS conducted a second Summer Implementation Workshop involving 40 participants, who in turn conducted regional workshops.

Although ESS has directed its major thrust at inservice education, it is beginning to move more toward preservice education. It has, for example, made an arrangement with Wheelock College[8] (Boston) whereby some 30 freshmen students spend their six-week winter term half-time at ESS.

Through its workshops and preservice programs, ESS is actively involved in numerous teacher education activities. Furthermore, it is not merely concerned with preparing teachers to teach ESS materials. It is equally concerned with the important task of informing and acquainting supportive personnel (principals, supervisors, college instructors, and so on) with the ESS materials and ESS approach to educating children.

Evaluation

ESS is first and foremost an organization that exists for the purpose of developing instructional materials. It is very much concerned with

8. Wheelock is a private college for women that is devoted entirely to the preparation of elementary school teachers.

making sure that the materials developed are in fact appropriate for children's science learning and that the materials are being used as they were intended. Hence, a great deal of attention is given to the development process and to teacher programs.

ESS is, of course, concerned with evaluating children's learning. But the kinds of learning outcomes—interests, motivation, curiosity, attitudes, inquiry skills—it considers important are indeed difficult to measure. Some attempts have been made to assess the impact of ESS materials on children by tape-recording their responses to questions about provocative film loops they had just viewed. The purpose of the assessment was to see if children who had been exposed to ESS materials differed from non-exposed children (control group) in their pattern of response. The results were inconclusive.

ESS contends that while objective, quantified testing is one way to evaluate learning outcomes, the subjective impressions of teachers and administrators are also valid forms of assessment. According to ESS, the feedback gathered from teachers and administrators indicates that children who use ESS materials "like science, ask more questions, ask more perceptive questions, are more observant about things outside of school, and actively initiate projects."(22)

One of the most satisfying experiences ESS has had has been with the children involved in its Cardozo Project[9] in Washington, D. C.'s ghetto area. ESS reports that many of the Cardozo children who are "non-verbal" and generally unsuccessful in school have begun to read better and perform better in many of their school tasks(25). ESS attributes this improvement to the change in the child's view of himself; he has a healthier self-image, which gives him a greater sense of his own potential and power, not only with science but with other areas as well. If indeed this is a correct interpretation of this phenomenon, educators would do well to take a very close look at ESS materials, for a number of studies, including the Coleman Report(5), have found the state of a child's self-concept to be a variable significantly related to achievement.

The Role of the Teacher

To teach ESS materials as intended demands a certain view of teaching, of the learner, and of the learning process. The teacher's role in an ESS classroom is one of consultant, guide, and catalyst. The teacher advises, listens, diagnoses, and in Hawkins' terms, acts as an external loop, doing things for the child that he cannot do for himself(9). For this reason, the teacher must see the child as having an extraordinary ca-

9. *See* Mary Lee Sherburne, A Peach Tree Grown on T Street, EDC, 1967, for an informative account of the Project.

pacity for learning and believe that he learns best from his own activity. Teachers who already have this view of teaching, learning, and children are well suited to use ESS materials in their classroom, while others who do not share it might be persuaded to reconceive their role as teachers through sensitivity training, workshops, and reading.

Besides conceptualizing this role, the teacher needs to know how to operationalize it. He needs to see what an ESS-type classroom looks like, how the teacher attends to the details of classroom management, the mechanics of distributing and storing materials, and how the teacher works with a whole class, small groups, and individual children. Participating in an ESS workshop, viewing ESS teaching films, observing existing ESS classes, reading or viewing documentation[10] of how some teachers have developed their own style in teaching ESS materials are all ways of learning how to operationalize ESS concepts of teaching.

It is very difficult for an isolated teacher to go it alone in an innovative endeavor, irrespective of his commitment to the innovation. He needs the continued philosophical and material support of his superintendent, principal, and supervisor, as well as the good will of his teaching colleagues. Real and lasting curriculum change comes only when it proceeds on a broad front and when personnel at all levels are actively committed to the same goals.

Summary Statement

ESS has so far directed its major efforts at developing instructional materials, acquainting an assortment of educational personnel with the materials, and preparing teachers to use them. ESS has not proceeded in its development of instructional materials within the framework of a particular philosophy of education. Implicit in its approach to developing materials is a concern for the development of the whole child. ESS emphases—active involvement, freedom to pursue one's interests, imagination, individually—are aimed at developing self-directing, autonomous, and self-actualizing individuals. The materials include a great deal that is related to learning science concepts and developing intellectual skills. Intuitive as well as analytical thinking are cultivated. Thus, the cognitive domain is served well.

In the area of the psychomotor domain, ESS's emphasis upon children's manipulating concrete materials helps develop motor skills. But ESS's greatest strength is, perhaps, its contribution to the effective development of children. Children derive satisfaction from exploring, in their own individual ways, interesting materials, finding not only answers

10. An Interview with Dorothy Welch (EDC, 1969) in one such documentation.

and solutions but also that they have the ability to learn for themselves. Perhaps, too, children who find satisfaction in exploring will in time come to value and commit themselves to it.

REFERENCES CITED

1. Bertyne, David. "Conflict and Arousal." *Scientific American.* August, 1966.
2. Brown, Randolph. "Elementary Science Study." Education Development Center Annual Report 1968. Newton, Massachusetts, 1968.
3. Bruner, Jerome S. *Toward A Theory of Instruction.* New York City: W. W. Norton & Company, 1968.
4. Butts, David P. "The Price of Change." *Science and Children.* April, 1969.
5. Coleman, James S. et al. *Equality of Educational Opportunity.* Washington, D. C.: U. S. Government Printing Office, 1966.
6. Combs, Arthur W. "A Perceptual View of the Adequate Personality." *Perceiving, Behaving, Becoming.* Association for Supervision and Curriculum Development, Washington, D. C. Yearbook, 1962.
7. Dewey, John. *Democracy in Education.* New York City: The Macmillan Company, 1916.
8. Duckworth, Eleanor. "The Elementary Science Study Branch of Educational Services Incorporated." *Journal of Research in Science Teaching,* September, 1964.
9. Hawkins, David. "I, Thou, It." *Elementary Science Study.* Newton, Massachusetts, 1967.
10. Hawkins, David. "Messing About in Science." *Science and Children.* February, 1965.
11. Hein, George E. "Children's Science is Another Culture." *Technology Review,* December, 1968.
12. Holt, John. *How Children Learn.* New York City: Pitman Publishing Corporation, 1967.
13. Hull, William. Quoted in The Prepared Environment by Margaret Howard Loeffier. Casady School, Oklahoma City, 1967.
14. Hunt, J. McV. *Intelligence and Experience.* New York City: Ronald Press, 1961.
15. Isaacs, Susan. *Intellectual Growth in Young Children.* New York City: Shocken Books, 1956.
16. Kelly, Earl C. "The Fully Functioning Self." *Perceiving, Behaving, Becoming.* Washington, D. C.: Association for Supervision and Curriculum Development. Yearbook, 1962.
17. Maslow, Abraham H. "Some Basic Propositions of a Growth and Self-actualizing Psychology." *Perceiving, Behaving, Becoming.* Washington, D. C.: Association for Supervision and Curriculum Development. Yearbook, 1962.
18. Morrison, Philip, and Charles Walcott. "Enlightened Opportunism: An Informal Account of the Elementary Science Summer Study of 1962." *Journal of Research in Science Teaching,* March, 1963.
19. Morrison, Philip. "Experimenters in the Schoolroom." *ESI Quarterly Report,* Winter-Spring, 1964.
20. Morrison, Philip. "The Curriculum Triangle and Its Style." *ESI Quarterly Report.* Summer-Fall, 1964.
21. Piaget, Jean. "Development and Learning." *Journal of Research in Science Teaching,* September, 1964.
22. Personal Communication from ESS. June 23, 1969.
23. Rogers, Carl R. "Toward Becoming a Fully Functioning Person." *Perceiving, Behaving, Becoming.* Washington, D. C.: Association for Supervision and Curriculum Development. Yearbook, 1962.
24. Sears, Robert. "Process Pleasure" in Learning About Learning, ed. Jerome S. Bruner. Washington, D. C.: U. S. Government Printing Office, 1966.

25. Sixth Report of the International Clearinghouse on Science and Mathematics Curricular Development. Under the editorship of J. David Lockard. University of Maryland, College Park: Science Teaching Center, 1968.

OTHER REFERENCES

Education Development Center. "An Interview with Dorothy Welch." Newton, Massachusetts, 1969.

Elementary Science Advisory Center. "Science Equipment in the Elementary School." University of Colorado, 1967.

Elgammal, Attia. "Elementary Science Study at Macomb County Students' and Teachers' Reaction." Macomb Intermediate School District, Mount Clemens, Michigan, 1969.

Finley, Gilbert. "The Elementary Science Study." *Elementary School Science Bulletin.* February, 1963.

Hartley, Mary Lou. "Evaluation and Reflection After Attending the Elementary Science Study Summer School." *ESI Quarterly Report.* Winter-Spring 1964.

Hawkins, David. "ESI Elementary Science Activities Project." *Science Education,* February, 1964.

Hawkins, David. "Laboratory Science in Elementary Schools." *American Journal of Physics,* November, 1964.

Hawkins, David. "The Informed Vision: An Essay on Science Education." *Daedalus,* Summer, 1965.

Hawkins, David. "The Stuff from Which Questions Are Shaped." *Nature and Science* (Teacher's Edition), April 17, 1964.

Leodas, C. J. "The Elementary Science Study." *ESI Quarterly Report.* Winter-Spring, 1964.

Moss, Penrod. "An Elementary Science Study Report from California." *ESI Quarterly Report,* Winter-Spring, 1964.

Nichols, Benjamin. "Elementary Science Study—Two Years Later." *Journal of Research in Science Teaching,* December, 1964.

Walcott, Charles. "Elementary Science Study." *Science Education News,* AAAS Miscellaneous Publication. December, 1962.

Webster, David. "How To Help Children Make Mistakes." *Science and Children,* May, 1964.

Webster, David. "Making a Chicken Skeleton." *Nature and Science.* May, 1964.

Zacharias, Jerrold R. "Learning By Teaching." *Instructor,* January, 1966.

Zacharias, Jerrold R. "What's Ahead in Elementary Science." *Instructor,* January, 1967.

---

1. Whereas other curriculum projects are quite concerned with science content, ESS seems to be more highly concerned with attitudes, values, etc. that represent the affective side of learning. Is this a defensible position?

2. Is it defensible for one to say that learning about magnetism and electricity in elementary school is more important than learning about a fly?

3. In reference to the Shulman paper in Part II, would you say ESS is more closely correlated with discovery or guided learning?

29 BARBARA S. THOMSON AND ALAN M. VOELKER

Programs for Improving Science Instruction in the Elementary School: Part II, SCIS

Another of the "major" elementary science curriculum projects is described in this paper. Because the director of SCIS held certain beliefs about scientific literacy, this science program reflects those beliefs. While ESS was not concerned with scientific literacy in the same sense, SCIS identified conceptual schemes that were supposed to communicate the nature of science to children. It is interesting to note that SCIS also identifies its goals, methods, etc. with the work of Piaget. Two distinctly different approaches to elementary school science seem to claim the same psychological base for their development. It is left for the reader to decide whether or not one of the programs seems to be more compatible with the ideas of Piaget about the intellectual development of children. Unfortunately, the actual classroom conditions that are established by teachers using ESS or SCIS are not compared. The extent to which children engage in discovery learning and independently creative endeavors should be researched in much greater detail.

A few years ago when the elementary school science curriculum projects were first being funded by the National Science Foundation (NSF) and other foundations and agencies, educators adopted a "wait and see" posture in order to give the program advocates an opportunity to provide careful development and evaluation. Administrators, classroom teachers, curriculum workers, as well as college personnel are seeking various types of information for making crucial decisions regarding adoption, adaptation, or rejection.

This article is the second in a series of articles prepared by the ERIC Center for Science Education in which the authors present descriptions of elementary school science projects sponsored by NSF. The article consists of a review of the Science Curriculum Improvement Study

Reprinted from *Science and Children*, Vol. 7, No. 8, 1970, pp. 29-37, by permission of the editor. Dr. Thomson is with the Science and Mathematics Education Department at Ohio State University. Dr. Voelker is Assistant Professor of Science Education at the University of Wisconsin at Madison.

(SCIS). The basic rationale for writing this series of articles and the procedure utilized in acquiring the information can be found in the overview of the series, Part I, ESS.(31)

Introduction

The work of Karplus with the Elementary School Science Project, University of California (ESSP) in the late fifties raised three questions.

1. How can one create a learning experience that achieves a sure connection between the pupil's intuitive attitudes and the concepts of the modern scientific point of view?
2. How can one determine what children have learned?
3. How can one communicate with the teacher so that the teacher can in turn communicate with the pupils?(9)

It was Karplus's feeling that the only reasonable way for him to answer these questions was to try to familiarize himself with the point of view children take toward natural phenomena by actually teaching science to some elementary school classes on a regularly scheduled basis. The outcome of this experience coupled with his work with ESS and Minnemast (and other programs attempting to improve science instruction in the elementary school) served as a frame of reference for the basic SCIS work.

A succinct historical summary of the project from its conception to the present time is located in the Clearinghouse report. It states:

> The Science Curriculum Improvement Study was established in the winter of 1962 by Robert Karplus, a Professor of Theoretical Physics at the University of California, Berkeley, as a result of his work with the Elementary School Science Project (ESSP) at that University. This experience had led Professor Karplus to the conclusion that science had not only to be simplified for the elementary school, but organized on a drastically different basis from the usual logical subject matter presentations to which the university scientist is accustomed.(19).

Nature of the Program

The objectives of the program have been carefully articulated by Karplus and Thier to include intellectual development and scientific literacy. The belief that the concept of literacy be the principal objective of teaching science in the elementary school permeates the total program. Thier's definition of "functional scientific literacy" states:

> The individual must have a conceptual structure and a means of communication that enables him to interpret the information as though he had obtained it himself. (9)

This objective of scientific literacy is pursued through concrete experiences whereby children acquire the concepts and communication skills essential to its development.(17) Concrete manipulation and interaction among students and teachers are important components and well developed in their laboratory approach. (See materials section, page 342.)

Another major objective is that of decision-making. It was emphasized in the 1968 *Clearinghouse Report* that:

> A second implication of scientific literacy is the development of a free and inquisitive attitude and the use of rational procedures for decision making. In the SCIS program, children learn science in an intellectually free atmosphere where their own ideas are respected, where they learn to accept or reject ideas, not on the basis of some authority, but on the basis of their own observations. Ideally, some of these experiences will carry over to other areas of life and incline the children to make decisions on a more rational basis after weighing the factors or evidence involved more objectively. (19)

Psychological Bases of SCIS

Educators such as Hunt(8), Piaget(12), Bruner(4), and Almy(15), who wish to capitalize on the learning potential of children, have conducted developmental research that has illustrated the importance of concrete manipulative experiences. The SCIS designers looked closely at these findings, the child, and his elementary years in order to develop an effective program of science instruction within a framework of elementary education. The belief was:

1. The child's elementary school years are a period of transition as he continues to explore the world he began in infancy.
2. He develops confidence in his own ideas.
3. He builds abstractions with which he interprets the world.

Utilizing this rationale and drawing upon the groundwork laid by Piaget, Hunt, Bruner, and Almy, it was concluded that the elementary school years should provide:

1. A diversified program based heavily on concrete manipulative experiences. (Used guidelines of Piaget)
2. These experiences in a context that helps to build a conceptual framework.
3. A conceptual framework that permits them to perceive phenomena in a more meaningful way, (i.e., integrate their inferences into generalizations of greater value than the ones they would form if left to their own devices.)(9)

Therefore, each lesson that has been developed fulfills one or both of two functions: to provide a new experience, and to establish or reinforce an abstract concept.

Although the cognitive aspects of the program seem to be of paramount importance, the other domains, i.e., affective and psychomotor have not been neglected.(2) A possible explanation is these domains are less tangible as evidenced by Kuslan and Stone. They describe the affective domain as:

1. Attitude—a willingness to approach or avoid environmental interactions
2. Appreciation—a measure of satisfaction in interacting
3. Interest—positively motivated and enjoys the experiences(15)

The role of the affective domain in student learning is illustrated in Figure 1. It is a continuous circular process whereby interested students become involved and if they experience feelings of success, their interest is again supported and continued via this route. The psychomotor domain encompasses the areas of physical development, neuromuscular coordination, and motor skills. The SCIS program provides numerous experiences for students to develop or improve their manipulative skills through concrete experiences.

The philosophy of the SCIS program certainly reflects all three domains but the key focus for program development seems to be on the cognitive domain. However, evaluation activities are being designed in the psychomotor and affective domains.

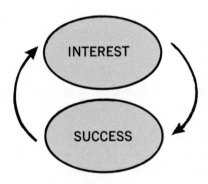

FIGURE 1.

The Learning Environment

The objectives, in conjunction with the SCIS rationale, resulted in a curriculum built around extensive laboratory experiences where the students are involved in exploring new experiences and phenomena. It is referred to as a *direct approach* to learning.

> What is needed to a large extent, especially at the elementary science level is a reversal of the premise that teaching is talking and learning is listening. Very frequently, teaching is listening and observing in order to understand the capabilities of each member of the group of learners. In a textbook or other abstract based situations, this interplay between teacher and learner is impossible. Science taught through the laboratory approach, however, simulates the natural way that children acquire understanding. (26)

An indirect approach to learning could be diagrammatically represented as in Figure 2 while a direct approach could be illustrated by Figure 3.

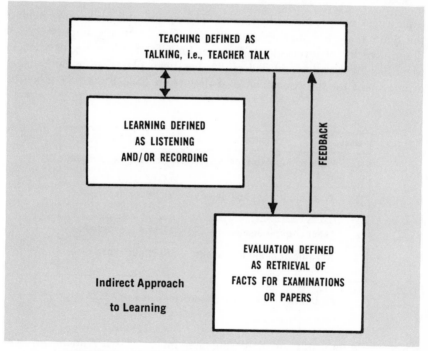

FIGURE 2. Traditional Diagram of Teaching/Learning.

The role of the SCIS teacher must evolve to a point whereby the teacher can function effectively with the type of interaction illustrated in Figure 3. Unless the teacher can function in this direct approach environment, a crucial aspect of this program becomes nonfunctional which in turn severely weakens the total program.

In order to make this technique operational, the "classroom" has to be designed so it becomes a laboratory in which children can have actual

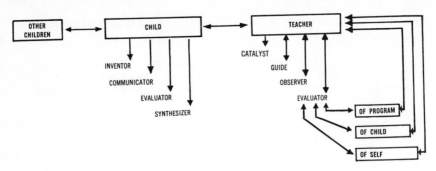

FIGURE 3. (Teacher/Student Partnership) Direct Approach to Learning —The SCIS Approach.

experiences with natural phenomena. The design and philosophy behind the SCIS materials dictates that *involvement* is of key importance. A descriptive list of levels of involvement for effective learning of science, identified by Karplus and Thier(12), has been placed in a hierarchical arrangement for the convenience of discussion (See Figure 4). Each of

LEVEL	INVOLVEMENT	EXPERIENCES
4	Pupil manipulates, observes, acts	Firsthand experiences
3	Teacher and/or pupil demonstration	Vicarious experience
2	Teacher-pupil discussions	Vicarious experience
1	Reading or being told about science	Vicarious experience

FIGURE 4. Levels of Science Involvement—SCIS.

these levels indicates an increasing amount of active student involvement with level four approaching the SCIS "ideal." It is essential in the SCIS scheme that the learning environment include the elements depicted at level four of Figure 4 and in Figure 3. They need to become operational before the full potential of this program can be realized.

Instructional Materials

All materials are carefully focused toward meeting four explicit goals: (1) Scientific Literacy, (2) Intellectual Development, (3) Rational

Decision Making, and (4) To Produce Favorable Pupil Attitudes Toward Science. Hurd and Gallagher have stated:

> The subject content of SCIS is based upon science concepts chosen for their wide applicability and potential usefulness. Instruction is designed to reach pupils at their level of development and help them acquire these concepts. (17)

The concepts around which the materials have been developed are representative of the "big ideas" in science, (i.e., organism, ecosystem, matter and energy: property, reference frame, system, and model). The first four are major scientific concepts while the latter are process oriented concepts.

These "big ideas" form a conceptual framework that cuts across the traditional disciplines forming a structure that illustrates the unity of the sciences.(27) The lessons focus upon concepts related to the "big ideas" and provide a sequencing of experiences. Thus, a conceptual framework for a student can be built enabling the student to organize successfully subsequent science experiences as the instructional materials have been designed to reach pupils at their level of development and to provide an experience base to help to acquire a conceptual framework.

Because each lesson builds upon previous classroom work, it is essential that the materials development portion of the program progress through a complex system of trial testing evaluation and rewriting. According to Karplus the work on one unit progresses:

1. Preparation of teaching plan and design of experiments
2. Exploratory teaching in public schools by SCIS staff
3. Completion of trial materials, i.e., guide, manuals and kits
4. Classroom trial (one to two years)
5. Revisions and additional teaching by SCIS staff
6. Second classroom trial by regular teachers
7. Revisions and preliminary commercial publication
8. Classroom trial in several centers across the United States

At the conclusion of these steps plans for a final commercial edition are put into operation.

At the present time there are four preliminary editions and four final editions with completed kits available from Rand McNally and Company;[1] i.e., Preliminary Editions—*Life Cycles, Relativity, Populations, Position and Motion*. Final Editions—*Material Objects, Organisms, Interaction and Systems, Subsystems and Variables*. Trial editions con-

---

1. D. C. Heath and Company, Lexington, Massachusetts, prepared some of the preliminary editions of SCIS materials. That contract has since been terminated.

sisting of a teacher's guide and student manual can be ordered directly from SCIS. A kit is available for each unit which includes all the necessary materials for the teacher and 32 students. Expendables can be purchased from Rand McNally for replacement in the kits (see list of addresses). Some of these expendables can be purchased at various local stores but for the convenience and time of the teacher, it seems advantageous to purchase these supplies as refill packages. Thus, the necessary student materials can always be complete and ready for use.

Materials are of four types:

1. *Teacher's Guide.* This guide provides a rationale for the unit, a list of objectives, a list of necessary materials, useful suggestions from other teachers, and helpful techniques.
2. *Pupil Manuals.* Each pupil is provided with a manual that serves as an organizational aid to assist him in keeping records. This manual is not the traditional type of workbook but specifically designed to promote organizational skills and to keep records. The utilization of these books occurs only after concrete experiences.
3. *Laboratory Materials.* These are the materials that allow children to have firsthand concrete experiences. Kits are prepackaged so all needed equipment will be available when needed; expendable materials can be purchased in refill packages. The kits have been field tested along with the other materials in order to identify weaknesses and strengths in their use.
4. *Films.* Motion-picture films (16-mm sound films) for all the SCIS units in Preliminary Edition are also available either on a rental basis from the Extension Center or they can be purchased through the SCIS office. Films available for use with the *Material Objects* unit are: "Observing Liquids" (Activity 18), 15 minutes; "Experimenting With Air" (Activity 29), 15 minutes; "Material Objects Overview" (5 classrooms), 14 minutes.

Other films currently available are:

Interaction: "Making Cooper Chloride Solution" (Interaction Documentary). 11 minutes; "Interaction Overview" (4 classrooms), 11 minutes.
Relativity: "Relativity" (4 classrooms), 17 minutes.
Systems and Subsystems: "How Cold is Ice?", 10 minutes.
Position and Motion: "Flip Books," 12 minutes.
Organisms: "How Can We Find Out?", 9 minutes, Color.
Life Science Program: "Don't Tell Me, I'll Find Out" (representative activities from Organisms, Life Cycles and Populations), 22 minutes, Color.

Pre-Service and In-Service Films: Piaget developmental theory films by Robert Karplus and Celia B. Lavatelli. "Classification," 17 minutes; "Conservation," 28 minutes.

The units are sequential which means that activities are built upon knowledge acquired in previous lessons. The trial editions integrate the life science, the physical sciences, and quantitative comparisons, but the interrelationship becomes more obvious to the older students. This sequential aspect causes the development of materials to progress at a slow rate since refinement at each level is imperative for a strong program.

The trial editions currently available for purchase from the SCIS office are:

1. Environments
2. Communities
3. Energy Sources
4. Periodic Motion
5. Models for Electric and Magnetic Interaction
6. Ecosystems

The commercial editions available from Rand McNally are:

1. Material Objects
2. Organisms
3. Interaction and Systems
4. Life Cycles
5. Subsystems and Variables
6. Relativity
7. Populations
8. Position and Motion

Program Implementation

A description of the implementation process can be found in a recent SCIS Newsletter (Fall, 1969).

The SCIS implementation program is designed to train science educators starting SCIS projects in their communities. Each *one* or *two* week visit is tailored to the interests and needs of the participant. Classroom visits acquaint the participant with the concepts and materials of SCIS units. Informal discussions and meetings with members of the staff allow the visitor a close look at the evolving SCIS program. Prospective participants should write Jack Fishleder.(26)

Educators who are not able to attend an implementation program prior to initiating the use of SCIS materials can obtain the names of persons in their area who can assist them. A list of these persons can be obtained by contacting Jack Fishleder, Implementation Program Leader, at the SCIS office. The SCIS office keeps an up-to-date roster of:

1. Participants in a summer leadership workshop
2. Trial Center Coordinators
3. Implementation Program participants
4. Others having a special understanding of the program

With the initiation of this service, SCIS is working toward improving its implementation program.

As Rand McNally releases the final editions, the company is planning to introduce a number of services. For those who purchase these materials the size of the school system, number of children, and number of teachers involved will determine the type of workshop their resources can provide. The proposed workshops will most likely be of three types:

1. Regional Workshop for leadership training
2. Workshop for School System Adoptions
3. Sample Kit—An orientation, training kit to assist a school in making a decision to try SCIS and to orient teachers to the SCIS program and philosophy

The Educational Products Information Exchange Institute (EPIE) has an Information Unit which is a package of materials (i.e., filmstrips, tapes, program description booklets) that was developed as an aid to use in curriculum selection and teacher training. The SCIS program is one of the six presented in this unit.

Evaluation

In curricular development one of the essential integral components is evaluation. Since this is a time-consuming, expensive task requiring specialized personnel for test development, analysis, etc., it is often the most neglected part of a program. SCIS has attempted to circumvent this problem by establishing a strong task force to pursue evaluation. This is particularly vital for this project due to its sequential nature. It would be unrealistic to expect students to advance to a new level of learning if they had not achieved the learnings and outcomes of the previous unit. A program with a sequential structure requires a large amount of evaluation time since some of the evaluation aspects may not become apparent until a student has progressed an entire school year from one grade to another. At that time a weakness may become evident which would require the modification of certain experiences in the materials used during a previous year. This type of structure also implies that schools would best start this program in kindergarten or grade one adding one more level each year over a period of 5 to 6 years. Therefore, total K-6 evaluation for this project will take longer than programs that are adopted across the K-6 span in one year.

Although the SCIS program is still less than a decade old, the quality and quantity of the studies indicate that this aspect of development has not been neglected. The information gleaned from the various studies has been classified into two categories (1) descriptive feedback and (2) experimental.

Descriptive Feedback

This category includes studies where data have been collected through observation of and/or discussion with teachers, illustrative of what occurs in the classroom. In some instances the teacher is the observer and evaluator while at other times an outsider fulfills this role. A major function of these data has been to modify and improve existing materials.

Ness(10), Flory(10), Tresmontan(10), and Vivian(30) all collected data of these types and utilized the information either for revising instructional materials or increasing teacher sensitivity to pupils and their interaction with these materials. The first three investigators summarized their findings in an SCIS publication, *What Is Curriculum Evaluation?*

Ness(10) collected data from teachers who were using the unit *Organisms*. (Each coordinator sends a quarterly report from the SCIS Trial Centers to the headquarters office). A variety of information was accumulated ranging from suggestions for specific unit revisions to an attempt to discover if climatic differences (e.g., Hawaii, Michigan, New York) affected the behavior of organisms in the classroom. Resulting information was used for revision purposes and preparing of an Organisms Feedback booklet to help teachers acquire information concerning students' understanding of the material. Student responses were used by the classroom teachers as an aid in planning future lessons. Positive comments about this device, as well as student feedback, indicated a satisfactory level of concept understanding.

Ness discovered that teachers are an invaluable source of critical analysis of materials; and may have been a major resource in this project. By having them collect information for the project staff, they are able to help themselves too.

Flory(10) in an observational study of 28 classrooms discovered that a large percentage of the time was being spent at the discussion level which is in contradiction to the SCIS philosophy. The major outcome of the study seems to be that teachers need to have inservice training when working with a program of this type.

Tresmontan(10) conducted an exploratory study and SCIS in an attempt to determine the needs of teachers as well as pupils and identify ways that SCIS could provide beneficial services for them. The investigator conducted observational studies, bi-weekly sensitivity training sessions, and interviews. An attempt was made to change teacher attitudes and behaviors by helping them understand their roles in relation to the SCIS program. This study points up that content background is necessary, and it could best be provided by an inservice program in conjunction with the adopted program. Also it seems that once teachers accept the confidence of the people with whom they are working, they are open to talking and are very interested in the improvement of instruction. Thy accept and use constructive criticism when they are respected as knowledgeable persons.

A final study submitted by Vivian(30) describes a checklist evaluation scheme for SCIS materials. This checklist provides a vehicle for classroom teachers to focus their attention on some of the cognitive and affective behavioral outcomes of the SCIS program. Vivian's study again points out that teachers are very responsible persons, are an extremely valuable resource, and are far more perceptive than some people believe, provided they are involved in the planning and decision-making processes.

Experimental

In this area specifically constructed measurement devices are employed to determine whether the SCIS goals or objectives are being met; i.e., resultant learning outcomes. A definition of "desirable behavior" is determined prior to constructing or administering a test.

A series of doctoral dissertations by Bruce(3), Moon(20), Neuman(21), and Kondo(13) fit the research category. Bruce(3) taped a non-SCIS science lesson of 15 teachers prior to participation in a three-week SCIS workshop and all the participants (33 teachers) SCIS lessons on returning to their classrooms. An analysis of the tapes indicated that higher level questions, requiring more thinking, were asked after the workshop and the initiation of an SCIS program.

Moon(2) did a comparative study between 16 teachers who taught in a conventional program and 16 who were teaching an SCIS program after all completed a three-week SCIS workshop. The SCIS teachers used a greater number of higher level questions which was also supported by the Bruce(3) study.

An investigation by Kondo(13) focused on an analysis of the relationship between questioning behavior of the teacher and different types of SCIS lessons (i.e., *Invention and Discovery*) front four lessons found in the unit *Material Objects*. The results indicated that the way the lesson is approached (e.g., teacher demonstration, children handling materials), has a greater influence on the type of question the teacher asks than the type of lesson.

Neuman(21) attempted to measure intellectual growth of first-grade children utilizing the *Material Objects* unit. He found that the group of SCIS girls scored significantly higher on a post test. Various comparisons were made within the SCIS group as well as with first graders in a conventional program.

Besides these studies, Wilson(32), Rowe(24), Coldispoti(26), and Gilbert(26), have also researched in the area of questioning and verbal behavior. Wilson(32), using SCIS materials as a vehicle, discovered that the SCIS teachers used a significantly higher level of questioning than the non-SCIS teachers. His findings support those completed by the other researchers.

Rowe(10) describes a study conducted with eight SCIS and eight non-SCIS second graders. After they examined two different systems (i.e., aquarium and an SCIS whirlybird) through observations, the examiner disagreed with all statements made by these students. Six of the SCIS students argued their point of view but only one from the non-SCIS group even attempted a second experiment to support his argument.

In an inner-city school study Rowe(10) found that the children demonstrated a verbal deficiency that posed problems for the development of conceptual skills, (e.g., missing final sounds makes comparisons impossible, greater, larger, etc.) Her study showed that after sampling numbers of sentences spoken during SCIS science, language arts, and math that the most spontaneous language and the most subject relevant talk occurred in the SCIS science lessons; the science talk exceeded language arts by 200 per cent. No comparison was made with other types of science classes.

After reviewing the preceding studies the indications are that the SCIS approach to teaching science seems to have an effect on students' behavior, what they do, how open they are in discussing things, and the kind of responses they give. It appears the teachers become more flexible and make changes in their teaching behavior, (e.g., questioning).

Other aspects of teacher behavior have been investigated by researchers at the Far West Laboratory for Educational Research and Development in Berkeley, California(16), the Magnolia Elementary Schools in cooperation with Southern State College(6), Haan(16), and Fisch-ler(7). Each of these investigators has selected a different area for analysis, but all provide information in the area of teacher behavior.

The initial research conducted by the Far West Laboratory(16) was considered exploratory in nature. SCIS and non-SCIS first-grade teachers were observed using their own teaching styles. Those students whose teachers employed teaching styles that were in accord with the SCIS style descriptions demonstrated improved performance in a variety of SCIS tasks. Perhaps more consideration needs to be given to the induction as well as the maintenance of SCIS teachers.

When should in-service work occur? The Magnolia Elementary Schools in conjunction with Southern State College in Arkansas(6) conducted an NSF Cooperative College-School Science workshop which provided an initial three-week workshop as well as seminars and conferences throughout the year. When the teachers were provided with supportive assistance throughout the year; they emerge confident that they had done a good job and had positive feelings about their efforts. It appears that in-service work should not come in large segments, but initial introductions should be followed by continuous and regular contacts.

Fischler(7) at Nova University used SCIS materials as a vehicle for teacher preparation. It appears that inherent in SCIS is embodied a philosophy of teacher behavior which is useful in preparing teachers to be self-critical and self-analytical of their behavior. The SCIS lessons along with video-tape equipment facilitated this investigation.

Haan(16) has a belief that the SCIS program may have some effect on self-concepts and self-determination. She is doing research in this area. A study of children working with *Material Objects* unit lends support to this hypothesis.

Currently there are many studies in areas related to concept development, the SCIS program is no exception. Siegelman and Karplus(10), Thier(29), Allen(1), Stafford(28), and Raven(23) have all been exploring concept development with the SCIS materials although they have approached it from a variety of directions.

Siegelman and Karplus(10) utilized the information from their study to make revision decisions about the unit *Relativity*. Out of the five unit objectives it was found that only partial attainment was made in three. Data collected helped to initiate the necessary revisions.

Thier(29) investigated first graders' understanding of the concept matter using the Material Object unit. When a lack of understanding was identified as being significant, this portion was submitted to SCIS for revision; conversely, aspects that were effective were recommended for retention.

Allen(1) found that middle-class students do not develop any better classification skills as a result of working with the classification skills and activities in SCIS than they would as a result of their general experiencial background and; therefore, it may not be contributing to the total program.

Stafford's(28)research focused on the question of accelerating concept skills in the area of conservation. The experimental group showed greater growth[2] in each of the six areas tested (i.e., conservation of number, length, liquid amount, solid amount, weight, and area). Stafford is presently involved in an evaluation of the SCIS *Material Objects* unit at the kindergarten level.

Raven(23) used SCIS as a vehicle to investigate concept development. The purpose of the study was to determine the developmental sequence necessary for the understanding of momentum. The results supported Piaget's findings that children understand concepts about matter before they understand concepts about speed. SCIS supported this research in an attempt to assist them in determining sequencing of certain concepts because what may be logical sequencing for the discipline may be inconsistent with the psychological development of the learner.

In the book, *A New Look at Elementary School Science*(9) the authors indicate that additional research is continually being pursued. Karplus and Thier describe in detail two examples of evaluation studies as an illustration of the work that precedes publication of student materials. For example, the following information they obtained from their research caused revisions to be made:

1. SCIS student who have completed the unit *Relativity* have a greater understanding of relative motion than non-SCIS students.
2. There was little difference between groups on either configuration or the spatial perceptives test.
3. The *Solutions* unit helped to develop mastery of experimental techniques and an understanding of concentration.
4. Children need experience with the repeated use of measure, displacement, and deformation of objects in the *Variation and Measurement* unit.
5. In *Variation and Measurement* the lessons on diameter, perimeter, and area need to be clearer.

Studies of this nature are time-consuming for the curriculum staff, but the outcomes indicate revisions that lead to stronger more effective materials which are more apt to meet the intended objectives of the pro-

2. There is no indication that the control group dealt directly with these concepts.

gram. All of the work done in the area of evaluation should eventually be reflected in stronger programs.

Role of the Teacher

The units are structured in such a way that children are to have (1) first-hand experiences, (2) a laboratory setting, and (3) be able to explore natural phenomena in small groups or individually, depending upon the activity. The developers believe that the teacher should provide substantial guidance and help with discussion. Thus, the development of erroneous ideas is circumvented. The teacher should then provide opportunities for children to extend their learnings by applying those concepts with which they were working in a new context. The materials are structured in such a way that the teacher is provided with equipment and suggestions for the extension of these concepts. It is imperative with a program such as SCIS that the teachers assume a role of guide instead of the more conventional information giver. This aspect of teacher behavior becomes of prime importance if the program is to be successful.

Summary

The SCIS project's staff is attempting to produce materials that *are effective* in meeting the objectives of elementary science education. These outcomes have been identified by Hurd and Gallagher:

1. An understanding of science principles.
2. Skills for acquiring knowledge.
3. Favorable attitudes toward science.

In making SCIS program selection decisions, it is important to see if the instructional package effectively helps students obtain these outcomes. The SCIS program is time consuming since it takes more time than elementary school teachers have traditionally spent on science, but it is a different kind of experience where the teacher is a guide and the children pursue their learnings. Also, this program is more expensive than simply purchasing a single text for each child since kits of equipment accompany the materials.[3] This aspect does save teacher preparation time as well as insure that the appropriate materials are available for each lesson.

3. The David Butts article. *The Price of Change* (5) published in *Science and Children* is helpful when considering current costs of programs. (The reader should note that there may be some fluctuation in prices since this article was prepared.)

Selection decisions need to be made on the basis of compatibility with local plans keeping in mind whether or not it will be effective for local needs. This review has oriented the reader to the SCIS program and has provided a review of the literature and research currently available. Although this program is of recent origin there is substantial information available, which, along with the objectives for elementary science education should provide a basis for wise decision making.

Addresses

Science Curriculum Improvement Study
Lawrence Hall of Science
University of California
Berkeley, California 94720

School Department
Rand McNally and Company
P. O. Box 7600
Chicago, Illinois 69680

Educational Products Information Exchange Institute
386 Park Avenue South
New York, New York 10016

REFERENCES

1. Allen, Leslie Robert. "An Examination of the Classificatory Ability of Children Who Have Been Exposed to One of the New Elementary Science Programs." (Unpublished doctoral dissertation, University of California). 1967.
2. Bloom, Benjamin S. et al. *Taxonomy of Educational Objectives*. New York: David McKay Company. 1967.
3. Bruce, Larry R. "A Determination of the Relationships Among SCIS Teachers' Personality Traits, Attitude Toward Teacher-Pupil Relationship Understanding of Science Process Skills and Question Types." (M)*, 1969.
4. Bruner, Jerome S. *Toward A Theory of Instruction*. New York: W. W. Norton and Company, 1968.
5. Butts, David. "The Price of Change." *Science and Children*, April 1969.
6. Final Report on SCIS Activities for the 1968-69 School Year at the Magnolia Public Schools. Magnolia, Arkansas. 1969.
7. Fischler, Abraham S. "Change in Classroom Behavior Resulting from an in-Service Program Utilizing Television." *School Science and Mathematics*. April 1967.
8. Hunt, J. McK. *Intelligence and Experience*. New York: Ronald Press, 1961.
9. Karplus, Robert, and Thier, Herbert D. *A New Look at Elementary School Science*. Chicago, Illinois: Rand McNally and Company, 1967.
10. Karplus, Robert. What is Curriculum Evaluation? Science Curriculum Improvement Study, Berkeley, California, 1968.
11. Karplus, Robert, Powell, Cynthia Ann, and Thier, Herbert D. "A Concept of Matter for the First Grade." *Journal of Research in Science Teaching*. December 1963.

*(M) denotes University Microfilm, Ann Arbor, Michigan.

12. Karplus, Robert, and Thier, Herbert D. "Science Teaching is Becoming Literate." *Education Age*. January/February 1966.
13. Kondo, Allan K. "The Questioning Behavior of Teachers in the Science Curriculum Improvement Study Teaching." Paper presented at the NARST Meeting, Pasadena, California. February 1969.
14. Kusian, Louis I., and Stone, A. Harris. *Readings on Teaching Children Science.* Belmont, California: Wadsworth Publishing Company, Inc., 1969.
15. Kusian, Louis L., and Stone, A. Harris. *Teaching Children Science: An Inquiry Approach.* Belmont, California: Wadsworth Publishing Company, Inc., 1968.
16. Haan, Norma. *An Exploratory Investigation of the Effect of an Initial Experience With SCIS's Material Objects Unit on First-Grade Children and Their Teachers.* Far West Laboratory for Educational Research and Development, Berkeley, California. 1968.
17. Hurd, Paul DeHart, and Gallagher, James Joseph. *New Directions in Elementary Science Teaching,* Belmont California: Wadsworth Publishing Company, Inc., 1968.
18. Lerner, Marjorie, and Victor, Edward. *Readings in Science Education for the Elementary School.* New York, New York: Macmillan Company, 1967.
19. Lockhard, J. David (Ed). Sixth Report of the International Clearinghouse on Science and Mathematics Curricular Developments. College Park, Maryland: University of Maryland and AAAS. 1968.
20. Moon, Thomas Charles. "A Study of Verbal Behavior Patterns in Primary Grade Classrooms During Science Activities." (Unpublished doctoral dissertation, Michigan State University) 1969.
21. Neuman, Donald B. "The Influence of Selected Science Experiences on the Attainment of Concrete Operations by First Grade Children." Paper read before 42nd meeting of the National Association for Research in Science Teaching, Pasadena, California. February 1969.
22. Piaget, Jean. "Development and Learning." *Journal of Research in Science Teaching.* September 1964.
23. Raven, Ronald J. "The Development of the Concept of Momentum in Primary School Children." *Journal of Research in Science Teaching,* Vol. 5; 1967.
24. Rowe, Mary Budd. "Science, Silence, and Sanctions." *Science and Children.* March 1969.
25. Sanders, Morris M. *Classroom Questions.* New York: Harper and Row, 1966.
26. Science Curriculum Improvement Study, Newsletter, Nos. 1-18. Science Curriculum Improvement Study, Lawrence Hall of Science, Berkeley, California: University of California.
27. Showalter, Victor. "Unified Science, An Alternative to Tradition." *The Science Teacher,* February 1954.
28. Stafford, Don. "The Influence of the Science Curriculum Improvement Study First-Grade Program on the Attainment of the Conservations." (Unpublished dissertation abstract) 1969.
29. Thier, Herbert D. "A Look at a First Grader's Understanding of Matter." *Journal of Research in Science Teaching.* March 1965.
30. Vivian, V. Eugene. "An Evaluation Scheme for Elementary Science." Glassboro State College. Paper read before the National Science Teachers Association, Dallas, Texas. 1969.
31. Voelker, Alan and Rogers, Robert. "Programs for Improving Science Instruction." *Science and Children.* January/February 1970.
32. Wilson, John H. "Differences Between Inquiry-Discovery and the Traditional Approaches to Teaching Science in the Elementary Schools." (Unpublished doctoral dissertation, University of Oklahoma) 1968.

1. Describe what you think the classroom conditions might be in a SCIS oriented program. This might include teacher behaviors, student behaviors, etc.
2. After reading the descriptions of both ESS and SCIS, can you compare the goals of each?

30 JOHN R. MAYOR AND ARTHUR H. LIVERMORE

A Process Approach to Elementary School Science

The first major *elementary science curriculum project was developed by a special commission within the American Association for the Advancement of Science. It was a great departure from the regular textbook program for three main reasons:*

1. *Textbooks were eliminated.*
2. *Science processes replaced the normal emphasis on content.*
3. *Manipulative materials were a central part of the curriculum.*

Science processes were identified by these scientists, science educators, etc., who worked in various developmental phases of the project. Behavioral objectives are very much a part of Science: A Process Approach (S-APA). The program is hierarchical in nature, with all children proceeding in a step-by-step fashion through each exercise in any grade level. Just as the previous two papers do not really communicate the real nature of what would happen in the classroom, this description also falls short. It should help, however, if you recall what Shulman said of Robert Gagné's position in a previous paper, because Gagné exerted a strong influence on the structuring of the hierarchy and the evaluation system of S-APA.

Development of the Program

In the spring months of 1961, the American Association for the Advancement of Science sponsored conferences in Berkeley, St. Louis, and Washington to explore the feasibility of course content development projects in elementary and junior high school science. The conferences emphasized the urgency for new programs in science for elementary and junior high schools and the desirability of foundation support of developmental projects in several centers. The conferences proposed the establishment of a national commission to encourage and

Reprinted from *School Science and Mathematics*, Vol. 69, No. 5, 1969, pp. 411-416, by permission of the editor. Dr.'s Mayor and Livermore are with the American Association for the Advancement of Science.

support these projects and recommended that the commission and course content development staffs be representative of scientists, and school administrators and teachers.

In response to the feasibility study recommendations, AAAS appointed a Commission on Science Education in the spring of 1962. In order to seek advice from a broad spectrum of scientists and school people, the Commission sponsored two conferences in the summer of 1962. From these conferences came recommendations which have determined the Commission's program during the past six years. The principal recommendation was for the development of an experimental program in elementary school science (grades K-6), which has come to be known as *Science—A Process Approach.*

Science—A Process Approach has been developed by five summer writing teams of scientists and teachers working for six-to eight-week periods beginning in the summer of 1963. It consists of texts for teachers and kits of teaching aids for use by the children. Over 100 scientists and teachers from 30 states have contributed during one or more of the sessions. Following each summer of writing, the program has been taught in 11 or more tryout centers, representative of school systems throughout the country. After the first summer, the materials were revised in subsequent summer writing sessions as recommended by the tryout teachers and as suggested by results on regularly administered tests provided for each exercise. These tests, called competency measures, have been an integral part of the program from the beginning and now are available for general use along with the printed teacher text materials and kits of teaching aids.

The summer writing teams have also produced a *Commentary for Teachers,* published in a third experimental edition in May 1968, a *Guide for Inservice Instruction,* and several films to be used with the Guide.

The Processes

Two basic premises have served as guides in the development of *Science—A Process Approach.*

The first premise is that a scientist's behaviors in pursuing science constitute a complex set of skills and intellectual activities that can be analyzed into simpler skills and activities. The second premise is that these skills and intellectual activities can be learned, and that it is possible to begin the instruction in the early grades.

The processes in which skills are developed in grades K-3 (Parts A-D) are:

Observing	Using Numbers
Measuring	Using Space/Time Relationships
Classifying	Inferring
Communicating	Predicting

These are the basic processes.

Most of the exercises for grades 4-6 (Parts E, 6 and 7) develop skills in the following integrated processes:

Formulating Hypotheses
Defining Operationally
Controlling Variables
Interpreting Data
Experimenting

There are between 20 and 25 exercises in each Part (grade level), and each exercise emphasizes the development of skills in a particular process. Skills developed in one exercise are basic to the next exercise in sequence in a particular process. For example, the first exercise in Observing develops the child's ability to identify and name six basic colors. The second exercise in Observing, *Observing Color, Shape, Texture and Size,* gives the child an opportunity to use his skills in identifying and naming colors. This exercise also requires the child to use skills in identifying and naming common two-dimensional shapes. He developed those skills in an earlier exercise on the process of *Using Space/Time Relationships.*

An exercise in Part Seven, *Experimenting 7, Density,* provides an example of dependence on skills developed in prior exercises. Before a pupil can perform successfully in the activities of this exercise he must be able to do the following:

1. Measure the mass of an object on an equal arm balance using metric units.
2. Determine the volume of an object by measuring the volume of water it displaces.
3. Plot data on a graph.
4. Construct a best fit straight line through points on a graph.
5. Construct an operational definition.
6. Construct and demonstrate a test of a hypothesis.

Skills in measuring mass and volume and in graphing were developed in a series of exercises which started in first grade. Four exercises on *Formulating Hypotheses* and six on *Defining Operationally* in Parts Five and Six have produced in the pupils two of the skills they will need to use in the exercise on *Density.*

Science Content

Science—A Process Approach is like a fabric in which process is the warp and content is the woof. A particular process skill can be developed using content from different fields. Skill in observing and describing change, for example, can be developed equally well with an expanding balloon, a melting ice cube, or a moving animal. It is to give children experience in content from different areas of science rather than because certain topics are considered important for children to "know about," that the science content of the program is drawn from the physical and biological sciences, earth science and behavioral science.

The titles of a few exercises in each Part are listed in Table 1. These titles illustrate the variety of science content in the program.

Evaluation

In the earliest planning for *Science—A Process Approach* beginning with the 1962 summer conferences it was decided that objectives of the program should be stated in terms of performances of children. Tests for determining if the children achieve the objectives were prepared from the beginning along with the writing of each exercise and used in the development of the program. In the commercial editions these tests, that have undergone several years of tryout and subsequent revision, are an important part of the *Science—A Process Approach* sequence. It seems fair to claim that in no other curriculum for any other subject or level, has evaluation played such an important role from the beginning of the developmental work.

Science—A Process Approach is organized into seven Parts, for kindergarten through grade 6, each Part containing 20 or more exercises. For each exercise objectives state what the child should be able to do after completing the exercise. In the primary grades, each exercise includes an appraisal activity which the teacher uses to see how well her class has progressed in achieving the exercise objectives, and an individual competency measure to assist the teacher in determining just what an individual child is able to do.

Both a competency measure to be administered to individual children and a competency measure to be given as a group test are prepared for each exercise in Parts E and Six, usually taught in grades 4 and 5. There are no appraisal activities in these Parts. The terminal Part of the program, Seven, consists almost exclusively of exercises on the process of experimenting. Four exercises in experimenting constitute the measures of achievement in this Part.

Table 1.
Some Exercises from Science—A Process Approach Selected to Show
the Variety of Science Content.

Part	Process	Title of Exercise
A*	Observing	Observing Temperature
	Observing	Observing Solids Changing to Liquids
	Classifying	Classifying Animals
B*	Observing	Observing the Weather
	Observing	Observing Some Properties of Magnets
	Observing	Observing Color and Color Change in Plants
	Observing	Observing Mold Gardens
C*	Measuring	Measuring Forces with Springs
	Classifying	The Solid, Liquid and Gaseous States of Matter
	Communicating	Using a Sundial to Describe Shadow Changes
	Observing	Observing Animal Responses to Stimuli
	Predicting	Surveying Opinion
D*	Predicting	Describing the Motion of a Bouncing Ball
	Measuring	Measuring Rate of Evaporation of Water
	Inferring	Loss of Water from Plants
	Measuring	Describing and Representing Forces
E*	Controlling Variables	Liquid Movement in Materials
	Interpreting Data	Guinea Pig Learning in a Maze
	Inferring	Inferring Connection Patterns in Electric Circuits
	Classifying	Classifying Minerals
	Communicating	Force and Motion
6	Defining Operationally	Determining the Direction of True North
	Controlling Variables	Effect of Practice on Memorization
	Interpreting Data	Effect of Temperature on Reaction Time
	Controlling Variables	Human Reaction Time
	Interpreting Data	Moon Photos
7	Experimenting	Temperature and Heat
	Experimenting	The Growth of a Root
	Experimenting	Variation in Perceptual Judgments: Optical Illusions
	Experimenting	Semipermeable Membranes
	Expermenting	Plants and Light of Different Colors
	Experimenting	Communication Among Ants

* Commercial Edition.

The statement of objectives in performance or behavioral terms,
serves another purpose, equally important with that of evaluation. Each
exercise is designated by one of the eight basic processes or one of the

five integrated processes. The collection of all of the objectives of exercises comprise the definition of the process of Observing in this science program. Similarly the collection of exercises designated by any of the other processes comprises the definition of that process in the program.

The objectives of the Observing exercises are arranged into a hierarchy of competencies in Observing. A small part of the Observing hierarchy is shown in Figure 1.

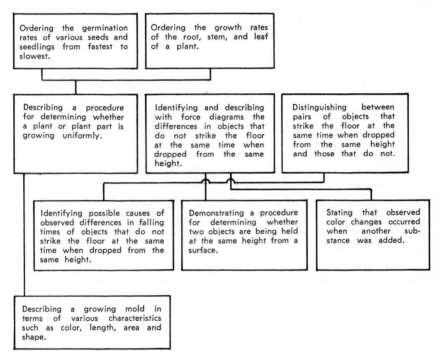

FIGURE 1

The ordering implies that the acquisition of a given skill depends upon the previous acquisition of skills at a level below it in the hierarchy. Thus the hierarchy determines the order of teaching the Observing exercises. For the eight basic processes, seven hierarchies have been determined—the process of Communicating and Predicting are combined into a single hierarchy. A composite chart, showing these seven hierarchies, has been prepared using a color coding scheme of great value to the teacher in determining the prerequisites for each exercise, in identifying future exercises for which a given exercise is a prerequisite, and in graphically showing relationships and interdependencies among the several hundred process skills.

Associated with each process hierarchy is a test covering all skills in the hierarchy. These tests, seven in all for the basic processes, are contained in a single test booklet, called the *Science Process Instrument,* to be published in 1969. The tests can be administered at any time during a school year so that a profile of a child's competencies in the processes of science may be constructed. If a teacher chooses, the tests can be administered again a year later as a measure of the child's growth.

In summary, tests of children's achievement of the objectives of instruction in *Science—A Process Approach* are provided for immediate assessment of accomplishment in each exercise (competency measures) and for long-term assessment (*Science Process Instrument*). Furthermore, the ordering of the objectives in hierarchies for each process determines the sequence of the program. The hierarchies provide for easy identification of prerequisite skills and of what is yet to come.

Summary

Science—A Process Approach is an interdisciplinary science program for elementary schools in which the primary purpose is the development of skills in the processes of science. The program is sequential. The order of exercises and activities is determined by hierarchies of process skills. The skills are stated as behavioral objectives. They describe what the child can be expected to do after he has carried out the activities of the program. Probably in no course of study for any level of instruction or any subject matter have behavioral objectives been so specifically and so comprehensively stated.

The program includes exercises from the biological, physical, and social sciences and exercises in mathematics when a skill in using numbers, such as in graphing, decimals, or probability, is needed in a science investigation before the skill is likely to have been included in a school's mathematics program. The emphasis on behavioral objectives, sequencing in terms of complexity of behaviors, interdisciplinary considerations and evaluation provide a model of curriculum development that may have wide application.

---

1. Of the three programs, ESS, SCIS, and S-APA, which do you think might provide the greatest opportunity for the child to structure ideas for himself?
2. Of the three programs, which one most emphasizes evaluation?

PART FOUR

Evaluation–Objectives

In his recent book, *Crisis In The Classroom,* Silberman refers to "mindless" education in this country as a kind of "nonthinking" behavior that leads to curricula that are inappropriate for children. Another critic of our schools, John Holt, is even more emphatic (and emotional) in *How Children Fail* about the irrelevant damaging aspects of most classrooms. What are the purposes of elementary school education and how can we decide whether or not the goals are being achieved? Specifically, what is the place of *science* in this whole scheme of things and how should educators determine the "success" of the science program?

Decision-making should be based upon the best available evidence. Evidence regarding how children think for example should be incorporated into the decision-making processes involved with curriculum and instruction. Most important, we should be consistent with what we say the science program will do and the instructional strategies used to accomplish such goals and objectives. If one goal is to "encourage independent thinking" and the strategy used involves the teacher telling children what to do and how to do it seventy-five percent of the time, either the goal or the strategy needs to be changed. As another example of goal-strategy consistency, if the goal in science involves helping "concrete operational children" understand the properties of objects or events and the method is talking about the same, seventy-five percent of the time, then a change is required.

Evaluation methods in education can be used to evaluate programs and teaching strategies as well as children. The choice of evaluation methods should also be such that the system of evaluation is compatible with objectives and strategies. If it is somewhere stated that individual differences, in terms of how children think, will be taken into account and then all children are "graded" relative to a single scale of some sort, there is an inconsistency in the overall strategy.

Internal consistency within the various systems of the educational process is highly desirable and decisions should be based on the best available evidence. The papers in this section deal with various aspects of objectives in science programs and evaluation methods that can be used to assess their effectiveness.

31

CHARLES C. MATTHEWS

Classroom Conditions, Instructional Objectives, and Evaluation in Elementary School Science

This paper by Dr. Matthews emphasizes the interrelatedness of goals, classroom conditions and evaluation methods in elementary school science. Various studies are referred to in this paper that provide some information about various classroom conditions, particularly the effects of teacher behaviors on student behaviors. The fact that teaching patterns have a corresponding effect on student classroom behaviors has been well-established by scores of studies.

Behavioral objectives are mentioned in terms of the curriculum developer and the teacher. What are the effects of communicating specific behavioral objectives to children in a science curriculum? These and other questions regarding objectives, etc. can be answered in general by reading, in more detail, the studies that are referred to in this paper.

If one accepts a definition for science which involves Bridgman's "doing one's damnedest with one's mind, no holds barred"(1) or Feynman's notion that in science the individual "suffers no inhibitions of precedent or authority, but is completely free to adopt any course that his ingenuity is capable of suggesting to him"(2), then one can make some rational decisions regarding the classroom conditions, instructional objectives, and evaluation procedures in elementary school science. If one accepts Piaget's statement that "physical experience consists of acting upon objects and drawing some knowledge about the objects by abstraction from the objects,"(15) then certain biases are established that influence decisions regarding classroom conditions, instructional objectives, and evaluation procedures in elementary school science.

Prior to this rational decision-making, one must identify some goals related generally to elementary school programs and specifically to the elementary school science program.

This paper was presented at a symposium on elementary science at the forty-third annual meeting of the National Association for Research in Science Teaching, 1970 and is published with the author's permission. Dr. Matthews is Associate Professor of *Science* Education at Florida State University.

Most professionals associated with elementary education accept the following goals statement:

"Learning how to learn" is of major importance to the elementary school child and can be facilitated by school experience. Self-actualized learning is a major goal of education.

The following general goals for elementary school science relate rationally to this broad goal, to the previous "definition" of science, and to the child's cognitive characteristics:

1. A major goal of science in the elementary school curriculum is the enhancement of the thinking of children. Developing the ability to think systematically and creatively is more basic to "learning how to learn" than the traditional skills of "reading, writing, and arithmetic."
2. A second important goal of science in the elementary school curriculum is the facilitation of the child's positive self-concept with regard to independent learning.
3. An elementary school science program must facilitate maximum cognitive progress of individuals; this involves a self-determined pace from manipulation of concrete objects to manipulation of symbols and other abstract ideas and to the concommitant higher mental processes of problem solving.
4. An elementary school science program must facilitate *individual* development of interests, attitudes, personality and creativity which enhance the continued development of individuality in the learner.
5. An elementary school science program should encourage a child's tendency to accept the existence of individuals who have ideas and values which are different from his own.

If we begin with acceptance of these goals as worthy goals and assume that it is possible to achieve these goals, then perhaps some rational statements regarding classroom conditions, instructional objectives, and evaluation procedures can be derived.

Classroom Conditions

Let's begin with "classroom conditions." If we accept the foregoing general goal statement for elementary education and the slightly more specific goal statements of elementary school science education, then what can be decided for "classroom conditions"?

Although no conclusive research data is available to specify precise conditions under which learning is maximized, we are not left without strong indications of the sets of conditions which are associated with different outcomes of education. Probably the largest "body" of research relating to classroom conditions is that research commonly referred to as "classroom interaction analysis" or "systematic classroom observation." This field of research has been extremely valuable because it has operationally defined "teaching" and "learning" as different activities. It has attempted with considerable success to empirically associate certain "teaching behaviors" with certain "learning behaviors," or "outcomes of education." Various researchers have been impressively successful in identifying these "associations," or relationships.

B. O. Smith's early work with "closed episode" versus "open episode" teaching, for example, leads to the following conclusion:

> It is not difficult to see that episodes of the closed type lend themselves very easily to programmed instruction such as that used in so-called teaching machines where the situations are so structured as to reduce the chance of incorrect responses. In sharp contrast, episodes of the more open forms lend themselves to manipulation by those teachers who wish to encourage originality and flexibility in their students. It seems reasonable to suppose that the openness of episodes tends, in the various sciences, to encourage creativity and, in those fields with social concerns, to stimulate the growth of wisdom. (16)

If rationality is as Rogers(2) defines it, "the use of the most effective means to reach a given end," then the science program will employ "open episodes," which "encourage a great variety of responses,"(16) as opposed to the "closed episodes," which involve only one correct response.

The earliest systematic studies of "classroom climate" are those of Anderson and his colleagues (3, 4, 5, 6). These studies of preschool and elementary school classrooms involved different teachers and extended over several years; they revealed that the teacher's behavior set a pattern which spread throughout the classroom—influencing the behaviors of children even when the teacher was not present. These student behaviors even persisted into the following school year. If the teacher dominated, the students adopted dominating behaviors; if the teacher was integrative, so were the children. Anderson's studies also revealed that initiative, spontaneity, and problem-solving were enhanced by integrative teacher behavior. The students of dominative teachers were more easily distracted from schoolwork and showed greater compliance to, as well as rejection of, teacher domination.

A rational decision is to establish and maintain integrative teacher behaviors, or those behaviors which increase the alternatives of children —behaviors which do not command children. These conclusions were supported in the independent investigations of Lippitt and White(8).

Flanders(9) found that dominative teacher behaviors were consistently disliked by pupils, reduced their ability to recall, and produced disruptive anxiety revealed in galvanic skin response and changes in heart beat rate. Perkins(10) found that greater learning took place if the teacher used integrative techniques; Cogan's work(11) even revealed that students did more assigned and extra schoolwork when they perceived their teacher's behavior as integrative.

Lewin has found that "objectivity cannot arise in a constraint situation; it arises only in a situation of freedom." (12) *Constraint teacher behaviors produced a high level of dependency of students on their teachers.*

This powerful work of Anderson has been pursued by many "followers" into the current research of Withall, Joyce, Flanders, and many others who followed the Flander's "model." The 1968 "Anthology of Classroom Observation Instruments," repeats and emphasizes the composite findings of the last thirty years of research on classroom teacher behaviors:

> Teachers who behave in an integrative (supportive) fashion tend to have students who behave integratively, and conversely, dominative teachers have students who are dominative, aggressive, and non-sharing. (13)

"Goal clarity" was introduced by Flanders(14). His research suggests that dependency does not increase in students if the instructional goals are clear to them—even when the teacher exerts "direct influence" over the activities of students. However, *if the goals are not clear to students, a high level of dependency develops when teachers were "directive."*

Instructional Objectives

Some comments on "instructional objectives" seem to be in order. The extent to which the instructional objectives are clear to the learner would influence our decision with regard to the teachers' directiveness. If we derive some statements of objectives from the previously-stated general goals of elementary school science, they could sound something like this:

A beginning science program should have objectives associated with both affective and cognitive learning. The cognitive objectives should be associated with the goal of communicating to children what science is and how creative and systematic thinking relates to solving self-perceived problems. *The child who completes a K-6 science program should be able to design activities (without suggestions) and do activities (without instructions) in which he: (1) manipulates objects in a way that is dependent upon the properties of the objects, (2) identifies rela-*

tionships among the properties of "static objects" or among the factors which affect the behaviors of "dynamic systems," and (3) manipulates objects to test the usefulness of the relationships which he has identified.

The affective objectives should be associated with the development of a positive self-concept with regard to independent learning. *The child who completes a K-6 science program should identify himself as a person who can be successful in science and who chooses to use science. He should describe science in terms of activities which make sense to him. He should state his own explanations for natural phenomena and should modify these only when they cease to be compatible with his own interpretations of his environment. He will frequently state alternative explanations for an observed phenomenon and will identify "tentativeness" as an important characteristic of scientific knowledge.*

These objectives can be broken into numerous specific objectives associated with specific behaviors of the learner. If we take a rational or even an empirical approach to the analysis of the objectives given above, it is quite likely that the activity would yield objectives which sound something like:

1. The child will be able to classify objects into two groups by color.
2. The child will be able to measure the length of a table (or some other object).

What, then, does the teacher do in order to achieve these objectives? What classroom conditions facilitate the most efficient accomplishment of these objectives? It is at this point that a critical error is often made because the teacher or the curriculum developer loses sight of the general goals. The decision is often to tell and/or show the child how to exhibit the desired behavior—or to exert some other rather "direct influence" over the activities of the students.

"Direct teaching practices" have undesirable effects on the learner —*since the goals of an elementary school science program cannot possibly be clear to the students.* A student who does not have a concept of classification cannot possibly understand a goal which involves developing a concept of classification. A student who does not understand iteration cannot possibly have an understanding of a goal which involves measurement of length with a rule. Therefore, it seems uncompromisingly clear that classroom conditions must involve freedom of the student to choose and direct his own activities. The teacher must not tell or show the student how to do the activity—nor even tell him which activity to do. This imposes severe, but challenging, limitations on the materials which may be designed for children. The child must have a spontaneous affinity for the materials! The science concept and process objectives must be communicated to the child via his own interpretations of and actions on the sets of objects which are available to him.

Since different children will have affinities for different materials and will have different cognitive levels, there must be a variety of objects available and there must be a variety of "activity opportunities" with each. I am not suggesting that behavioral objectives should not be stated but I am suggesting that this practice has frequently resulted in "direct teaching" of behaviors and the resultant increase in dependency of the child—not to mention many other disadvantages of a rigid set of specific expectations of children.

Behavioral objectives are clearly useful for the curriculum developer. The teacher has often been intimidated and frustrated by her misunderstanding of how the behavioral objectives relate to her role in the classroom.

Evaluation

Time and space limitations do not permit a thorough discussion of the evils and values of evaluation in elementary school science. Of course, evaluation is necessary to the curriculum developer. Evaluation of his program—not of his subjects—is an integral part of his research and development activities.

The evaluation of a child's achievement in elementary school science cannot be rationally justified. What is the standard to which he will be compared? Should he be compared to his local peer group? Should he learn that he cannot achieve in science—simply because he's a few months behind his neighbor in cognitive development? The only rational recommendation that can be given to teachers is: Do not evaluate (and certainly do not "grade") children in elementary school science.

REFERENCES

1. Bridgman, P. W., "Prospects for Intelligence," *Yale Review*, 34 (1945): 450.
2. Feynman, Richard P., "What is Science," A paper presented to the 1966 Annual Convention of the National Science Teachers Association.
3. Rogers, Everette M., *Diffusion of Innovations*. New York: The Free Press, 1962.
4. Anderson, Harold H., "The Measurement of Dominative and of Socially Integrative Behavior in Teachers' Contacts with Children," *Child Development*, Vol. 10, No. 2, June, 1939.
5. Anderson, Harold H. and Brewer, Helen M., *Studies of Teachers' Classroom Personality, I: Dominative and Socially Integrative Behavior of Kindergarten Teachers.* Applied Psychology Monographs, No. 6, 1945.
6. Anderson, Harold H. and Brewer, Joseph E., *Studies of Classroom Personalities, II: Effects of Teachers' Dominative and Integrative Contacts on Children's Classroom Behavior.* Applied Psychology Monographs, No. 8, 1946.
7. Anderson, Harold H., Brewer, Joseph E., and Reed, Mary Frances, *Studies of Teachers' Classroom Personalities, III: Follow Up Studies of the Effect of Domi-*

native and Integrative Contacts on Children's Behavior. Applied Psychology Monographs No. 11, 1946.

8. Lippitt, R. and White, R. K., "The Social Climate of Children's Groups," *Child Behavior and Development.* Edited by R. G. Barker, J. S. Kounin, and H. F. Wright, New York: McGraw Hill, 1943.

9. Flanders, Ned A., "Personal-Social Anxieties as a Factor in Experimental Learning Situations," *Journal of Educational Research,* Vol. 45, October, 1951.

10. Perkins, H. V., "Climate Influences Group Learning," *Journal of Educational Research,* Vol. 45, October: 1951.

11. Cogan, M. L., "Theory and Design of a Study of Teacher-Pupil Interaction," *Harvard Educational Review,* Vol. 26, No. 4, Fall: 1956.

12. Lewin, Kurt, *Dynamic Theory of Personality,* New York: McGraw Hill, 1935.

13. *Mirrors for Behavior, An Anthology of Classroom Observation Instruments* (Edited by Anita Simon and E. Gil Boyer) *Classroom Interaction Newsletter.* Research for Better Schools, Inc., Philadelphia, Vol. 3, No. 2: 1968.

14. Flanders, Ned A., "Teacher Influence in the Classroom." Paper Presented at the First Teachers College Conference on Research and Theory in Teaching, April 13-14: 1962.

15. Piaget, Jean, "Development and Learning," Part I of "Cognitive Development in Children," *Journal of Research in Science Teaching,* Vol. 2, No. 3, 1964.

16. Smith, B. O., "Toward a Theory of Teaching," *Theory and Research in Teaching,* edited by Arno A. Billack, New York: Bureau of Publications, Teachers College, Columbia University, 1963.

---

1. Can you analyze the five general goals stated near the beginning of the paper in terms of the nature of science and the nature of children?

2. How should behavioral objectives be used by teachers and how might such usage affect the science program?

3. What conclusions regarding teacher behaviors can be drawn from this paper?

32 RONALD D. ANDERSON

Formulating Objectives for Elementary Science

Stating educational objectives in terms of behavioral or performance criteria has become increasingly popular in recent years. The first of two papers by Anderson is devoted to the strategies involved in writing objectives for elementary science. Bloom's Taxonomy of Educational Objectives *was used by the author to establish the various domains of human development, with an emphasis on the cognitive domain. The six learning levels of knowledge, comprehension, application, analysis, synthesis, and evaluation are explained and used as a basis for considering behavioral objectives in elementary school science.*

The Key to Good Evaluation

The objectives of an instructional program and the program's evaluation are intimately related. Without well-stated objectives there is no basis for making any judgment as to whether or not the program has achieved the desired goals (objectives). Before examining evaluation practices and procedures, it is first necessary for us, as teachers, to be sure we have a set of objectives which is an adequate basis for our evaluation. In this first of a series of two articles on evaluation, attention will be centered on the formulation of such objectives.

Stated objectives for elementary school science, as well as other parts of the curriculum, are found in abundance in textbooks, curriculum guides, and courses of study. In most cases, however, they are so general and vague that they are of little help to the classroom teacher either in determining what he will do in teaching science to his children at 10:25 A.M. Tuesday, or in evaluating the success of his efforts. For example, a frequently identified objective in science is that children should develop problem-solving skills. Although it is agreed that this is a worthwhile and important objective of science instruction, it is so

Reprinted from *Science and Children*, Vol. 5, No. 1, 1967, pp. 20-23 by permission of the editor. Dr. Anderson is Assistant Professor of Science Education at the University of Colorado at Boulder.

general and vague that it is of little worth to a teacher in determining specifically what he will do with the children. Also this vagueness makes it almost impossible to determine at the end of a unit whether or not the objective has been achieved. In sharp contrast to the above-mentioned objective is this specific one concerning observation and classification: Each child will be able to separate a group of twelve different leaves into four groups according to their size and shape.

At this point some readers are probably asking, "Why be so specific?" The answer is simple. Unless an objective is stated precisely, it is not clear what steps should be taken to achieve the objective. Some teachers teach science only because it is part of the school program or because it has always been taught in their school. They have not stopped to consider carefully *why* science is taught. Whereas, the reasons why science is part of the curriculum determine what aspects of science will be emphasized, what approach will be used, and what objectives will be realized. Without clearly defined reasons, which in turn determine the objectives, teachers have no basis for deciding the questions of "what aspects" and "how." A broad objective such as "to develop problem solving ability" may be a good starting point but it must be broken down into a more detailed description before decisions are made about "what aspects" and "how" for classroom use. In the grouping of leaves activity, the broad objective has not been rejected, only stated in much greater detail, i.e., classifying objects is part of solving some problems.

Basically, science is included in the curriculum because it is such a large and influential part of our culture. Of course, science is much more than a body of knowledge about the material universe. To understand science the process of science (the means of investigation by which the body of knowledge is acquired) as well as the products of science (the body of knowledge that results from the investigations). Since a basic objective is for children to understand science, our specific objectives for each unit or day should reflect this basic and far-reaching objective. The precise objectives that are formulated for each class period should reflect the fact that a basic and overriding objective is that children will acquire an understanding of both the products and processes of the scientific enterprise.

Make Provision for All Objectives

A basic consideration in preparing objectives is that provision must be made for instruction in and evaluation of all the important desired outcomes of science instruction. The stated objectives which serve as the basis for instruction and evaluation should reflect all of the desired outcomes. A brief look at a classification of educational objectives might be useful in determining if the objectives are limited and unimaginative. Such a classification is Bloom's *Taxonomy of Educational Objectives.*[1] In this scheme, all objectives have been classified into one of three "domains"—*cognitive, affective,* and *psychomotor.* The objectives which are generally given most attention by the teacher of elementary science fall within the cognitive domain which includes the recognition and recall of information and also the development of various intellectual abilities. Many of the objectives which are included in textbooks and curriculum guides, but to which teachers less often direct their teaching, are part of the affective domain. These pertain to the development of attitudes, values, interest, and appreciation. Physical, manipulative, and motor abilities are part of the psychomotor domain.

Since the cognitive domain receives most attention, it will be examined here in greater detail. A look at the various levels of this domain will give some insight into the level of sophistication of objectives.

The first and lowest level in the cognitive domain is the *knowledge* level. It includes the recall of specifics (e.g. ice is a form of water), structures (e.g. the skeletal structure of vertebrates), or scientific processes (e.g. a control is an important part of an experiment). The knowledge level emphasizes that which would be described as remembering. Of course, the examples given here could be understood at a deeper level. They are classified at this level if it is only a matter of being able to remember the information rather than a deeper understanding such as being able to apply it to a new situation or synthesizing several items of knowledge. These deeper understandings are dealt with in other levels of this classification system. The entire taxonomy is a hierarchy in which each lower level of understanding is necessary before understanding at the next higher level is possible.

The second level is *comprehension* which includes translation from one form to another. Examples would be drawing a graph of daily temperature changes from a list of temperatures recorded over a period of days or weeks, or explaining verbally what is meant by a statement which is expressed in mathematical symbols.

Application, which is the third level, requires the ability to apply abstract ideas in a concrete situation. Examples would be the ability to use a knowledge of the relationship between heat and the expansion and contraction of liquids to explain how a thermometer works, use a knowledge of classification to classify a group of seashells according

1. Benjamin S. Bloom, Editor. *Taxonomy of Educational Objectives. The Classification of Educational Goals, Handbook I: Cognitive Domain.* (New York City: David McKay Company, Inc., 1956).

to size, shape, or color, or use a knowledge of electric circuits to cause a light bulb to light using a cell, bulb, and pieces of wire.

Analysis, the fourth level, involves breaking down an idea into its various parts and determining the relationship between the parts. Determining which statements about an experiment are facts and which are hypotheses, or determining which factors led to an unexpected conclusion of any experiment would be examples.

Snythesis, the fifth level, includes taking parts and putting them together to form a whole such as skill in expressing verbally or in writing the results of an experiment using an appropriate organization of ideas. Other examples would be formulating a hypothesis to explain why some animals are less active in the daytime than at night or why water poured on a fire will often put out the fire.

Evaluation, the highest of the six levels in the cognitive domain, includes making judgments. An example is the ability to state the falacies in an analysis of an experiment. Another example is the ability to evaluate popular beliefs about health.

The reason for looking at this classification of objectives is to gain some insight into the sophistication of the objectives we actually are endeavoring to reach in our teaching. Is teaching aimed at the remembering of facts and ideas or are children expected to be able to apply these facts and ideas? Do some children arrive at junior high school without having been challenged to analyze, synthesize, or evaluate ideas? Do the children gain a greater interest in science or a better appreciation of its place in society? If this classification of objectives has caused the readers to think critically about the objectives of their science program, it has served the purpose for which it was included here.

Objectives Should Be Behavioral

So far, it has been pointed out that objectives should be specific, in keeping with the area of study at hand, and not be limited to the knowledge level. In addition, objectives should be stated in a manner that permits a judgment about the attainment of the objectives. To make this possible, objectives should be stated in terms of the behaviors which will be exhibited by the children. Objectives stated in this form are often spoken of as behavioral objectives or performance objectives. Behavioral objectives have been talked about for years, but recently they have received renewed and closer attention. For example, *Preparing Instructional Objectives,* a small book by Mager,[2] is devoted entirely

2. Robert F. Mager, *Preparing Instructional Objectives.* (Palo Alto, California: Fearon Publishers, 1962.)

to the "how" of writing good behavioral objectives. *Science—A Process Approach*,[3] the experimental elementary science program sponsored by the American Association for the Advancement of Science, has behavioral objectives set up for each lesson in the program. In addition to providing a basis for the teacher's efforts in aiding student learning, the behavioral objectives provide the basis for the extensive evaluation which is being conducted by the sponsors of the program.

In order to understand what is meant by a behavioral objective, let us look at some of the basic ideas presented by Mager. First of all, an appropriate objective is *not* a description of what the lesson is about, but is a statement of what the learner will be able to *DO* at the end of the learning activity. For example, "a study of the kinds of materials that are attracted by magnets" is a description of what is to be included in a certain science lesson. It is not an objective. In contrast, although in some ways incomplete, the following is an objective: "At the conclusion of this lesson the children will be able to state what kinds of materials are attracted by magnets." It describes what the children will be able to do. Thus, the first step in formulating good behavioral objectives is deciding what the child should be *DOING* when the instruction has been successful.

A key to writing good objectives is the verb which describes what the child will be able to do. Some are vague and open to many interpretations. Others have clarity and convey a definite meaning. Consider carefully the chart of examples from Mager:[4]

Words Open to Many Interpretations	*Words Open to Fewer Interpretations*
to know	to write
to understand	to recite
to *really* understand	to identify
to appreciate	to differentiate
to fully appreciate	to solve
to grasp the significance of	to construct
to enjoy	to list
to believe	to compare
to have faith in	to contrast

3. *Science—A Process Approach.* American Association for the Advancement of Science, Washington, D. C., 1966.
4. Mager, *op. cit.,* p. 11.

There is nothing wrong with teaching children to "understand" and "enjoy," but clear communication of ideas requires that objectives be stated in terms of what they will be *DOING* that indicates they "understand" or "enjoy." How else will teachers know if children are "understanding" or "enjoying?"

After determining what behaviors are the object of instruction, a second major question can be considered. Under what conditions will these behaviors be observed? The answer to the question will progress one step further toward a precisely stated performance objective. Consider this objective: At the end of this lesson, the child should be able to identify constellations in the night sky. Does it state the conditions under which the objective is to be reached?

It does not indicate whether the child is expected to make the identification with or without the aid of a star chart or other reference. It does not state whether the student is given a list of the names and asked to assign these names to the appropriate constellation or whether the student is expected to produce the names from memory. Therefore, the objective should be restated.

A third major question that should be considered in formulating performance objectives is "How well is the child expected to perform?" or "What is the minimum acceptable level of performance?" Look again at the objective above on identifying constellations in the night sky. Is the objective stated in such a way that this kind of question is answered? It does not tell *how many* constellations the child is expected to identify. Also, in the case of some objectives, it may be desirable to indicate *how long* the child has to attain the objective.

Now the objective concerning identification of constellations can be restated in a more precise form: At the end of this lesson the child should be able to identify at least five constellations when given a star chart as a guide. This objective answers the three basic questions: What is the behavior? What are the conditions? and What is the minimum acceptable level of performance?

Can Objectives Be Made Behavioral?

Readers are no doubt asking "Can all of our objectives be stated in behavioral form with the conditions and minimum level of performance clearly indicated?" It may not always be easy. For example, a common objective of science education is the development of interest in science. It must be asked what behaviors on the part of the child will indicate that this interest is present. Would behaviors such as

reading books on science, visiting a local science museum, or building
a simple telescope for observing the stars and planets be indicators of
this interest? Difficulties may be encountered in giving the *conditions*
and *minimum level* of performance for such an objective, but the objectives can be framed in terms that will allow teachers to make judgments on the basis of student performance. A teacher's objective might
be: the child will pursue his interest in astronomy by such means as
reading library books on astronomy, visiting the local museum, and
making night-sky observations.

As another example, there is certainly a place in the elementary
school science curriculum for free exploration on the part of children,
such as "playing around" with magnets in an undirected fashion or
observing mealworms for an extended period of time without definite
directions concerning what they should observe. Such activities often
lead to the posing of interesting questions and interesting hypotheses
that might answer the questions as well as creating means of testing
hypotheses. Objectives for such activities should reflect *why* the children are being encouraged in this direction. Objectives might be: by
the end of the class the child will have posed two or more questions
concerning magnets, or by the end of the class the child will have posed
two or more hypotheses as possible answers to questions concerning the
behavior of mealworms, or the child will design an experiment for testing
a hypothesis concerning the behavior of mealworms. Here again, there
may be some difficulties stating conditions and minimum levels, but the
children's behavior can be used as the referent in determining if the
activity was worthwhile. It must be granted that educators cannot always
state their objectives as precisely as they would like, but they can certainly do better than they often have done in the past.

Objectives are dynamic not static. They are based on more than the
structure of the subject and thus they change as a result of experience
with children in the classroom. The teacher may find that an objective is
not realistic in view of the level of maturity of the children or a classroom experience may suggest a different objective which is more profitable to pursue than the one originally stated. It is necessary to begin
by carefully specifying objectives, but to be flexible enough to alter
them as experience indicates. Careful stating of objectives provides an
aid to the clear thinking and planning which must continue throughout
the duration of the science instruction.

This article has been concerned with the formulation of objectives
for the elementary school science curriculum. After they are formulated,
the next step is to teach to attain these objectives. That is the job of
the reader. The next article will deal with using meaningful objectives
as a basis for evaluating the success of the teaching.

1. Of Bloom's six cognitive levels, which one do you think is emphasized most by the typical elementary school science program?
2. How does the affective domain (attitudes, values, etc.) affect the cognitive domain and vice-versa?
3. Are there objectives that might be difficult to formulate in behavioral terms?

33 RONALD D. ANDERSON

Has the Objective Been Attained

After objectives have been formulated, how does one decide if they are achieved? This second paper by Anderson deals with this question of evaluation and raises many important issues. It might be interesting to think about the three elementary science curriculum projects described in Part Three in terms of evaluation methods described, while reading this paper. What are the reasons for evaluation? Is it evaluation of children or curriculum? If children are evaluated relative to one another, what general results should be expected if we look at Piaget's work on cognitive development? These and many other questions will probably arise since evaluation is directly related (or should be) to program objectives and instructional strategies.

What are the reasons for evaluation and how can one decide if goals and objectives are being achieved? These questions are considered in this paper and many implications for curriculum and instruction in elementary science are apparent. If the purpose of evaluation procedures is to provide feedback about the effectiveness of curriculum materials, then certain things are implied. If the purpose of evaluation is to provide feedback to parents about their children, then the circumstances are very different. Can attempts to find out if the objectives have been attained, influence the nature of the instructional program?

In Part I of this two-part article (*S & C,* September 1967, page 20), guidelines were given for formulating specific behavioral objectives. In the first article attention also was called to the importance of formulating specific performance objectives for each day on which science is taught. Broad general objectives are important to give general guidelines, but if they are to serve as an adequate basis for planning either teaching or evaluation, they must be translated into specific objectives for each day. In fact, if specific objectives for the day are formed, a great deal of the planning for the teaching and evaluation

Reprinted from *Science and Children,* Vol. 5, No. 2, 1967, pp. 33-36, by permission of the editor. Dr. Anderson is Assistant Professor of Science Education at the University of Colorado at Boulder.

already has been done. The evaluation, in particular, is aided by stating as part of an objective, the conditions under which the behavior is expected and the minimum acceptable level of performance.

Reasons for Evaluation

The most important reason for conducting careful evaluation of the science program is to locate learning difficulties that individual children are encountering and aid them in overcoming these difficulties. To accomplish this purpose, the evaluation must be a continuous activity that is done each day and not put aside until the end of a unit when a formal evaluation is made. It may be difficult in a large classroom, but the teacher must continually attempt to determine what obstacles, if any, each child is encountering.

A second important reason for careful evaluation is to enable the teacher to change and alter her teaching practices and procedures in the manner that will best improve the learning situation. The idea that appeared promising before trying it in the classroom may, in practice, be a complete failure in terms of the objective it was expected to accomplish. Or possibly the objective itself is unreasonable when viewed with respect to the classroom experience. An evaluation at the end of the unit should show if the promising idea "fizzled." Here again, the continuous day-to-day evaluation of the teaching techniques is important so that revisions can take place.

A third reason for evaluation is as a base for reporting a child's progress to his parents and other members of the school staff who work with him. Usually this is referred to as grading, although the report may include more than just a grade. Grading or reporting of student progress is a matter of importance but is not our major concern. Even though it is one of the reasons for evaluation in elementary school science, the focus of this article is on the evaluation itself.

Types of Evaluation

It might be helpful to discuss two types of evaluation which can be referred to as informal and formal. Formal evaluation refers to paper and pencil tests, or other devices such as individual tasks which are administered uniformly to all the children in the class. This type of evaluation will be discussed in detail in the following sections. Much of a teacher's evaluation is more informal and is based upon her observations while the usual classroom activities are underway. The responses that children make to the teacher's questions and the questions that children ask are noted by the perceptive teacher. In addition to verbal statements and questions, the actions of children as they work with equipment provide important information for informal evaluation.

It is important that the teacher's informal evaluation be centered on those behaviors which are her objectives and that she not be unduly influenced by unrelated behaviors of the children. If one of the objectives for the day's work is that children be able to formulate hypotheses concerning a particular phenomenon, such as the breaking of rocks during freezing weather, the teacher should be listening for statements that indicate that a hypothesis has been suggested. The central objective is for the children to develop their ability to formulate hypotheses. The behavior that is indicative of this should be of major concern to the teacher rather than verbal fluency or discussion of the breaking of rocks in freezing weather which is unrelated to hypotheses concerning the phenomenon.

Informal evaluation of the type described above is dependent upon a certain type of teaching. The teacher who does not have much student involvement (for example, the discussion of thought-provoking questions), often is not in a position to observe student behaviors which are indicative of whether or not an objective has been reached. This indicates clearly the close "tie-in" between objectives, teaching, and evaluation. Ample evidence is available to show that student involvement is important for science teaching, particularly for objectives related to the processes of science. This student involvement also is important for the informal evaluation in which a teacher evaluates on the basis of what students *DO* on a day-to-day basis. What is good teaching practice also is generally advantageous for evaluation.

Cover All Objectives

The more formal evaluations such as paper and pencil tests should be planned carefully to insure that all objectives are given proper attention and that the measurement planned actually does measure the stated objectives. The first step, specifying the objectives, was discussed in the first article. It is well to remember, however, that teaching is a very dynamic and flexible activity, and as a result of interaction with the children, the objectives may have been altered or given a different emphasis. Now that preparations are being made for the evaluation, it is time to consider again exactly what goals *have* been sought.

The next step is to weight the various objectives according to the relative emphasis given to them during the teaching. For example, if two days were spent on the measurement of temperature and one day on formulating hypotheses concerning the change of state water from one form to the other, the former should receive twice as much emphasis in the evaluation. If it is a paper and pencil test, the number of items or questions should be in proportion to the time spent on the objectives which they are designed to measure.

A crucial step is the selection of the evaluation technique which will be used to measure the various objectives. The technique used is dependent upon the nature of the objective. Many teachers use a particular type, e.g. an objective paper and pencil test, regardless of their objectives. Sometimes a particular evaluation technique is appropriate; many times it is not. This teacher then asks herself, "What are some items that are related to the topics that have been considered?" There are at least two things wrong with this approach. First, the achievement of the objective at hand may not be measurable with this technique. Second, just because the test items chosen are on the same topic as the objectives, does not insure that the items actually measure the students' achievement of the specific objectives.

The first type of error is shown by the following example. One of the objectives for a unit is that children should be able to classify a group of leaves into three groups on the bases of color, size, or shape. Paper and pencil items are probably not the most appropriate means of evaluating whether or not this objective has been achieved. In this case, each child could be given a group of leaves and asked to classify them. It may be possible to devise paper and pencil items using pictures that test such an ability, but a teacher is more likely to devise a means of measuring the stated objectives by the above technique than by objective test items which she devises.

The second type of error is shown by a teacher's evaluation of the following objective: Given data showing the daily fluctuations in temperature over a two-week period, the child should be able to construct a graph which shows the relationship between time and temperature. In this case the teacher constructed this true-false item which referred to a graph of time vs. temperature: The graph above shows the relationship between time and temperature. This item was on the same topic as the objective, yet it was not a measure of the students' achievement of the objective. The item required that the student be able to determine what had been plotted on the graph, but the objective stated that the child should be able to construct a graph. In this case, it would have been more appropriate to give the student some data and ask him to construct a graph.

Variety of Formal Evaluation Techniques

Two main types of formal evaluation techniques have been referred to thus far—paper and pencil tests and the systematic use of situations in which individual children are presented a situation which includes the use of material objects. The latter type is used very extensively in the evaluation program of *Science—A Process Approach.*[1] Each child is individually presented with a standard situation and given specific directions for indicating his responses on a check sheet. Some of their items and the objectives they were designed to assess will serve as good examples of this evaluation technique.

One of the objectives for a lesson on color in Book One is that the child should be able to "identify the following colors by sight: yellow, orange, red, purple, blue, and green."[2] A competency measure designed to assess the achievement of this objective has the following directions:

> Show the child each of three blocks—a yellow (1), a red (2), and a blue (3) one, and say to the child, WHAT IS THE COLOR OF THIS BLOCK? Repeat for all three blocks. One check should be given in the acceptable column for each correct name.[3]

In Book Four is a lesson on communicating entitled "Describing an Experiment." The objectives of this lesson are:

> The child should be able to describe any one of the following portions of an experiment which he has just observed or conducted:
>
> 1. the question to be answered.
> 2. the method or approach used.
> 3. the apparatus and procedures used.
> 4. the results obtained, as observed.
> 5. the answer to the original question.[4]

The competency measure designed to assess the achievement of this objective is as follows:

> Tell the child: I AM GOING TO EXPERIMENT TO SEE WHAT HAPPENS TO A PENCIL FLOATING IN WATER WHEN SALT IS ADDED TO THE WATER. I WANT YOU TO WATCH ME CAREFULLY SO THAT YOU WILL BE ABLE TO DESCRIBE WHAT I DID. Fill the test tube with water and place a pencil in the tube. Place the test tube next to a ruler and record the reading

---

1. Commission on Science Education, *Science—A Process Approach,* American Association for the Advancement of Science, Washington, D. C. 1965 and 1966.
2. *Ibid.,* Book One, p. 1.
3. *Ibid.* Competency Measures, Parts One and Two, p. 11.
4. *Ibid.,* Book Four, p. 95.

either at the bottom or the top of the pencil. Pour salt (two table-spoons) into the test tube and record the reading again. (Change in level will be about one half centimeter.) Ask the child: WRITE DOWN OR TELL ME IN WORDS ALL THAT YOU CAN ABOUT THIS EXPERIMENT. Give him one check for each of the following steps that he includes:

1. question to be answered.
2. proposed method or approach.
3. apparatus and procedures required.
4. results obtained, as observed.
5. answer to the original question.[5]

Note some characteristics of these examples. In contrast to informal evaluation, this is a carefully defined standard situation which is the same for each child. There is a close correlation between the stated objectives and the items used for evaluation. It is apparent that the evaluation items were designed specifically to measure the correspond-ing stated objective. Also, these items are not dependent upon either the child's reading or writing ability. In both cases the child does not read anything. In the second example the child may write his answer but only if he prefers this method to telling the teacher his answer.

An obvious difficulty with this type of evaluation is the time required to administer the assessment to each child in the class individually. On the other hand, its freedom from dependence on writing and reading ability gives it an advantage over paper and pencil tests. The reading difficulty of paper and pencil tests is a major problem when employing them at the elementary school level. Both varieties of assessment devices have their advantages and disadvantages. In choosing between them the basic question should be, "What can I use that will determine if my objective has been attained?" As a result, an assessment of the student's achievement over a fairly long period of time will probably include some of both types.

The situation evaluation technique, with some modifications, can be used with groups of children rather than individuals. When used with groups, the children generally are required to give their responses on paper rather than verbally. This is a useful form of evaluation in that it combines the flexibility of the situation technique with the efficiency of paper and pencil tests. Because of these dual advantages, some teach-ers find this technique to be the most useful of all the evaluation tech-niques which they employ.

The higher the grade level, the more paper and pencil tests are likely to be employed. This is understandable, since as the child's

5. *Ibid., Competency Measures.* Parts Three and Four, p. 85.

reading and writing abilities increase, the better able he is to respond to this kind of examination. At present it is the most widely used type of evaluation for elementary school science. Since science is being tested, every effort should be made to reduce the influence of the child's reading ability upon his score. This influence is greater than most teachers realize. One helpful procedure is to project the test on a screen with an overhead projector and read each item to the children as they respond to the questions on their own copy of the test. With the modern equipment which many schools have today it is relatively easy to make an overhead projector transparency of any printed material.

The construction of good essay, matching, true-false, completion or multiple choice items is not a simple matter. An adequate discussion of this topic would require far more space than is available here. For helpful information on the construction of good items, the reader is referred to one of the many good books in this area such as those written by Stanley[6] or Ebel.[7] If the reader is not thoroughly familiar with the principles of constructing good test items, he should spend time studying the relevant chapter or chapters of such a book.

In summary, the key to good evaluation is carefully defining objectives and then devising a means of determining if the objectives have been achieved through informal and formal evaluation.

---

1. In Part Three, the paper by Bruner, "The Act of Discovery," identified certain characteristics of the *process* of discovery. How might behavioral objectives "fit into" a science program based on discovery learning?
2. What might be some purposes of written tests for elementary science and would they have any effect on the overall science program?

6. Julian C. Stanley, *Measurement In Today's Schools*, Fourth Edition, Englewood Cliffs, N. J.: Prentice-Hall Inc., 1964.
7. Robert L. Ebel, *Measuring Educational Achievement*, Englewood Cliffs, N. J.: Prentice-Hall, Inc., 1965.

34 J. MYRON ATKIN

Behavioral Objectives in Curriculum Design: A Cautionary Note

Performance-based testing, which is a part of the larger issue of accountability in education, has advantages and potential disadvantages. Dr. Atkin's paper is an attempt to get people to look at the entire educational process, beyond specific, isolated skills that can be assessed using performance-based criteria. He cautions against accepting an idea or technique simply because it is easily measurable. The method of evaluation and its interaction with the instructional strategies are also discussed, with specific reference to performance testing. The priority of objectives should never be determined by the ease with which they can be measured.

In certain influential circles, anyone who confesses to reservations about the use of behaviorally stated objectives for curriculum planning runs the risk of being labeled as the type of individual who would attack the virtues of motherhood. Bumper stickers have appeared at my own institution, and probably at yours, reading STAMP OUT NONBEHAVIORAL OBJECTIVES. I trust that the person who prepared the stickers had humor as his primary aim; nevertheless, the crusade for specificity of educational outcome has become intense and evangelical. The worthiness of this particular approach has come to be accepted as self-evident by ardent proponents, proponents who sometimes sound like the true believers who cluster about a new social or religious movement.

Behavioral objectives enthusiasts are warmly endorsed and embraced by the systems and operations analysis advocates, most educational technologists, the cost-benefit economists, the planning-programing budgeting system stylists, and many others. In fact, the behavioral objectives people are now near the center of curriculum decision making. Make no mistake; they have replaced the academicians and the general cur-

Reprinted from *The Science Teacher*, Vol. 35, No. 5, 1968, pp. 27-30 by permission of the editor. Dr. Atkin is Dean of the College of Education at the University of Illinois.

riculum theorists—especially in the new electronically based education industries and in governmental planning agencies. The engineering model for educational research and development represents a forceful tide today. Those who have a few doubts about the effects of the tide had better be prepared to be considered uninitiated and naive, if not slightly addlepated and antiquarian.

To utilize the techniques for long-term planning and rational decision making that have been developed with such apparent success in the Department of Defense, and that are now being applied to a range of domestic and civilian problems, it is essential that hard data be secured. Otherwise these modes for developmental work and planning are severely limited. Fuzzy and tentative statements of possible achievement and questions of conflict with respect to underlying values are not compatible with the new instructional systems management approaches—at least not with the present state of the art. In fact, delineating instructional objectives in terms of identifiable pupil behaviors or performances seems essential in 1968 for assessing the output of the educational system. Currently accepted wisdom does not seem to admit an alternative.

There are overwhelmingly useful purposes served by attempting to identify educational goals in non-ambiguous terms. To plan rationally for a growing educational system, and to continue to justify relatively high public expenditures for education, it seems that we do need a firmer basis for making assessments and decisions than now exists. Current attention to specification of curriculum objectives in terms of pupil performance represents an attempt to provide direction for collection of data that will result in more informed choice among competing alternatives.

Efforts to identify educational outcomes in behavioral terms also provide a fertile ground for coping with interesting research problems and challenging technical puzzles. A world of educational research opens to the investigator when he has reliable measures of educational output (even when their validity for educational purposes is low). Pressures from researchers are difficult to resist since they do carry influence in the educational community, particularly in academic settings and in educational development laboratories.

Hence I am not unmindful of some of the possible benefits to be derived from attempts to rationalize our decision-making processes through the use of behaviorally stated objectives. Schools need a basis for informed choice. And the care and feeding of educational researchers is a central part of my job at Illinois. However, many of the enthusiasts have given insufficient attention to underlying assumptions and broad questions of educational policy. I intend in this brief paper to highlight a few of these issues in the hope that the exercise might be productive of further and deeper discussion.

Several reservations about the use of behaviorally stated objectives for curriculum design will be catalogued here. But perhaps the fundamental problem, as I see it, lies in the easy assumption that we either know or can readily identify the educational objectives for which we strive, and thereafter the educational outcomes that result from our programs. One contention basic to my argument is that we presently are making progress toward thousands of goals in any existing educational program, progress of which we are perhaps dimly aware, can articulate only with great difficulty, and that contribute toward goals which are incompletely stated (or unrecognized), but which are often worthy.

For example, a child who is learning about mealworm behavior by blowing against the animal through a straw is probably learning much more than how this insect responds to a gentle stream of warm air. Let's assume for the moment that we can specify "behaviorally" all that he might learn about mealworm *behavior* (an arduous and never-ending task). In addition, in this "simple" activity, he is probably finding out something about interaction of objects, forces, humane treatment of animals, his own ability to manipulate the environment, structural characteristics of the larval form of certain insects, equilibrium, the results of doing an experiment at the suggestion of the teacher, the rewards of independent experimentation, the judgment of the curriculum developers in suggesting that children engage in such an exercise, possible uses of a plastic straw, and the length of time for which one individual might be engaged in a learning activity and still display a high degree of interest. I am sure there are many additional learnings, literally too numerous to mention in fewer than eight or ten pages. When any piece of curriculum is used with real people, there are important learning outcomes that cannot have been anticipated when the objectives were formulated. And of the relatively few outcomes that can be identified at all, a smaller number still are translatable readily in terms of student behavior. There is a possibility the cumulative side effects are at least as important as the intended main effects.

Multiply learning outcomes from the mealworm activity by all the various curriculum elements we attempt to build into a school day. Then multiply this by the number of days in a school year, and you have some indication of the oversimplification that *always* occurs when curriculum intents or outcomes are articulated in any form that is considered manageable.

If my argument has validity to this point, the possible implications are potentially dangerous. If identification of all worthwhile outcomes in behavioral terms comes to be commonly accepted and expected, then it is inevitable that, over time, the curriculum will tend to emphasize those elements which have been thus identified. Important outcomes which are detected only with great difficulty and which are translated only rarely into behavioral terms tend to atrophy. They disappear from the curriculum because we spend all the time allotted to us in teaching explicitly for the more readily specifiable learnings to which we have been directed.

We have a rough analogy in the use of tests. Prestigious examinations that are widely accepted and broadly used, such as the New York State Regents examinations, tend over time to determine the curriculum. Whether or not these examinations indeed measure all outcomes that are worth achieving, the curriculum regresses toward the objectives reflected by the test items. Delineation of lists of behavioral objectives, like broadly used testing programs, may admirably serve the educational researcher because it gives him indices of gross achievement as well as detail of particular achievement; it may also provide input for cost-benefit analysts and governmental planners at all levels because it gives them hard data with which to work; but the program in the schools may be affected detrimentally by the gradual disappearance of worthwhile learning activities for which we have not succeeded in establishing a one-to-one correspondence between curriculum elements and rather difficult-to-measure educational results.

Among the learning activities most readily lost are those that are long term and private in effect and those for which a single course provides only a small increment. If even that increment cannot be identified, it tends to lose out in the teacher's priority scheme, because it is competing with other objectives which have been elaborately stated and to which he has been alerted. But I will get to the question of priority of objectives a bit later.

The second point I would like to develop relates to the effect of demands for behavioral specification on innovation. My claim here is that certain types of innovation, highly desirable ones, are hampered and frustrated by early demands for behavioral statements of objectives.

Let's focus on the curriculum reform movement of the past 15 years, the movement initiated by Max Beberman in 1952 when he began to design a mathematics program in order that the high school curriculum would reflect concepts central to modern mathematics. We have now seen curriculum development efforts, with this basic flavor, in many science fields, the social sciences, English, esthetics, etc. When one talks with the initiators of such projects, particularly at the beginning of their efforts, one finds that they do not begin by talking about the manner in which they would like to change pupils' behavior. Rather they are dissatisfied with existing curricula in their respective subject fields, and they want to build something new. If pressed, they might indicate that existing programs stress concepts considered trivial by those who practice the discipline. They might also say that the curriculum poorly reflects styles of intellectual inquiry in the various fields. Press them further, and they might say that they want to build a new program that more accurately displays the "essence" of history, or physics, or economics, or whatever. Or a program that better transmits a comprehension of the elaborate and elegant interconnections among various concepts within the discipline.

If they are asked at an early stage just how they want pupils to behave differently, they are likely to look quite blank. Academicians in the various cognate fields do not speak the language of short-term or long-term behavioral change, as do many psychologists. In fact, if a hard-driving behaviorist attempts to force the issue and succeeds, one finds that the disciplinarians can come up with a list of behavioral goals that looks like a caricature of the subject field in question. (Witness the AAAS elementary-school science program directed toward teaching "process.")

Further, early articulation of behavioral objectives by the curriculum developer inevitably tends to limit the range of his exploration. He becomes committed to designing programs that achieve these goals. Thus if specific objectives in behavioral terms are identified early, there tends to be a limiting element built into the new curriculum. The innovator is less alert to potentially productive tangents.

The effective curriculum developer typically begins with *general* objectives. He then refines the program through a series of successive approximations. He doesn't start with a blueprint, and he isn't in much of a hurry to get his ideas represented by a blueprint.

A situation is created in the newer curriculum design procedures based on behaviorally stated objectives in which scholars who do not talk a behavioral-change language are expected to describe their goals at a time when the intricate intellectual subtleties of their work may not be clear, even in the disciplinary language with which they are familiar. At the other end, the educational evaluator, the behavioral specifier, typically has very little understanding of the curriculum that is being designed—understanding with respect to the new view of the subject field that it affords. It is too much to expect that the behavioral analyst, or anyone else, recognize the shadings of meaning in various evolving economic theories, the complex applications of the intricacies of wave motion, or the richness of nuance reflected in a Stravinsky composition.

Yet despite this two-culture problem—finding a match between the behavioral analysts and the disciplinary scholars—we still find that an expectation is being created for early behavioral identification of essential outcomes.

(Individuals who are concerned with producing hard data reflecting educational outputs would run less risk of dampening innovation if they were to enter the curriculum development scene in a more unobtrusive fashion—and later—than is sometimes the case. The curriculum developer goes into the classroom with only a poorly articulated view of the changes he wants to make. Then he begins working with children to see what he can do. He revises. He develops new ideas. He continually modifies as he develops. *After* he has produced a program that seems pleasing, it might then be a productive exercise for the behavioral analyst to attempt with the curriculum developer to identify *some* of the ways in which children seem to be behaving differently. If this approach is taken, I would caution, however, that observers be alert for long-term as well as short-term effects, subtle as well as obvious inputs.)

A third basic point to be emphasized relates to the question of instructional priorities, mentioned earlier. I think I have indicated that there is a vast library of goals that represent possible outcomes for any instructional program. A key educational task, and a task that is well handled by the effective teacher, is that of relating educational goals to the situation at hand—as well as relating the situation at hand to educational goals. It is impractical to pursue all goals thoroughly. And it does make a difference *when* you try to teach something. Considerable educational potential is lost when certain concepts are taught didactically. Let's assume that some third-grade teacher considers it important to develop concepts related to sportsmanship. It would be a rather naive teacher who decided that she would undertake this task at 1:40 P.M. on Friday of next week. The experienced teacher has always realized that learnings related to such an area must be stressed in an appropriate context, and the context often cannot be planned.

Perhaps there is no problem in accepting this view with respect to a concept like sportsmanship, but I submit that a similar case can be made for a range of crucial cognitive outcomes that are basic to various subject-matter fields. I use science for my examples because I know more about this field than about others. But equilibrium, successive approximation, symmetry, entropy, and conservation are pervasive ideas with a broad range of application. These ideas are taught with the richest meaning only when they are emphasized repeatedly in appropriate and varied contexts. Many of these contexts arise in classroom situations that are unplanned, but that have powerful potential. It is detrimental to learning not to capitalize on the opportune moments for effectively teaching one idea or another. Riveting the teacher's attention to a few behavioral goals provides him with blinders that may limit his range. Directing him to hundreds of goals leads to confusing, mechanical pedagogic style and loss of spontaneity.

A final point to be made in this paper relates to values, and it deals with a primary flaw in the consumption of much educational research. It is difficult to resist the assumption that those attributes which we can measure are the elements which we consider most important. This point relates to my first, but I feel that it is essential to emphasize the problem. The behavioral analyst seems to assume that for an objective to be worthwhile, we must have methods of observing progress. But worthwhile goals come first, not our methods for assessing progress toward these goals. Goals are derived from our needs and from our philosophies. They are not and should not be derived primarily from our measures. It borders on the irresponsible for those who exhort us to state objectives in behavioral terms to avoid the issue of determining worth. Inevitably there is an implication of worth behind any act of measurement. What the educational community poorly realizes at the moment is that behavioral goals may or may not be worthwhile. They are articulated from among the vast library of goals because they are stated relatively easily. Again, let's not assume that what we can presently measure necessarily represents our most important activity.

I hope that in this paper I have increased rather than decreased the possibilities for constructive discourse about the use of behavioral objectives for curriculum design. The issues here represent a few of the basic questions that seem crucial enough to be examined in an open forum that admits the possibility of fresh perspectives. Too much of the debate related to the use of behavioral objectives has been conducted in an argumentative style that characterize discussions of fundamental religious views among adherents who are poorly informed. A constructive effort might be centered on identification of those issues which seem to be amenable to resolution by empirical means and those which do not. At any rate, I feel confident that efforts of the next few years will better inform us about the positive as well as negative potential inherent in a view of curriculum design that places the identification of behavioral objectives at the core.

---

1. At this point, can you differentiate between behavioral and non-behavioral objectives?

2. What do you think are the three most significant arguments used by Atkin against the overall use of behavioral objectives?
3. Can you identify any advantages or disadvantages with regard to the use of behavioral objectives, not already stated at this point?

35 RONALD G. GOOD

Accountability and Conceptual Learning: Some Considerations

The issue of the use of behavioral objectives in education is a part of the overall issue of "accountability." This paper looks at some recent curriculum developments, including Elementary Science Study, in terms of how accountability applies in such cases and how the programs would change if a stereotyped interpretation of accountability were imposed. Conceptual learning and skill learning are compared in terms of accountability. Conceptual learning is identified with the type of thinking researched by Piaget that is most characteristic in science and mathematics curricula. Skill learning is associated more closely with such things as reading, writing, computational arithmetic, etc.

Educational accountability has been receiving more attention during the past two or three years by educators and lay people alike.(1, 2, 3, 4, 5) Being accountable undoubtedly means different things to different people. To the educator, it should be apparent that the accountable product varies among content areas. The type of "skill" learning involved in a shorthand course differs from conceptual learning that is more characteristic of a physics course, for example. Even within the physics course, however, the teacher can emphasize skill-type learning over conceptual learning. Memorizing words and formulas can replace experimentation and "grappling" with data.

Pressures of accountability can lead to an emphasis on memory and skill-oriented factors in place of learning that is more difficult to measure. Assessing the speed with which an individual can read is far easier than testing for comprehension. Further, testing for comprehension is far easier than determining the extent to which a person is developing a positive attitude toward reading that will affect later reading habits.

This paper was written for use in the science education program for prospective elementary school teachers at Florida State University. Dr. Good is an Assistant Professor of Science Education at Florida State University.

Curriculum projects in science education over the past decade have deemphasized memory and verbally-based learning in favor of conceptual learning centered around manipulative materials. One elementary curriculum project in particular, the Elementary Science Study, offers only that evaluation of the success of individual science units should be judged by the interest and excitement exhibited by the children.(6) Since manipulative materials rather than written materials comprise the vast majority of that curriculum, the learning that results must be in the nonverbal, conceptual category. How does accountability fit into such a curriculum?

Man: A Course of Study represents a curriculum project in social studies education that attempts to explore the question: What is human about human beings?(7) While the content is much more heavily oriented toward verbal learning using printed materials and discussions than is the Elementary Science Study, social attitudes, enthusiasm, and other affective outcomes are highly valued by Bruner and the other developers. How does accountability fit into this program? The easily isolable "content" does not by itself characterize the broad objectives of Man: A Course of Study.

The desire to "fit" the entire curriculum into an accountability model that can be managed by a computer program poses a real threat to creative projects such as the Elementary Science Study, Man: A Course of Study, and other attempts to provide alternative approaches to education. Since human beings have different physical, emotional, and intellectual characteristics, it should not be surprising that children in a classroom would differ in their conceptual learning if they are given the opportunity to structure ideas for themselves. They will show a greater conformity when dealing with skill-oriented learning than with conceptual learning that is dependent upon developmental aspects of the cognitive and affective domain.

The State Department of Education in Florida represents one of the more comprehensive attempts for dealing with the accountability issue. An analysis of the First Annual Report of the Florida Research and Development Program (1970) reveals that learning will be defined in terms of performance criteria.(8) Hierarchies of subordinate abilities are to be coordinated into "domain" charts that will indicate the order with which performance objectives are to be accomplished. Under ideal conditions, the domain would enable the interested observer to see "where the student has been" and know "where he needs to go."

There can be no doubt that schools should be able to account for certain kinds of learning in a way that is suggested by the plans of the Florida R and D Program. Skills in reading, writing, vocational education and certain computational skills are examples of these "certain kinds of learning." A substantial portion of learning in many areas cannot be so neatly programmed, however. Domain charts have a certain finality and absoluteness that are incompatible with the uncertainties and imperfections in people. The outstanding leader in the field of cognitive development research, Jean Piaget, has suggested that a person understands things only to the extent to which those things are reinvented by him.(9) This discovery or reinvention process following different paths and time schedules with different people. Many "mistakes" are made during the process of reorganizing previously known ideas that provide valuable information. Especially where children of elementary school age are involved, the reorganization of ideas is difficult to monitor or account for. This is because the ideas must originally be generated through personal interaction with concrete objects. Abstract or formal thinking is generally not available to the child before about 12 years of age, and with no certainty afterwards.(10) Freeing children to think their own thoughts when interacting with manipulative materials will result in a wide variety of activity and a similar variety of measurable outcomes. What is to be accounted for and how, no longer corresponds neatly with the lines of a domain map. When discrete learning "units" vary from the "master plan" of a domain map, an individual's short term progress becomes less accountable in terms of predetermined performance criteria.

Conceptual learning is tied directly to an individual's characteristic state of cognitive development. Skill learning can be relatively independent of such development, especially at the secondary school level. The present state of accountability in education lends itself more appropriately to skill learning. A skill can be programmed as a series of discrete, predetermined learning units. The most important objective in such learning is the outcome or skill that can be performed. The nature of the learning process is deemed relatively unimportant when compared to the demonstrable outcome.

Conceptual learning brought about by the learner's interaction with objects and events must be much more concerned with the process. Jerome Bruner (1960) has been most closely identified with the emphasis on *process* in learning.(11) If his message is to be taken seriously, we in education must not develop tunnel vision when it comes to the accountability issue. The conditions under which learning occurs surely affects the learner's attitudes, values, etc., toward further learning in that area when formal education ceases. The nature of developments in science, mathematics, and social studies curriculum projects over the past decade indicates an awareness of the importance of the processes of learning. *Doing* science has dominated the more passive role of reading about science. Such process-oriented curricula where students identify problems and design investigations will seldom be as "efficient" in terms of narrowly conceived concepts of accountability. Different learning types will require different interpretations of the approach to accountability.

Schools *should* be accountable for what they say they are doing. A master plan of accountability through which all learning progresses and is assessed, however, would seem to provide undesirable limitations to certain types of learning. Disregarding "humanistic" aspects of education because they offer severe problems to the domain map builders and the computer programmers will hardly solve the problem of relevancy that is facing every phase of education today.

REFERENCES

1. Grieder, C. "Educators Should Welcome Pressure for Accountability." *Nations Schools* 85 (May, 1970): 14.
2. Lessinger, L. M. "Accountability for Results: A Basic Challenge." *American Education* 5 (June, 1969): 2-4.
3. Austin, G. R. "Educational Accountability—Hallmark of the 1970s." *The Science Teacher* 38 (April, 1971): 26-28.
4. "ERIC Cites Concern Over Accountability." *Report on Education Research* 2, Number 26 (December 23, 1970): 2.
5. Davies, D. "Relevance of Accountability." *The Journal of Teacher Education* 21 (Spring, 1970): 127-33.
6. Rogers, R. E. and Voelker, A. M. "Programs for Improving Science Instruction in the Elementary School, ESS." *Science and Children* 7 (January/February, 1970): 35-43.
7. Dow, P. B. "Man: A Course of Study—Science in the Social Studies." *The Science Teacher* 38 (April, 1971): 33-4.
8. The First Annual Report of the Florida Educational Research and Development Program. State of Florida, Department of Education, February 24, 1970.
9. Jennings, F. G. "Jean Piaget: Notes on Learning." *Saturday Review,* May 20, 1967.
10. Inhelder, B. and Piaget, J. *The Growth of Logical Thinking.* Basic Books, Inc., 1958, 334-350.
11. Bruner, J. S. *The Process of Education.* Cambridge, Massachusetts: Harvard University Press, 1960.

1. Could you identify nonverbal, conceptual learning in elementary science by giving specific examples?
2. What part of the school day would you guess is devoted to helping children engage in conceptual learning?

36

EVELYN H. WILSON AND GEORGE J. PALLRAND

The Tyranny
of Terminology

In an earlier paper in this section by Anderson, the lowest level of educational objectives was referred to as the "knowledge" level. From that lowest level of cognitive functioning, one can go to comprehension, then to application and upward to the sixth level, evaluation. This paper by Wilson and Pallrand takes a critical look at terminology, which is at the knowledge level of the above classification system. Learning scientific terms is substituted for science in a great many, probably a majority, of our science classrooms. Yet, few teachers would admit that learning words is a primary goal they hold for their students in science. It is easy to substitute words for understandings and one of the reasons involves the ease with which word definitions can be evaluated. Electricity can be defined by an eight-year-old if he is first given the "correct" words to say, even though he is unable to conceptualize the meanings of the words.

Ours is a culture which relies chiefly upon language, spoken and written, for the transmission of knowledge and information. The belief that words always convey ideas is such a fixed notion in the society that facility with words becomes the basis of some important judgments about people. The extensiveness of vocabulary is a way of appraising not merely social background but, more importantly, intelligence as well. A command and easy flow of words are considered equivalent to profound understanding.

Students also are judged by their language. The vocabulary of the classroom is commonly considered the indicator of what is being learned therein—the more sophisticated the implied ideas, the more one is pleased. Thus, when children speak of Hamlet and Oedipus Rex, of sets and subsets, of DNA and hydrogen bonding, everyone is impressed with how much schools are teaching young people these days.

Reprinted from *The Science Teacher*, Vol. 36, No. 7, 1969, pp. 41-44, by permission of the editor. Dr. Wilson is Associate Professor of Science Education and Dr. Pallrand is Director of the Science Education Center, both at the Graduate School of Education, Rutgers State University.

In a visit to almost any science classroom, these general impressions are readily confirmed and reinforced. Observing and listening to the process of the teacher posing questions and students giving answers, one marvels at the complex ideas with which children seem able to deal. If this traditional procedure is fairly informal, and if the classroom has a relaxed atmosphere in which students seem free to raise questions and comment, most observers will be satisfied that, educationally, all is well: "Learning is taking place."

A nagging suspicion persists, however, that the mere presence of a lively verbal exchange between teacher and student is not an adequate criterion for judging the effectiveness of an educational program. The possibility that the use of appropriate vocabulary is a simplistic standard for evaluating what is being learned is certainly suggested by the fact that student understanding is usually judged by the degree of word similarity between the response of the student and the presentation of the textbook or the teacher.

What are student and teacher actually saying to each other? An examination of the substance of an exchange is as important as an examination of its dynamics. For example, consider a dialogue heard recently in a tenth-grade biology class during a lesson on photosynthesis:

Teacher: What happens when light hits *chlorophyll a*?
Student: The chlorophyll absorbs energy.
Teacher: Right. What does *chlorophyll a* do with this extra energy?
Student: It moves the electron shell farther out from the nucleus.
Teacher: Yes, and what do you call energy that has to do with the position of objects?
Student: Potential energy.

Chlorophyll a, electron, energy, light are certainly "right" words in the sense that they symbolize ideas associated with the very complex phenomenon of photosynthesis. But only those totally unaware that among these words are represented some of the most abstract ideas in science as well as incompletely understood phenomena could possibly believe that there is substance to this exchange or that much of anything is understood. An allusion to atomic structure (using an outmoded model at that), an operational definition of potential energy to encapsulate the subject, and a science-flavored vocabulary become a substitute for understanding.

Science classes abound in similar examples which suggest that words, rather than their meanings, are frequently the product of instruction; that familiarity with the terminology of a discipline is taken to mean an understanding of the ideas the terminology represents; that the ability to name a phenomenon is mistaken for the knowledge of the phenomenon itself.

This characterization may invite objections on the ground that such educational practices belong to an era now past in science education. One might argue that the many recent curriculum efforts, with their emphasis on students becoming involved in and using a "discovery" approach to the learning of fundamental ideas, have eliminated from teaching the use of meaningless verbalizations. Unfortunately, not much evidence for such claims is found in classrooms where these programs are in use. Even when the curriculum itself minimizes terminology, one generally sees a situation in which old habits are being superimposed on new materials.

That the names, rather than the ideas, associated with phenomena are often the only "discovery" actually made can again be illustrated by a classroom sequence. In this sequence, a group of fifth-grade students was observed as it worked in what the teacher reported was an area of considerable interest—electricity. The particular lesson was based upon materials rather recently developed by one of the national curriculum projects.

After a few introductory remarks in which learning something about electricity was clearly identified as the object of the lesson, the teacher pointed out that there were two fundamentally different kinds of electricity—static and current. Static electricity, she explained, was obtained by rubbing certain objects together; and the second, current electricity, was obtained from batteries. Discussion was then limited to the "current type" of electricity. The attention of students was directed to the two knobs on the battery, and they were asked to name these knobs. After several "incorrect" suggestions were made by the students, the teacher provided the "right" word, namely "poles." She also volunteered the information that these poles had something to do with passing electricity from the battery. The teacher then proceeded to cut a short section of plastic-coated wire and, while she removed the plastic at each end, she explained that the wire was coated with a material called insulation which served to keep the electricity inside the wire. The middle portion of the wire was then wrapped around a common nail, and the ends of the wire were connected to the battery. In response to the teacher's demonstration that the wire-enveloped nail could now pick up a few tacks, students readily stated that the nail had become magnetized. Students were then given batteries, wire, nails, and tacks and asked to "discover" how to increase the magnetism of the nail.

The implications of the reference to two kinds of electricity, although of interest and importance, will be omitted from the present discussion in favor of the more pertinent question of the pedagogical significance of using such terms as battery, poles, insulation, and magnetism. Was the interjection of these formal names into the discussion really necessary? Did it help in developing some simple but fundamental understanding of electricity and magnetism? Actually, the introduction and use of terminology in this lesson appeared to stifle class discussion. The teacher had imposed a certain viewpoint on students by herself establishing the parameters within which the discussion of how to make the nail more magnetic was to proceed. This procedure, which effectively "turned off" students and limited involvement to matters which could be related to the terminology, failed to elicit a host of interesting and profitable questions, some of which were painfully obvious: How does electricity in the battery get out? What does the presence of the wire have to do with the electricity in the battery? If electricity leaves and returns to the battery, why do batteries run down? How, if at all, is the magnetism which appeared in the nail related to the electricity in the wire? What is electricity made of? The "right" words had displaced attention from, and got in the way of, investigating the phenomenon itself. Students apparently viewed the terminology as the end product and all that needed to be considered. The terminology seemed to exert a subtle kind of tyranny.

Those sensitive to the problems of communication, especially with young children, will recognize that an instructional focus on terms has implications more serious than just the inhibition of student involvement. The phenomena dealt with in this lesson are hardly simple even though they were being demonstrated with simple equipment. Many very learned men spent the better part of their professional lives developing understanding of electricity and magnetism. And while the understanding of a young student certainly cannot approach that of a scholar in the field, an understanding *at some level* does seem to be the reason for introducing the material in the first place.

In the approach described, the use of special and unfamiliar names in itself presents some learning obstacles. But worse, the complex ideas involved are mistakenly thought to be simple and easily understood because the words used to represent them are relatively simple and readily learned. Familiarity with words masquerades as an understanding of the realities represented. And in confusing the symbol for the concept, students come to believe they understand the substantive ideas of the subject when, in fact, they only know the appropriate vocabulary.

A third-grader's homework paper provides, perhaps, the ultimate in anecdotes of how the "proper" vocabulary can be a misleading guide to what is actually understood. The work is an amusing and probably deserved culmination to a sequence of events that occurred in another elementary school science class.

The teacher had asked students to write a paragraph incorporating certain words they had learned in previous science lessons. These are the words which the students were expected to use:

air pollution	cow
ants	house fly
atoms	photosynthesis
bees	protein
carbohydrate	rain
clouds	steaks
community	trees

No one can fail to be awed by this vocabulary list because the level of science work implied is extremely advanced for any third-grade class. In fact, such highly sophisticated ideas are symbolized by some of these words that one must wonder what understanding of them even the most intellectually gifted eight-year-old can reasonably be expected to have. The arrangement of these words into some kind of coherent relationship might prove challenging to even an accomplished scientist. The following story was the response of one member of the class to this assignment:

THE HOUSE FLY

Once upon a time there was a little *house fly*. It had very many friends and these are some of them. Peter *Rain*, Anne *Protein*, Mark *Community*, Mary *Trees*, John *Air Pollution* and Cindy *Cow*. One day *House Fly* had a birthday and he invited all his friends and they ate so many *ants* and *steaks* and *bees* and *atoms* that it was really hard to believe. They got so sick that they caught a sickness called *Clouds*. They all had to have some medicine called *Photosynthesis* and then they all caught a sickness called *Carbohydrate* and they all died.

The spelling is impressive. The sentence structure and paragraph structure organization are at least acceptable for a child of this age. But while the story is delightful and full of charm, it nevertheless reveals a lack of understanding of the meanings generally associated with these terms.

If terminology does obscure meaning and impede understanding, one must certainly wonder at its extensive use in the classroom. Tradition, undoubtedly, is largely responsible—we teach as we were taught. Perhaps a more important contributory factor stems from the role in which the teacher is cast in the typical teacher-pupil relationship. The teacher customarily is viewed as all-knowing, the fountainhead and dispenser of all information. Under such a burden, the use of any technique that will maintain a facade of knowledgeability is entirely understandable.

Teachers who are insecure in a subject may also find terminology a handy crutch. That the terminology of a discipline intimidates the uninitiated is well known; it is, therefore, not surprising to find teachers, when uncertain or unclear about a subject, concealing their shortcomings with this same terminology. The use of elaborate words may impress some students and account for the often-heard student comment that a given teacher is brilliant, but he just cannot get his subject across.

Obviously, teaching and learning must rely upon words for the communication of ideas. How, then, should terminology be handled? One possible approach is to provide some contextual setting in which students can generate their own terms—terms that are personal and relevant for them. As they expand and deepen their understanding of the meanings associated with such personal terms, they may become sensitive to the need for a refinement of their initial selection of words.

For example, an experiment now widely used in school science programs calls for periodic temperature readings of a liquid as it cools and a subsequent construction of the substance's cooling curve. Students, recording the steadily decreasing temperature, usually are startled when the temperature of the liquid abruptly stops falling, remains fixed for a brief period, and then resumes its decline. When encountering this strange event for the first time, most students are convinced they have a defective thermometer whose column temporarily became stuck. In discussing this phenomenon, some students have generated the descriptive term "stick-point." And even though this name focuses attention upon the behavior of the instrument rather than on any property of the substance, "stick-point" is quite a descriptive, specific term that is meaningful in relation to real events.

As the discussion proceeds, the appropriateness of this term will come into question. The teacher may help students see the need to move from a limited examination of individual data to a consideration of the findings of the whole class. Once students recognize that all groups in the class found the same results, attention begins to pass from the instrument to the substance itself. The phenomenon of the temperature of a cooling liquid dropping steadily down to, and then temporarily remaining at, a particular point is seen as a characteristic of the substance and not an idiosyncrasy of the measuring instrument.

The meaning of "stick-point" expands further when another event is noted and related—at the "stick-point" temperature, the liquid changes to a solid substance. Students may then reflect their focus on the behavior of the substance by suggesting a new term "solidification temperature." More generalized meanings will become associated with the phenomenon if the cooling behavior of a number of different liquid substances is explored: Students will then be in a position to argue that the temperature of any substance remains unchanged during the liquid-to-solid transformation and that the temperature is a characteristic of the substance. Thus developed, the personal term acquires associations and meanings beyond specific events.

How far a teacher proceeds along such lines would depend largely upon the nature of the class and the overall educational program. Further study of the question of the "solidification temperature," for instance, might be worthwhile. If students go on to investigate the temperature behavior of a solid as it is warmed and converted to a liquid, they will again observe a pause in the changing temperature—this time when the solid is liquefying. The finding that a solid substance changes to a liquid at the same temperature that the liquid form changes to a solid is usually unanticipated and may lead students to once more revise their personal term—changing it, perhaps, to "reversible temperature."

In the example given, the names used to represent the concept were evolved contextually. Although the particular words initially selected were arbitrary, they did have meaning in terms of what students encountered in their investigations. As students proceeded with their work and related additional ideas to the phenomenon, the meaning of the term was extended. Finally, when the meaning of the personal term "reversible temperature" was well understood, it was readily translated into conventional terminology. Thus, terminology was placed in perspective—not a mystique but a necessity for general communication.

Eventually, students must be exposed to at least some of the "accepted," standard terminology in a field if they are to communicate with and understand those outside the classroom. But dealing in the manner described, with even a few terms, may be argued against as being so time consuming as to seriously limit the amount that could be taught. However, this may well be a case of doing more by doing less. From relatively few such efforts it may be possible for students to begin to recognize what terms stand for, how they are coined, and how they are used. In that case, the ideas associated with each formal term would not need to be developed situationally, and specific experiences would not have to precede introduction of each term.

Clearly, there is a need for research in this area. Some complex questions require examination and study. New educational practices must be developed that facilitate the association of meaning with words. In a system utterly dependent upon words for conveying ideas and knowledge, pedagogical procedures must allow words to promote, not interfere with or substitute for, understanding. In terms of the total educational program, decisions must be made as to whether the "right" word should be used at all and at what point it should be introduced.

Much needs to be learned about the relationship between cognition and language in children. Questions about *when* may prove as much a key to the issue as those about *how* to introduce terminology. Piaget's early work on children's language and thinking seems to have great relevancy to these questions.[1] For example, his studies indicate that a large proportion of the language of children between six and eight years old is egocentric and does not have the primary intent of communication. Because of these egocentric factors children at this age are poor listeners and apparently do not completely understand information even when it is appropriately transmitted. The work of Piaget certainly suggests that, in educational programs for young children, stress on the use of language in the development of thought structures is quite misdirected.[2]

Finally, a set of basic criteria is needed for judging, perhaps, justifying, the inclusion of terminology in a given curriculum. For instance, if just one of such criteria was the probability that students would again encounter the term or need it in the future, a host of formal names would disappear from science lessons at all levels: First-class levers, magnetometers, and variometers would cease to confuse and confound. The consequent development of a more relevant, personal language in the science classroom might augur well for the achievement of deeper and richer understandings.

---

1. Choose a few "scientific" terms such as energy, force, atom, conservation, electricity, vacuum, chemical energy, equilibrium, etc. and compare your definitions with those of fellow students.
2. If children are available, try asking them to define some scientific terms and then try to get at their understanding of what they mean.

1. J. H. Flavell, *The Developmental Psychology of Jean Piaget.* Princeton, New Jersey: D. Van Nostrand Company, 1963. Chapter 8.
2. Edward A. Chittenden, "Piaget's Research and Science Experiences for Young Children." Address before the Fifteenth Annual Convention of the National Science Teachers Association, Detroit, Michigan, March 1967.

37 RONALD G. GOOD

Analysis of "Science" Activities: Non-Verbal Learning

How would you define "learning"? One's definition would more than likely influence decisions about curriculum and instruction in elementary science. Learning is typically defined in rather narrow ways with an emphasis on the "verbal" aspects. This should not be surprising since most of us associate schools with learning, and schools mean books. Textbooks use symbols to communicate ideas and all is well if the reader can structure ideas using symbols. Unfortunately, the research on cognitive development strongly suggests that conceptual learning for most children of elementary school age develops through the experience of the personal manipulation of concrete objects. This paper presents some ideas (in a verbal way) about the nature of nonverbal cognitive learning with systems in science. "Static" and "dynamic" systems are explained in terms of their appropriateness for elementary school children.

If you would ask somebody to define "learning" as applied to elementary school science, the chances are very good that verbal learning would be predominate in the response. Science facts and concepts that are labeled with special words would constitute the learning. It is not difficult to see why this tendency toward verbal learning is with us in education today. Textbooks in elementary school science have generally emphasized names and definitions because a textbook *is* a verbal presentation.

Science—A Process Approach, Elementary Science Study, Science Curriculum Improvement Study, and a few other elementary school science curriculum projects represent attempts to de-emphasize the restricted verbal approach to learning as exemplified by textbooks. Manipulative materials replaced in whole or in part the verbal materials.

This paper was written for use in the science education program for prospective elementary school teachers at Florida State University. Dr. Good is Assistant Professor of Science Education at Florida State University.

Science—A Process Approach exchanged what children could say for what children could do. Science process behaviors were identified by the developers of that program as the goals. The role of the teacher included trying to get children to exhibit certain predetermined process behaviors. When a certain percentage of the children in the class could exhibit these behaviors, the lesson was considered successful.

A somewhat different approach to elementary school science was taken by the *Elementary Science Study*. Although manipulative materials made up the core of the science, specific process behaviors were not required of the children. Science was defined more as a process of total involvement using one's mind and hands in finding out about things. Specific outcomes were not defined in terms of *either* words to say *or* behaviors to exhibit. This is the point when many people involved in education might question if any learning at all is occurring. When children are permitted to structure their own learning in a given situation, the assessment of that learning becomes very difficult.

Analyzing science activities in terms of the possible intellectual involvement and learning that might result provides some answers. With systems of manipulative materials rather than language-based (verbal) materials, the thinking is of the logical-mathematical type. Classifying objects according to physical characteristics does not require that a name be attached to the objects or to the characteristics. One need only detect the shape, size, color, texture, etc., of the objects in question. To understand the concept of "chairness" does not require the term, chair.

Suggestions for Analyzing "Science" Activities

A few example science activities might serve to analyze the non-verbal learning possibilities inherent in selected sets of materials. For young children, a set of materials developed by one of the curriculum projects and known as "Pattern Blocks" provides opportunities for a variety of non-verbal learning types. The set of "blocks" includes polished wooden pieces of various geometrical shapes that can be fitted together to form a multitude of shapes. Although the pieces are only about 3/8 inch thick, they can be used for making three-dimensional structures. Each shape has a specific color and the sides of the pieces are the same length (side of the red trapezoid is doubled, 2 inches). Large metal mirrors (about 4" x 6") are also in the set.

Children will do many different things with sets of these materials if given the opportunity for free, independent activity. Let's try to identify some of the possible activities in which 7- or 8-year-old children might engage and the resultant learning.

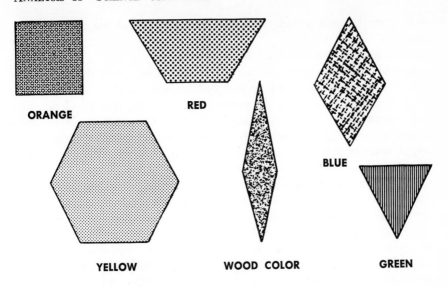

ORANGE

RED

YELLOW

BLUE

WOOD COLOR

GREEN

1. *Group Pieces by Color or Shape (Classifying).* Although a child may put the pieces together by what seems to be color, he may only discover later that all of one shape are also the same color.

2. *Make a Design Representative of a House, Flower, Person, Etc.* Possible intellectual involvement: Attribute discrimination; classifying; symmetry concepts; counting; parts-whole relationship; length-area relationships; comparing angles of sides; spatial transformations; topological relationships such as nearness, openness, surrounding, etc.; one-to-one and one-to-many correspondence of sides; measurement in one, two, and three dimensions.

3. *Make an Abstract Design.* Possible intellectual involvement: Similar to items under 2 with more emphasis on noticing how all the pieces can fit together. In making a house, flower, etc., some of the pieces might "necessarily" be excluded by a child because they are not the correct shape or color. In an abstract design, however, there might be more of an attempt to use all of the shapes (colors).

4. *Use Pieces of One Shape to Make Designs.* Possible intellectual involvement: In addition to many items in 2 and 3, emphasis would be on noticing patterns with successive rearrangement and addition of pieces. Using squares, for example, the child might notice that 4 squares can be arranged to make another square; 9 squares for the next, etc. The limitations of using only one shape would also become apparent. A triangle cannot be constructed using only squares and vice-versa. Opportunities for quantitative thinking using numbers would probably be more likely for this activity. Older children would be more likely

to deal more quantitatively with the characteristics of the patterns they make.

5. *Use a Mirror to "See" the Reflection of a Pattern.* Possible intellectual involvement: The mirror would tend to focus a child's thoughts on symmetry and spatial transformations of pieces and patterns. Tilting and rotating the mirror can cause unexpected changes in the mirror image that can lead to further investigations. With two mirrors taped together, one piece can produce multiple images that might lead to counting activities as well as observing the importance of the angle concept between the mirrors.

6. *Construct Three-Dimensional Structures.* Possible intellectual intellectual involvement: The length of a side and size of the angle would be noticed by the child who is trying to build a structure. The diamond shaped pieces are difficult to use because of the large angles in these four-sided shapes. The four-sided square, however, is a stable piece to use. The characteristics of the square, hexagon, and trapezoid cause them to be "good" building materials for tall structures. Creative thinking is encouraged if the child attempts to incorporate all of the pieces into a structure. All the pieces can be used in fitting together a structure if open-ended, trial and error procedures are attempted by the child. These attempts tend to require a closer inspection of relationships among the sides and angles of the pieces.

7. *Filling in Outline Shapes.* Possible intellectual involvement: Using outline shapes as a "puzzle" to complete can be a challenge and great fun. The length of each side of the shape would be multiples of the side lengths of each piece. In a problem-solving situation such as this, the child would use many of the processes identified in number 2. Coordination of perspective is heavily involved as are length-area relationships. Angle comparison and combinations of "parts" to make "wholes" would reflect a more quantitative approach to the "puzzle."

8. *Making Up Games.* Possible intellectual involvement: The process of making up a game requires an understanding of many of the items listed under number 2. As an example of this, a child would need to have had experience with various problems involved with filling in outline shapes with the pieces before he could make "proper" outlines. Although the word "game" suggests something very basic, often times it requires more sophisticated thinking than might be assumed. It is left as a challenge to the reader to invent games that can be played using the pattern pieces. How many different games can you invent? Of these, what type of intellectual involvement is required to "play" the game? Which of the games might be appropriate for 7 or 8-year-old children?

The eight categories of activities are certainly not the only activities possible with these manipulative materials. They represent many of the things that 8-year-old children might do when allowed to structure their own knowledge.

A Different Kind of Set of Materials

The pattern blocks represent a sort of "static" set of objects that do not require sophisticated mental characteristics and a logical approach to problems to engage in productive activity. A "dynamic" system of equipment involves the interaction of the different components of the system. When one characteristic of the system is changed, other parts of the system might also change. This variable kind of interaction among system parts requires a more systematic approach to learning about the nature of the system.

An activity using batteries, bulbs, wire, and miscellaneous materials is widely incorporated into many elementary school science curriculum projects. Characteristics of circuits can be studied by using one battery, one bulb, and one piece of wire or by using larger numbers of each item. Very complex systems can challenge even the most sophisticated elementary school child (and teacher) and provide a highly interesting format for the systematic study of problems. An attempt will be made here to identify some of the various activities possible with such equipment and the corresponding intellectual involvement for an 11- or 12-year-old child.

1. *Try to Light the Bulb with Only 1 Battery and 1 Wire.* Possible intellectual involvement: Identifying variables that might affect the behavior of the system becomes very important in dynamic systems. A need to combine variables of a system is also present when trying to determine the effects of one or more parts on other parts. Although only 3 objects comprise this system, each object may represent more than one variable. The bulb has at least 3 distinct parts: the glass bulb, the contact at the tip, and the metal casing adjacent to the glass. These areas may be used to connect the wire and/or battery together in determining the important or controlling variables.

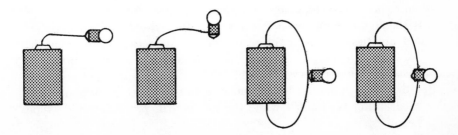

Only four of the possibilities are shown in the previous figures. After identifying the variables that could affect the lighting of the bulb, the 10-year-old child might systematically go about identifying all the possible combinations to find out if he was correct. The chances are quite good, however, that the 10-year-old will not approach the problem in a highly systematic manner. Trial and error will likely characterize his methods.

A systematic approach to solving problems that includes 2 or more variables requires that the problem-solver understand and be able to use the fundamentals of logic. Four operations that are necessary include conjunction, disjunction, negation, and implication:

1. conjunction—outcome affected by .... *and* ....
2. disjunction—outcome affected by .... *or* ....
3. negation—affected by *neither* .... *nor* ....
4. implication—*if* not affected by ...., *then* it must be ....

Here, the blanks represent variables that might affect the outcome or behavior of the dynamic system being studied. For the battery, bulb, and wire system the "position of the battery" and the "length of the wire" could be variables that might affect the outcome, which is the lighting of the bulb.

Adding one more piece of wire to the original three allows for many more combinations. Can you compare the number of combinations using only one wire with the number possible using two wires?

2. *The Child Uses Bulbs, Batteries, and Wires to Construct More Sophisticated systems.*

As with the system using only 1 bulb, 1 battery, and 1 piece of wire, the child is confronted with many possible arrangements. Systematic investigation is complicated as the number of variables of a system increases. The processes of observing, classifying, measuring, using spatial relations, making inferences and predictions, and controlling variables are continually used in systematic investigations using equipment such as batteries, bulbs, and wires. Concepts of equivalency, reversibility, combinations and correlations, and the various mental processes involved in logical thought are also required to analyze "dynamic" systems where the interaction of variables occurs.

It should be emphasized again that a 10-year-old will have rather limited abilities to pursue problems in a systematic, logical manner. The development of the ability to deal in logical ways with problems is a relatively slow process. Dynamic systems like the one anlyzed here offer the child opportunities to continue this intellectual development. Verbal learning is minimal while the non-verbal, problem-solving type of learning is enhanced. Some science processes and concepts used in the development of logical thinking are listed as examples of essentially non-verbal learning. Perhaps you will be able to identify many more that fall into the non-verbal category.

1. Observing
2. Classifying
3. Measuring
4. Using Length-Area-Volume Relations
5. Using Time and Sequence Relations
6. Making Hypotheses
7. Making Predictions
8. Identifying Variables
9. Controlling Variables
10. Using Number Concepts Such As: Ordering, Seriation, Identity, Equivalency, Correspondence, Combinations, etc.
11. Relativity of Position and Motion
12. Weight–Density Concepts
13. Equilibrium
14. Spatial Transformations
15. Analyzing Variations and Correlations
16. Using Logic Operations Such As: Conjunction (and), Disjunction (or), Negation (neither, nor), and Implication (if, then).

No attempt was made in the previous list to identify facts and concepts in chemistry, physics, biology, etc. This type of content would be used to provide opportunities for the child to engage in processes that help him to further develop his ability to interpret physical causality in more rational, logical terms. The *words* to be learned in the various sciences take a back seat to the *processes* that are exemplified by the two examples already discussed. Different sets of materials offer various potential for science processes in particular and logical thought processes in general.

Teaching children words to say is of little consequence in their total intellectual development. Knowledge is not the word itself. It is understanding what the word means in terms of the learner. Unless the child already has developed the necessary mental structures that enable him to attach meaning to a word, the word is an empty kind of knowledge.

Science activities of the non-verbal type offer much potential for allowing children to structure the meanings first, and add the verbal labels at the appropriate time. The kind of false sense of security that adults can derive from hearing children repeat words back to them must be exchanged for a more rational sense of security. The security of seeing children engaged in manipulating static and dynamic sets of equipment will have to replace the word game before the classroom becomes a place that helps children acquire real knowledge.

———————

1. Can you compare other "static" and "dynamic" systems in science?
2. Try to analyze a science activity (investigation) in terms of the probable non-verbal learning involved.
3. Check a few elementary science textbooks and try to find examples of non-verbal learning.

38 CALVIN W. TAYLOR

Creativity and the Classroom

Creativity is always among the goals in our schools and yet how much is known about the conditions which foster creative thought and actions? In this paper, creativity is viewed within the context of education and some implications for teaching science are suggested. Are children creative thinkers before they get to school and if so, how did they get that way? How is discovery learning related to creativity? How is guided learning related to creativity? Hopefully, this paper will raise more questions than it will answer and you will continue to pursue these questions on your own.

Research in the area of creativity has tended to indicate that we are not on target with our present talent measures. Most school programs do little to help identify and develop creativity in our science students.

Evidence to date tends to indicate that grades in school are generally not good predictors of later creative performance, many of them having nearly zero validity. In a few special areas of the curriculum, grades may have some value as forecasters of future creative performances. On the whole, however, more creative activities have to be requested of students and their resulting performances have to be deliberately scored for creativeness if grades are to have greater value in predicting later creative performances.[*]

Creativity and the IQ

A similar type of picture is found when we inquire about intelligence test scores as indicators of creative potential. At best, such scores prob-

Reprinted from *Science and Children*, Vol. 1, No. 8, 1964, pp. 7-9, by permission of the editor. Dr. Taylor is Professor of Psychology at the University of Utah, Salt Lake City.

[*]Further research evidence on nearly all points in this article can be found in the references listed at the end of the article.

ably account for only a small percentage of the total phenomenon of creativity. Typical intelligence tests do not call for much that can be considered to be productive or creative thinking. Since intelligence tests tend to be highly verbal in nature (at least verbal materials are the most heavily weighed in them), I suspect that such scores will have little relationship to creativity in nonverbal fields. Furthermore, research at the University of Utah suggests that the current education of science students is more verbal in nature than is the research performance of scientists in research development (R&D) laboratories. In addition basic research on human abilities has indicated that there are at least 61 separate intellectual talents in our students, but a typical intelligence test tends to measure a subset of no more than 6 or 8 of these 61 high-level talents that are measurable to date.

Several of these new types of talents are likely to be of some importance in creative thinking. These abilities include the sensing of problems, originality, flexibility that is spontaneous, flexibility that is adaptive, fluency of ideas, fluency of associations, fluency of expressions, ability to redefine things in a different way than they are usually defined, ability to juggle several ideas in the mind at one time, penetration, visualization, elaboration, and certain abilities in the broad areas of foresight and evaluation. Questioning and other curiosity-in-action abilities, plus an ability to think at right angles to the mainstream of thought, and an ability to become broadly diffused in one's attentional processes while working and thinking on problems may also be important.

Exploratory searches for creative potential have certainly not been limited to these many intellectual abilities. They have also included, often more fruitfully, studies of biographical, motivational, and other personality characteristics. From our studies of nearly 2000 NASA and Air Force Research Center scientists, we have found that our well constructed biographical inventory (after being thoroughly analyzed through computer programs and revised several times) is clearly our best single measure of creative potential. It has continued to be the best single indicator as we have moved our studies from mature scientists backwards to the high school level to date.

Some other promising scores have included a self-rating on creativity, inner-directedness, drive, professional self-confidence, intellectual thoroughness, aspiration to make theoretical and original contributions, high self-sufficiency, openness to the irrational in oneself, intuition, awareness of one's own impulses, resourcefulness, adventurousness, complexity as a person, interest in unconventional careers, dedication and involvement in one's scientific work, liking to think, liking to toy with ideas, need for variety and autonomy, preference for complexity and the challenges therein, a striving for better and more comprehensive answers, need to improve upon currently accepted systems, need to adjust their environment (not adjust to it), tolerance of ambiguity, and resistance to closing up and crystalizing things prematurely which is coupled with a strong need for ultimate closure.

Implications for Teaching

Both science textbooks and teachers have tended to focus on what is *known* far more than upon what is *not known*. They may have also set the stage for learning by authority and imitation much more than for learning by creative processes. Creative learning and experiences in dealing with the unknown are often missing, even though, as we have found, a largely different subgroup of students excel in such activities. The fascinating research participation programs for high school students (supported by the National Science Foundation) have strikingly demonstrated the readiness of high school students to engage in the research adventure of delving into the unknowns. Jablonski has successfully pioneered such research participating programs in the Pittsburgh public schools both during the summer and for the entire academic year. He has then extended this research participation program back to the elementary school level where he found that fourth, fifth, and sixth-graders are more prepared to do research than even he suspected; in fact they have successfully been helping him do cancer research. Should not the younger generation be joining in cancer research as soon as they are ready and capable of doing so?

These programs, plus our research findings, tend to reverse the question about "readiness of students for school programs" to one of "readiness of schools for students." Another question that has emerged is whether our science courses are offered in ways that tend to repel rather than attract those who like to do creative thinking about a subject matter field. Too often, we are teaching the "dead corpse" of past knowledge without giving our students any chance to experience the excitement and living adventures that researchers experience when new scientific knowledge is being discovered and produced.

At the University of Utah's 1962 creativity research conference, Jablonski reported that if these young students did not understand the scentific language used in research work, they asked what each word meant and soon learned the language as readily as they learned English. He also described the case of a high school student with an IQ of 86 who could not read very well. But this student produced some ideas of his own during the summer research program that the other student researchers picked up and worked on during the entire year in several high schools. (Some university people are working on the chain of ideas he opened up.) This case is cited as a challenge to our current educational system which would say he is without much promise and should not be allowed to go much further along the educational ladder.

In searching for what we might try in education, Gallagher of Illinois has used an effective technique for having teachers think about the environmental features that might affect creativity. He has reversed the question by asking "How would we design a classroom program that would be most effective for hindering, stifling or even killing creativity in our students?" After the teachers have named several features that they feel would be effective in curtailing or blotting out creativity, he reports that they gradually discover that many of these negative features they are describing may already be present in our classrooms. Have we somehow ignored creativity in designing our classroom programs or have we even gone further and allowed forces that might work against creativity to be strongly built into many of our programs?

Our own research approach has been to study creativity in those adults in whom it is hopefully in "full bloom." An alternate approach used by some others is justified by their saying that they study creativity "in its more natural state," in children before it may become wilted or even blotted out by various features of our world, including some educational programs.

In our educational theory, we state that creative thinking can deliberately be developed to some degree in our educational programs even while students are learning subject matter if teachers so desire. In other words, we feel it is possible for teachers to find ways of developing the creative talents of students while students are simultaneously acquiring the subject matter. Stated alternately, course content can be the stuff on which the creative processes of the mind can feed and grow.

A dissertation completed in 1964 by Hutchinson, at the University of Utah, verifies this educational theory. This study involved a two-week unit of language arts at the junior high where Hutchinson was principal. Four teachers first taught one class by their traditional method. Then a new teaching method was tried which yielded an interesting shift. In this case, the principal took an effective educational leadership role by giving in-service training to the teachers for most of one week. This in-service training brought about positive and stimulating results in the classroom. The teachers were told to conceive of their students as being thinkers (not merely learners) who were to do productive thinking while learning the subject matter. In the second set of four classes, the students were matched on mental ages with the first set of students. In this latter productive-thinking setting, instead of asking the teachers "what do I do and how do I do it?" the students responded largely by receiving and reproducing knowledge, especially by increasing in their thinking responses and in producing something of their own (new ideas, etc.) as they worked with the subject matter. The students were more actively participating and were using more of their thinking processes than they were in the earlier traditional classroom. They were also learning as much or more subject matter, so there was no loss, but if anything, there was a slight gain in amount learned. The students were more active and more interested in school under the latter productive-thinking conditions.

In the traditional classroom, IQ scores were related as usual to the increased subject matter learned, but in the new kind of classroom practice, other processes of the mind were being used; in the latter case, test scores on creative thinking were related to amount learned, whereas IQ scores correlated zero with how much material was being learned. In the traditional classroom, we feel that the goldlike IQ abilities, which are effective in receiving and reproducing knowledge, were being used. In the second type of classroom, the uraniumlike creative-thinking abilities were being used and developed and a new group of students emerged as star performers. This study demonstrates that teachers can structure the situation in school so that creative thinking abilities can be identified and fostered in the classroom while the students are learning the required subject matter.

As teachers, we can join in these challenges of trying to find various ways of conducting our classes so that our students can display and develop their different creative thinking abilities and characteristics while they are also growing in subject matter knowledge. Instead of acting like the uncreatives who want "pat answers" as to what to do (even before such answers exist), let us join in the challenging exploratory search for alternate and better ways of conducting our total science education programs.

REFERENCES

Taylor, Calvin W. *Creativity: Progress and Potential.* New York City: McGraw-Hill Book Company, Inc., 1964.

———. *The 1962 Utah Creativity Conference Report.* (Mimeographed manuscript ready for 1964 publication.)

———. *Widening Horizons in Creativity.* New York City: John Wiley and Sons, Inc., 1964.

———. and Frank Barron. *Scientific Creativity: Its Recognition and Development.* New York City: John Wiley and Sons, Inc., 1963.

1. What conditions in elementary science would tend to encourage creative thinking? Discourage it?
2. To what extent do you think creativity is "in the genes" and to what extent does the environment influence it?

Bibliography

SCIENCE AND SCIENCE EDUCATION

Baker, Adolph. *Modern Physics and Antiphysics*. Reading, Massachusetts: Addison-Wesley, 1970, 261 pp. (paperback).

Modern developments in physics are treated from the viewpoint of a humanities student and explain why he should be interested in physics. Interrelationships between science and society are continually considered.

Bronowski, J. *Science and Human Values*. New York: Harper Torchbooks, 1965, 119 pp.

Also a short paperback, this book is a philosophical approach to such things as creativity and truth. The author sheds light on the humanistic aspects of science and how science relates to society. He is an outstanding scientist as well as a fine writer.

Calder, Nigel. *The World in 1984*. (2 vols.) Baltimore: Penguin Books, 1965, 215, 205 pp. (paperback).

The author presents a collection of articles that predict advancements that will have occurred by 1984. Scientific as well as nonscientific topics are utilized for such predictions.

Deason, Hilary J. (ed.). *A Guide to Science Reading*. New York: New American Library, 1966, 288 pp. (paperback).

Over 1300 paperback books in most areas of natural science, mathematics, psychology, anthropology, etc. are reviewed in this handy resource book. Each book is classified according to four levels of difficulty, from junior high school through graduate school. The prices, lengths, addresses of publishers, and other pertinent information are included.

Dethier, Vincent G. *To Know a Fly*. San Francisco: Holden-Day, 1962, 119 pp.

This is an excellent short paperback book that gives an account of how one can get to know a fly. The author describes his own experiments in humorous, non-technical language that effectively communicates the processes of scientific enquiry. It suggests that much of science entails patience and careful thinking with an occasional good idea.

419

The ESS Reader. The Elementary Science Study of Education Development Center, Inc., 55 Chapel St., Newton, Mass. (paperback).

As a series of previously published papers related to elementary science, this book explains some of the ideas behind ESS. The ideas, however, are not limited in application to a singular curriculum project.

Fischer, Robert B. *Science, Man, and Society.* Philadelphia: W. B. Saunders, 1971, 112 pp. (paperback).

Science as a human activity is described by the author. The language of science, motivations of scientists, limits of science and "truth" in science are among some of the topics discussed. Science is also analyzed in terms of its relationships with technology, higher education, public policy, and the individual. A good reference section at the end of the book identifies almost 100 books and articles that should have relevance for the interested reader.

Gamow, George. *One, Two, Three . . . Infinity.* New York: The Viking Press, 1961, 340 pp. (paperback).

Well-known and widely read, this book, deals with many fascinating phenomena of the universe. The method of presentation manifests the most outstanding feature of this material.

Santayana, George. *Reason in Science.* New York: Collier Books, 1962, 277 pp. (paperback).

This is a somewhat more technical explanation of man's efforts to discover order in nature. The past achievements are used to predict future possibilities.

School Science and Mathematics. Central Association of Science and Mathematics Teachers, P. O. Box 246, Bloomington, Indiana.

Also issued monthly, this journal is designed for teachers of grades K-12 in both science and mathematics. It frequently contains articles on elementary science.

Science and Children. National Science Teachers Association, 1201 Sixteenth St., N.W., Washington, D. C.

This is the official monthly journal of the NSTA for those interested in elementary science education. It contains suggestions for teaching and general articles of interest for the elementary school teacher.

Scientific American. New York: Scientific American Co.

A monthly journal that is devoted to publishing scholarly but nontechnical papers in all areas of science and mathematics. It is written for the interested student and contains articles by many outstanding scientists.

Scientific American, Editors of: *Lives in Science,* New York: Simon and Schuster, 1957, 274 pp. (paperback).

Eighteen biographies of scientists, such as Galileo, Newton, Ben Franklin and Charles Babbage, are contained in this book, with a look at their accomplishments and insights into their personal lives. The history of science is viewed as a series of personal achievements of such men.

Watson, James D. *The Double Helix.* New York: The New American Library, 1968, 143 pp. (paperback).

This Nobel-prize winning author was one of the two men who were credited with the discovery of the structure of the most important of all "life-giving" molecules, DNA. The account of events leading to the discovery is written in a way that reflects the human emotions and "inside" views of scientists who are usually seen as rather cold and emotionless individuals.

GENERAL

Bruner, Jerome. *The Process of Education.* New York: Vintage Books, 1960 (paperback).

As the leading spokesman for "discovery" learning in science and mathematics curricula, Bruner set forth many of his ideas in this short book. It is a compilation of some ideas that resulted from a conference of scientists and educators at Woods Hole on Cape Cod in 1959. It deals with structure of subject matter, readiness for learning, motivation, and various kinds of thinking.

Holt, John. *How Children Fail.* New York: Dell Publishing Co., 1964 (paperback).

This critical analysis of our schools has led the way to a deluge of books criticizing education. It is extremely sensitive to problems facing children in school and is widely found in bookstores. It is well-worth reading.

Kozol, Jonathan. *Death at an Early Age: The Destruction of the Hearts and Minds of Negro Children in the Boston Public Schools.* Boston: Houghton Mifflin Co., 1967 (paperback).

The title tells the story of a follow-up type of book to *How Children Fail.* The author was a substitute teacher in the elementary schools of Boston.

Neill, A. S. *Summerhill: A Radical Approach to Child Rearing.* New York: Hart Pub. Co., 1960 (paperback).

Summerhill is the name of a "live-in" school in England, operated by Neill, where children are essentially allowed to make decisions for themselves. The only rules are: (1) they cannot destroy property, and (2) they cannot interfere with the freedom of their peers. This experiment in living was founded in 1921 and has spread to schools in our own country through the efforts of individuals with similar beliefs. A very provocative book.

Neil, Postman and Charles Weingartner. *Teaching as a Subversive Activity.* New York: Delacorte Press, 1969.

A well-written book that presents examples of teaching as subversive to the development of the minds of children.

Silberman, Charles E. *Crisis in the Classroom,* New York: Random House, 1970.

This book contains the results of a three-and-a-half-year study commissioned by the Carnegie Corp. and conducted by Silberman and a staff of four. It has been highly recommended as one of the most worthwhile books ever written about education. The combination of a readable writing style and interesting research results make this a very unique work.

COGNITIVE DEVELOPMENT

Ginsburg, Herbert and Sylvia Opper. *Piaget's Theory of Intellectual Development: An Introduction*. Englewood Cliffs, New Jersey: Prentice-Hall, 1969 (paperback).

A thorough, readable introduction to the ideas about intellectual development of Jean Piaget.

Inhelder, Barbel and Jean Piaget. *The Early Growth of Logic in the Child*. New York: W. W. Norton, 1969 (paperback).

This book is the result of eight years of research work with over 2,000 children. The processes of classification and seriation are analyzed and, as with most of Piaget's works, many conversations with the children are used as examples of various kinds of thinking. The two processes—classification and seriation—are viewed as forming the basis for the child's reasoning ability.

Inhelder, Barbel and Jean Piaget. *The Growth of Logical Thinking: From Childhood to Adolescence*. New York: Basic Books, 1958 (paperback).

The extensive use of symbolic logic makes this book somewhat more difficult to read than *The Early Growth of Logic*, but the information on the development of logical thinking is valuable. Children do experiments to indicate their abilities to eliminate contradictions, separate and control variables, exclude certain variables, deal with possible combinations, and generally deal with the operations of formal logic (disjunction, conjunction, implication, etc.). This book, combined with *The Early Growth of Logic*, provides an in-depth view of the gradual development of logical thinking in children from the ages of about 2-3 to 14-15 years.